A Guide to Reading Herodotus'
Histories

Sean Sheehan

BLOOMSBURY ACADEMIC
LONDON · NEW YORK · OXFORD · NEW DELHI · SYDNEY

BLOOMSBURY ACADEMIC
Bloomsbury Publishing Plc
50 Bedford Square, London, WC1B 3DP, UK

BLOOMSBURY, BLOOMSBURY ACADEMIC and the Diana logo are trademarks of
Bloomsbury Publishing Plc

First published in Great Britain 2018

Cover image: Paris Abducting Helen, c1782–c1784. Found in the collection of
the Pushkin State Museum of Fine Arts, Moscow.
Photo by Fine Art Images/Heritage Images/Getty Images

A catalogue record for this book is available from the British Library.

Library of Congress Cataloging-in-Publication Data
Names: Sheehan, Sean, 1951– author.
Title: A guide to reading Herodotus' histories / Sean Sheehan.
Description: London ; New York : Bloomsbury Academic, 2018.
Identifiers: LCCN 2017040899| ISBN 9781474292665 (pb) | ISBN 9781474292672 (hb)
Subjects: LCSH: Herodotus. History–Appreciation.
Classification: LCC D58.H473 S54 2018 | DDC 930--dc23 LC record available
at https://lccn.loc.gov/2017040899

ISBN: HB: 978-1-4742-9267-2
        PB: 978-1-4742-9266-5
        ePDF: 978-1-4742-9269-6
        eBook: 978-1-4742-9268-9

Typeset by RefineCatch Limited, Bungay, Suffolk
Printed and bound in Great Britain

To find out more about our authors and books visit www.bloomsbury.com
and sign up for our newsletters.

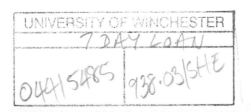

In Memory: 2008–2014

CONTENTS

Book Two: Egypt   89

Book Three: Cambyses, Samos and Darius   111

LIST OF BOXES

Book Five

Book Six

Book Seven

Book Eight

Book Nine

AUTHOR'S NOTE

Most quotations from Herodotus in English, and all those in Greek, are based on the four volumes of the Loeb Classical Library edition, translated by Godley. This translation, alongside early twentieth-century commentaries by How and Wells and by Macan, is available online at the Perseus Digital Library (www.perseus.tufts.edu). Godley's translation is also available through Hestia (http://hestia.open.ac.uk). Other translations which are referred to – by Sélincourt, Waterfield, Blanco, Holland and Mensch – are listed in the bibliography under the translator's name. Quotations and references to Homer are based on the Lattimore translations and quotations from other ancient Greek writers, unless otherwise stated, are based on those available at the Perseus Digital Library.

All dates referring to the ancient world, unless otherwise stated, are BCE.

Approaches to Herodotus

A literary historian

The word 'unfolding', explains Walter Benjamin writing about Kafka in 1934, has two meanings: there is the unfolding of a bud into a blossom and the unfolding of a paper boat which becomes a flat sheet of paper.[1] Two years later, writing 'The Storyteller', he says how storytelling is rooted in oral tradition and how the story does not expend itself in the telling but, by integrating itself with the listener's experience, lives in the memory and is repeated to others. Storytelling preserves what gives it life and meaning and the example that he cites is one of Herodotus' tales, about the Egyptian king Psammetichus (3.14), noting its ability to provoke 'astonishment and reflection'.[2] It unfolds, to use his image, like a bud.

Egypt has been conquered by the Persians and Psammetichus is forced to watch as his enslaved daughter is compelled to fetch water in a pitcher, accompanied by other girls whose fathers are also compulsory spectators. Psammetichus is the only one who does not cry out and he also remains silent as his son, roped and bridled like an animal, passes by on his way to execution. It is only when he sees one of his servants, now reduced to begging for a living, that he is stricken with grief and bursts into tears. Benjamin suggests possible reasons – perhaps the servant is the catalyst for the release of his pent-up grief – but observes how Herodotus offers no explanations. Commenting on the absence of psychologizing or emotive reporting, he acclaims how it 'shows what true storytelling is'[3] and compares the story to seeds of grain that after centuries in chambers of the pyramids retain their power of germination.

The *Histories* has been around for 2,500 years without losing its ability to enliven audiences and, central to its continuing appeal, its storytelling. Penguin's first edition of the *Histories* appeared in the Fiction series, published in a dark period of the Second World War when readers had enough non-fiction to contend with and when imagining the author as a patriotic teller of tall tales, a racy raconteur, might have been welcoming. Here was a conversationalist who enjoyed embellishing his accounts while professing disbelief in what he is about to share with his audience, as in a tale of a precocious child who will become king Cambyses of Egypt, pledging revenge on behalf of his mother aggrieved by a slight from another woman.

Having enjoyed the telling of the tale, Herodotus informs us that he finds it unconvincing (3.3). He presents empirical information but with imagination and flair and a modern parody of how he sometimes drew unfounded conclusions brings out what is also beguiling about his writing: 'England being a very cold country, the Londoners live on a food they call curry, eating it all day long, for it makes their entire bodies feel warm, and when they begin to feel cold again, they eat some more. This food they get from India and it is carried from there on the backs of the dogs one sees all over Britain. This, it seems to me, must be the reason for the great affection the Britons bestow on dogs' (Roberts 2011: 59).

Precious little is known for certain about Herodotus' life and while there is no agreement about the extent or duration of his travels[4] it is very probable he left his home city, travelled widely, was exiled at least once and spent his last years in south Italy. He was 'the product of the culture of walled cities' but his authority as a historian and ethnographer derives 'from passage beyond the walls' (Greenblatt 1992: 123).[5] The language and imagery of travel pervades his work and characterizes its opening and concluding sections. The proem (1.1–5) covers a series of sea journeys as abducted women are carried far and wide and the last chapter of the book sees the Persians discussing where to travel to and why (9.122). An authorial voice brings the kidnapped women's voyages to an end, only to announce another type of movement: 'I will go forward in my account, going alike through cities small and great' (1.5). The phrasing carries a Homeric echo: the *Odyssey* opening with the poet asking the Muse to sing of the man 'who was driven far journeys' and saw 'the cities of many men, whose minds he learned' (1.1–3). Herodotus is not an armchair traveller but one who keeps on the move, amassing layers of information as he takes byways and diversions, prepared to be a slowcoach but keeping a destination in mind, eschewing short cuts in favour of minor lanes and detours.[6] He is ready to be lured into narrative outings by tales of the uncanny and the fabulous, places and people on the rim, rerouting on the hoof if an interesting excursion suggests itself and creating his own signposts as he maps previously unknown or obscure connections.

Herodotus as a traveller collects stories, learning about the inseparability of the present from the past, and his journeying, listening and storytelling become equally inseparable. A term that brings together a set of such traditionally unrelated temporalities and spatialities is 'hodology'. The study of pathways in geography, hodology can also refer to connections in parts of the brain – a coming together of the physical and the cerebral that can be seen taking place as a result of social interactions and the exchange of stories arising in the course of following a path or a trail. We make sense of the world as we move through it, and we follow a story like a trail. In both cases there is an ordering of material, the physical steps of the traveller on the ground mirrored in cognitive movements arising from social exchange during a journey. A call for a new class of mapping that would build on this performative aspect to knowledge unites components that can be seen at work in Herodotus: 'Knowing is a form of travelling, of moving through space; and travelling, like knowledge, is also a form of narrative' (Turnbull 2007: 143). Dewald (1987: 149) writes of Herodotus' *logon hodos* ('route of the *logoi*) that the reader is guided along as the stories calmly proliferate.

The status of Solon as a great sage is bound up with his reputation as a traveller, his wisdom associated with his wandering after his self-exile from Athens, his 'love of knowledge' (*philosopheōn*) motivating him to 'travel widely' for the sake of 'seeing the world' (1.29–30). The word for his sightseeing, *theōria*, means 'a looking at, viewing' before it became a word for 'a thinking about', linking intellectual movement with physical movement.

If the *Histories* were a website it would be littered with hyperlinks as Herodotus meanders, branches off and loops back on himself as connections are made across time and space. His journeys, real and textual, become a form of web drifting as one link leads to another – with the reader sometimes wondering what the starting point was – and while the interruptions are productive the process does not lend itself to static placements on the type of map that was shown to the Spartans. Aristagoras, hoping to persuade the Spartans into supporting a revolt in Ionia, displays a map of the Persian world and points to it as he talks about the great riches that are waiting to be seized by its conqueror (5.49). When the Spartans find out what the map cannot show them, a journey time of three months to reach the Persian capital, they reject the proposition. Herodotus is also interested in adding the dimension of time to the plotting of places on a cartographic representation, not like the Spartans in wanting to know the temporal duration of a journey but because he is aware of how time changes places, concluding his proem with the knowledge that big cities become small and vice versa (1.5). The spring-like structure of his narrative expands and contracts the journeys contained within it according to the ways in which time has affected the subject matter. The failure of Aristagoras' map to impress the Spartans is due to an excessively schematic representation of space, something Herodotus found laughable about cartographical displays of the world: drawing the world 'as round as if fashioned by compasses' and depicting Europe and Asia as of equal size (4.36). The challenge for Herodotus in his 'showing-forth' of world history is to avoid an overemphasis on overly abstract representations of space by accommodating non-cartographic aspects like the temporal and the cultural.

The *Histories* is an outstanding, multiplex text, its discursive sinuousness captured in the first decade of the twentieth century by an image of Macan's in his sharp commentaries, advising readers that they will find 'wares of widely different values side by side in the Herodotus bazaar' (2013: xcv–xcvi). Another picture has been evoked in the attempt to pin down the quality of his achievement in combining a love of truth with a passion for telling fictional stories: a 'literary centaur [with a] human forepart . . . [but] the body indissolubly joined to it is something out of the faraway mountains, out of an older, freer and wilder realm where our conventions have no force'

(Herington 1991b: 8). For Dewald (1987: 147), Herodotus is a warrior from an epic who wrestles like Menelaus, not with the shape-shifting Proteus (*Iliad* 4: 400–64) but with the polymorphous nature of the material he brings together in his text. These three images are symptomatic of an awareness that the *Histories* cannot be read as an organic, mimetic text in the manner of a conventional novel or work of history. Its author does not withdraw from the scene, providing the reader with an uninterrupted immersive experience and, as Dewald (1987) shows in her examination of the authorial first person in the text, what emerges is an alternative voice that distinguishes itself from the *logoi* being recounted. This authorial voice, the *histōr* (inquirer), is seen as wanting the reader to engage with the difficulty of the writing task, speaking on over 200 occasions about the author's efforts to deal with his own narrative (164).

Intellectually, it is a work of conceptual sophistication, a 'showing-forth', to use the author's expression, of world history and its achievements that are worth recording. This is his stated intention and it is in the unpacking of what he means by the achievements of humankind that his writing attains remarkable levels of quality. His reporting of a historic event, notable in itself simply because it occurred, can include moments that bring to mind what Virginia Woolf called 'moments of being', something she never defined but a phrase which looks to brief but intense instants that set an experience apart from the opaqueness of ordinary life. As the Greeks prepare themselves in their camp before the Battle of Thermopylae, a spy is sent to secretly observe the scene and report back to Xerxes what he has seen: some Spartans, their weapons against the wall, combing and arranging their traditionally long hair (7.208). The spy is astonished, Xerxes is incredulous, and the reader, like both of them, is allowed a glimpse of something quite private: one of those rare moments in certain individuals' lives when their existence is defined, owned and redeemed. It is a revelation only for the reader; the men are preoccupied with arranging their hair and preparing to die.

The *Histories* is a work of a literary artist, a historian and a cultural critic; a work that brings together in a highly coherent manner topics and interests that now tend to be confined to separate disciplines. His achievement and his reputation as a writer of distinction was recognized in the ancient world, confirmed in the celebratory lines of verse of the Salmakis inscription found off the coast of Bodrum, naming Herodotus as 'the prose Homer'.[7] Although the magnitude of his achievement remains secure there was a period when his status as a serious historian was relegated in favour of Thucydides, but now, following the renaissance in Herodotus studies over the last few decades, his best years as a literary historian are ahead of him. If Benjamin is correct in charting a decline in the craft of storytelling in the modern world – 'the web in which the gift of storytelling is cradled' is 'unravelling' (Eiland and Jennings 2002: 149) – the value of Herodotus is greater than ever before.

The form of the *Histories*

The word Herodotus uses to describe his own work is *logos* and the term used to mark sections of it is *logoi*; they can vary in length from a short story within the narrative to a lengthy section within a book, like the Scythian *logoi* of Book Four, or even an entire book as with the Egyptian *logos* that constitutes Book Two. A task for the reader – it can sometimes feel like a tease – is following the dizzying loops and connections between different *logoi*. A Persian general Megabazus learns that Histiaeus, a Greek who helped keep a vital bridge open after the king had crossed it at the start of his Scythian campaign, has been rewarded with the grant of a city in Thrace, to the north of Greece (5.11). Megabazus, alarmed at the prospect this poses for the security of the empire, warns the king of the danger and Histiaeus is deceived into travelling to Susa, the Persian capital (5.23–4). Here he is kept under virtual house arrest on the pretext that the king wants to keep such a good friend close to him. There is an unexpected sequel because the detention motivates Histiaeus to stir up a rebellion in Ionia (5.35), helping to bring about the very outcome that Megabazus had feared and hoped to prevent. The reader needs to remember that another Greek, the physician Democedes, was also kept in Susa against his will and, anxious to return home, is able to have Darius persuaded into planning an invasion of Greece (3.132–4), something the king had never before contemplated and which in the course of time will lead to his defeat by the Greeks. The irony of unintended consequences and the strange workings of contingency that connect these two stories create another link, to the story of Croesus and his son (1.34–45) where, just as with Megabazus, the wish to avoid something undesirable happening is precisely what causes it to take place. Then there is the story of Astyages, king of the Medes, fearful of a precognitive dream that his grandson, a Persian named Cyrus, will depose him. The king orders his servant Harpagus to kill the infant but the servant avoids doing so and when Astyages finds out he kills Harpagus' only child and feeds him to his father in a meal. As a result of this macabre horror, Harpagus defects to the Persians and encourages Cyrus to conquer the Medes (1.107–19, 123–30) and in this way Astyages brings about the very danger he feared by trying to avoid it.

The form of the *Histories* is to be found in the symmetries, doublings, echoes and inversions that constantly arise in the reading of it and the connections just noted between the stories of Megabazus, Democedes, Astyages and Croesus' son are just one example of this form at work. One wonders sometimes whether a particular connection that can be plotted is one consciously charted by the author or whether it arises from the workings of a literary mind that intuits the aesthetic value of a particular embellishment. Aristagoras visits Sparta to try to persuade the city to support an Ionian revolt and does so with the visual aid of a map engraved on a bronze plate (5.49) and it is easy to forget that on three previous occasions encounters have taken place between an Ionian and the Spartans, all as unsuccessful as Aristagoras' and involving some kind of prop (1.152, 3.46, 3.148).

A method of writing known as ring composition, a characteristic of Homer's epics,[8] is used by Herodotus to provide a framing device and an aid to the reader negotiating his text. Ring composition, working through the repetition of motifs, situations, characters or vocabulary, returns the reader to an earlier moment in the text and in this way links the start and end points of a piece of writing. The opening sentence of 1.7 introduces the story of Gyges – 'the kingdom passed from the Heraclids to the Mermnadae in the following way' – and the first sentence of 1.14 rounds off the account of the previous six chapters: 'This was the way the Heraclids took power from the Mermnadae.' An example of ring composition at work over a short stretch of writing can be seen at the beginning of 6.121, introducing the allegation that the Persians had secret support from the Alcmaeonid family in Athens, and the end of 6.124 where the topic is mentioned once again and brought to a conclusion. In Book Three, the existence of unusual phenomena in remote regions of the world is mentioned at 3.106 and the matter is returned to at the end of 3.116, with the ring composition providing an envelope for the material in between these two points. On a larger scale, encompassing the *Histories* as a whole, a series of episodes that brings the work to a close in Book Nine can be seen as completing a ring composition that began in Book One. At the very start of the work, for instance, a voice is given to the Persian perspective whereby all of Asia is its territory, geographically and politically separate from Europe (1.4), and this finds an acerbic echo in one of the final chapters of the *Histories*. A scandalous Persian governor impiously steals treasure from a sanctuary and manages to do so by telling Xerxes he is expropriating the house of a Greek who dared to attack Persian territory. The Greek in question, Artayctes, is a legendary hero credited as the first Greek to have died at Troy, but while Xerxes doesn't know this he is able to be hoodwinked because 'Persians believe all Asia to belong to themselves' (9.116), so, technically, Artayctes was guilty and therefore liable for reparation.

Metaphors and similes are needed to help grasp the extraordinary intricacy of Herodotus' patterning of what could otherwise come across as a congeries of tales, anecdotes, legends, exotic folklore, genealogies, oral tradition, historical events, eyewitness accounts – his own and other people's – and metaphysical reflections. Griffiths' image for the accomplishment comes from the quality of a fine piece of worked wood: 'The knots and burrs in the growth of Herodotus' narrative grain are not defects, but intrinsic to the attraction of the timber's polished surface' (2006: 134). Gould (1989: 58) finds an analogy in Herodotus' remark about the Euphrates looping so much in its course that the same village is passed three times on successive days (1.185); another picture, that of fractals, comes to mind given the way mininarratives recursively echo themes and patterns. Comparing the work to an elaborately woven tapestry employs a familiar image but it usefully conveys the idea of the representation of a whole that depends for its pictorial clarity on a multiplicity of different coloured threads being skilfully interlaced. The embedding of links on an online site has been mentioned above and the analogy with an electronic web supplements that of the spider's that Stadter may have had in mind when he wrote of 'a dense web' of common themes and patterns, a technique where for him 'everything seems connected to everything else' (2002: 40). Taken as a whole, these attempts to express what is happening in the *Histories* have in common a conviction that the themes at work make up the terrain of its discourses.

The stories within the *Histories* are not to be regarded as a narrative equivalent to a salad dressing, added for the sake of piquancy or the picturesque. Embedded and integrated into the main narrative, they contribute immensely to the complex layers of meanings that the work enshrines, and the topmost level of meaning is shaped by the fact that Herodotus is a history-teller at the same time as he is a storyteller. One part of an awareness of how he works as a historian, equally important in understanding how his writing unfolds like a bud and not a paper boat, is appreciating the content and positioning of some of the stories. When Xerxes and his huge army are setting out to conquer Greece there is a story about the rewarding and then dreadful punishing of Pythius (7.27–9, 38–9); much later in time, when the defeated king is returning to Asia, there is a tale about a sea captain who is also rewarded but only at the cost of his life. The first story (see p. 228) is more multilayered than the second but their point of similarity, dramatizing the arbitrary power of an authoritarian political system, arises from a shared historical context.[9]

Herodotus declares in his opening sentence that his work is the result of his 'inquiry' (*historiē*). It is unlikely that he invented the word *historiē* but in using it on more than twenty occasions the context is usually one of investigative questioning on his part and it is only later that the meaning of the word shifts from an inquisitive activity to the results of an inquiry, the meaning 'history' as we now understand it.[10] *Historiē* opens doors for Herodotus into many rooms – now labelled history, ethnography, geography, cultural studies, comparative religion, philosophy – and the result is a complex, literary work of a historian.

The structural framework is provided by a clash between East and West: the East comes to be represented by a single empire whereas the West is a collection of Greek states characterized by their lack of unity. Lydia, the dominant power in the region at the time, is the first to do wrong to Greeks by subjugating the Ionian Greeks and this is where the main narrative begins. The defeat of Lydia by Persia requires backtracking to explain how its king, Croesus, came to be captured by Cyrus, the first ruler of Persia, and the continuing expansion of the empire under Cyrus, Cambyses and Darius is unfolded in chronological order. Countries and states attacked and usually conquered by these kings are each described as and when they encounter the imperial might of Persia. These descriptions cover customs and geography as well as politics. The history of the Greek states does not lend itself to a similarly systematic treatment. This is partly due to the lack of an equivalent overarching chronology, with each state having its own history of development which often consists of quarrels with its neighbours, and different cities are introduced by way of digressions at various points in the main narrative.

As the Persian advance into Greece the pace of the story undergoes a change, becoming more focused and dramatically concentrated as the existential danger facing the Greek city-states is experienced by them with a mixture of foreboding, dissension and courage. Their fissiparous history up to now has been one of infighting and arguing among themselves and suddenly there is an urgent need to come together in solidarity and rally their forces against a common enemy. It doesn't happen overnight.

The sense of Herodotus' personality that emerges from his text, where precious little personal information is ever given, is bound up with his literary style. His capacious text charts variegation and it embodies the multifaceted and pluralistic mentality of a writer whose omnivorous inquisitiveness is always on display. His curiosity has no bounds, ranging from inquiries into the course of a river, family genealogies and people's sexual practices, and he switches from the recondite to the ridiculous, from the empirically exact to the gossipy anecdotal, without any crunching of narrative gears.[11] A nativist at times but with a breadth of perspective that also marks him as an internationalist, his writing indicates a man who is unsnobbish and humane. His readiness to use the second person draws an audience into a subject under discussion, as, for example, when noting the Babylonian custom that has every woman offer her body to a complete stranger once in her life, he adds how afterwards she will never again countenance such behaviour: 'no matter what you offer, she will refuse you' (1.199).

Herodotus can also be self-reflexive and cerebral, searching for meanings just as the agents in the stories he tells are so often doing: consulting oracles, making sacrifices, attending to auguries, having dreams that require interpretation, noting cryptic signs and epiphanies. His diversified series of observations become a sometimes sublime meditation on life's strangeness and sadness while on other occasions they allow him to make wise and philosophical generalizations. Reacting to conflicting views on why Argos refused to join the alliance of Greek states prepared to oppose the invading

Persians, Herodotus jadedly steps back from the arguing and, in a rare recourse to metaphor, makes a statement about happiness per capita: if everyone brought their domestic troubles to market in the expectation of exchanging them for a neighbour's less onerous misfortunes, one look at what was on offer would have them gladly returning home with their own (7.152).

Herodotus states his purpose in the preface: he wants to record what people have accomplished in the past because time erases human memories. It is not time in the abstract, not an arbitrary universal time of the type established at Greenwich, but a lived time that always leaves the lived past behind. By experiencing time as a threat, feeling the need to counter it with a written record of the past, Herodotus' reputation as the 'father of history' is validated. He seeks to preserve what is worth remembering about Greeks and non-Greeks and, in particular, the way in which they came into conflict with one another. In order to prevent his work being just a succession of 'one-damn-fact-after-another',[12] he needs to find an artful way of organizing and presenting it, and the result is a literary history written in prose. In the earlier age of archaic Greece, verse is the predominant and authoritative form not just for literature but also for political discourse, religious celebration and philosophical inquiry: Homer, Hesiod, hymns, choral odes. An intellectual revolution on the west coast of modern Turkey, where the Greeks had founded colonies as early as the eleventh century, gave rise to a new form of writing and the first writers to use prose are a number of shadowy figures from Ionia.[13] Thales, Anaximander and Anaximenes are names from the first half of the sixth century but little remains of their avant-garde work and the same is true of Hecataeus, a writer who along with Thales is mentioned by Herodotus and whose ethnographic and geographic interests most probably influenced his own writing. The art of oratory and disciplines such as philosophy, science and geography are attached to these pre-Socratic thinkers but such categories were not perceived as such at the time and Herodotus elides the boundaries that a later age draws between them. He applies intellectual concerns and processes of the pre-Socratics, who inquired into nature (*physis*), to the world of human behaviour. Historiography, ethnography, literature: all are watered by Herodotean springs.

Herodotus the historian

'There was no Herodotus before Herodotus' (Momigliano 1966a: 129): he created the historiography by which he is now judged and enjoyed, making his moment an inaugural one in the writing of history. It does not mean that before him no one wrote anything that could be called history but it does mean that Herodotus was the first to achieve in writing the expression of a historical consciousness with the intellectual scope of the *Histories*.[14] This historical consciousness is crystallized in his declaration at the end of the proem: 'For many states that were once great have now become small; and those that were great in my time were once small' (1.5). History is taken as a process, not inert but dynamic, and the changes that occur – in this citation the reversal of states' power – will be seen not as the result of something extraneous – brought in from the outside as a simple opposition – but as arising from within, immanent, self-driven by contradictions. The lives of individual people and the course of political and identities will be seen as subject to changes emanating from their own natures. The Lydian state, once locally great, will become small by overreaching itself; the power of Persia, once insignificant, will become great by its own commitment to expand. The perception of a dialectic at work underlies the claim that Herodotus is 'the father of history'.

In 1913 an almost book-length entry on Herodotus, written by Felix Jacoby in a German encyclopaedia, was hugely influential and it established an issue that would be at the heart of Herodotean scholarship for a long time. Jacoby questioned whether The *Histories* might be the result not of a unified design but of a stitching of geographical and ethnographic material into a historical account when its author realized the significance of Persia's war against Greek city states. Jacoby's article encouraged a picture of Herodotus as an itinerant raconteur who gave entertaining readings about his travels, grouped into topics like Egypt and Persia, and who over time, after chronicling the development of the Persian Empire and then the Persian Wars, put it together as one text. Writing more than half a century after Jacoby, another influential study with the same concerns recognizes that an intellectual development on Herodotus' part could have shaped the final form of his work. Different interests, Fornara accepts, may well have been central to Herodotus' interests at different stages of his life, but he succeeds in integrating historical and ethnographic material 'like the heads of the hydra in the body of that mythical beast' (1971: 3). The negative implications of a genetic approach, seeing the *Histories* as a patchworked text cobbled together, have largely come to be rejected[15] but disagreement remains about its standing as a work of history. There is an undeniable difference between the experience of the reading the first three books of the *Histories* and the final three and this allows for a tendency to judge its author's credentials as a *histōr* – using the form of the original Greek term – based on a modern conception of how a 'proper' historian works.[16]

Herodotus' sources and methodology

In the same year that Fornara's book, *Herodotus: An Interpretative Essay*, defended Herodotus against the charge that he merely conglomerated a collection of diverse material, a book was published in German that reignited a debate about his status as a historian. Fehling's book, *Herodotus and his 'Sources': Citation, Invention and Narrate Art* (its English title when translated and published in 1989), argued that Herodotus was not only insufficiently critical by misinterpreting some of his source material but that he invented some of it when it suited his purposes. For example, Fehling finds it peculiar that when Herodotus comes across a temple in Memphis dedicated uniquely to 'Foreign Aphrodite', and having heard that Helen of Troy spent time in Egypt, he deduces that it was built in her honour (1.112). The source of the account that follows, of how Helen came to spend the years she is assumed to have spent in Troy actually in Egypt, is attributed to the temple's priests but Fehling is not convinced. For him, Herodotus has decided that the temple is dedicated to Helen and a picture of him 'hurrying off to secure confirmation in the form of a few uncomprehending nods to be extracted from guides devoid of any knowledge of Greek' is conjured up to show how he arrived at his 'deduction' (1989: 65).

Fehling's contentions have proved fraught but not fruitless, generating a lively debate around his criteria which some have found wanting,[17] and disquiet about Herodotus' veracity has a history of its own that may go back to Thucydides. The methodologically more explicit author of *The Peloponnesian War* (2009) makes a point of distancing himself from poetic and prose accounts of the past that are 'written more to please the ear than tell the truth' (1.21), and this could be a slightly veiled criticism of his predecessor. Plutarch, writing half a millennium later, did not restrain his ire in *The Malice of Herodotus*, and accuses the Greek author of having a slanderous agenda of his own that distorts the truth, as he sees it, in favour of character assassination and favouritism towards non-Greeks.[18]

Fehling's argument that there is a fictional quality to the citing of sources by Herodotus is a serious charge, attacking the credibility of any ancient or modern historian, and it has helped focus attention on how Herodotus goes about collecting and presenting information about the past. In the course of his inquiries he is regularly meeting with and listening to people who can relate their memories of events, sometimes seeking out credible informants, especially officials at sacred places, perhaps sometimes using interpreters as Cyrus does (1.86). There were Persian-speaking Greeks in Babylon and Greek-speaking Egyptians and Herodotus characteristically refers to himself as 'hearing' reports; the *logioi* that are mentioned three times as a source (1.1, 2.3, 2.77) are tellers or keepers of stories. He listens to genealogical traditions from aristocratic families and traditional accounts of an oral kind belonging to a local community, and not just Greek ones; informants are rarely named and a source attribution like 'the men of Delphi' or 'the Corinthians' is the norm.

Social memory, mediated by group identities as individuals' memories are by various subjective factors, has suffered devaluation as a source of information in the modern world, making the power, complexity and retentiveness of communal memory in the world that Herodotus inhabited easily underplayed.[19] It is also easy to misunderstand what Herodotus means when he provides a source and it is important not to think of his referencing as being of the kind that a modern historian would make. Herodotus is dealing with community-based traditions and social memories of a local and shared kind and it is not appropriate, or expected by his audience, for him to pinpoint the provenance of each piece of information he collects. There is a need, as Luraghi puts it, to 'de-emphasise the concrete meanings of these source references' (2002: 146).

At the same time, there are places where it is legitimate to query the way Herodotus refers to sources, and an example of this is his account of the city of Babylon. He refers to unnamed Chaldean priests on three occasions (1.181–3), though not always believing them, and implies that he has visited the city for himself (1.185, 193). What is said about the city, and what he omits to say, gives grounds for wondering if he actually saw Babylon for himself and whether he had first-hand sources within the city or used material that reflects a Greek paradigm of what a very foreign city might be like (Kuhrt 2002: 478–82). Some of what he says is not supported by Mesopotamian material and the story about every woman having to prostitute herself once in her life (1.199) may be more a piece of titillating exotica than an authentic fact based on a credible source. Perhaps Herodotus is well aware of this but finds it too good a tale to bury. He declares in Book Two how 'these Egyptian stories are for the benefit of whoever believes such tales' and goes on to say that his business is 'to set down what is told me [*tauta legonta*]' but not necessarily to believe it (2.123). The same circumscription around *tauta legonta*, repeated at 2.130 and again at 6.137 and 7.152, comes to the fore when he is writing about Cyrus, the founder of the Persian Empire. He knows of three other versions but asserts how he will 'tell the true story [*ton eonta legein logon*]' (1.95) and at the end of the story returns to the question of credibility: 'Many stories are told of Cyrus' death; this, that I have told, is the most credible' (1.214).

Scepticism is natural when there are competing versions of the same event – Cyrus can only have died in one way – and an expression of doubt about the veracity of what he hears may underlie the way Herodotus sometimes refers to his sources. Only rarely does he identify by name his source of information[20] and far more characteristic of his approach is the manner in which he begins the account of what happens when Cyrus changes his mind about having Croesus burnt to death: 'The Lydians say ...' (1.87). As Waterfield points out (2009), there were no established historiographical standards for fifth-century writers to follow and so it is possible that when Herodotus mentions a general source he is not doing so out of professional duty or pride but because he wants to convey a measure of doubt or mistrust.

In Book Two, writing about Egypt, it is noteworthy that he twice pauses to divide up his material, not according to subject matter but with reference to the type of sources he is using. The first division occurs when he states that his accounts thus far have been based on 'my own observation [*opsis*], judgement [*gnome*] and inquiry [*historiē*]', but that from this point on he will be recording what is told to him by Egyptians, supplemented by what he sees for himself (2.99).[21] The second division occurs when he flags a departure from relying on what Egyptians say and a turn to 'what other people, with whom the Egyptians agree, report about the history of the country' (2.147). The vocabulary in the authorial statement of 2.99 is an important guide to how Herodotus sees his own work and his elevation of *opsis* above hearsay (*akoē*) as a source of information. Material evidence that can be seen will help verify or disprove what he is told and so, for example, the story of Arion and the dolphin is supported by the bronze statue of a man riding on a dolphin in the city where the story begins and ends (1.24). When Herodotus is inquiring into the numerical size of the Scythian population, he admits that accurate information is beyond his reach but he deduces that the figure must be high based on the huge size of a bowl into which one of their kings ordered each of his people to deposit one arrowhead (see n133). What is important is that his source for this anecdote showed him the bowl (*apephainon moi es opsin*), he saw it with his own eyes, and this is the basis for his deduction.

The questioning of informants (*historiē*) involves listening, but the process is investigative and critical in its nature, categorized on an equal basis with observation and judgement, and to be distinguished from merely reporting what is heard. On nearly a hundred occasions Herodotus expresses doubt about something he reports and more than forty times he interrupts his narrative to question the veracity of what he is recording (Dewald 1987: 151, 163). An emphasis on sources, drawing attention to how something of a historical nature is established, is particularly characteristic of the first four books of the *Histories* and such a weighting is not found in what has survived from the works of his contemporaries or predecessors. The desire to establish his credentials as an investigative inquirer is a characteristic that emerges in the early books (see p. 93) and sometimes he goes to extraordinary lengths to track down a story: looking into whether the proper provenance of Heracles is Greek or Egyptian, he states that having heard there was a temple to Heracles in Tyre in Phoenicia he sailed there solely for the purpose of research (2.44).

For the new discourses emanating from Ionia, especially in science and medicine, there is an innovative stress on rational scrutiny and a willingness to criticize earlier authors and authorities. Confident of his methodology, Herodotus often feels he can speak with authority on a subject that his audience will not be so well informed about, declaring in relation to Persian culture that he knows about the customs he is going to describe (1.131). The verb he uses, *oida* ('I know'), is in the perfect tense, connoting a certitude on his part that goes beyond just hearsay, and after listing and commenting on a number of such customs he stresses the accuracy and reliability of his report: 'having observed them', he says, 'I can speak about them precisely [*atrekeōs*]' (1.140).

As a historian, Herodotus employs an epistemological sliding scale: with Persian customs he is dealing with Rumsfeld's 'known knowns' but he accepts that sometimes there will be 'known unknowns'. In gathering oral-based information, Herodotus is aware of its limitations and his remarks about the difficulty of ascertaining the source of the Nile – 'I have reported as much as it was possible to learn by inquiry' (2.34) – and knowledge of a remote region north of the Black Sea – 'I have not met anyone who claims to have actually seen it' (4.16) – are not untypical.[22] Concerning a huge bronze bowl that never reaches its intended destination, he is responsive to the existence of rival traditions that reflect their different sources. Spartans say the bowl was stolen by Samians, but on Samos he hears that the Spartans in charge of the bowl's transport sold it to private buyers. Herodotus withholds a final judgement but notes that if the bowl had been illicitly sold then it is believable that the sellers would claim they were robbed (1.70). In this case, Herodotus may not be unduly worried about two conflicting interpretations if his intention is to highlight Greeks' propensity for lying and trying to deceive one another.

Herodotus can be forensically aware of the prevalence of variant versions, and Lateiner (1989: 78) attests to this by listing well over a hundred instances of alternative accounts. On occasion, Herodotus provides a version which he knows or regards as untrue (8.119, 1.75) and when alternative versions are irreconcilable, with no authorial indication as to which one to trust, it is left to the reader to make a judgement and become the interrogative *histōr*.[23] An example is when, having given two motives for a plan to capture the ruler of Samos and put him to death (3.120–1), the reader is invited to believe whichever one he prefers (3.122). When two accounts are provided of Cambyses' murder of his wife, the absence of a clue as to which one to believe seems unnecessary because both versions highlight his violent and unstable nature.

In the lengthy account of the foundation of Cyrene, three separate traditions are identified and drawn on for information (4.145–8); while different accounts of how Cyrus died are acknowledged, only one is used: 'I have given the one I consider most plausible' (1.214). When he hears a story that he feels is patently untrue, like an account purporting to explain how the daughter of Mycerinus died and why a statue has no hands, he dismisses it as 'nonsense' (2.131). He is more diplomatic over the question as to who on the Ionians side conducted themselves bravely at the Battle of Lade and states that it is impossible to answer because the sailors blame each other (6.14): 'Thus Herodotus makes clear that though he is not sure which were brave, he is quite sure some were cowards' (Flory 1987: 75).

Mythical time, historical time, folk tales

Central to the epistemological sliding scale that has been mentioned is the time-based distinction between a remote past, remembered in stories and poetry, and a temporally closer historical past that remains within the span of human memory.[24] When at the start of his work Herodotus moves away from the legendary tales of female abductions – Io, Europa, Medea and Helen (1.1–3) – he turns to 'the man I know [*oida*] to have wronged the Greeks' (1.5) and thereby stakes a claim for objective knowledge about the past. He 'knows' because the man in question, Croesus, is fully recognized as the king who ruled Lydia a century earlier and his existence is within a reliable range of orally-transmitted human memory. The enormous mixing bowls, the silver wine jars and water basins that Croesus sent to Delphi can still be seen (*opsis*) and their locations are specified (1.51). The Lydian king's existence can be validated in a way that the abduction stories cannot and Herodotus endeavours to draw a line between these types of stories and a Lydian king who is 'the first of whom we know [*protos ton emeis idmen*] who subdued the Greeks' (1.6).

Croesus belongs to the middle of the sixth century, three generations earlier than Herodotus, and so also does Polycrates, a ruler of Samos, whom he says 'is the first Greek of whom we know of to seek control of the sea' (3.122). When Herodotus visits Egypt and finds accounts of kings stretching back over a period of 11,340 years (2.142), none of whom are considered gods, he allows himself to be seriously impressed because, as opposed to just oral authority, material evidence in the form of statues and a list on a papyrus roll are there to be seen.[25]

Herodotus sometimes struggles over where and how to draw a dividing line between an age of myths which may be unreliable and later times when there are more trustworthy sources of information.[26] When it comes to the figure of Heracles, a god for the Egyptians but a legendary hero for Greeks, Herodotus faces a knotty chronological problem as he tries to reconcile different accounts.[27] As a historian concerned with causation this is of epistemological concern for him – uncertainty exists about what happened long ago – but Herodotus is also bothered by an ontological issue that attends such problems: what sort of time was it that existed in the remote past? Polycrates is named as the first of what 'can be called the human race' (3.122), and this passage has exercised scholarly debate and division about the extent to which Herodotus distinguishes between a time of unverifiable myth and history proper and what degree of importance he attaches to any such distinction.[28]

A 'floating gap' has been identified in societies where knowledge of the past depends on memory and oral tradition and there is some evidence of this in Herodotus (Thomas 2001). Accounts are available for the very distant past, often relating to a group's origins, but the record then jumps to the most recent past, going back two or three generations.[29] A chronological line, imagined vertically, bulges at the top and bottom but with a gap in the middle where much is forgotten. As the recent past moves forward in time, the gap also moves, hence 'floating'. So, the founding of Greek cities in Ionia is described (1.145–7) but then the timeline jumps to their subjection to Lydia (1.14–22) and then Persia (starting in 1.141). Thomas gives other examples, relating to Sparta, Athens and Egypt, and views the chronological gap as often veiled because of the way oral tradition, with which Herodotus is working, prefers to follow a trail dictated by episodes of revenge and retaliation. A pattern of vengeance takes the place of chronological connections and provides a series of links between one event and another from the distant past. The long-lasting animosity between Aegina and Athens (5.81–9) is a good example of this.

Something that Herodotus is not aware of but which is of historiographical significance is the presence of folk tale motifs in accounts which he takes to be of a historical nature. Oral tradition can shape and colour what is remembered with motifs and patterns of a mythic kind; it will be noted how tales he reports share a kinship with Greek, biblical and Mesopotamian myths as well as with the category of stories collected by the Grimm brothers. The childhood and coming to power of Cyrus (see pp. 78–81) is embroidered with legendary and mythical elements, and the stories around Croesus are another prime instance. The historicity of the Lydian king is not disputed but facts are adulterated with elements common to oral tradition, from his historically improbable (if not impossible) meeting with Solon to the tragic tale of his son (see pp. 75–6). The story of Croesus and his son is 'as prolific a hothouse of communication as the tale of Oedipus' in the words of a commentary that reads it as an 'intricate and abstract statement' about the nature of communication (Sebeok and Brady 1978: 12–14), and it is generally agreed that there is more going on in the story than the history of an unfortunate incident concerning a king's son. The same is true of another story of a ruler and his son, Periander and Lycophron (p. 3.50–3), and a tendency to convey folk tale-freighted narratives in information purporting to be about historical characters raises doubts about its historical value.

Questions and doubts can be met with recognition of how such stories are informed by political and philosophical reflections that are not mutually incompatible with kernels of historical truth. The story of Croesus amplifies a signature concept for Herodotus: happiness cannot be taken for granted, the wheel of life guarantees impermanence (1.107), and consequently kingdoms will fall as surely as they rise (1.5). The conversation between Solon and Croesus may be an invention originating in oral tradition, but it functions as a paradigm for underlying themes of importance to Herodotus' view of history. Similarly, the antagonism that divides parent and child in the Periander and Lycophron story reflects the colonizer–colonized relationship that mars dealings between Corinth and Corcyra. None of this is to deny that there are occasions when non-historical material of a popular storytelling kind finds its way into a chronicle. The pharaoh Rhampsinitus dispatches his daughter to a brothel to track the robber of his treasury (2.121) and, if this is not improbable enough, a page later his successor Cheops is seen acting in a similarly scandalous manner (2.126).

Causation

At a simplistic level, causation is how one event explains a temporally sequential event and, unlike writers of fiction, historians are not allowed to make up what happens or invent the characters who are the agents in a sequence of events. E. M. Forster in *Aspects of a Novel* notes that in saying 'the king died and then the queen died' and 'the king died and the queen died of grief' the time sequence remains the same but in the second case a 'sense of causality overshadows it' (Forster 2005: 87). The aim of the historian can be seen as bringing to light underlying causes that explain the course of real events and real characters and so we have a Herodotus who asks questions, looks for evidence and sets out to explain the causes of what takes place.[30] Such an approach has a scientific flavour and for some philosophers of history Herodotus is the inventor of scientific history (Collingwood 1994: 20); for others, causality in history is 'a metaphorical notion taken from natural science' and as a modern notion is inappropriate for Herodotus (Immerwahr 2013: 157). Both these judgements have their validity when they are assessed in the light of particular passages in the *Histories*. For the author of *Studies on Collingwood, History and Civilization* (Van der Dussen: 2016), when Herodotus addresses the overflowing of the Nile he employs in an exemplary manner – even though the problem is not a historical one – a methodical and thoroughly scientific approach to a question of causation (162–3). Even though the river had been overflowing for millennia, it appears that no one in Egypt had searched for the cause of the phenomenon; no one had looked for a connection between the river annually flooding and other facts which would explain this. Kuhn in *The Structure of Scientific Revolutions* says how discovery starts from the awareness of an anomaly, with 'the recognition that nature has somehow violated the paradigm-induced expectations that govern normal science' (1970: 53). This is how Herodotus begins with the Nile and he puts forward three theories, examines but rejects them and then gives his own considered opinion,[31] a procedural set of moves from hypotheses to evidence to the causation in question: 'It [discovery] closes only when the paradigm theory has been adjusted so that the anomalous has become the expected' (Kuhn 1970: 53).

On another level, one that is not 'scientific' in the above sense, Herodotus works from a deep awareness of the power of the past as a hermeneutical passkey for an understanding of historical causation. There is a broad understanding, never made an explicit causal principle, that the Persian Empire's drive to expand, beginning with the conquest of Lydia, exists at a foundational level in his archaeology of the present. This never becomes schematic and is seen to be nuanced by the presence of metaphysical notions.

The preface to the *Histories* famously declares that the inquiry will look into the question of cause, or responsibility (*aitiē*), for the conflict between the Greeks and the barbarians. The noun *aitiē* is usually translated as 'cause', and Immerwahr (2013: 160) quotes a breakdown of the fifty-one times the word is used, listing 'reason why' twenty-two times and 'charge, fault, blame' the same number of times. He qualifies this breakdown on the grounds that even when it carries a sense of 'reason why' it is nearly always in a human context, always based on motivation and nearly always an unfavourable motive. Herodotus is seen to pay relatively little attention to underlying economic and social cause, preferring to rely on stories about characters, sometimes quite minor ones, driven by grudges and a desire for revenge. The conclusion is that the notion of causation is not used with the modern understanding that historians bring to it but, instead, with a juridical sense of 'responsibility' or 'Who is to blame?' Vengeance is seen to be a decisive factor in causation for Herodotus by Immerwahr (168), but because it is built into the reporting of the events themselves it is seen not to lend itself to the kind of rigorous patterning that modern historians bring to causation. For the philosopher Ricoeur, the historian makes the explanatory form 'autonomous', removing it from its immanent presence within 'the fabric of narrative', making it the 'distinct object of a process of authentication and justification' (1984: 175).

If vengeance as a causal factor is located within the stories and not made as historiographically explicit as some might like, there is a danger of trivializing its explanatory importance, reducing it to a feature of the narrative and as such a rogue arrow in the historian's quiver. Gould (1989) has contributed a valuable correction to this misapprehension by situating vengeance within a larger frame of causality, that of reciprocity, which structures what happens around 'obligations of gratitude and revenge' (65).[32] His first example is the beginning of Book Three where the Persian king's invasion of Egypt is traced back to a grudge on the part of a physician that eventually leads to Cambyses, the Persian monarch, seeking his own revenge by attacking the country (3.1), An alternative account, mentioned above, is that Cambyses made a promise when he was a child to revenge an insult to his Persian mother by turning Egypt 'upside down' (3.3). For good measure, a contributory factor is the desertion to the Persians of a mercenary who, motivated by a grudge of his own, provides valuable military advice for the invasion (3.4). It is an elaborate set of causes but the common factor here, the motivating force of reciprocal action that requires the taking of revenge, is found throughout the *Histories*, along with its obverse which is the fulfilment of a debt of gratitude. A particularly fine example, almost arcane with its complicated tale of cult statues and unfulfilled promises, has to do with the strained relations between Athens and Aegina (5.82–7, see pp. 168–9). In another case, Athens takes revenge against the Boeotians for helping their enemy, the Chalcidians, and this leads to a city in Boeotia, Thebes, wanting her revenge. The Thebans ask Aegina for assistance, who oblige by attacking Athenian territory (5.77–81); later, the Athenians see an opportunity to get their revenge against Aegina (5.89), and so it goes on (6.87–9).

The exercise of reciprocity is not just something that arises in the course of telling stories but an elementary level of explanation for why, sometimes allegedly, things happen. After the Battle of Marathon, Athens grants Miltiades seventy ships and he lays siege to Paros, claiming the islanders are going to be punished for having contributed a trireme to the Persians. This is just a pretext, asserts Herodotus with confidence, disguising a personal grudge he bears against a Parian (6.133). A Persian governor of Egypt uses as an excuse for wishing to subjugate Libya the wish to help the mother of a Cyrenean king who has been killed (4.167). When those responsible for her son's death are handed over to Pheretime, she carries out an excessively brutal and disproportionate act of revenge (4.202); reciprocity is used to legitimise violent acts that in other circumstances would be considered unlawful and unjust.

Even when driven by vengeance, individuals are seen looking after their particular interests in the best way they can, given the circumstances they find themselves in, unaware of larger consequences resulting from their subjective agency. Cyno has a stillborn child and begs her husband not to let die the infant Cyrus that her husband brings home, under orders to expose the baby on a mountainside (1.111). Her intervention allows Cyrus to survive and ultimately defeat the Medes and absorb their territory into a Persian empire (1.130). Democedes, a Greek physician held in Susa, pines for home, and his scheme for returning to his country leads to Darius contemplating an invasion of Greece and sending a spying mission to the country: 'the first Persians to come to Greece from Asia' (3.129–38).

Two brothers from Paeonia, in the far north-west of the Greek world, have a plan to become local rulers with Persian backing. They use their sister to capture Darius' attention, in the expectation that the king will approve of her industry and consequently support her brothers' bid for power. When

Darius sees how industrious the girl is and how such talent is wasted in her homeland, he orders the mass deportation of all Paeonians to Phrygia in Asia where they will be able to contribute more to the Persian state (5.12–15).

Contingency, the absence of necessity, in these episodes seems to be at the heart of causation, but it is also the case that individuals are seen following their own agendas and effecting change while unaware of larger forces shaping the causes and consequences of what they do. In the Ionian revolt *logos*, Aristagoras wants to become ruler of the island of Naxos (5.30), and a family relation, Histiaeus, wants to leave Susa where he is being kept against his will (5.35). These are the motives that cause them to act on their own initiatives and pursue private agendas, but what they do and achieve is inseparable from the political and social context of Ionia, a region that wants democratic rule and independence from Persian rule. Histiaeus was the tyrant of Miletus, a Greek colony on the Ionian coast under Persian control, and was one of those left by Darius to protect the escape route during his Scythian campaign. When Darius was retreating from his unsuccessful campaign, Scythians wanted Histiaeus and other Ionians rulers to destroy a bridge that would then maroon the Persians in their territory and allow them to pick off the enemy in their own time. The Ionians, for their part, would gain their freedom from Persian rule. Histiaeus, placing his class interest above ethnic allegiance, points out to his fellow tyrants that without Persian backing his city and others 'would be sure to choose democracy in preference to despotism' (4.137). He successfully persuades them to keep the bridge open, is rewarded by the king but then detained in Susa, from where he encourages an Ionian rebellion in the expectation that Darius will then order him back to Ionia to deal with the situation (5.37). He becomes, along with Aristagoras, a key player in an Ionian revolt even though he is no supporter of democracy.

What individuals like Histiaeus make of the world remakes them in turn or, as Marx put it, 'Men make their own history, but they do not make it just as they please, in circumstances they choose for themselves; rather they make it in present circumstances, given and inherited' (Cowling and Martin: 2002: 19). Sometimes an individual is well aware of what is 'given and inherited' and acts in the conscious knowledge of this awareness. The 'circumstances' that Marx is referring to in the quotation from the *Eighteenth Brumaire of Louis Napoleon* are not so much a set of underlying economic considerations but the very factor that causes Xerxes to set about an invasion of Greece: 'Tradition from all dead generations weighs like a nightmare on the brain of the living' (Cowling and Martin 2002: 19). Xerxes feels that it is his country's manifest destiny to conquer foreign lands and expand its imperial rule; it is Persian tradition that dictates what he as a king has to do (see p. 201). Cyrus, the first king, rebelled against the Medes and conquered Lydia and Babylon; his son Cambyses conquered Egypt, Phoenicia and Cyprus; Darius subjugated Samos in the Aegean, Indians and Thracians. When Xerxes reconsiders and decides not to invade Greece, he has a dream of a 'tall and goodly man' standing over him and warning him to abide by his original decision (7.12), and the apparition later reappears and warns him that he risks imperilling his status as a great king in the tradition of his forefathers (7.14). As Marx also put it – he is referring to people engaged in a revolutionary project but the words are apposite – 'they nervously summon up the spirits of the past, borrowing from them their names, marching orders, uniforms' (Cowling and Martin: 2002: 19). Xerxes takes his 'marching orders' from an imperial tradition he has inherited.

Causal relationships in Herodotus can be bound up with another set of traditions arising from aspects of Greek thought and religion. There is a description of how Egyptians sacrifice bulls (2.38–9) for which an obvious parallel is the biblical scapegoating ritual (Leviticus 16.21), but a detail notes how the head of the bull is given to Greek traders if they are in the vicinity. This suggests a willingness to transfer guilt to another party – and, in this instance, reveal Egyptians' condescension to Greeks – and a similar thought process can be seen in the Spartans' decision to offer up to Xerxes the lives of two of their citizens in an attempt to carry away the culpability arising from their earlier mistreatment of Persian heralds. Xerxes refuses to execute the two Spartans, saying he will not free the city from its 'guilt' (*aitiēs*, 7.136), but the accrued guilt is later paid for by the sons of the two Spartans when they die in circumstances that on the face it are completely unrelated to their fathers (7.137). In a consideration of this type of adjacency, Stern (1991) looks at the religious context of such events, seeing the consequences of mistreating heralds as a secularized equivalent, expressed in political and military language, of the Egyptian sacrifice of bulls.[33]

In *The Historical Method of Herodotus*, Lateiner (1989: 191–6) regards Herodotus' use of analogies as one of his ways of explaining causal relationships – with the principle of *tisis* (retribution) being an important type of analogy. References to the operation of *tisis*, 'payment by way of return or recompense, retribution, vengeance' (Liddell and Scott 2002), can be found in all of the Books except Four and Nine. It is the optic through which the acts of abductions recounted in the proem are thematized and the idea runs through the tale of Gyges. The oracle that confirms Gyges' place on the throne of Lydia adds that in the fifth generation the Heraclids, the family whom he has replaced by killing Candaules, will have their revenge (*tisis*, 1.13). When, four generations later, Croesus is deposed by the Persians he feels he has been tricked by the divine, but the priestess at Delphi tells him he has paid the penalty for the crime of Gyges (1.91). In Egypt, another oracle correctly foretells how Psammetichus will have his revenge (*tisis*) and regain rule of Egypt (2.152). In Book Three, retribution is observed operating in nature when the female snake that kills its mate by biting through his neck during insemination 'suffers in return [*tisin*]' when she is killed by her young eating through her womb (3.109).[34] Not long after the murder of Polycrates, 'atonement overtook' the killer (3.126), and in Book Five the brother of the tyrant Peisistratus in Athens is warned in a dream that no one escapes 'without paying the penalty' (5.56); the following day he is slain in public. *Tisis* is used to explain how a man who helps depose a Spartan king is punished for his role in the conspiracy (6.72), and Xerxes uses the word when talking of taking revenge on the Greeks for burning a temple in Persian territory (7.8). At the Battle of Salamis the word appears again when explaining how the Persians seek to trap the Greek ships in order to take revenge for the earlier Battle of Artemisium (8.76). Hermotimus is famous for taking the cruellest revenge (*tisis*) ever known (8.105).

Acts of sacrilege and subsequent misfortunes affecting the perpetrators are seen to reflect a concern for retribution by the divine: Cambyses dies of a wound in the same part of his body where he had struck a sacred bull (3.29, 3.64, 3.66); the madness and death of Cleomenes is related to his desecration of temples (6.75), though not everyone accepts this explanation (6.84); the injury that Miltiades suffers after illicitly entering a temple leads to his death (6.134–6); Themistocles is of the opinion that the Persians are defeated in Greece because of their acts of impieties (8.109) and credence is given to an oracle expressing a similar proposition (8.77). Mikalson (2003: 143) takes issue with Harrison (2000) over the extent to which the divine exacts retribution, asserting that the cases where divine intervention punishes an individual are always matters of impiety alone.

There are other manifestations of the divine (*to theion*) in Herodotus. Events involving oracles, dreams, sacrifices, portents and divinations abound, functioning as a ready-to-hand mode of thinking. The background presence of the divine as a way of being in the world needs to be accepted as such; it is not like the vital clue that the detective realizes makes sense of the crime scene and solves the case. The divine for Herodotus is neither a convenient substitute for a nexus of causal relations nor an alibi for not having one; his primary interest remains that of human behaviour. The gods may provoke, mislead, send signs, display partiality and intervene on occasion, but people are seen making decisions for themselves.[35] Croesus blames the oracle at Delphi for his decision to invade Persia but, fearing the growing power of Cyrus (1.46), his pre-emptive strike is in accord with his earlier, aggressive foreign policy. Moreover, there is a personal obligation involved (1.28, 73). It is also true that Herodotus does not rule out the effects of a divine agenda on human affairs: he notes that 'if' the rumour of the simultaneity of the battles of Plataea and Mycale is true then clearly the gods do take part in the affairs of humans (9.100) and he attributes the failure of the Greeks at Troy to realize that Helen was not inside the city to a divine plan: to show 'that vengeance [*timōriai*] from the gods for terrible wrongdoing is also terrible. This is what I believe and I state it.' (2.120) There is overdetermination in Herodotus, a habit of 'accumulating different causal explanations' of which the comingling of the human and divine is a 'refined example' (Pelling: 1991: 139). The Cretans will not join the anti-Persia alliance because in the past Greeks had failed to avenge the murder of Minos when he was in Sicily looking for his son. Later, after giving assistance to Menelaus when he took revenge against the Trojans for the loss of his wife Helen, they returned to Crete and the consequences. Their land suffered from plagues and famines, seen as a sure sign of Minos' displeasure for their failure to repay the obligation they owed him (7.169–71).

Retribution is one wheel in a complex cycle of reciprocities that entails responsibilities and obligations, usually of a personal kind and shaped by ties of kinship which can be inherited across generations. Reciprocity has a positive pole – the giving and receiving of gifts and favours and the bonds of guest-friendship (see p. 75) – and, in the exacting of revenge, a negative one. It is part of the complicated syntax of chronicle and causation in Herodotus, an intricate archipelago of explanations – rules of reciprocity, chance, fate, guest-friendship, the gods, the past, imperialism, pathologies and compulsions of individuals – with gaps and discontinuities between them but all part of the same historical landscape. This openness to multiple perspectives and competing discourses has been seen as a characteristic of Herodotus that sets him apart from Thucydides despite an important similarity. Both historians, for Pelling (2000: 82–6), provide an explanatory historical account with three shared concerns: imperialism's drive to expand, the causes of a state's loss of power being inseparable from the qualities which fuelled its success, and a set of psychological and ideological factors. Thucydides is seen to bring these strands together in a tightly cohesive story that leaves no gaps or uncertainties whereas Herodotus accommodates several interpretations in a way that allows for the employment of Bakhtin's term 'dialogic'.[36]

Herodotus the ethnographer

Book One of the *Histories* covers the emergence of Persia as a state and the development of its imperial ambitions; the final Books draw to a close as that empire comes face to face with an alliance of Greeks states resisting absorption into its realm of power. The history in between, from the mid-sixth century when the empire first establishes itself to the years 490–479 when the Persian–Greek battles take place, is filled with matters of ethnographic interest. When reading Herodotus, it is inevitable that at times the pattern into which these cultural excursions are woven will be lost, but the book's larger design is flexible enough to accommodate the ethnographic and other cultural material. Each account of a foreign campaign by Persia includes digressions on the people targeted for conquest, encompassing a variety of observations on their ways of life. These accounts are not blatantly ethnographic and nor are they those of an apologist for imperialism: inquiries into foreign forms of living are not invested with assumptions of cultural supremacy, justifying conquest by identifying the perceived inferiority of others. Herodotus is extraordinarily absorbed by the cultures of non-Greeks, hence Plutarch's denigration of him as a *philobarbaros* ('lover of barbarians').

Aspects of Lydian society are folded into the history of its military defeat by Persia; those of Babylon and the Massagetae into the history of Cyrus' endeavours to extend his imperial sway; the nature of Scythian lifestyle fits into the attempt by Darius to conquer that country.[37] In the case of Egypt, the reader momentarily forgets the geopolitical context – the Persian occupation of the country – given the plethora of everyday topics that are included: 'shopping practices, weaving, transporting burdens, urination and defecation, organization of the priesthood, care for the elderly, coiffure and practice related thereto, living arrangements with animals, bread-making, the kneading of dough and mud, circumcision, habits of dress, sail-making, and writing' (Lloyd 2002: 433). Culture becomes an inclusive field and embraces aspects of the animal world, especially where there is interaction between human and non-human worlds. Ibises are accorded respect by Egyptians because of the way they ambush the winged snakes that fly through a narrow pass from Arabia (2.75), and there are gold-digging ants in India whose benignity to anthropoids cannot be taken for granted (3.102,105). At the extremes of the known world, information of an ethnographic kind becomes scarce and Herodotus is unable to gather even the scantiest of rumours about Europe's westernmost areas: 'I have no knowledge of the Tin Islands where our tin is brought from' (3.115), a possible reference to Britain. Far to the east, by contrast, there are from the perspective of Greeks – monogamous consumers of cooked cereals and meat – alarmingly strange and lurid reports of Indian cultures where food is not cooked and sex takes place in the open 'just like cattle' (3.101). A map of Herodotus' world would look like one of those *mappae mundi*, a medieval map with depictions of fantastical creatures decorating the edges of the known world.

In the Greek, 'Herodotus' is the first word of the *Histories* and it is followed by 'Halicarnassus' (modern Bodrum), a Greek colony in a region of Asia Minor known as Caria. Halicarnassus, where Herodotus grew up speaking and writing Greek (though Carian or Carian-influenced names are found in his family), was a multicultural city, although Caria was part of the province of Lydia and had come under Persian suzerainty by the time he was born there. This made him part of a Greek diaspora and a subject of the Persian Empire. The Persians, the masters of central Asia, were a people who had expanded their territory in the previous century from their homeland in what is now southern Iran. This Persian Empire had a road network that linked the coast of Asia Minor with its capital at Susa, near the head of the Persian Gulf, enabling 'a distance of more than 1,600 miles to be covered in the course of a week' (Frankopan 2015: 2). Along these roads, the value of which Herodotus highlights (8.98), travelled armies, merchants and nomads and with them came gossip, tales, legends, customs and ideas. There was interaction between the Mediterranean and the Near East and the geography of the region was not politicized in the way it would come to be: a unidimensional East–West division, the Occidental and Oriental schism, with ancient Greece portrayed only as a 'prehistoric Miss Liberty, holding aloft the torch of moral purpose in the barbarian night' (Wolf 2010: 5); but, as Wolf goes on to point out, more Greeks fought in the armies of Darius and Xerxes than for the Greek city-states that opposed them on battlefields.[38]

The shadow cast by Hellenocentrism over the cultural achievements of Persia has now been lifted by contemporary scholarship.[39] The Persian Empire stretched from the eastern end of the Aegean, taking in the Black Sea and the Caspian as well as Egypt, Palestine, Syria, encompassed modern Iraq, Iran and Afghanistan and reached to Pakistan and the Indian Ocean. The Persian monarchy boasted of its domain's vast dimensions[40] but no known history of the empire was written about from a Persian perspective. Herodotus is the most important written source of information and he bears witness to some of the many cultures over which Persia exerted, or sought to exert, imperial sway. His home city was a cultural borderland between

Asia and Europe, intermarriage between descendants of the original Greek settlers and the Carians who lived inland was common and such a mixing of race and culture mirrors what would have occurred in other parts of the empire. People from Asia Minor worked in Babylon, Carians in Egypt (2.61), Jews were stationed at a garrison at Aswan (Hornblower 2011b: 68), Greeks travelled to Susa. It is not surprising to find Herodotus frequently pointing to cross-cultural resonances, deflating Greek ethnocentrism in the process, and the first sentence of the *Histories* announces his intention to record the achievements of non-Greeks as well as Greeks. His first piece of historical data (1.1) records the origins of the Phoenicians, migrants from what he calls the Red Sea (the Persian Gulf), and it is noteworthy that he nowhere proclaims the uniqueness of the Greeks (Munson 2001a: 76)

Herodotus can be journalistic but he is never jingoistic. He likes superlatives – 'the happiest of men' (1.30); marvels 'more remarkable than those produced by any other country' (2.35); the 'greatest of all military expeditions' (7.20); the cruellest act of vengeance 'ever known' (8.105), and so on[41] – but also likes pointing to cross-cultural influences: the Lydians were the first to use gold and silver coinage and may have invented games played by Greeks (1.94); army divisions were first developed by the Medes (1.103) but helmet crests and other devices on shields were invented by Carians (1.171); yoking four horses to a chariot came from Libya (4.189); writing was brought to the Greeks by the Phoenicians (5.58). He notes similarities between Spartan customs and those of Persia (6.58–9) and Egypt (6.60). The names of the Greek gods are traced back to Egypt (2.50, 2.53)[42] as well as various religious customs (2.58 and 2.64). Herodotus enjoys the role of cultural cartographer, stepping back and comparing two cultures, especially when one of them is his own. He avoids disparaging other cultures; unlike the first Persian king in the story he tells about a Spartan mission with a message for Cyrus (1.152–3). The Spartans warn him to avoid harming any Greek city and Cyrus replies with a threat and a rude remark about the Greek practice of allotting a set space as a marketplace (*agora*). He identifies a feature of a foreign culture that is not found in his own country and wrongly interprets it as a place of organized fraud. The Other is not the barbarian but the Greek as seen from a Persian perspective.

Herodotus travels the world and takes note of differences in lifestyles and mindsets among the different groups of people he encounters or hears about and inquires into, always aware of the plural perspectives of other people and remarkably critical in his attitude to questions of apparently stable ethnicities.[43] He is struck by differences in the normative realms peculiar to each society and the reader comes to perceive a sophisticated mind capable of understanding and empathizing with cultures very different to his own but without feeling threatened. At times he comes across as an investigative journalist, but he is not tied down to current events and speculates on philosophical and anthropological matters, driven by curiosity, imagination and open-mindedness. He is an intellectual, unaffiliated, and he does not naively believe everything he hears, rejecting, for example, reports of one-eyed men (3.116), a tribe who sleep for half the year (4.25), werewolves (4.105), the phenomenon of the sun being on the right after sailing around the south of Africa (4.42) and the existence of a river called Ocean encircling the world (2.23).[44] Sometimes he reports something that looks to require a suspension of disbelief, as with the Arabian sheep fitted with miniature wheeled carts to keep their very long tails off the ground (3.113), but which doesn't.[45] Herodotus is broadminded and humane but does not hesitate to express a personal opinion where he feels it necessary, finding it morally distasteful that most people are sanguine about sex taking place in temples (2.64) – the Greeks and Egyptians being noble exceptions – but praising a Babylonian practice designed to improve the chances of people recovering from medical problems (1.197). When he reports facts but withholds an opinion where one might be expected, his silence can be pregnant with meaning: noting how some Greek states that did not participate in the Battle of Plataea – 'the finest victory of all those we know of' (9.64) – erected empty sepulchres on the battlefield to hide their shame (9.85), he remains tight-lipped; similarly, no comment follows his gruesomely detailed description of human sacrifices by the Scythians (4.62).

The scale and depth of his undertaking is so breathtakingly ambitious that it comes across as churlish when Herodotus is criticized for not being the kind of historian someone wants him to be. Briant, writing a landmark history of ancient Persia, finds him wanting because he 'treats it [Darius' campaign in Scythia] only very superficially. His main interest is in fact describing the different Scythian peoples . . . One digression leads to another' (2002: 142). It is true that Herodotus is writing before the long footnote became a tool for historians, but what the complaint ignores is the way that ethnographic and other material can be pleated into historical concerns and this is clear from Redfield's analysis of 'hard' and 'soft' cultures (Redfield: 2013: 281–2). This theme in the *Histories* will be looked at below but the point to be made here is that the cultural differentiation into 'hard' and 'soft' ways of life also plays itself out on the historical stage and takes on ideological freightage: political autonomy is a privilege of the 'hard' and they are never conquered by a 'soft' people.

Jacoby's view that the ethnographical material was composed at an earlier time in Herodotus' career, before he became absorbed by the Greek–Persia conflict, need not be rejected in its entirety. Between the early books of the *Histories* and the last three that tighten the focus on the military progression of Xerxes' invasion, there is a perceptible change in emphasis and many would sympathize with Fornara's judgement that 'every reader . . . has sensed the relative independence of his account of Egypt' (1971: 3). A drawback to this way of thinking – archaeological in its temptation to separate strata and allocate them temporally – is a forgetting that the Persian Wars are only one part of the declared brief in the programmatic statement at the start of the *Histories*. Greeks and non-Greeks are to be accorded equality of treatment in the face of time's corrosive ability to render everything evanescent unless it is recorded for posterity. Such equality covers both the historical and the ethnographic and this latitude allows for an extended look at Egyptian culture but within the context of a historical inquiry: a relatively young Persian Empire imposing hegemony over a very ancient civilization.

The *Histories* as literature

For Jacoby, Herodotus is an ethnographer who evolves into a historian and then strings his previously separate *logoi* together but leaves the seams showing. For many first-time readers, consternation is not caused by an apparent muddling of genres per se – after all, some brands of postmodernism would like to regard this as passé – but by the bewildering sensation of simply losing one's bearings with a narrative possessing a cast of over 900 named individuals and nearly 700 locations.

Assistance with locating the names of places in the text is available through Hestia (http://hestia.open.ac.uk). The reader becomes accustomed to taking stock of the narrative, making mental if not written bookmarks, and needs to do so from the very beginning. The history of Lydia and its subjection by Persia is the first historical account in the story of the Persian Empire's expansion, but as soon as it gets going with the mention of Croesus (1.6), there is a flashback (1.7–25) explaining how the kingdom first passed into the rule of Croesus' ancestors. The reader can feel sidetracked by the various tales and the first digressions, dealing with Athens and Sparta and not continued until Book Five, have to be taken in before the narrative arrives at the point where Lydia comes into conflict with Persia (1.71). Readers know that the Persia–Greece conflict is to come but Herodotus is busy making other plans, laying out the expansion of the Persian state and its encroachment into Europe, first in Scythia in Book Four, and then the consequences of the Ionian revolt. The end (*telos*) is always in sight and the overriding theme of tyranny versus freedom circulates intermittently in Book Three with the Constitutional Debate (3.80–3) and events on Samos (3.142–3).

There is now no shortage of excellent scholarship that shows how reading the *Histories*, far from being a perplexing experience, is enriched by the structure and style of the book. A parallel, as de Jong indicates (2013: 268), can be usefully drawn with the *Odyssey*. Homer's epic covers only forty days as reported through the central narrator, but flashbacks and flashforwards turn this into ten years. The *Histories* covers around eighty years, from the middle of the sixth century to 478, but this unrolls into a far longer period that stretches back to pre-Greek times. The parallel is not meant to be exact because Herodotus' flashbacks, unlike Homer's, take the reader into territory and topics not previously covered and they are occasioned both by the narrator and by characters introduced into the narrative. There are also many more of them than found in Homer, and in Book Five they come particularly thick and fast.

The difficulties can be exaggerated. Most readers do not begin on the first page and continue reading as if making their way through a long novel and, while the flashbacks and embedded micro-narratives may sometimes recall Proust's time shifts, Herodotus' sentences are rarely convoluted or difficult to follow. His style of writing is paratactic – from the Greek (*parataxis*) for the orderly arrangement of troops in a battle line – using straightforward sentences with consecutive clauses and a light use of conjunctions. Aristotle (*Rhetoric*, 3.9) described the style as *lexis eiromenē* ('continuous style'), the word *eiromenē* meaning 'to fasten together in rows, to string'. A notable exception to this style, but no less lucid, is the final sentence in the story of Adrastus, a fratricide who is cleansed of the stain of homicide by Croesus only to go on and accidently kill the king's son. Standing by the burial place of the son, he delivers a self-inflicted verdict on the misery of his misfortune: 'Adrastus, son of Midas and grandson of Gordias – the man who became the slayer of his brother and murderer of the man who had purified him, when silence fell upon those around the tomb, recognising himself to be the most ill-fated of all men he knew, cut his own throat upon the mound' (1.45). As Gould remarks, the man's ancestry and life-story are 'gathered in to define him in the moment of his death' and he falls 'with the weight of an axe-blow across the culmination of the story' (1989: 54). The edge of this figurative axe is one word in Greek – '*barusumphorōtatos*' (the 'most ill-fated') – and is used only once by Herodotus and quite possibly for the first time in ancient Greek literature; nearly all occurrences of the word after Herodotus are also superlatives, suggesting that his use created a literary benchmark.[46]

The literary style adapts in some degree to the needs of the narrative and in this respect there is a noticeable difference between the early and late books. In building up the background to the Greek–Persian conflict there are many anecdotes and short stories, but as the conflict moves centre stage there are long speeches advocating various courses of action and tightly written accounts of military engagements. The syntactical style of the speeches, nevertheless, is remarkably similar to the rest of the *Histories*; the writing style of Herodotus remains a constant.

The narrative point of view, called focalization in narratology, also changes in the telling of events and there can be secondary focalizations taking place within a story. Xerxes, having returned to Susa after his defeats in Greece, falls in love with the wife of his brother Masistes before switching his attention to her daughter, Artaynte. The tale of what takes place (9.108–13) begins from Xerxes' point of view, but when his wife, Amestris, finds out that a shawl she embroidered for her husband has been gifted to

Artaynte the perspective shifts. Now the reader follows Amestris' revenge-seeking plotting. After the horrendous mutilation of Artaynte's mother, the focalization shifts again, this time to Masistes, and the tale comes to an end with the impersonal, controlling voice of the author: 'Such is the story of Xerxes' passion and Masistes' death' (9.113).

Telling stories

A decisive moment in the life of Croesus and the history of Persia comes when he crosses the River Halys with his army, committing his country to a war which leads to its defeat by Cyrus. Herodotus states in a few words that he is of the opinion that Croesus used a bridge that was in place at the time. He then devotes fifteen lines to an alternative story, which he does not believe to be true, about how Thales of Miletus cleverly devised a way of crossing the river without the use of a bridge (1.75). Something similar occurs in the writing with the homeward journey of Xerxes after his defeat at the Battle of Salamis. He reaches the Hellespont and crosses it in a ship, the bridge that had been built for the invasion having been shattered by storms (8.117). This is what Herodotus believes to have happened but it does not prevent a far lengthier account being provided, an alternative version that becomes a short story about a sea captain who is rewarded for saving the life of his royal passenger but then executed for the manner in which he did so (8.118–19, see p. 228). Herodotus enjoys telling a story that has a basis in fact – Croesus does cross the Halys and Xerxes does cross the sea in a ship – but with fictional adornments that are characteristic of other anecdotes fuelled by the rich storytelling tradition that Herodotus inherits. A clever solution to a problem, like Thales' engineering project, or a tale with a punchline as in Xerxes' two summary judgements being delivered almost simultaneously – especially one that allows for a touch of the author's black humour to be added – are typical of a story that gets retold for its entertainment value.

Gérard Genette, a literary theorist who influenced narrative theory,[47] introduced the terms analepsis (flashback) and prolepsis (flashforward) and they are germane to the way linear time in the main narrative of the *Histories* can be interrupted by multiple micro-stories that regularly intrude into the main chronicle. The temporal ordering of events in the overarching narrative discourse follows the succession of Persian kings, from Cyrus through to Xerxes, but this temporal sequencing is not the same as the chronological ordering of events on the level of the mini-narratives. These smaller stories, expanding, explaining or providing background information, usually take the form of an analepsis or prolepsis. The discordance between the two time scales is called anachrony by Genette,[48] and de Jong (2013: 273–81) presents a case for describing the structure of the *Histories* as 'anacronical', looking at the Persian debate over whether or not to invade Greece as an example (see pp. 197–201).[49]

Authorial assistance in negotiating the frequent narrative detours is provided by short statements that are not part of the story being told and which form a different level of discourse. These metanarrative comments serve to introduce or summarize material which represents a departure in time or place from the preceding narrative. When the story of Croesus has been told, concluding with his defeat by the Persians under Cyrus, the reader is addressed: 'My account [*logos*] now obliges me to inquire who this Cyrus was by whom the empire of Croesus was destroyed . . .' (1.95); or, more succinctly: 'We now turn to their [Babylonian] customs' (1.196).[50] Sometimes the metanarrative remark becomes more communicative and prepares the reader for an interpretation of what is to follow. A dream experienced by Croesus (1.34) will set in train a course of events that will destroy the happiness that he feels so confidently endowed with, but before this story is told the reader is given an indication of why his life is going to suffer a terrible reversal: 'After Solon had left, divine indignation [*nemesis*] from god fell heavily on Croesus: as I guess, because he supposed himself to be blest beyond all other men' (1.34).

The short stories invite appreciation and enjoyment as a narrative art form in their own right, varying in length and register, weaving direct and indirect dialogue and speeches into a narrative pattern created by the measured voice of the author. The proem, dealing ostensibly with the roots of Greek–Persian enmity, offers a hint of what is in store for the reader. In place of dry historical data presented impersonally, there is a conversational, anecdotal style of delivery – 'or six days later when they were nearly sold out, a number of women came down to the beach to see the fair' – that would not be out of place in a novella. Incidental details are keenly observed – the women are 'standing about near the vessel's stern' (1.1) – but the reader does not wonder about the source for such pictorial precision. In the tale about Gyges, pictorial exactitude in the interior space of the royal bedroom lends conviction to what unfolds: there is a door behind which the bodyguard must stand in order to be able see the king's wife undress; a chair on which she will 'lay each article of her clothing as she takes it off, and you will be able to look upon her at your leisure' (1.9). The most memorable parts of the Croesus *logos* are the short stories embedded within it, tales told with verve by a practised narrator: 'He likes the incremental triple, which repeats the basic pattern for increasing impact, as in Croesus' triple rejection of Solon's advice' (Gray 2002: 297).

Given the proliferation and form of short stories in Herodotus, a comparison has been made with *One Thousand and One Nights* because of the way in which the frame story in that collection, the relationship between Shahryar and his wife Scheherazade, is eclipsed by the multitude of all the other stories within its frame (Curthoys and Docker 2006: 30). A mini-tale in Herodotus can sometimes be nested within a tale which itself is part of a larger frame and, like a Russian *matryoshka* doll, they fit together for no other ostensible purpose than the joy of matching and unmatching them.

Some, like the tale about Arion and the dolphin (1.23–4), are very short but memorable while the rise of Cyrus is a veritable short story choreographed into Persia's political history. Others are remarkably elliptical, like the unfortunate Aminocles who became rich by retrieving treasure chests from shipwrecks of a Persian war fleet but who had to live 'with the grief of having killed his son' (7.190); Herodotus gets that, and says nothing more about him. Aminocles' fate mirrors the change in fortune that marks far lengthier accounts like the one about Polycrates, a complex tale with micro-stories nested within it (3.39–43, 120–5). Whatever their length, stories come to life with visual and verbal moments of memorable import, ranging from the ending of the Atys and Adrastus episode quoted above to the humorous verbal felicity of the lighter tale of the banished Samians. They request help from the famously terse Spartans but their speech is too lengthy and deemed incomprehensible. Being smart and resourceful they return with a sack and merely state that the sack needs flour, only to be informed – with the laconic style of the author's delivery perfectly matching the dry and deadpan wit of the Spartans – that they could have dispensed with the word 'sack'(3.46). Herodotus' sense of humour can be as dry and understated as the Spartans', as when he tells of the incredible 16-km underwater swim by Scyllias and remarks with faux seriousness that his own opinion is that 'on this occasion, he made his way by boat' (8.8).[51]

Direct speech is also used to make a story memorably vivid, with the reader becoming a spectator listening and observing the scene, as with the tale of the Persian envoys' encounter with the long-lived Ethiopians (3.17–25). In the story about Periander there is the heartfelt plea of his daughter to her brother, begging him to return home and bring the family together once more: 'Come back home and stop punishing yourself . . . Our father is an old man now. Don't abandon your property to strangers' (3.53).

The short stories found throughout the *Histories* bear testimony to the tremendous influence of oral tradition at the level of composition and content. Many of them share motifs from folk tales, like the story about Rhampsinitus (see p. 107), and the recurrence of certain themes suggest a popular interest, shared by Herodotus, in topics like the need to make a difficult decision in the face of a shocking dilemma. The wife of Intaphrenes can only save the life of one member of her family (3.119) and the wife of Sesostris realizes that her family can only be saved if the lives of two of her sons are sacrificed (2.107). Herodotus, far more than a conduit for popular stories and folk tales, chooses and shapes from a pool of material that he collected according to his own literary desires. This can be established when, as in the case of the Gyges story, a different version is known from an account by Plato (see pp. 68–9). The existence of a magical ring that confers invisibility on its wearer is discarded in favour of a more real-life drama where lack of visibility is a stratagem designed by a husband who wants his wife to be seen naked by another man. In the tale of Arion and the dolphin (1.23–4), it might be expected that the lyre player would consciously call on his patron god Apollo for assistance, but a supernatural rescue is replaced by a fabulous one. This allows the emphasis to stay focused on the theatricality of the moment and Arion's death-defying decision to end his life in a manner than befits his calling (see pp. 69–70).

Literary influences

The *Iliad* and *Odyssey* constitute one of the two most important literary influences on Herodotus and their gravitational pull is persistent both conceptually and verbally.[52] Examples will be highlighted in the commentary on individual books of the *Histories* while at a general level a noticeable influence of Homer is detectable in the way Herodotus enlivens his chronicle with theatrical renderings of scenes and speeches and the skilful dramatization of key narrative moments. This is well illustrated in the conversation between Solon and Croesus (1.30–2) and in the Macedonian dinner party (5.17–22). At the compositional level, Homer's subject – the war between Greeks and Trojans – finds a correspondence in the war between the Greeks and Persia, the greatest of events for Herodotus and his contemporaries just as the fighting at Troy was for those who lived in the distant past. On more than one occasion, though, he shows a willingness to rework material from the epic poet[53] and when he does relate a truth about Helen's whereabouts during the siege of Troy, which Homer declined to mention, he notes that the epic poet's choice to leave it out was because it was 'not so suited [*euprepēs*] to epic poetry' (2.116). The meaning of *euprepēs* takes in the aesthetic ('appealing, well-looking') and the literary ('seemly, appropriate'), and by the same token Herodotus' reasons for keeping Helen in Egypt throughout the siege could also be literary in nature.

The theatrical aspect that Herodotus brings to his text has dual influences and Attic drama is likely to have been as much, if not more, of an inspiration as Homer. Herodotus is believed to have spent time in Athens and there are records that indicate he knew Sophocles;[54] points of contact between Herodotus and the dramas of Aeschylus, Sophocles and Euripides will be noted when they occur. In the story of Atys and Adrastus, to take one example, there are various reminders of conventions and poetic idioms from Athenian tragedy: scenes are marked by the arrival and departure of main characters; an unknown messenger arrives with unexpected news; there is a supplication and a burial procession; and like Oedipus, Croesus tries to avoid the portent of a family tragedy but only succeeds in facilitating its execution.[55]

In the Gyges story (1.8–12), the ethically inflected choice facing the king's most trusted bodyguard is really no choice at all – Gyges can only save his life by taking someone else's – but it is not dissimilar to the sort of dilemmas found in Greek tragedy: Agamemnon either sacrifices his daughter Iphigenia or his Zeus-directed mission to Troy; Orestes must avenge his father but only by killing his mother. A papyrus fragment indicates a drama was written around the Gyges story and, even though the fragment is now thought to have been influenced by and written after Herodotus, it points to the tale's tragic potential. When dialogue within the tale is also taken into account along with the oracle's pronouncement that vengeance will descend on a future generation (1.13 and 1.91), suggestive of the accursed houses of Atreus and Laius, the result is more reminiscent of poetic drama than a historical event (Saïd 2002: 132–4). Yet the Heraclid dynasty did come to an abrupt end around the late eighth/early seventh century and Herodotus does want to offer an account of a dramatic coup d'état. The transition in power from Candaules to Gyges suggests itself as a Greek parallel to a reflection by a character in Joyce's *Ulysses* on an incident in Roman history, something that happened in the past but was subject to the distortions of time: 'Fabled by the daughters of memory. And yet it was in some way if not as memory fabled it' (Joyce 1984: 2.7–8).

One way of approaching a reconcilement of the *Histories* as a work of high literary value with its achievement as a major work of history is by looking to aspects of theories that blur the distinction between historiography and literary texts. For Hayden White, a key figure in this respect, the two discourses of literature and history may be seen as ontological cousins, with the writing of history engaging with and depending on the imaginative faculty as well as empirical research. The consanguinity is very close: 'The differences between a history and a fictional account of reality are matters of degree rather than of kind' (White 1973: 296, n. 27).[56] Plot, taken as a temporal ordering of events and driven by a compulsion for narrativity, is common to fiction and historiography and in both cases is usually understood to involve causal links and a consideration of motives. For Hayden White, the work of the historian in arranging events and sorting them into a hierarchy of meanings involves an essentially poetic dimension.[57] Although the facts themselves are not invented, they are constructed in so far as their meaning and significance is shaped into a set, a completed story, and White explains this by way of three approaches: emplotment, argument and ideology (2014: 7–28). The intricacies of his taxonomy need not be taken on board but his distinction between the aesthetic nature of emplotment and the cognitive quality of argument and ideology is illuminating. Emplotment is White's term for the developmental story that emerges from the way events are framed, forming an aesthetic that is different in kind from the intellectual and philosophical orientations that characterize the other two modes, argument and ideology. The possibility of a different make of story emerging from the same events induces epistemological anxiety and charges of relativism.[58] Choices are made about what is worth writing about, causality is considered and what unrolls is a narrative chain of events that we call history but which is also a story shaped aesthetically and cognitively by the author. Each fact does not possess its own precisely determinate atomic weight: they can be enlarged or shrunk, take on huge or minimal significance, depending on how – temporal succession notwithstanding – they are joined up. This is something that may be shaped by literary choices on the part of the author and the facts themselves may be affected by the way they are written about. The process can be seen as akin to the observer effect in physics, as shown by an incident during the Battle of Salamis that Herodotus records. During the battle Xerxes takes up a hillside position to watch events, but his presence as spectator affects the course of the battle: each of his men think the king has his eye on them and when some of the Persian ships try to withdraw the scale of losses is compounded because those stationed behind the fleeing ship press forward in the hope of performing valorously before the king and they collide with the leading ships that are on their side (8.86–90). Just as the observation of an event can affect what is observed, the historiographical act affects the subject matter that is being written about.

Themes and patterns

Postmodern questionings of history do not necessarily entail a wholesale abandonment of knowledge claims regarding the past, although this was how they were represented and responded to at the time.[59] What once caused controversy has now acquired a patina of acceptance, the ability to provoke has faded and, while factualism never was denied by Hayden White, the idea that historical knowledge is to some extent rendered by the historian's composition of it is no longer a shocking proposition. Fixing the borders of the extent is open to contention around issues of the past's recoverability and the ahistorical implications that come with thinking of the past as an artefact crafted by literary minds. What is more acceptable is that historians do author their work by arranging – or, more polemically, fashioning – their material into a narrative. Narrative is not the prerogative of a literary mode of discourse; the unswerving arrow of time makes it an imperative for historians, but there is a degree of prefiguring in the crafting of an interpretative pattern for understanding the past. At the same time, one view of the world can be privileged over another and regarded as a more truthful historical account even if both views are perspectival. It is not necessary to throw out a literary-historical plane of interpretation with the postmodernist bathwater. Herodotus does not lay down a priori lines connecting points on the map of human history, but there are narrative idioms, topoi and categories of thought that affect the form and content of his writing. Bearing historical as well as literary weight, these matrices function like a leaven in the text; and an important pattern is created by variations on the motif of fate, with repetitions in the way certain situations and events are described.

Fate

If one end of the spectrum of meanings attached to *tisis* is plain revenge, the other reaches out to a realm of cosmic justice and the workings of fate. Notions of such ultimacy possess explanatory power and this is sensed by Herodotus when he connects the deaths of the sons of Bulis and Sperthias with the divine (7.137), allowing for correlation to morph into causation. When Croesus is complaining to the oracle at Delphi, the priestess refers back four generations to Gyges' usurpation of the throne and the paying of a penalty. Her words evoke a doom-laden, pagan belief that no matter what, we cannot escape the consequences of past acts. Individuals are not cognisant but consequences follow them like ghostly footsteps and sooner or later catch up and demand that the debt be settled. The priestess speaks of Gyges' appointed lot, using the word *moira*, saying this is something no one can escape, 'not even a god' (1.91). *Moira* is usually translated as fate and if even a god cannot escape it then its power is truly cosmic, transcending the divine. Such an idea, by no means peculiar to Herodotus, stretches back to archaic Greece and earlier, suggesting there is an ordered arrangement in the world, governed by necessity (*anankē*). Fragments of the pre-Socratic Heraclitus refer to 'measures' which even the sun has to acknowledge (Barnes 1982: 100). The word *moira* means a portion, a part, and thus one's portion in life is one's fate or destiny.[60] Yet Herodotus also insists on showing how individuals freely make their own decisions and are responsible for what they do. Leonidas is praised for his decision to remain at Thermopylae and die fighting (7.220) and although this happens to fulfil an oracle there is no suggestion that it is any less a personal choice than Ephialtes' was to lead the Persians around the mountain so they could entrap the Greeks. Human responsibility has no hiding place, unlike an only child who excuses some tangle of their making by talking about the powers of an unseen friend, but there is a methodological dualism available to Herodotus: the realm of the divine and the historiographical realm of human causation.

There is a puzzling episode in Book Six that hinges on ineliminable issues of fate and freedom, and if it fails to arrive as a satisfactory explanation this is down to intrinsic perplexities with the ideas at play and not some ineptness on the writer's part. The Athenian Miltiades is unsuccessfully trying to besiege Paros and is willing to follow the advice of a minor priestess of a temple, Timo. Assured by her of success, he enters a sanctuary, with impious intentions which are never made clear, but is spooked by something and injures himself when rushing to leave. The siege fails and the Parians consult the oracle at Delphi about their intention to execute Timo for her treacherous behaviour, only to be told she is not to blame. Miltiades was fated to die, pronounces the oracle; it was an 'apparition' or an 'appearance' (*phanēnai*) of Timo that led him to enter the sanctuary. Sure enough, back in Athens, a humiliated Miltiades dies from the wound he received when leaving the sanctuary (6.134–6). Herodotus remains studiously noncommittal about the story's truth, stating that the Parians are his only source for what happened on the island. The vignette has a degree of similarity with a later one set in Apollonia, a remote region in north-west Greece. An appointed guard, Euenius, falling asleep and failing to prevent the killing of a number of sacrosanct sheep by wolves, is brought to court and blinded for his offence. Later, with harvests failing and sheep becoming barren, it is clear that the gods are offended and oracles inform the Apollonians that their punishment of Euenius was unjust and recompense must be made. It was, say the oracles, the gods themselves who had sent the wolves (9.93). This is another puzzling tale, not least because of the way the Apollonians fulfil the gods' demand for recompense (see pp. 241–2),[61] inhabiting a world where an individual or a group act for their own ends but unwittingly bring about the realization of some higher, ulterior purpose. As in the popularized understanding of Hegel's 'cunning of history', which can be seen as a secular version of the opaque workings of fate, subjective intentions of a self-aggrandizing kind achieve aims that have an objective purpose not comprehended by the historical agents involved.[62] Miltiades, caught in 'the cunning of reason' by a limited horizon of meaning, follows Timo's advice and by failing fulfils his role.

There is no consensus about the importance or exact meaning that the locutions surrounding the concept of fate held for Herodotus. The term *moira* is not often used by Herodotus and, for Lateiner, fate only *appears* to function as a form of causality but it lacks explanatory force and only in retrospect does it takes on the mantle of destiny (1989: 197).[63] Nonetheless, there are references to intimations of fate, an inevitability surrounding what is about to happen to Apries (2.161), Polycrates (3.43), Scycles (4.79), the city of Corinth (5.92) and Artaynte (9.109). Such moments have a literary or theatrical value by engaging the reader with insider information about what is about to happen, not unlike the way certain camera angles or editing techniques in a film prepare the viewer and create dramatic tension.

Adrastus, whose story has been mentioned above, has a name linguistically connected with *adrasteia* (inescapable), an epithet for the goddess Nemesis, and his inability to escape implacable fate is entwined with a similar failure on the part of Croesus, the man who tries to help him. Croesus is anxious to avert his son being killed in the way his dream foretells, but it is his attempt at prevention that actually brings it about (1.34–43). The story is a variation on the theme Žižek refers to as truth arising from misrecognition, which he illustrates by the myth of Oedipus and by the story about the 'appointment in Samarra', to show how a prophecy becomes true *because* the attempt to evade it is what allows its realization. In Somerset Maugham's retelling of a Mesopotamian story, a servant is terrified by the gaze on the face of Death when he encounters him in a Baghdad market. The servant borrows his master's horse and flees to Samarra and the master goes to the market place to find Death and reproach him: but Death says how he didn't intend to scare the servant but was only greatly surprised to see him there because he had an appointment that night with him in Samarra (Žižek 1989: 57–8). A paradox to do with fate is at work in the way Cambyses meets his end. He kills his brother Smerdis in order to eliminate a threat to his rule that a dream tells him will come from someone of that name but it is another and unrelated Smerdis who will actually conspire against him. In the attempt to deal with the real threat, he accidentally injures himself mounting his horse and later dies from the wound at Ecbatana. This was to be the place of death as foretold in an oracle but he had always assumed it referred to Ecbatana in Persia, not another place with the same name in another land; either way, it was his 'assigned end' (*peprōmenon teleutan*) and he comes to realize this before he dies (3.64–5). The circumstances leading to the deaths of Adrastus and Cambyses are uncanny, and evoking fate can be seen as the bringing of an Ockham's razor to them, the quickest way of accounting for unsettling coincidences that defy probability, what the surrealists called 'objective chance'.[64]

In order to account for what happens, events can be retrospectively positioned so as to produce a causal chain that makes the result appear inevitable. The event, the effect of something contingent, can be explained by positing necessity as its organizing force. Necessity, fate, is retrospective and the inevitability it imposes comes about because of an intrinsically accidental event; something that is perhaps there in the background when we speak of 'as a simple twist of fate', the inexplicable moment that determines that which follows and in a way that could never be foreseen – unless you are Apollo. The circumstances of Cambyses' fated death make a satisfying narrative conclusion to the life of a man who is presented as cruel and ruthless, someone who in the ends gets what he deserves (see p. 121), and such a coupling of fate with characterization is often the case. Croesus' downfall, notwithstanding the oracle's reminder that he is fated to fall because of what happened generations earlier, is linked to his overconfidence. Amasis brings his relationship with Polycrates to an end because 'he perceived that no man could save another from what was going to happen' (3.43), but accompanying this fatalism is the realization that in time Polycrates' acquisitive nature will meet its match. Amasis knows that sooner or later Polycrates will experience some chance event that will point to the fickle nature of fortune (as it does, 3.120–5). Uncertainty about fortune and fate, the ups and downs of life and sudden reversals in one's luck, are seen in the *Histories* as fundamental forces at work in the human universe and this is what Amasis realizes about Polycrates. He pushes his own wheel of necessity and assumes his fate.

Life, luck and everything

A work of history as well as a work of literature can show forth a philosophy, and in reading the *Histories* there emerges, at historical and literary levels, a feeling of how life as a whole is viewed by the author. There are occasions when Herodotus is supremely sensitive to the transitory nature of life and the pain of its wrenching contingencies. Philosophical reflections of this order dominate the encounter between Solon and Croesus (see pp. 72–3) and they are a topic of conversation between Xerxes and Artabanus when the king unexpectedly starts to shed tears and Artabanus remarks that we have only a taste of how sweet life could be before the gods become envious (see p. 205). To be overjoyed and exceedingly happy (*perikharēs*) about something carries a health warning in Herodotus; on almost every occasion the word's use refers to a character about to suffer grief or a disappointment (Chiasson 1983). Harpagus feels *perikharēs* at the honour of being invited to dinner with the king where he will unknowingly be served the flesh of his own son (1.119); the same word is used to describe the Persian Oeobazus' delight at the prospect of his sons (who will be executed) being exempted from service in his country's Scythian expedition (4.84); Xerxes is *perikharēs* on hearing that a solar eclipse foretells defeat for the Greeks (7.37).[65]

Alongside this tragic awareness, there is an equally fine attunement to what gives dignity and meaning to life, a sentiment that lies behind Herodotus' declaration that he knows the names of all the 300 who died at Thermopylae (7.224) or in his story of Arion's leap (see pp. 69–70).[66]

Solon says the 'happiest' (*olbiōtatos*) man he has ever known is Tellus an Athenian and, while *olbos* can mean wealth, the man's happiness is due to more than material prosperity. The first reason, explains Solon when asked by the disgruntled Croesus who thinks the display of his treasury should earn him the award, is that Tellus came from a flourishing city and the second reason is that his children outlived him and he had grandchildren. This cannot be said for many of the citizens of communities who become victims of wars and imperial aggression: Cambyses executes 2,000 Egyptians after his conquest of the country (3.14); Pelasgians are subjected to ethnic cleansing (6.137);[67] the Paeonians are forcibly deported (5.12); and after the failure of the Ionian revolt the men are killed and the women and children sold into slavery (6.18). The human cost of war, the unconscionable suffering of individuals in these impersonal multitudes, are not ignored by Herodotus, and his acute and sympathetic awareness of personal anguish often comes to the fore. There is the eloquent plea of the Greek woman, forced into becoming a sex slave for a Persian, who asks a Spartan general for consideration of her plight (9.76); for Psammetichus, the overwhelming grief he feels is beyond the power of words to express, 'too great for tears' (3.14).[68]

Croesus tells Cyrus that no one would choose war over peace – 'in peace, sons bury their fathers; in war, fathers bury their sons' (1.87) – but Herodotus bears testimony to how frequently this is negated by the choices individuals and states do make; as a chronicle of many wars, international and local, the *Histories* is also a register of deaths and atrocities so terrible that at one point he refuses to go into details: Polycrates dies 'in a way not fit to be told' (3.125).

Underlying the unspooling of life's ups and downs, there is a cognizable mindfulness in Herodotus of the persistent role of good luck (*tuchē*) in averting misfortune. A future ruler of Corinth escapes being killed as an infant because he happened to smile at his would-be murderer (5.92), and Sylsson's spontaneous gift of his cloak to the young Darius proves fortuitous when he later needs assistance (3.139). In these two instances, the phrase 'divine chance' (*theiē tuchē*) is used, adding a touch of providence, but on another occasion, when the exiled Spartan king Demaratus is being pursued by his enemies, he only manages to successfully make his way to Asia 'by luck (*tuchē*, 6.70). One translation (Mensch) renders *tuchē* in 6.70 as 'fate', but in another (Holland) it becomes 'twists of fortune' and this is more accurate. Solon's insight into what makes a happy life is predicated on *tuchē*, for without it a person's life cannot end well: 'for man', he succinctly summarizes, 'everything is happenstance' (*pan esti anthrōpos sumphorē*, 1.32). In the military preparations at Thermopylae, the Phocians are partly persuaded to contribute troops by being reminded that Xerxes is only a man and therefore necessarily born with the likelihood of encountering misfortune (7.203).

Tuchē, occurring far more often in the text than *moira*, works against the operations of an implacable fate determining the course of individuals' lives because chance, like the throw of a dice, can work in one's favour or against it, but there is no telling which; the subjunctive is a part of reality's grammar.[69] Artabanus spells this out when he is trying to persuade Xerxes to think very carefully about his intention to invade Greece, warning him that luck can bring success or failure (7.10). He immediately goes on to talk about the envy of the gods when someone is too successful, conflating chance with the divine. E. R. Dodds in *The Greeks and the Irrational* notes such a zone of cohesion in Herodotus who, along with Pindar and Sophocles, possesses a 'deepened awareness of human insecurity and human helplessness'. For Dodds, this zone of cohesion has a correlation in religion: hostility from the gods who begrudge success and happiness when it threatens their prerogative' (1951: 29).[70]

Luck may be seen at times as a metaphysical force at work in the universe and as the Persian threat to Greece's future becomes increasingly more tangible there are intimations of supernatural interest and even intervention in the outcome (see above and see p. 220), but luck is more usually a matter of material happenstance. Cyrus feels he is destined for great deeds, regarding his birth as 'something more than human' (1.204), but a military defeat sees his head being dunked in a bag of blood (1.214). There are limits to human ambitions of a naturalistic and not incorporeal kind, as the history of the Persian Empire exemplifies. It grows to become the largest empire the world had ever known, 'from Sind [in Pakistan] to Sardis [western Turkey]' as an inscription by Darius boasts,[71] but Cambyses is thwarted by the Ethiopians (3.17–25), Darius by the Scythians (4.125–140), and Xerxes by the Greeks. What Herodotus says of cities in the proem applies equally well to empires and life generally: those 'great in early times have become small . . . those that were great in my time were small . . . knowing human happiness never abides in the same place. I will memorialize both alike' (1.5).

The rise and fall of cities and empires overlaps with a pattern that relates to the consequences of systems of government where power resides with one person. The rulers of Persia are not called tyrants, a semantically loose term in the Greek political vocabulary, but the country's kings become emblematic of a type of absolute power that is set against the political systems of the Greek cities.[72] The opposition cannot be configured as an East–West, clash-of-civilizations conflict – the Peisistratids rule over Athens, Polycrates is tyrant of Samos as Periander is in Corinth – and relates more to issues of power and how it is distributed. Criticisms of despotic rule, Asian and Greek, are found in the Deioces story (1.96–100, see pp. 76–7), the Constitutional Debate (3.80–82, see pp. 122–4) and the speech of Socles (5.92, see pp. 170–1). The tyrants of the Greek cities in Ionia depend on Persian backing for the maintenance of their arbitrary rule and know full well that the people do not support them (4.137). Herodotus feels sure that the military success of Athens is related to its democratic system of government bringing out the best in everyone and not, as in an autocracy, encouraging a slavish mentality (5.78, see p. 168).

Nomos

Nomos can be translated as 'law' or 'custom', a term that encompasses formally enacted legislation as well as customs that have become so well established within a community that they function as social laws which are expected to be followed. *Nomoi* provide the fabric of socially defined knowledge and the set of rules governing a community's behaviour and speech and they can be viewed as regulatory, providing subjects with a consistent sense of his or her identity. The range of *nomos* stretches from the merely cosmetic to the purely existential: the Spartans who comb and arrange their hair before the Battle of Thermopylae do so because it is their custom (7.209), and it is *nomos*, as will be seen, that accounts for a fundamental difference between Greeks and Persians.

Any discussion of *nomos* in Herodotus is likely to reference the affective drama of Darius' experiment to establish the power of cultural norms: inviting Greeks to eat the corpses of their fathers, reacted to with horror because their custom is to practise cremation, and finding similar outrage on the part of the Indian Callatiae tribe, who do happen to eat their dead, when asked if they would burn the bodies of their fathers. This confirms for Herodotus that 'custom is king of all' (3.38). Such an insight, based on Darius' ethnographic experiment and gleaned from many observations of his own, is not one of cultural relativism (see pp. 118–19). On the contrary, it is what allows him to make an objective assessment about the state of Cambyses' mental health: only a deranged individual would wilfully disrespect *nomos* so blatantly as to desecrate a tomb, jeer at images of a god and burn them (3.38).

Herodotus' non-combative attitude towards the religious beliefs of non-Greek communities is unconditional, and in Egypt, after conversing with many priests there, he declares his unwillingness to reveal what he has been told: 'I do not think that any one nation knows much more about such things than any other' (2.3). It is a cagey, non-denominational statement, allowing for there being an absolute truth, albeit one that might be apprehended or negotiated with in different ways by humans. Different cultures will have particular modes of awareness for contact with the divine, enshrined in practices like sacrifices, festivals and oracles. The observance or participation in certain practices has the force of *nomos* and Cambyses' outrage, ridiculing the Egyptians' worship of the Apis bull by attacking it with a knife (3.27–9), is to undermine by a secular act what *nomos* has rendered sacred. Herodotus' respect for foreign *nomoi*, unqualified when they touch on matters of religion (see p. 92), is tested when he strives to maintain an even-handed approach to the nature of Salmoxis, a god to the Getae in Thrace but a charlatan to the local Greeks (4.94–6, see pp. 141–2). He avoids making a judgement but the reader senses his scepticism towards what he has been told, by both sides, and vexation at himself for not knowing more about the matter.

What consistently emerges in the *Histories* is the power of *nomos* as an intersubjective system – memes rather than genes – determining how individuals in particular communities think and behave. There are normative realms of expectation that transcend the conscious selves of individuals, and Herodotus, always alert to what is habitual and taken for granted by a society, enjoys describing a community's common way of living. He can be fascinated by aspects of everyday life for non-Greeks but he very rarely tries to romanticize them, and there is a curious anecdote about the pharaoh Amasis that brings out the arbitrary element in the nature of social mores. Amasis breaks up a foot-bath which has been used for washing and urination and has the pieces turned into a cult statue (*agalma*) and placed in a suitable city location. It comes to be venerated by Egyptians and accepted as a part of their *nomos*, a phenomenon that Amasis explains to show how the people will come to revere him as their king if they honour and treat him with similar respect (2.172). Behaviour, material practice of an everyday kind, will generate ideological commitment.[73]

The way people choose to live is very much governed by the *nomoi* of their society, but people's cultural norms and political arrangements are bound up with material factors, a complex conjuncture that can be traced in the theme of 'hard' and 'soft' lifestyles, a cultural physiognomy that has been presented as an opposition at work in the *Histories* (see p. 30): 'soft' people have a penchant for luxuries, are prone to tyranny, their women tend to be commodified and their cultures are 'confusing and seductive, difficult to leave once visited'; by comparison, 'hard' people are tough and resilient, politically less centralized and, less open to outsiders, they 'fall short of civility' (1985: 281–5). No 'soft' people – the Lydians, Babylonians and Egyptians – conquer a 'hard' people like the Scythians, Massagetae or Ethiopians, but the division is not rigidly schematic and cultural fluidity allows for change. Croesus saves his people from mass enslavement by the Persians by persuading Cyrus to force the Lydians to wear luxurious clothes and spend their time playing music (1.155–7). Losing their warlike propensities, they become docile and no longer pose a potential threat to their new Persian masters.

Earlier, when the Lydian Sandanis is trying to persuade Croesus not to attack the Persians he urges him to consider what might happen. The Persians are a hardy people who live frugally, their clothes are made from animal skins, their land is not bountiful and their diet so plain that they even lack figs for dessert. If they conquer Lydia they will grow accustomed to luxuries, warns Sandanis, and they will never willingly abandon them (1.71, see pp. 86–7). By the time of the invasion of Greece, the Persian army that marches westwards has thousands of infantrymen carrying spears topped with golden and silver pomegranates (7.41), and Sandanis' cultural prognosis is proved correct to judge by the reaction of the Spartan general, Pausanias, after the defeat of the Persians at Plataea. Gold and silver furniture and basins are discovered inside their tents while scimitars with golden hilts and clothes richly embroidered are found on Persian corpses on the battlefield. Pausanias orders Persian cooks to prepare a meal in their customary fashion and serve it to Greek commanders alongside a typical meal of their own, joking that the enemy came to Greece to rob its people of their poverty (9.82).

Demaratus, an ex-Spartan king exiled in Persia, had earlier tried to explain to Xerxes the nature of the enemy he is facing and he began with the harsh material conditions of their country. Poverty in Greece, he asserts, is endemic and a state of deprivation is inherited by each generation, but when sound judgement and 'strong law' (*nomou iskhurou*) is put to work in these circumstances Greece is able to defend itself against 'poverty and despotism' (7.102). Speaking of his fellow Spartans, he asserts that custom (*nomos*) is their master (*despotēs*) and this will guarantee their resolve to stand and fight (7.104). A basic difference between Greeks and non-Greeks is registered by Xerxes' laughter – what Demaratus has said is beyond the Persian's comprehension – but pinning down the nature of a Greek–Persian polarity in Herodotus is open to discussion. For some it is a primary antithesis that can be traced in the *Histories*, an opposition of cultural and political *nomoi* that amounts to an accident waiting to happen: despotic autocracy versus forms of civic government, servitude against liberty. In a classic presentation of such an antagonism (Cartledge 1993: 60–2), Herodotus is seen in 7.104 as endorsing 'a negative stereotype of the barbarian Other'; it has been noted, however, that this passage refers only to Spartans and is more about adherence to *nomos* than a cultural clash of libertarian and authoritarian values (Gruen 2011: 22).[74] For Forsdyke (2001: 348), the courage of the Spartans that Demaratus highlights is 'socially enforced through shame' – underlined by the plight of those who happened not to die at Thermopylae (7.231–2) – and Millender (2002: 40), who sees the Spartans as driven by 'compulsion and obedience', goes further by drawing a parallel between their motivation and that of the soldiers in Xerxes' army.[75]

There is a later conversation between a Persian and Greeks that does focus on a conflict of values. Two Spartans, travelling to see the Persian king on a mission which they know will probably cost them their lives, explain en route to a puzzled Persian commander, Hydarnes, that he only understands what it means to be a slave. He has 'never tasted freedom' therefore cannot know 'whether it is sweet or not' (7.135). It does not follow, given how what is supposedly a self-evident polarity in the text is more fluid than fixed, that this is the all-important message of the *Histories*. The reader will come across examples of intolerant Greeks and barbarous behaviour on their part just as there will be situations showing high-minded and self-aware Persians. After their conversation with Hydarnes, the two Spartans present themselves bullishly to Xerxes but he declines to order their execution and allows them to return home (see p. 210) – unlike the Greek states who throw Persian envoys into a well and a pit (7.133). It is noted elsewhere that the customary behaviour of Spartans and Asians when one of their kings die is remarkably similar (6.58), and Ionian claims to racial purity (1.146–7) are scoffed at. Herodotus is a diffusionist who accepts acculturation as something that can be observed in the world around him[76] – Persians like to adopt foreign customs (1.135) – and while at times a Greek–barbarian cultural schism suggests itself as a leitmotif, the consistency of such an opposition is unpicked on other occasions. The inquiry into foreign *nomoi* vis-à-vis Greek customs is complex and sophisticated, with Herodotus seeing what is praiseworthy and objectionable in both cultures. Some values are shared, some overlap and others unambiguously divide them.

The absence of Hellenic chauvinism is especially apparent in Herodotus' recognition of cross-cultural links and similarities between different societies.[77] *Nomos* divides people, indicative of deep differences in forms of life but it also reveals underlying uniformities. Some *nomoi* can be common to a set of different peoples, as with the denigration of manual work in favour of the military arts that is noted in Thrace, Scythia, Persia and Lydia, and which has been adopted by the Greeks (2.167). There is a particular song which is found in Egypt, Phoenicia, Cyprus and elsewhere and Herodotus finds this inexplicable (2.79, see p. 101). Polygamy is practised by the Massagetae and by the Nasamones (2.216, 4.172) although their geographical separation (the western side of North Africa and north of the Black Sea) makes it unlikely one culture influenced the other.

The quixotic tale of the Amazons and their amorous encounter with a group of Scythian men (see p. 143) is the most appealing story that allows for the possibility of happy co-mingling of people from societies with very different *nomoi*. Countering this, there is also the story from Scythia of Anacharsis and Scyles, two men who pay for their lives because of their adoption of foreign *nomoi* (see pp. 139–40). Although the Amazons and their Scythian partners do successfully negotiate a settlement, the power of *nomos* is not something to be ordinarily trifled with. It goes all the way down, to fundamental questions of identity and the possibility of civilized life. Somewhere beyond Scythia, reports Herodotus, the Androphagi inhabit a space, living as nomads and eating human flesh as part of their diet. They are beyond the pale, not knowing about justice (*dike*) and living without *nomoi* (4.106).

Notes to Approaches

1 Jennings, Eiland and Smith 1999: 802.

2 Eiland and Jennings 2002: 148.

3 Ibid.

4 For the biographical traditions in the ancient world about his life, see Priestley 2014: 19–50; for examples of the contested issue of Herodotus' travel – possibly to Egypt, the littoral of North Africa, the Black Sea region, Syria, Palestine and Babylon – see Armayor 1978a and 1978b.

5 Greenblatt goes further, linking Herodotus' commitment to travel and his attention to cultural margins with the nomadism of the Scythians that so interests him in Book Four. Taken together, these aspects come to represent his openness as a historian to move between opposed 'cultural constructions of reality' (127) and legitimate a place for the historian to live with uncertainties and doubts.

6 For Ryszard Kapuściński (2007: 259), a writer who himself juggles documentary-style reportage with literary narratives, the *Histories* is 'world literature's first great work of reportage' and its author has 'a journalistic eye and ear'.

7 For the reception of Herodotus in the Hellenistic world, see Priestley 2014.

8 For examples of ring composition in Homer, see Douglas 2007: 101–24.

9 The Persian king Darius, at the start of his campaign to conquer Scythia, behaved in a way similar to his son (4.84), reinforcing a connection between the exercise of extreme violence and their authority as wielders of a power that is accountable to no one but themselves.

10 For the shift in meaning, see Press 1982: 23–34; for *historiē* in Herodotus, see Bakker 2002: 13–9.

11 Examples range from describing the use of mosquito nets (3.95) to the colour of a people's semen (3.101).

12 A view of history as a series of damn facts, popularly associated with Arnold Toynbee and gaining fresh currency when expressed in the vernacular by the schoolboy Rudge in Alan Bennett's *The History Boys*.

13 For Greek accounts of Eastern history before Herodotus, see Drews 1973: 20–44, and Scanlon 2015: 11–14, 17–21.

14 It is clear from a passage in Dionysus of Halicarnassus, writing in the late first century or possibly early in the first century CE, that there was a number of what could very loosely be called historians before Herodotus. For a view of

ancient Greek historiography before Herodotus, see Marincola 2012: 3–11; Osborne 2011; and Boedeker 2011. For the range of different methods and models of non-Greek historical inquiry before Herodotus, see the chapters on Mesopotamia, ancient Egypt and ancient Israel in Feldherr and Grant 2011.

15 de Jong (2002), like Fornara, argues firmly for the unity of the *Histories*.

16 Grant (1995: 4–6, 93–5), for example, is full of praise for Herodotus as an entertaining writer of history but not as a historian. For O'Malley (2015: 244), not himself a historian, Herodotus is the 'problematic founder of the discipline of history', while for Fehling he is the writer of 'pseudo-history' (1989: 179ff.). West (1985) finds 'something disingenuous' about Herodotus' use of inscriptions and attributes the unprofessionalism to an oral culture and less than rigorous use of logic and standards of accuracy.

17 Fehling is critically discussed by Pritchett (1993); see also, Fowler 1996: 80–6; for Herodotus' source material and how he uses it, including a rejection of Fehling, see Hornblower (2002).

18 For an overview of negative judgements in Plutarch, Thucydides and other pre-modern writers, see Evans 1968; for Herodotus' reputation in antiquity as a liar, see Priestley 2014: 209–19.

19 For a general background to oral memory and the transmission of social memory, see Fentress and Wickham 1992: 41–86; a more difficult book on the subject is Assmann 2011.

20 The three prophetesses who provide him with one of the two versions of how the oracle at Dodona was founded are each named (2.55, see p. 258, n19 for a classic refutation by Fehling); he meets the grandson of the Spartan Archias whose exemplary bravery in the capture of Samos is described (3.55); he names Tymnes, a steward of a Scythian king, as someone he spoke to (4.76); and Thersander is the first-hand source of information for a conversation that took place at a dinner attended by Thebans and Persians before the Battle of Plataea (9.16).

21 For a historiographical discussion of 2.99, see Schepens 2007: 43–5.

22 An equivalent temporal difficulty to these geographical ones, arising when the long passage of time makes knowledge uncertain, is acknowledged when Herodotus is discussing the Carians and their degree of integration into Minos' maritime empire (1.171). When comparing different military expeditions (7.20), he distinguishes between those 'we know of' and those like the one to Troy that are told about in stories (*kata ta legomena*).

23 Baragwanath writes of Herodotus 'enfranchising' his readers (2008: 20) and speculates that, well aware of how an Athenian audience would have been well versed in listening to opposing speeches in court cases, he encouraged active reactions to his text. Baragwanath is influenced by Iser's reader-response theory, whereby a text's indeterminacy stimulates readers into engaging with a text, and she makes interesting observations by applying a form of literary criticism to a work of non-fiction.

24 Unlike Homer, Herodotus will not call on the Muses for knowledge of a time that is ordinarily beyond our scope; see Feeney (2007: 74) for the interesting Homeric reference (*Iliad*, 2.485–6) in this respect.

25 See p. 108.

26 Minos of Crete could be seen to straddle the divide, for while on one occasion his historical identity is regarded as questionable (3.122) his verifiable existence is later dated to three generations before the Trojan War (7.171). This is the view of Harrison (2000: 203, 205), but, as Feeney points out (2007: 74), the second passage is in direct speech and an authorial voice cannot be taken for granted.

27 See pp. 97 and 135–6).

28 For the many discussions around the extent to which Herodotus makes a distinction between a time of myth (*spatium mythicum*) and of history (*spatium historicum*), see Feeney's clear-sighted account (2007: 70–7); see also, p. 264 (n39); for the historicity of the Trojan War in the *Histories*, see Saïd 2012: 88–90, who concludes that Troy 'anchors' Herodotus 'somewhere between epic tradition and fifth-century rationalism' (105).

   A comparison may be made with the writers of the Hebrew Bible, parts of which, the Pentateuch, are thought to be based on a number of earlier written sources that were combined by an unknown author or authors sometime between 520 and 400. Events that supposedly took place around 1800 are recorded and for some of those who wrote the source material used in the compilation of the Pentateuch there is an aetiological impulse, trying to explain the creation of life and the origins of Israel's tribes and neighbours. Theodicy, the vindication of present tribulations with a theological explanation, is also strongly at work in creating Israel's exceptionalism; as expressed by one scholar of Jewish history, 'If Herodotus was the father of history, the fathers of meaning in history were the Jews' (Yerushalmi 1982: 8). The narrative is based upon a body of traditions that promote the sense of a corporate, divinely-endorsed identity among various people living in the land of Palestine, and matters of historical probability do not arise; its value as a cultural memory is immense but its value as history is open to doubt and the archaeological support, or lack of it, is contentious; for some recent summaries, see Stavrakopoulou 2016, Van Seters 2011 and Brettler 2014.

29 Murray (2001: 20) finds modern and ancient evidence for the time span of oral tradition being up to two centuries.

30 For Herodotus' distinction between surface and underlying causes, see p. 267 n27.

31 See pp. 95–6.

32 For an overview of revenge and reciprocity in Herodotus, see Fisher 2002: 209–17; for reciprocity as 'a defining criterion of social relation itself' and the way it combines with Herodotus' interest in the wondrous to make 'extraordinary reciprocity' a key to the *Histories*, see Braund 1998.

33 For Stern, the idea that guilt or pollution cannot be transferred when the carrier's purpose is rebutted, as is the case when Xerxes refuses to execute the two Spartan citizens, has an echo in his later unwillingness to execute Athenian spies (7.146–7); Zopyrus' self-mutilation (3.154), which becomes 'an emblem of the danger he transfers from the population he leaves to the city which accepts him' (1991: 308), also exhibits the scapegoat pattern.

34 Similarly, timid animals breed prolifically in return for their vulnerability to relatively unproductive predators (3.108).

35 Where there are stories of direct communication between mortals and gods, Herodotus tends to express either outright disbelief or maintain a distance by

specifying his source and reporting it in indirect discourse: Rhampsinitus' dice game with Demeter (2.122); Philippides' encounter with Pan (3.105); the 'god' Salmoxis (4.94–6). For false gods and 'sham messengers of the divine', see Lateiner 1990: 235–40. For the importance in Herodotus of personal motives overriding issues of fate for his sense of causation, see Derow 1994: 74–9.

36 Boedeker (2003: 30–1) refers to Pelling in her use of Bakhtin and the applicability of 'dialogism' to Herodotus; Dewald (2002: 275–6; 2015) recalls Bakhtin when describing the way the *logoi* of others are presented as 'dialogic'. There is, however, another way of looking at the open-mindedness of Herodotus' non-coercive approach, one that positions a 'withdrawal from arrogant self-assertion' as part of a 'rhetoric of authorization' (Goldhill 2002: 28). Herodotus asserts his position as a historian by a show of disengagement and disaffiliation from partisan versions enshrined in the *logoi* of others. By not too readily and arrogantly asserting his own point of view, he is working at convincing his readers that he is able to offer an authoritative interpretation of events.

37 'The effect is similar to that achieved by Edward Gibbon more than two thousand years later in his *Decline and Fall of the Roman Empire*, as he successively introduces the people who will overwhelm the Roman World' (Burrow 2007: 14). A difference is that the people Herodotus introduces do not manage to devastate the Persian Empire, although some of them successfully resist incorporation into it.

38 The construction of an East–West divide, with the West extolling the individual, personal freedom and rational inquiry as against a less individualist and more communitarian East, has been seen by some to originate with Herodotus (Lewis and Wigen 1997: 73, 94). Differences between Persians and Greeks – political, cultural and ethical – are drawn by Herodotus but were amplified and extended by later generations; see Cartledge 1993: 36–55.

39 A repositioning of the Persian Empire is accepted as a necessary corrective to clichés of Oriental despotism even if it sometimes results in a too rosy picture of Persian power. The seismic break with previous scholarship took place over thirty years ago, associated with Heleen Sancisi-Weerdenburg, Amélie Kuhrt and others. Pierre Briant's *History of the Persian Empire*, first published in 1996, is testimony to this rewriting of Persian history using new approaches and new material. See Sancisi-Weerdenburg and Kuhrt 1987; Briant 2002; Llewellyn-Jones 2013; Morgan 2016; and http://www.achemenet.com (accessed 16 November 2017). For a potted account of Persian history, see Bowie 2007: 1–6; for how historians of Achaemenid Persia underestimate the nuanced approach by Herodotus to the Persian–Greek wars, see Harrison (2011); for an insightful look at Greek visual representations of Persians, see Gruen 2011: 40–52.
　　Gore Vidal's novel *Creation* (1982) is set at the height of Persian power and though necessarily dependent on Herodotus (except for sections about India and China) it successfully maintains a Persian narrative point of view.

40 A Persian inscription reads, 'Darius the king says: this is the kingdom which I hold: from the Scythians who are beyond Sogdiana [Tajikistan and Uzbekistan] to Ethiopia, from Sind to Sardis' (quoted in Bowie 2007: 1).

41 For the rhetoric of wonder (*thōma*) in Herodotus, see Munson 2001a: 232–65.

42 What is remarkable to modern readers is the way Herodotus readily identifies the gods of foreigners with Greek names of deities, although there are exceptions (the odd case of Salmoxis (4.94–6), and Pleistorus (9.119) to whom the Apsinthians offer human sacrifices). Over fifty foreign gods are recognized as being identical with Greek deities and in more than half of them the barbarian name is not given (Hall 1989: 183). Herodotus and his peers take it for granted that the gods worshipped by non-Greeks are the same as theirs and the particular nomenclature employed has no special significance. The idea that different groups could quarrel and kill one another over rival taxonomies and claims to be the true god would have startled Herodotus and maybe warranted an anthropological investigation. For the naming of gods, see p. 98).

43 For Herodotus' highly sophisticated attitude to issues of ethnicity, see Munson 2014.

44 The exception that proves the rule is his gullible acceptance that an inscription (possibly graffiti) on a pyramid records the huge amount of money spent feeding the labourers with radishes, onions and cloves of garlic (2.125).

45 A sub-species of sheep, identified as Barbery sheep by How and Wells in their 1912 commentary, and as 'fat-tailed sheep of the Middle East' in Goodridge (2006) who notes references to the use of tail-trolleys from ancient Mesopotamia to a 1980s' Bruce Chatwin essay.

46 Chiasson 2003: 14, n. 30.

47 For narratology, the study of narrative as a genre with the objective of describing 'the constants, variables and combinations typical of narrative', see Fludernik 2009: 8–12.

48 For anachrony and the kind of 'retrograde' movement that Genette first illustrates by way of the opening lines of the *Iliad*, see Genette 1983: 35–47. Anachronies are described in an introduction to narratology as simply 'chronological deviations' (Bal 1997: 83), and Barthes, observing the phenomenon in Herodotus, describes the effect as 'zigzag history' (1986: 129).

49 Grethlein (2009b: 160–4, 172–3) provides a narratological reading of the Croesus *logos* to show how Herodotus' handling of time and characters' perspectives creates a contrast between a strong sense of contingency and 'the safety of the reading experience'.

50 There are many examples of Herodotus informing readers of what he intends to relate: 1.192, 1.194, 2.14, 2.24, 2.38, 2.51, 2.147, 2.156, 3.6, 4.14, 4.45, 4.82, 4.99, 4.145, 5.22, 5.65, 6.55.

51 At Thermopylae the curt humour of the Spartans has a dark side (7.226), but at Plataea (9.55) there is a verbal pun (with the Greek word for the stone that Amompharetus drops on the ground to register his dissent playing with the word 'to vote') which has the effect of deflating the deadly seriousness of the Spartan. For more examples of the Herodotean sense of humour, see Dewald 2006.

52 For the possibility that Herodotus was also influenced by Simonides' narrative verse elegy about the Battle of Plataea as a poetic source, see Boedeker 2001.

53 See de Jong (2012a), Vandiver 2012, and Grethlein 2006.

54 For the view that there was a close personal relationship between Herodotus and Sophocles, see Ostwald 1991: 143–7.

55 For points of correspondence between the story and Attic drama, and how Herodotus adapts the model from Attic theatre through the use of indirect discourse and by his handling of the Croesus-on-the-pyre scene and the suicide of Adrastus, see Chiasson 2003.

56 Facts do not speak for themselves – 'the documentary record does not figure forth an unambiguous image of the structure of events attested in them' (White: 2014: 30) – and the historian has to prefigure what set of events will count as knowledgeable. For White, this is a poetic act and 'constitutive of the structure' that will be offered as an explanation for what happened and why (White: 2014: 30).

57 The recognition of a poetic dimension in the writing of history is not a twentieth-century invention. Hegel in *The Philosophy of History* outlines three modes of historical writing, the first of which, 'original history' (1956: 1), includes Herodotus as one of the historians who operates like a poet 'upon the material supplied him by his emotions; projecting it into an image for the conceptive faculty.' (1956: 1).

58 In White's seminal work *Metahistory*, first published in 1973, 'the past' is a construct, a set of politically and socially determined discursive practices mediated by language, ideology and aesthetics. The relativism this allows for was propagated vigorously, some would say disruptively, by postmodern historiographers like Keith Jenkins, leading to dissolution of the distinction between history (facts about the past) and historiography (writing about the past). For a carefully reasoned response to aspects of White, see Ricoeur 1984: 161–8; for an intemperate and now dated reaction to White and a host of thinkers who are seen to be threatening the autonomy of the historian, see Marwick 1995. For Marwick, aligning the writing of history with the natural sciences and the 'systematic analysis of the primary sources', not 'spinning narratives and telling stories' (12), Herodotus would probably struggle to be accepted as a historian.

59 For a response at the time to what was seen as an attack on history as a discipline, see Evans 2001.

60 For a discussion of the meanings of *moira* and its occurrences in Herodotus, see Eidinow 2011: 39–43, 96–9; for a wide-ranging examination of Herodotus' religious beliefs and attitudes and the influence of poetic conventions on religious topics, see Mikalson 2002: 136–65.

61 The two tales are briefly referred to by Adkins because of a similarity with Aeschylus' exploration of the inherited curse of the houses of Laius and Atreus in *Seven Against Thebes* and *Agamemnon* (1960: 120–3).

62 'It is what we may call the cunning of reason that it sets the passions to work in its service, so that the agents by which it gives itself existence must pay for the penalty and suffer the loss' (Hegel 1975: 89). For a non-reductive account of 'the cunning of reason', see Dale 2014: 207–15.

63 In a similar vein, locating notions of fate in traditions of 'poetic speculation' rather than religion as it was practised, see Mikalson 2003: 147–50.

64 'Objective chance' was a term used by the surrealists for eerie coincidences that signal a connection between moments in the external, objective world

and a subjective, psychic need that somehow influences and helps bring about them about.

65 These uses of the word – and other occurrences at 1.31, 3.53, 3.157, 5.32, 8.215, 9.49 and 9.109 – are discussed by Chiasson (1983).

66 For an overview of the *Histories'* moral universe, see Hau 2016: 172–93.

67 When the Pelasgians arrive on Lemnos they proceed to do likewise with the island's inhabitants (4.149), only for some of these dispossessed people, the Minyans, to prove no better when they drive out the people living in a western region of the Peloponnese and occupy their land (4.148).

68 Herodotus' keen awareness of human sorrow and sympathy for life's victims is the subject of an article by Renehan. He notes with regret how the words that concluded the entry on Herodotus in the first edition of *The Oxford Classical Dictionary* (1948), and in the second edition in 1970, are omitted in the present edition (1996). The words in question, by Denniston, drew a parallel between Herodotus and Mozart: '[Herodotus] has suffered the fate which befell Mozart, His charm, wit, and effortless ease have diverted attention from the note of profound sadness and pity sounded not seldom in his History' (Renehan 2001: 187).

69 There is a tension that oscillates between something that has to be, because fate determines it so, and the sense that nothing has to be because chance determines everything; best seen, perhaps, as a case of parallax, where the two senses can never be reconciled because they are the same, though existing in different spaces.

70 For jealousy (*phthonos*) of the gods, see p. 199).

71 See n. 40 above.

72 For a discussion of Herodotus' critical gaze on the nature of autocratic rule, see Dewald 2003.

73 Amasis anticipates Pascal's advice to those who struggle to believe: behave as if you do believe, 'taking holy water, having masses said, etc.', and belief will follow in due course (Pascal 1995: 155–6). Habit, says Pascal, makes us believe 'without violence, art, or argument' and 'inclines our faculties to this belief (Pascal 1995: 148).

74 Pelling 2013b argues convincingly for a nuanced self-awareness in the *Histories* when it comes to a Greek–Persian polarity.

75 For a discussion of Millender, seeing the courage of the Spartans as portrayed with admiration by Herodotus (though not immune to criticism), see Balot 2014: 81–91.

76 See above, p. 29.

77 Very few Greek customs spread to non-Greek societies (pederasty and the Persians are an exception, 1.135), but aspects of Hellenic culture are learnt from Lydia (1.94, 4.189), Egypt (2.50, 2.81) and Caria (5.88).

Commentary

Book One: Croesus and Cyrus

The first book of the *Histories* covers the fall of Lydia under its king Croesus, the rise of Persian power under Cyrus and the expansion of a Persian Empire that embraces Asia Minor and Babylon. The book ends with the death of Cyrus, having covered a period of thirty years (560–530) since the rise to power of Croesus.

Proem

Herodotus' preface

On a first reading, it may appear that there is little that is puzzling about Herodotus' opening statement; it reads like a plain declaration of intent, a factual announcement by an author about to get down to the sober business of writing a history book. It is instructive, though, to consider the words alongside the openings of the *Odyssey* and the *Iliad*:

This is the showing-forth of the inquiry of Herodotus of Halicarnassus, so that human achievements may not be forgotten in time, and great and marvellous deeds – some displayed by Greeks, some by barbarians – may not be without their glory; and especially to show why the two peoples fought with each other.

Sing in me, Muse, through me tell the story of that man skilled in all ways of contending; the wanderer, harried for years on end, after he plundered the stronghold on the proud height of Troy.[1]

Sing, goddess, the anger of Peleus' son Achilles and its devastation, which put pains thousandfold upon the Achaeans, hurled in their multitudes to the house of Hades ...[2]

[1] Lattimore 2011: 75
[2] Lattimore 1967: 25.

BOOK 1, BOX A

Homer's epics begin with invocations to the Muses for inspiration whereas Herodotus starts by giving his name and place of origin, announcing the subject of his research and the motives for his inquiries. Homer seeks divine endorsement for his stories about the adventures of Odysseus and the wrath of Achilles; Herodotus, acknowledging that oral accounts of the past are doomed to perish in time, seeks to preserve their memory for posterity. The difference between the two authors might point to a simple contrast between a poet's need for inspiration versus the historian's desire to preserve a record of the past, indicative of two genres and their differing methodologies, but such an opposition occludes a mutuality that lies beneath an apparent divergence.

Homer and Herodotus share a rhetorical interest in engaging with their audiences and they each announce their chosen subjects with a degree of theatricality: declarative statements highlighting the dramatic importance of their subject matter. Equally importantly, they are both concerned with renown or glory (*kléos*): Homer is preoccupied with his warriors' desire for glory[1] – which can be a quasi-mystical quality in the *Iliad* – while Herodotus, bringing this concept down to earth, is motivated by a wish to ensure that what is marvellous does not lose its glory. The word 'marvellous' (*thomasta*) may be equally well translated as 'wondrous', while the word that appears here as 'achievements' (*genomena*) is more than just accomplishments and covers what could be called 'works', including material objects like monuments and natural phenomena.

Herodotus states that if human achievements and marvellous deeds (*erga*) are forgotten they will lose their glory and the Greek for this state of being without glory (*aklea*)[2] can also mean 'unsung': the song of the bard records great deeds. Here it is possible to infer the influence of archaic poetry on Herodotus, serving to remind us of moments like that in the *Iliad* (9.189) where Achilles is heard by his tent 'singing the famous deeds of fighting heroes' or in the *Odyssey* (1.338) where Penelope refers to songs that celebrate the deeds of gods and men. At the same time, though, Herodotus is also asserting his concern with notable events and investigating responsibility for the Greek–Persian conflict. These twin interests will combine the art of an epic narrator with the empirical concerns of a historically-minded observer; like Homer, Herodotus seeks to reach out to a truth that exists independent of the narrator, a truth bound up with warfare, and in doing so the historian's text assumes the mantle of the bard's song.[3]

Another presence in the opening sentence, very different to though not necessarily at odds with the Homeric influence, is that of a style of rhetoric associated with the sophist Gorgias. Following the first phrase ('this is the showing-forth of the inquiry') are two clauses expressing purpose with a parallel structure by way of negatives ('so that human achievements may not be forgotten . . . and great and marvellous deeds . . . may not be without their glory'). The use of isocolon, the term from ancient Greek rhetoric for this kind of symmetry,[4] suggests Herodotus's receptiveness to new intellectual currents and if so it sits alongside and counterpoises his awareness of a far older literary tradition. Throughout the proem there is movement and mixing between older forms of storytelling, often involving divine figures and superhuman mortals, and a newer resolve to record 'human achievements' without recourse to the miraculous or the divine.

The opening of the first sentence contains the first use by Herodotus of *historie*[5] ('inquiry') and the word is in the genitive case ('*of* the inquiry'), indicating its relation to the word translated here as 'showing-forth' (*apodexis*).[6] The word for 'showing-forth' comes from a verb meaning to display, demonstrate, perform, make known, and this allows it to be also translated as 'performance'. Using the word 'publication', as it is occasionally translated, may mislead given the particular cultural weight that we attach to that term. What is suggestive about translating *apodexis* as showing-forth, display or performance is the idea of Herodotus delivering excerpts of his work to a live audience, an entertainer of sorts, making public the results of his travels and research as he reads aloud from his text. Herodotus is part of a culture where the circulation of literature is still essentially oral, despite the 'published' nature of his written text.[7]

It is noticeable that Herodotus' declarative statement does not immediately or emphatically state his subject to be the Persian Wars. The contrast here with the opening of Thucydides – 'Thucydides, an Athenian, wrote the history of the war waged by the Peloponnesians and the Athenians against one another' – is significant. What we hear in Herodotus' reference to 'Greeks and non-Greeks' is an announcement of catholicity, a desire for a broad canvas that will take in the great works of an age. When, in the final clause of the preface, the war is mentioned it is the cause (*aitiē*), or responsibility, rather than the course of the conflict that merits his attention. Herodotus seeks answers to questions of who or what, when and where, and he probes into deeper queries about why people act and make decisions in the way they do. This curiosity blossoms in the *Histories* into a host of personal, political and cultural factors affecting causality and an important one – a desire for retribution, the restitution of parity kindled by remembrance of things past – is about to be touched upon.[8]

Abductions (1.1–5)

The inquiry begins by relating how learned men (*hoi logioi*) of Persia account for the conflict with Greece: Phoenicians abduct Io from Argos and Greeks abduct Europa from Phoenicia; a state of behavioural equality which is broken by Greeks kidnapping Medea, only to be redressed by Paris taking Helen to Troy (Box 1). An escalation in these two cycles of vengeance then takes place with the Trojan War, an invasion that in the course of time finds retaliation in the Persian invasion of Europe.

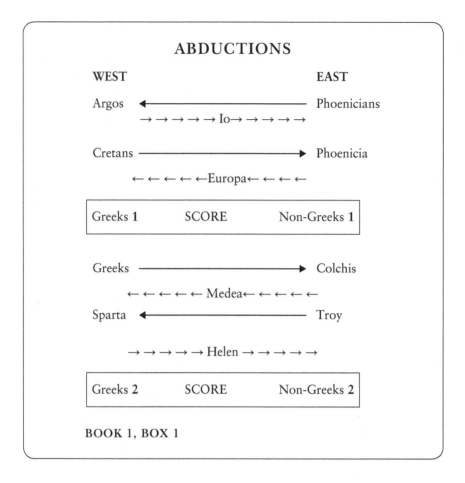

ABDUCTIONS

WEST   EAST

Argos ←———————————————— Phoenicians
         → → → → → → Io→ → → → → →

Cretans ————————————————→ Phoenicia
         ← ← ← ← ←Europa← ← ← ←

| Greeks 1 | SCORE | Non-Greeks 1 |

Greeks ————————————————→ Colchis
         ← ← ← ← ← Medea← ← ← ← ←
Sparta ←———————————————— Troy

         → → → → → Helen → → → → →

| Greeks 2 | SCORE | Non-Greeks 2 |

BOOK 1, BOX 1

The various seizures of women that take place are not experienced at the time in the schematic way represented in Box 1. The Greeks are not seeking revenge for Io when they kidnap Europa though it is seen as reciprocal by the unsentimental Persians whose account this is: 'So far, then, the account between them was balanced' (1.2). After Medea has been taken away by the Greeks,[9] the king of Colchis demands reparation and only now, with the Greeks harking back to Io and the lack of any compensation paid for her at the time, do both sides verbalize what is happening as a contestable score in terms of a due settlement being made. The carrying-away of Helen by Paris is seen by him as an adjustment that balances the score: Helen does not need to be paid for because Medea was never paid for by the Greeks. The Greek expedition against Troy is seen by the Persians as an intensification, political and geographic. An army from Europe, not a group of sailors or adventurers, sets out to invade and destroy a kingdom in Asia and this incursion is seen as a political affront by the Persians for whom the spatial movement of a Greek fleet becomes a territorial threat: 'Ever since then' there has been an irreparable breach, with Persians regarding Asia as their territory and thinking 'of Europe and the Greeks as separate' (1.4).[10] The Phoenicians are like the Persians in seeing the Greeks as overreacting to what are essentially minor bride-stealing affairs. Their version of Io's journey from Argos, fleeing from home to escape parental wrath after becoming pregnant from a liaison with a sea captain, supports the general Persian line that the Greeks allowed private goings-on between men and women to escalate into an international incident with their attack on Troy.

There are scholarly disagreements over the correct way to interpret 1–5 of the first book of the *Histories*. The fact that Herodotus has chosen to begin with these abduction tales indicates some purpose on his part but there is no consensus about his motivation and purpose. It has been argued that the reference to savants and their accounts of abductions, pointing to the use of a native Persian source by Herodotus, may be more of a narrative invention than the indication of an authentic body of opinion.[11] It is certainly the case that the abduction tales are pared down, rationalized, unpoetic versions of not Persian but Greek myths.[12] However, even if there is some basis to this claim, it does not firmly establish that Herodotus is fictionalizing a version of the past. He may be drawing on traditions involving reciprocal and inherited obligations to exact revenge, a motif about human interaction found in many of the narratives of the *Histories*. This approach needs to take account of the differences within and between the pairs of abductions: it is only the Persian *logioi* who claim the Europa incident balances the Io kidnapping; the Cretans who snatch Europa are not seeking revenge or retribution. With Medea and Helen, it is only characters within these tales who speak of reciprocity and compensation, but they are not seeking revenge. Paris steals Helen not to settle a score but because he feels certain he can get away with it (1.3).[13]

Another point of view discerns 'a parody of the type of history purveyed by Hecataeus and other early prose writers, which focused upon the genealogical and heroic subject matter of Greek myth and saw the myths and legends as offering sufficient explanations for later events' (Thomas 2000: 268).[14] Such a perceived note of mockery is seen as 'historiographically sophisticated comedy, but comedy nonetheless' Dewald (2006: 147): an intellectual awareness on Herodotus' part of the mythic nature of causality in these abductions allowing him to marshal such material as a foil for his own historically-minded account of the origins of East–West enmity.

The geographical arabesque marking the toings and froings of abducted women undoubtedly possesses a humorous dimension but there is also a serious sense of countries and cultures interacting and impinging on one another's identities. Persians find it difficult to register shock at the kidnapping of women; Io is a Greek princess whose worship in Egypt will coalesce with veneration of the goddess Isis; Europa is from Tyre in Asia but another continent comes to be named after her. Women become a currency for cultural exchange in an unstable world where 'what was earlier big becomes small, and what was big in my time was earlier small' (1.5).

What underlies the various interpretations is the awareness that Herodotus is *questioning* his source. The Persians have their accounts, pointing to a world spatially divided by the landmasses of Europe and Asia, while for the Phoenicians Io's departure from Argos was a purely private affair. Having recounted claims about who in the distant past is guilty of having started the intercontinental enmity, he declares in 1.5 an unwillingness to adjudicate between the claims and counterclaims. The legendary rapes of Io, Europa, Medea and Helen have been demythologized into self-serving tales of sordid goings-on arising from commercial and marital greed and Herodotus can be seen to be distrusting these partisan tales as emanating from Asiatics adversarily debunking traditional stories to protest their innocence.[15] What is important to Herodotus is being able to state who he *knows* to be the first to commit an unjust act against the Greeks. An epistemological concern comes into play with a contrast between 'certain knowledge' of Croesus' act of aggression against Greeks and uncertainty of knowing what really happened in the distant past.[16] Mythical tales may have been rationalized and opposing divinities removed from their telling but Herodotus is not going to believe them just on these grounds. In this way, Herodotus can be viewed as marking a division between logographers, content to record tales of the past, and an inquirer like himself.

While legendary accounts may lay the onus of responsibility on the Greeks – invading and making war on Troy even though the various abductions of women had rendered a net balance between Greeks and non-Greeks – the historical period restores a kind of equivalence by placing a degree of blame on the non-Greek Croesus. This mention of a known unjust act against the Greeks, not one shrouded in unreliable tales of a fabled past, brings to the fore a moral concern on the part of Herodotus. For one scholar, what emerges here is 'the *moral partisanship*' of the *Histories*, something that can be characterized as a 'guiding motif' to the work as a whole (Stahl 2012: 132–3). What is undoubtable is an assertion of authorial presence and this broadens out in the conclusion to a philosophical reflection on the instability of cities' prosperity and human affairs generally (1.5) – a theme of vital value in the *Histories* and one which will be developed and amplified in what is to come.[17]

The final paragraph of 1.5 registers an important change in tone, from talk of snatched princesses to that of time's erosion of human prosperity, and a change in chronology as the narrative shifts from a legendary past to historical events. Now that Herodotus is able to refer to 'certain knowledge' about a known historical figure, a methodological swing is detectable – or, at the very least, a distinction introduced between what people say happened in the past and what can be stated about the past with a degree of conviction.

Story of Croesus

The story of Croesus, the king of Lydia, is lengthy and can be divided into the account of Lydian kings before Croesus (1.6–25) and the reign of Croesus himself (1.26–92). More importantly, it is worth noting at the outset that the story as a whole does not unfold in a chronological sequence; it is 'interrupted' in a number of places with digressions and forays into related matters and throughout the story there is a pronounced genealogical dimension – the combined effect of all this is likely to bewilder the reader at times. In particular, lines of family descent that come readily to Herodotus can seem intrusive at times for, as Gould observed, there is a 'capacity of Herodotus and his audience to think more or less instinctively in terms of relationships which for us have to be elaborately reconstructed and committed to writing as a "family tree" before they can be raised to consciousness' (Gould 1989: 46–7).

There is another aspect to this first *logos* which is not confusing but is puzzling when it is recalled that at the end of the proem Herodotus declined to adjudicate over the competing claims and counterclaims has regarding kidnapped women and announced that instead of *chercher la femme* he will turn to the individual, Croesus, 'whom I know to have been the first to wrong the Greeks' (1.5). This logically follows from his stated intention in the preface to investigate responsibility for the war between Greeks and non-Greeks. No surprise then, when he comes to the reign of Croesus, to find him beginning with the Asian king's aggressive policy towards Greek cities on the coast (1.26–27). As the story unfolds, however, this hostility to the Greeks does not recede so much as disappear altogether; Croesus emerges as a friend and patron of the Greeks, suggesting the possibility of a change in Herodotus' plan for his first *logos*.[18] It is easy for this disjunction to slip by unnoticed because most readers will find themselves far more absorbed in the mini-narratives that begin with the tales of Candaules and Gyges and then Arion and the dolphin, continuing with Croesus' conversation with Solon and the grim story of Atys and Adrastus.

Throughout Book One there are numerous occasions that remind us of the important part played by myth and legend in Herodotus and his receptivity to narrative elements from the world of folklore. Characters deliver pithy maxims, make gnomic declarations, practise clever tricks and ruses. The role of oracles is especially prominent in the story of Croesus – the oracle of Apollo at Delphi occurs eight times and thirteen others are also mentioned – and there are six indications of divine intent that range in their manifestations from a sickness, a dream and fulfilled prayers to horses eating an inexplicable influx of snakes (Dewald 2012: 76–7).

Lydian kings before Croesus (1.6–25)

The story begins briefly with Croesus (1.6) before quickly going back in time to his great-great-grandfather Gyges, his great-grandfather Ardys,

---

LYDIAN KINGS BEFORE CROESUS

1.6:   Introduction to Croesus

1.7:   Lydian dynasty going back to Heracles

1.8–13:   Gyges and Candaules

1.14–22: Aggression with Greek cities of Asia
          Minor: Gyges (14), Ardys (15),
          Alyattes (16–22)

1.23-4:   Tale of Arion and the dolphin

1.25:   End of reign of Alyattes (father of Croesus)

BOOK 1, BOX 2

---

grandfather Sadyattes and father Alyattes. This is the royal line that replaced the ruling Heraclid dynasty and while Herodotus provides a genealogy for the last of these Heraclids, stretching back to the legendary Heracles (1.7), he does not do so for the usurper Gyges or for the king's very capable wife who is not even given a name.[19] This could be drawing attention to the illegitimacy of Gyges' place on the throne, his violation of law and custom (*nomos*) taking the form of a transgression within marriage of the rule that 'one must look at one's own' (1.8), 'nearly the first aphorism in the *Histories*' (Lateiner 1989: 14):[20] 'I beg you not to require of me what is unlawful' (1.8). Modern readers will be more struck by the verve and characterization in a tale that mixes factuality with fatalism, folklore with a frisson of eroticism. It is a narrative cocktail with heady ingredients: an oracle prophesying vengeance in the fifth generation (1.13) blended with a husband in the thrall of a desire to have his wife seen naked in their bedroom by another man,[21] garnished with motifs and material from myth, legend and drama.[22] The Gyges tale is about desire, shame of the body, human frailty and unforeseen consequences, features which also appear in the Phoenician and Persian stories of Io and Helen and, although the presentation is very different, both accounts share a concern with human motivation. The Gyges tale conveys mixed emotions and desire-driven subterfuge, staging everything within the confines of a palace bedroom; the other stories are told unsentimentally and soberly and have for their stage the whole Mediterranean. The abduction tales make no reference to destiny, but questions of fate and guilt surround the bedroom story and there is a strong sense of individual characters at odds with one another. Candaules' insistence – 'you must see her naked' (*gumnēn*) – causes Gyges to cry out in alarm at the unsoundness of a preposterous proposition – 'that I should see my mistress naked!' (*gumnēn*) – with each man pronouncing the word 'naked' according to their state of mind: an illicit command by a king who dearly wants a third party to see his wife undressed; an unthinkable scenario for a bodyguard shocked and fearful of a situation he is being coerced into.[23] The woman, no longer a commodity to be shipped around the Mediterranean at the dictates of men, becomes the player in the action who assumes executive control. She takes the precaution of having members of her household standing ready when she orders Gyges to attend her (1.11) and has meticulously planned how her vengeance will be enacted, wanting her husband's killer to stand behind the same door in her bedroom and, with the coolness displayed by Lady Macbeth, arranging for the dagger to be at hand for the assassin.

One of a number of versions of the tale, told by Plato a century later, has Gyges as a shepherd who becomes king with the help of a magical ring that confers invisibility, aiding him in the seduction of the queen and murder of her husband to become king.[24] The visible/invisible leitmotif and the violation of a boundary between proper and improper conduct between males and females, common to the versions in Herodotus and Plato, hark back to a mythic strain of fantasy, but for modern readers what holds attention in Herodotus' telling of the tale is the weaving of rationalism and voyeurism, a libidinously driven king and a telling use of words that renders pictorial clarity ('there is a chair set near the entrance of the room . . . gaze upon her with your leisure') and a dramatic force to the dialogue ('Now, Gyges, you have two roads before you; choose which you will follow . . . You shall come at him from the same place whence he made you see me naked').

Chapters follow dealing with Lydia and Greek cities of Asia Minor (1.14–22), before another tale interrupts the historical vector: Arion and the dolphin (1.23–4). Its abrupt appearance seems arbitrary – 'hung precariously on the chronological hook of the reign of the Corinthian dictator Periander' (Griffiths 2006: 133) – depending as it does on Arion's patron, Periander, being a *xenos* (guest-friend) of the ruler of Miletus, the city which has been at the heart of the preceding chapters. This time the tale mixes a layer of judicious rationalism, via the ruler of Corinth in the role of investigative judge, with a sense of the fabulous that cannot be explained away by way of commendable accounts of dolphins' intelligence and their encounters with humans: 'Though a boy can pirouette on a dolphin's back for half-an-hour, he cannot circumnavigate half the Peloponnese' (Asheri 2007b: 92). The tale shares with the story of Gyges the element of a choice that is no choice – Arion can stay on board and be killed or jump into the sea – and, while it lacks any ethical dilemma, it has for Herodotus the virtue of being an anecdote of what in his preface he called the marvellous (*thomasta*). The story is told in indirect speech without any dialogue – 'Thus then, the story runs' (1.24) – making clear that Herodotus is not claiming authorship yet surely it is his own sense of wonderment that leads him to emphatically draw attention to a histrionic picture of 'the best singer in the world' decked out in his professional outfit – 'all his singing robes about him . . . putting on all his adornment and taking his lyre' (1.24) – and singing on the poop of the ship before throwing himself into the sea still clad in his robes.

Arion's leap is all, a supremely theatrical moment that relegates to the periphery not just Periander, provider of the notional basis for telling the story, but also the dolphin's quixotic contribution. The sea rescue could have been central if Arion's gift for entrancing listeners extended to all mammals, unintentionally drawing the dolphin to him or summoning it by a charm as a stratagem for escape, but this part of the tale is merely mentioned in passing. It is Arion's suicidal leap that crystallizes the tale's dramatic import, an existential decision to die as he has lived, calmly defeating his assailants by his comportment, his dressing himself in his professional costume and playing his lyre for one final song, owning his own death by a gesture of defiance.[25]

Croesus as king (1.26–94)

The *Histories* now picks up on what was demarcated earlier (1.5–6) – Croesus as the first Asian ruler to systematically conquer Greeks – only to soon pause yet again, though keeping to the subject of Croesus himself. The reader is first detained by the visit of the Athenian Solon to Croesus' capital at Sardis and secondly by the story of Adrastus and Croesus' unfortunate son. After these tales the storyline switches to Croesus' preparations for a confrontation with Persian power, but again there are a number of digressions – dealings with Delphi and the politics and history of Greek states (principally Sparta and Athens) – before the narrative eventually returns to the conflict with Persia and Croesus' defeat by Cyrus. The long stretch of chapters dealing with Croesus' search for Greek allies (1.46–70) is disproportionately lengthy in comparison to the main storyline, due to its own digressions into Athenian and Spartan history, and it is forgivable for a reader to feel banjaxed at times and wonder where the narrative is going or what place in it has been reached (see Box 3). It is, though, worth noting that the lengthy discussion of Sparta and Athens as potential allies has a long-term function in that it flags at the outset the two Greek cities that will play the most central roles in the Persian invasion of Greece.

There is an account, 1.56–8, involving 'that imaginary people [Pelasgians] invented by early Greek logographers to explain who lived in Greece before the Dorians and Greeks arrived' (Thomas 2013: 351), of how indigenous Athenians once spoke a non-Greek Pelasgian language and 'became Greek' when they adopted the Hellenic language (1.57).[26] There follows an account, 1.59–64, of what Croesus learns about Athens in his search for allies.

CROESUS AS KING

1.26–48: Croesus' reign before attacking Cyrus

        29–33: Dialogue with Solon
        34–45: Story of his son, Atys,
                     killed by Adrastus

1.46–70: Planning of war against Cyrus

        46–9:   Testing of oracles
        50–5:   Dealings with Delphi

1.56: Croesus seeks a Greek ally

        56–8:   Dorians and Pelasgians
        59–64: Peisistratus at Athens
        65–8:   Sparta
        69–70: Dealings with Sparta

1.71–6: War with Persia in Cappadocia and Battle of Pteria

        72:      Cappadocia's geography
        73–4:   Lydia and the Medes

1. 77–85: Cyrus conquers Lydia

        82–3:   Sparta's war with Argos
                causes delay in helping Croesus

1.86–91: Croesus' dialogue with Cyrus and information about Lydia

BOOK 1, BOX 3

Herodotus ridicules the tale of the dressing up of a tall woman as Athena and having her enter the city in a chariot with heralds proclaiming the support of the goddess for Peisistratus as tyrant (1.60).[27] Croesus learns of Sparta's military dominance and there is a digression into how this came about thanks to the bones of Orestes being transferred to the city (1.66–8).

The Orestes-Lichas tale offers another contrast with Athens for, unlike a self-serving politician using a false figure of Athena, the Spartans have a real hero entering their city with the genuine approval of the oracle at Delphi (Boedeker 1993: 164–77).[28]

An important narrative thread that is easily misplaced in this *logos* is that it is Croesus who initiates the Lydian–Persian war and it is this conflict that leads to the ruin of his dynasty. This collapse is what facilitates the unification of Persian power under Cyrus. An East–West conflict is less important to Herodotus here than the centralization of Asiatic power under Persia.

Importance has been attached to the story of Croesus occurring as early in the *Histories* as it does, given that it might have been more logical to have started with the Persian king, bringing in Croesus at the point where Cyrus conquers Lydia. As noted, though, Herodotus is following through on the fact that Croesus was the first to reduce the Ionians to tributary status, a point he concludes with at the beginning of 1.92. More than one scholar sees the early placement of the Croesus story as Herodotus establishing 'a paradigm in miniature for the rise and decline of the Persian empire' (Romm 1998: 64–5), the main subject which is to come. Croesus' life may indeed be seen as a precedent for the career of Xerxes, though that particular account is some way off, and other commentators find significance in the particularity of having Solon's exchange with Croesus placed at the beginning of the *Histories*. This can be seen as a programmatic parable – illustrating the likely consequences of unrestrained ambition for power – to be taken heed of by Athens especially (Moles 2002: 35–38) or as the setting out of a philosophical framework for Herodotus' whole project: 'setting forth basic assumptions about the nature of human life and its relation to the gods which could then provide a philosophical framework for the *Histories* as a whole' (Shapiro 1996: 362).[29] Croesus is, via Gyges, caught in the web of history like so many of the powerful individuals whose lives will unfold during the course of the *Histories*.

The element of theatricality in Solon's meeting with Croesus and the role played by oracles has also been seen as significant, linking to the influence of Greek tragedy on the Croesus *logos* (Saïd 2002: 134–5; Stahl 1968: 385–400). For Sophocles, the life of Oedipus is inseparable from what the oracle at Delphi predicts about his fate, elevating consequent events to a metaphysical plane of bafflement at the contingency that lies at the heart of causation. For Herodotus, Croesus' trust in oracles emerges as a function of an overconfidence which is related to his failure to acknowledge, until it is too late, the truth in Solon's remarks about the unpredictable nature of life. An awareness of life's uncertainties is an abiding one in Greek thought and the quality it lends to a sense of how life should be lived is rendered even more existential when contrasted, as it often is, with the unchallengeable power of a divine order which is usually indifferent to the plight of supremely vulnerable mortals. Such vulnerability is pointed to by Solon and ignored by Croesus – a wilful ignorance that can annoy the gods – until events compel him to acknowledge the gnomic wisdom of the Athenian who visited him in his days of glory.

Croesus was an historical figure whose fame spread across the Greek world: before Herodotus, Pindar and Bacchylides are testimony to his renown for piety and wealth while a depiction of him on a red-figure amphora, now in the Louvre, suggests – in contrast to Herodotus' account – that his death on a pyre was a ritual suicide. After his defeat by Cyrus in 547, tales about his life would have circulated widely and Herodotus, writing a hundred years later, does not feel the need to name sources except for the scene on the pyre when it is known conflicting accounts existed.[30] It would seem that for information on Croesus he relied heavily on Delphi (Flower 2013), the recipient of lavish gifts from the Lydian king which Herodotus goes into detail in describing, raising the question of why so many rich donations were made. A political motive on Croesus' part is likely – gaining an endorsement for Lydian sovereignty from a respected Greek authority – and it is possible that Herodotus travelled to Delphi and listened to the priests there. Another explanation for his keen interest in Croesus might be that Herodotus is fascinated by the tale of a Lydian monarch who paid such generous respect to a Greek sanctuary before going on to lose everything he had.[31]

The dialogue between the two men and Solon's accounts of Tellus and then Cleobis and Biton (1.30–2)[32] dramatizes an obvious dichotomy: measuring happiness by a quantitative assessment of material possessions versus a qualitative measurement of how well and for how long one has conducted a good life. Such an opposition of values, occurring as early in the *Histories* as it does, suggests the setting up of a philosophical matrix dear to Herodotus – the dimension of which is the instability of all life and the rule of chance – and which he puts into the mouth of Solon: 'I know how jealous is the divine and how it loves to trouble us. In a man's length of days he may see and suffer many things that he much dislikes . . . Croesus, the whole of man is but chance' (1.32). Such a belief is consonant with what has already found expression in the proem (at the end of 1.5), and similar reflections on this theme will be found later in the *Histories*.[33] Another angle on this motif is by way of a contrast between wisdom and power, represented by Solon and Croesus, and the difficulty of bridging the gap between them. Solon does not lecture his interlocutor for he only responds to what he is asked but his discourse is dismissed as the mark of an ignoramus (1.33). The story of Croesus unfolds around the difficulty of communicating and the difficulty of defining wisdom. Croesus is on the receiving end of a plethora of messages, riddles and advisers but nothing turns out according to his interpretations of the information he receives.[34] Solon's conversation with Croesus has received much comment and interpretation and is generally seen as programmatic and invaluable in understanding Herodotus' approach to life and history.[35]

After Solon leaves Sardis, Herodotus remarks how a 'divine indignation' (*nemesis ek theou*) 'fell heavily on Croesus: as I guess, because he supposed himself to be blest beyond all other men' (1.34). This is the only occurrence of the term *nemesis* in the *Histories* and too much should not too readily be assigned to its use here, especially when Herodotus qualifies his own thinking with 'as I guess' (*hōs eikasai*). Such hesitancy suggests a deduction on Herodotus' part, an attempt to tie up material from his main source with a story, that of Atys and Adrastus, which is not associated with any of Croesus' dedications to Delphi (Flower 2013: 146). Applying the term *hybris* (hubris) to Croesus is more misleading than enlightening and is not something that scholars agree on.[36] He may at worst be guilty of second-degree hubris, the result of an excessive overconfidence that is close to the overstepping of a natural boundary that separates corporeal men from omnipotent gods. In this way his behaviour anticipates, without being a carbon copy of, the temperament that leads an arrogant Xerxes to think he can act like a god and ignore the vicissitudes of life.[37] What happens to Croesus is *nemesis ek theou* because his presumption of blessedness provokes the indignation of the gods, even though Herodotus is not going to claim that he knows for sure the exact degree of culpability on Croesus' part. The idea of divine punishment, which will find more explicit expression later in the *Histories*, is not being raised here.

The Lydian monarch is a complex figure: the first Asian potentate to subjugate free Greeks yet a remarkably Hellenized ruler; someone who shrewdly if not cynically tests the veracity of oracles (1.46–9) in a manner Greeks would consider presumptuous if not impious; ruler of a small kingdom wanting to protect himself against Persian expansionism (1.46), a motive strengthened by a family relationship with Astyages, king of the Medes until conquered by Cyrus (1.73–4),[38] but also desiring to expand his own territorial rule (1.73).

Herodotus offers three possible motives for Cyrus' decision to put Croesus and fourteen Lydian children on a pyre (1.86) – the number of juvenile victims matching the number of days Sardis was under siege – one of which is a wish to discover if the renowned piety of Croesus might precipitate divine intervention and save him from immolation. This recalls the Lydian king's own experiment to test the veracity of oracles but what unfolds is far more remarkable than the results of a research project. Croesus on the pyre recalls the wisdom of Solon, and its heuristic value transmits itself to Cyrus who rescinds his decision and orders the fire to be extinguished. Croesus' learning curve has taken a long and tortuous course but Cyrus swiftly absorbs the insight that uncertainty governs everyone's life, including his own, and an outstanding display of compassion now occurs. The reader is made privy to the thoughts and feelings of the two men as Cyrus, inviting Croesus to sit by him, 'showed him much solicitude, marvelling as he beheld the man, as did all those present' (1.88). The scene recalls the affecting meeting between the mighty Achilles and the broken-hearted Priam: 'so Achilles wondered as he looked on Priam, a godlike man, and the rest of them wondered also, and looked at each other' (*Iliad*, 24: 483–4). What the two Homeric characters come to share – an acute awareness of human vulnerability and the sorrow it brings – is not dissimilar to the understanding that Cyrus and Croesus come to share.[39]

The ability of Croesus to appreciate the truth of Solon's gnomic advice (1.86–7) does little to diminish the cunningness of his advice to Cyrus to speciously claim a religious motive and stop his soldiers looting. Croesus' error is intellectual, reading the oracles in ways that only suited his own agenda (the beginnings of 1.54, 1.56 and 1.75), but his humaneness in forgiving Adrastus for killing his son (1.45) is magnanimous.

Another misinterpretation by Croesus, this time of a dream, underlies the story of Atys and Adrastus (1.34–45):[40] he assumes that if a spear were to kill his son it would be as a weapon of war and thus tries to protect his son by having him wed, but the marriage makes Atys want to impress his wife by joining a hunt (1.37). His non-military death, at the hands of someone asked to protect him, makes Adrastus doubly unfortunate for he was previously purified of his blood-guilt by Croesus after accidently killing his own brother and was keen to repay this act of goodness.[41] He is unable to escape his destiny as an involuntary killer just as Croesus is unable to resist his fate as the descendent of Gyges who must pay for that man's usurpation of power (1.91). The tale of Atys and Adrastus, a *mise enabîme* of Croesus' eventual plight, is a short story well crafted by Herodotus, replete with ironies and a grim illumination 'for his narratees [of] man's – tragic – grappling with fate' (de Jong 2013a: 291). The tale may also be seen as an example of the way Herodotus grounded his writing and gained authority for his new way of narrating the past by using concepts familiar to his audience, in this case protocol governing conduct between a host and guest. Such protocol, *xenia*, comes into play as a social bond between individuals as well as a political force affecting relations between rulers.[42] In Homer it works on both levels, and Vandiver (2012: 155–166) sees Herodotus using it to endow his writing with a reassuring Homeric echo, both conceptually and verbally. In 1.43, describing how Atys dies, Adrastus is referred to as 'the guest-friend (*xenos*)' who had previously been cleansed of 'the deed of blood'; now, by the slaying of someone he was honour-bound to protect, he becomes guilty of *xenoktonia* (the killing of a guest/friend). The distressed Croesus calls upon Zeus to witness what 'his guest [*xenos*] had wrought him' (1.44), yet he pities Adrastus' plight and in 1.45 addresses him personally as *xenos*, forgiving him for this second act of manslaughter because 'it is the work of a god, the same who told me long ago what was to be'. This resonates with the misfortune of Oedipus in Sophocles' drama as well as verbally recalling the words of Priam when he tells Helen it is the gods and not she who is to blame for what has happened (*Iliad* 3.164–5). Vandiver finds significance in the repetition of an Eastern ruler forgiving a foreigner who is accepted into the ruler's house only to consequently bring down disaster: 'Earlier in the *logos*, Croesus has addressed Solon as "Athenian *xenos*"; it requires his interaction with two *xenoi*, one of whom warns him against overconfidence in his good fortune and the other of whom enacts the nemesis that punishes that overconfidence, for Croesus to be able to understand that his son's terrible death is indeed *ek thou*' (Vandiver 2012: 163).

Story of Cyrus

The focus now shifts from the deposed Croesus to the man who defeated him,[43] and Herodotus prefaces his account with a statement of intent: he will not be swayed by aggrandizing accounts of Cyrus but will instead tell the 'true story' (1.95).[44] This declaration is followed by the information that the Medes successfully revolted against Assyrian rule and this sets the scene for the story of how Deioces emerged as the first Median monarch. He is succeeded by two other kings before Astyages becomes monarch (1.107–30) and in time Astyages provokes a rebellion that brings to an end the Median dynasty and its absorption in Persia's Achaemenid Empire.

The story of Cyrus gets underway with his birth and childhood (1.107–22) and continues with his revolt against Astyages (1.123–30) before an interruption of ten chapters (131–40) dealing with Persian ethnography. Before any of this, there is a short account of the Median kings before Astyages.

Kings of the Medes before Astyages (1.95–106)

The period between Deioces becoming king and the conquest of the Medes by Persia has been calculated as lasting 150 years but this is at odds with Herodotus' numbers for Median chronology. Modern scholars are inclined to doubt the historicity of the account of how Deioces became king, the whole idea of an integrated Median state and the nature of Scythian hegemony provided in this section (Asheri 2007b: 147, 149, 153; Thomas 2012: 245–6). At the same time, though, the story of Deioces is remarkably free of folklore touches and its cogency suggests a Hellenizing of a Near Eastern tradition about an autocrat's rise to power. The setting and some of the details are oriental – the building of Ecbatana with its seven coloured walls and Deioces' diktats about palace procedures[45] – but the explanation of how a state evolved from the coming together of a number of geographically related communities, synoecism, evokes the language of Greek political theorizing; a particularly close parallel is to be found in Thucydides (2.15).

The Medes, having shaken off the Assyrians, become independent (*autonomon*, 1.96) but then become subject to the rule of Deioces who, we are informed when he is first mentioned in 1.96, 'was in love [*erastheis*] with tyranny', using a tad ominously the same word that began the story of Candaules' fatal attraction when he 'fell in love' with his wife (1.8). The circumstances and the means whereby Deioces establishes a tyranny, a term

KINGS OF THE MEDES BEFORE ASTYAGES

1.95: The 'real story' after Medes revolt against Assyrian rule

1.96–101: Deioces, founder of the kingdom

1.102: Phraortes and his defeat by Assyria

1.103: Cyaxares extends Median power

1.104–5: Scythian invasion of Asia

1.106: Medes slay the Scythians, conquer Niniveh and bring down the Assyrian Empire

BOOK 1, BOX 4

from Greek political vocabulary,[46] is not unlike what Herodotus relates earlier about how Peisistratus became tyrant of Athens (1.59). Both men start from a worthy position: Peisistratus has fought well in a war with Megara and Deioces is 'a notable man in his own town' (1.96). The Medes suffer from 'lawlessness' (*anomia*, 1.97); the Athenians are 'divided into factions' (1.59). Both men ask for and receive bodyguards from their communities (1.59, 1.98) and each contrives to achieve autocratic rule: Peisistratus has a fake goddess to support his cause and Deioces has his 'friends' (*philoi*) to speak for him in the Median assembly. Having become tyrants, they both rule well: Peisistratus 'fairly and well' (1.59) while Deioces is scrupulous 'in the protection of justice' (1.100).

Attention has been drawn to the concern in the Deioces story with the administration and maintenance of justice (Thomas 2012: 249–51). When the future tyrant was first acquiring a reputation for fairness (1.96), the Medes are said to be suffering from 'lawlessness' (*anomiē*) and the term is used again when, as a result of Deioces withdrawing his labour, a fresh wave of *anomie* breaks out. The same term occurs in Greek political discourse and is used by Thucydides when he describes the consequences of the plague that afflicted Athens under siege by the Spartans (2.53). For Thomas, this is testimony to Greek theorizing about the role of the state in maintaining justice: 'It [the Deioces story] looks like a perfect case study for a sophistic theory about the development of tyranny, the creation of *polis* society, and the possible relation between lawlessness, *eunomiē* ("good order"), and the tyrant' (Thomas 250–1).

The account of the kings before Astyages concludes with the period when Median power was eclipsed by invading Scythians who made themselves 'masters of all Asia', including Palestine (1.104–5). Herodotus provides the only source for Scythians in Palestine and he reports how their plundering of a temple to Aphrodite at Ascalon (north of Gaza) is believed to have caused *thēleannouson* in the pillagers and their descendants who become known as 'Enareis' (1.105). A literal translation of *thēleannouson* is 'woman's sickness', ranging in modern editions from 'effeminacy' (Blanco) to 'hermaphroditism' (Waterfield); in Holland the Enareis are 'men who are also women' and, more coyly, the 'Sissies' in Blanco. The Enareis are mentioned again in 4.67 where they are noted for their method of divination, a contributory factor in their marginalized role within Scythian society.[47]

Cyaxares, the third Median king, brings Scythian hegemony to an end and restores a Median Empire after a twenty-eight-year interregnum. Cyaxares was first mentioned in the Croesus *logos* where it is told how he had treated well a band of Scythian nomads until a moment of ill temper on his part led to a gruesome dinner party where he was unknowingly served human flesh by disgruntled Scythians who then fled to Lydia. This led to a war between Medes and Lydians, the ending of which was sealed by the marriage of Croesus' sister to Astyages, the son of Cyaxares (1.73–4). Astyages proves to be the last of the Median kings and the course of his downfall is inextricably and fatefully linked to the rise of Cyrus. The story of this conjunction is the first of the two main sections constituting Herodotus' account of the Achaemenid Empire, founded by Cyrus around 550 and lasting until its conquest by Alexander the Great in 330.

Cyrus (1.107–30)

Herodotus' forte for storytelling returns in the tale of Cyrus' birth, childhood and conquest of the Medes and, as with other stories in the *Histories*, motifs from folk tales and myths are identifiable: puzzling, misinterpreted dreams, a prince exposed and left to die at birth, cunningly conveyed secret messages. The narrator's skill in the account of how Cyrus is saved resides partly in the way vital information is gradually released to the cowherd Mitradates, allowing the audience to share his astonishment and fear at what is happening. His wife's solution, substituting her stillborn for the baby he has been ordered to kill, emerges as a spontaneous reaction to the sight of a beautiful infant and, again, the audience only understands this as it happens.

The myth of Atreus and Thyestes was well known to Greeks, being the subject of lost plays by Sophocles and Euripides and alluded to in Aeschylus' *Agamemnon* and in *Electra* and *Orestes* by Euripides. It resonates in the macabre meal served by Astyages to his vizier Harpagus as punishment for not killing the infant Cyrus as he was instructed to do. In Greek mythology, Thyestes is punished by his brother Atreus by being unknowingly fed his own children, and some particular details of this myth are found in Herodotus' account of Astyages and Harpagus.[48]

Aspects of the story of Cyrus are also to be found in Athenian drama: an oracle in Sophocles' *Oedipus the King* prophesies to Laius that his son will endanger his future; Astyages' two dreams in Herodotus are interpreted to mean that his grandson will imperil his future. The lives of both Cyrus and Oedipus are saved in infancy by a herdsman, a figure who in both stories is interrogated before proving instrumental in revealing the truth. No one claims that such parallels show that Herodotus borrowed material from tragedies but the shared motifs have been seen to indicate that they 'at least have a cousinly relationship' (Evans 1991: 53). Perhaps 'at most' would better serve to qualify the connection, for matters like an incredible survival of a baby supposed to be left to die is not confined to Greek myth; aspects of Cyrus' birth and childhood are also to be found in a Mesopotamian foundation legend (Murray 2001a: 38).What can be surmised is that Herodotus can again be seen to be adopting a Hellenized legend from Persian sources, or shaping an Eastern tradition to suit a Greek audience, thereby 'intensifying the emotional impact of remote events by appeal to a well-known heroic paradigm of both cruelty and suffering beyond mere human capacity' (Chiasson 2012: 223).

Herodotus, though relying on Persian sources and knowing there are numerous tales surrounding the founder of the mighty Persian Empire, has nevertheless declared his resolve to present a true account of Cyrus (1.95). What he does deliver might seem to stretch credulity quite far enough but a hint as to the kind of even more far-fetched legends he has heard but chosen not to accept is evident in the rumour that the exposed baby Cyrus was suckled, Romulus-and-Remus style, by a bitch (1.122). Herodotus accepts that Cyrus' survival in infancy was remarkable – the timely arrival of Cyno's stillborn child is 'somehow ordained by providence' (*kōs kata daimona*, 1.111) – but dependent throughout on human factors. It is down to the moral cowardice of Astyages, Harpagus and Mitradates – each in their way relying on someone else to do what is their responsibility – and the fact that a woman 'is the only actor in the entire account who is willing both to give voice to the full range of practical and moral considerations ... and to accept responsibility for acting on them' (Dewald 2013b: 168–9).

The account of how Cyrus' true identity is revealed (1.114–6), the appalling punishment of Harpagus (1.115–9) and how this leads to Cyrus' revolt against his grandfather Astyages (1.123–7) is fanciful stuff. The steps that lead up to a charismatic Cyrus being recognized in childhood for who he truly is – nobility as innate; nature stronger than nurture – are familiar ground in the ideology of royalty, while the future king's heuristic method of gaining allies (1.126–7) indicates leadership qualities that mark him out as a natural ruler.[49] Walter Burkert's deft summary of the significance of the punishment dinner serves to remind readers of this and draws attention to the human factor that fascinates Herodotus about events of world importance: '[Astyages'] meal transformed him, if only inwardly, invisibly: for under the mask of the devoted servant, he was henceforth the inexorable

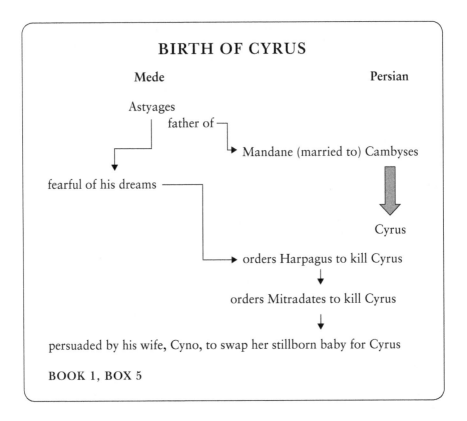

BIRTH OF CYRUS

Mede   Persian

Astyages
            father of
                        Mandane (married to) Cambyses

fearful of his dreams

                                            Cyrus

            orders Harpagus to kill Cyrus

            orders Mitradates to kill Cyrus

persuaded by his wife, Cyno, to swap her stillborn baby for Cyrus

BOOK 1, BOX 5

enemy of the king, unwilling to rest until Astyages had been overthrown . . . The parties were divided through the sacrificial meal, and their division determined the dynastic succession' (Burkert 1983: 109). Cyrus may have thought himself guided by the gods in his quest for power, telling potential allies 'I myself was born by a marvellous providence to take this work in hand' (1.126) – confirmed, it would seem, by the two dreams concerning Mandane's offspring[50] – but what facilitates him becoming the first Persian imperialist is another person's slow-burning desire for vengeance. Captive Astyages has the last word to say on the matter when he replies to Harpagus' taunt, calling him foolish and unjust, expressing his accusation in a clinically poised antithesis (1.129). The reader's sympathies will be with Harpagus but in one interpretation of this scene the surprise is 'the dignity of Astyages' bearing in defeat and the clarity of vision that he brings to the task of telling Harpagus a few home truths' (Pitcher 2007: 108). Herodotus' narrative skill is undoubtedly at work here but a reader may remain unmoved by the dispassionate reasoning of Astyages, struck more by the past event that has haunted Harpagus ever since joyfully informing his wife that his offence had been forgiven, pleased to send his only son off to the palace as requested (1.119).

CYRUS' GENEALOGY

Herodotus says:

1.107:	Cyrus' father, Cambyses, was a Persian from 'a good family'.
1.111:	Cyrus' grandfather was also called Cyrus.
1.125:	Persian kings came from the Achaemenid, a clan of Persian nobles but not royalty.

Babylonian and Persian sources say:

Cyrus' father, Cambyses, was a king of Anshan (modern Fars in Iran).

Teipes (Teispes) was the first king of Anshan, followed by Cyrus' grandfather, also called Cyrus, and then Cambyses, the father of Cyrus.

BOOK 1, BOX 6

Cyrus'genealogy (see Box 6) is sometimes at odds with what is known about the Achaemenid dynasty from Persian and Babylonian documents (Munson 2013: 323, nn. 6–9; Asheri 2007b: 157–8), but it does not cause problems for the historical summary that Herodotus provides in 1.130. Before the history of Cyrus continues there is an interlude on Persian ethnography.

Persian ethnography (1.131–40)

It seems clear from 1.107–30 and the individuality afforded to Cyrus[51] that Herodotus was using Persian sources of information and the impression that he has consulted and listened to Persians is reinforced when he comes to describe aspects of their culture. Their greeting etiquette is not just described in 1.134; an explanation is offered in terms of a mindset: 'for they deem themselves to be in all regards by far the best of all men'.[52] Herodotus is not criticizing them for being arrogant or overzealous in their self-esteem, simply reporting how, collectively, they think about non-Persians. There is an ontological guarantee to one aspect of their value system: not believing any child could kill one of its parents, they assert that any case of apparent matricide or parricide would, if properly investigated, prove that such children were illegitimate or adopted (1.137). Using negatives to describe another custom or culture can, consciously or not, reveal ethnocentrism, but with the listing of Persian *nomoi* the sense is more of Herodotus' awareness of a complete self-assurance enveloping their sense of identity: 'It is not their custom to make or set up statues and temples and altars but those who make such they deem foolish, as I suppose, because they never believed the gods, as do the Greeks, to be in the likeness of men' (1.131).[53] A consumerist and acquisitive mentality sees them enjoying large meals (1.133) and being desirous of many concubines (1.135) but Herodotus refrains from a negative judgement; the Persian emphasis on quantity over quality will be a hallmark of Xerxes' planning for the conquest of Greece and a limitation to this way of thinking will emerge in due course. Other aspects of Persian culture, the conviction that lying is heinous (1.136) and a restriction on a king's ability to inflict capital punishment (1.137), will be found wanting in the behaviour of later kings (3.72, 8.118).

The aspects of Persian sacrifices that are noted are those that depart from the protocols followed by Greeks: no fire is lit beforehand for roasting the meat, no altars are used or libations applied, no music or garlands or grains of barley (1.132). The unchallengeable authority of the Persian monarchy is not stressed and the law that Herodotus admires, whereby a king can no more execute someone for their offence than any Persian could his servant, is not a *nomos* borne out later in the *Histories*. It is the dictatorial power of the Persian monarch and royal punishments involving mutilation that will be reported later whereas here what is reported 'represents the assertiveness of the *ethnos* as a whole and places it firmly in control of its own *nomoi*' (Munson 2001a: 154).

The Ionia logos (1.141–76)

The chapters dealing with Ionia are ones that readers may occasionally be tempted to skim through in places because the various locations, their backgrounds and movements of people can befuddle (Box 7). The military comings and goings as the Persians set about establishing absolute control in Asia Minor are often less memorable than fleeting details that bear testimony to the human cost of their expansionism. There are the women who following the custom of their mothers eat separately from their husbands and never call them by name, acts of homage to the Carian menfolk killed by Ionian colonists in order to take their women for themselves (1.146). The guilty conscience of the people of Chios over Pactyes (1.160) lies behind their unwillingness to use barley from Atarneus, the place they accepted as a bribe for handing him over to the Persians. Throwing unground barley onto a sacrificial animal was an obligatory part of a Greek sacrifice, as was the offering of barley cakes to the gods, and the religious context framing their discomfiture indicates their sense that a sacrilege has been committed in the betrayal of a suppliant. Many of the Phocaeans who choose to flee rather than submit to Persian authority are overcome by

IONIA *LOGOS* AND PERSIAN EXPANSION

1.141–53: Ionia *logos*

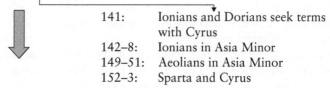

141:	Ionians and Dorians seek terms with Cyrus
142–8:	Ionians in Asia Minor
149–51:	Aeolians in Asia Minor
152–3:	Sparta and Cyrus

1.154–76: Persian conquests in Asia Minor

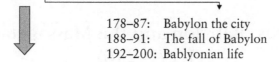

154–7:	Revolt in Lydia crushed
157–60:	Pactyes
161–8:	Persian campaigns; emigrations of Phocaeans and Teians
169–76:	Conquest of Ionia, Caria, Caunia and Lycia

1.177–200: Persia conquers Babylon

178–87:	Babylon the city
188–91:	The fall of Babylon
192–200:	Bablyonian life

1.201–16: Cyrus and the Massagetae

201–4:	Caspian Sea area
205–14:	Campaign to defeat Tomyris
215–16:	Massagetae culture

BOOK 1, BOX 7

homesickness and more than half of them break their vow never to return (1.165).

The chapters devoted to the ethnic history and politics of Ionia may not be very interesting for many readers today but they would have been for Herodotus' audience for whom migration and ancestry stories and questions of ethnic origin were bound up with issues of identity and self-perception. In some of what Herodotus says there is an indication of contentiousness on his part, as when he appears to ridicule those who would claim to be 'more truly Ionian' than others (1.146) or when he says 'seeing that they set more store by the name than the rest of the Ionians, let it be granted that those of pure birth are Ionian' (1.147). It is possible that the point of mentioning the killing of Carian males in 1.146 and the subsequent intermarriage with non-Greek women by Greek colonists is to belittle Ionian assumptions of racial purity.

Something similar may be going on with the complex lineage provided for the ethnic complexion of Lycia (1.173). It involves a quarrel between two Cretan brothers, sons of Europa.[54] One is the legendary Minos who drives out his brother who consequently settles in Lycia. There is a second set of quarrelling brothers, one of whom is the legendary figure Aegeus, the father of Theseus, who expels his brother who also ends up in Lycia. A reader familiar with the Greek myth of Theseus and the Minotaur will be struck by this earlier linkage between Minos and Theseus, a connection to which Herodotus does not feel the need to draw attention.[55] What would have been of interest to his audience were genealogies with mythic figures like Minos, Aegeus and Theseus and an account of Ionian identity that stresses the mixing of people and customs. Perhaps, as Thomas asserts, Herodotus takes 'delight in puncturing the myths of origin that embody ethnic identity for certain prominent Greek city-states' (2013: 356).

Cyrus, Babylon and the Massagetae (1.177–216)

Persian expansion under Cyrus started, after his rebellion against the Medes, with the conquest of Lydia – 'after this victory he became sovereign of all Asia' (1.130) – and this success motivates the subjugation of 'every nation, leaving none untouched' (1.191). This includes the fabulous city of Babylon and, in the words of one adjective-prone account, '[Cyrus] fixed his predatory gaze on that supreme goal of every conqueror's ambition, the wealthy flatlands of what is now southern Iraq, stretching from Assyria to the Persian Gulf, the stage for splendid cities since the very dawn of time' (Holland 2005: 18). Cyrus can be seen to be abrogating natural divisions effected by water in the incident where one of his 'sacred white horses' (1.189) is swept away in the Gyndes and he delays his campaign by a year in order to punish the river by having hundreds of canals dug into it to channel off water and weaken its power. An enigma, though, surrounds this event given the disproportional amount of time, an entire summer, devoted to achieving the punishment, if that is what it is. It is called *ergon* (work), the word used in the preface to the *Histories* to cover the 'great and marvellous deeds [*erga*]' that the author seeks to preserve. Gould, invariably astute in reading Herodotus, is left puzzled, wondering what sort of 'work' this is supposed to be if not a marvellous deed in the annals of the Achaemenid family: 'is this an act of atonement [for Persians, white horses were sacred to the sun], an "achievement", or rather a display of petulance and power by man encroaching on the boundaries that set him apart from god?' (Gould 1989: 109). Such speculation encounters only silence on the part of Herodotus.

Before the siege of Babylon is recounted, Herodotus gives a description of the walls and buildings of the city and if not awed by its scale he is certainly respectful of the achievement it embodies, an instance of what he said in his preface he was keen to preserve for posterity. It is built in the shape of a huge square, with the Euphrates flowing through the middle and a bridge across the river, and streets laid out in a grid plan. A palace stands in one half of the city and a temple, with a large ziggurat accessed by a spiral staircase, in the other. A moat surrounds everything and the walls are wide enough to accommodate a four-horse chariot. Hydraulic engineering by a queen, Nitocris, further protects the city; a queen who ranks as one of the three formidably self-reliant women in the first book of the *Histories*. The unnamed wife of Candaules was the first (1.8–13), and the third, Tomyris, is about to arrive on the narrative scene but neither can match the chutzpah of Nitocris who is prepared to have her tomb opened in order to mock a future greedy conqueror (1.187).

The archaeological evidence does not fully accord with Herodotus' description of Babylon and while it has been assessed as 'broadly reliable' (Kuhrt 2002: 480) the same scholar of Achaemenid history goes on to say that 'The picture of Babylonia and its capital which we can disengage from the sources differs in many fundamentals from that of Herodotus' (2002: 495). Apart from what Herodotus might have seen for himself, if he did visit Babylon, his main source of information on Babylon are the priests he calls Chaldaeans. It is difficult to know exactly who the Chaldaeans were, in distinction to other members of the Babylonian population, and given that Herodotus did not speak the language it is possible that, to some unknown extent, he was hoodwinked by exaggerated accounts provided by travellers who were acquainted with the city (Kuhrt 2002: 481–2).

After narrating the city's capture, Herodotus turns to Babylonian customs. He never states unequivocally that he visited the city although his tone of voice in 1.193 implies he did. Either way, he takes delight in the ingenuity of river trade between Armenia and Babylon – with donkeys and date wine carried by boats downstream and then boat parts carried by donkeys upstream – calling it 'the most marvellous thing in the country, next to the city itself' (1.194). He has no hesitation in approving of the exposure of the sick in public to facilitate the circulation of experienced advice (1.197) and describes two other customs which both involve the commodification of women's bodies but which produce opposite judgements on his part. He approves of the auctions of women that provide them all with a dowry (1.196), something which a little facetiously has been called a laudable application of market forces (Griffiths 2001b: 166).[56] Herodotus is just as earnest in condemning 'the foulest Babylonian custom' that in the guise of religion makes every woman prostitute herself once in her life (1.199). Such a negative judgement of a cultural practice is not characteristic of Herodotus and generally there is an absence of interpretative comments from his ethnographic observations. He prefers to present his information in a neutral manner, gently querying ethnocentric assumptions on the part of his audience by drawing out differences between a barbarian culture and his own but slipping in some similarities as well. With Babylonians, Munson describes and then summarizes what is said about their diet as 'exotic', their bride market as 'preposterous' and their boats as 'peculiar' but their ability to solve problems a talent that makes them similar to the Greeks (2001a: 8–12).

The conquest of Babylon does not satisfy Cyrus' imperial ambitions and he turns to the Massagetae that dwell on the north side of the River Araxes (the Alas in north-west Iran, forming the country's borders with Armenia and Azerbaijan). Cyrus still feels destined for superhuman deeds and buoyed up with his achievements feels confident about expanding his domain (1.204). The course of events that prove him gravely mistaken throws up a number of telling ironies and inversions in Herodotus' narrative, beginning with the advice of someone who himself lost an unnecessary war. Croesus' counsel to lure the Massagetae into a state of drunkenness (1.207), echoing Odysseus' ploy with the Cyclops, has only limited success and it leads to Tomyris' ultimatum.[57] Cyrus is defeated in a campaign that was no more essential for him to conduct than was the campaign mounted in the past by Croesus against him. At that time, a man called Sandanis had unsuccessfully tried to impart some sensible advice to the bellicose Croesus (1.71); now an ex-king, Croesus makes a prudent observation to the belligerent Persian king and, as with Sandanis' caution, it is ignored. Croesus' urging of restraint, premised on the cyclical nature of fortune (a wheel 'which in its turning suffers not the same man to prosper for ever' (1.207)), harks back to his own conversation with the sagacious Solon (1.30–3). Croesus realized too late the truth of Solon's wisdom (1.86–9) and now, on the eve of Cyrus' death, it is again passed on but unheeded.[58] In the proem (1.5), Herodotus himself draws attention to the inherent instability of human prosperity and the repetition and echoing of a single truth – that nothing is certain in life except death – lends credence to the belief that this is something the author of the *Histories* regards as a piece of important knowledge.

The advice proffered by Sandanis also has its place in a significant dynamic at work in the *Histories* between 'hard' and 'soft' lifestyles. It underlays Cyrus' stratagem for securing support in his planned revolt against the Medes, presenting fellow Persians with a choice between a life of toil or one of luxury (1.126), yet Sandanis cautions Croesus against an invasion of foreign territory on the grounds that the Persians are a hardy and tough people with nothing to offer Lydia. They wear clothes made of leather, do not drink wine or eat figs (as civilized people like the Greeks do) and if they were to defeat Lydia it will only give them a taste of the good life that can never be undone: 'for once they have tasted of our blessings they will cling so close to them that nothing will thrust them away' (1.71).[59] This would seem to have proved true for now it is the Massagetae who are the tough ones and Croesus' devious suggestion for their entrapment – getting them drunk – seeks to exploit their hardiness and use it against them: 'You see, a Persian-style good life and anything approaching real luxury is, I hear, something with which the Massagetae have no acquaintance or familiarity' (1.207). The wheel of fortune that Solon spoke of has made another turn. There is a final twist in the narrative: 'Cyrus' early victory over Astyages, a father (figure) alienated from his daughter, finds its antithesis in the king's final defeat by Tomyris, a mother avenging the death of her son' (Chiasson 2013: 230).

François Hartog, in his influential *The Mirror of Herodotus*, provides a geographical parameter for what he calls a moment of hubris, a transgressive act effected by moving beyond one's natural space into an alien one: 'the material sign of such transgression is the construction of a bridge over a river or, worse, over a stretch of sea' (Hartog 1988: 331). For Persian kings, the precedent is set by Cyrus when he orders the building of a bridge over the Araxes (1.205), and similar acts of contravention will be committed by Achaemenid kings that come after him.

Tomyris, a 'noble savage' who defends her land in a 'Homerically irreproachable fashion' (Dewald 2013b: 169), is not only a redoubtable ruler but one who demonstrates more honourable standards of military behaviour than her adversary. She articulates a creditable principle of peaceful international co-existence (1.206), one which the reader first sees being violated by Croesus, then by Cyrus and the Persian kings who come after him.

Book Two: Egypt

Introduction

The reader who has grappled with the digressions and time shifts in Book One may be relieved to know that Book Two remains focused throughout on a single topic – Egypt – but still wonder why it concerns itself with a wholesale diversion from the story of the Persians. Book Two is a lengthy excursus dedicated to all matters Egyptian: not just history but ethnography, geography, geology, zoology, architecture, society and religion. What holds this potpourri together is Herodotus' abiding commitment to what he announced at the very start of his work, his intention to celebrate the great and wondrous achievements of Greeks and non-Greeks. Book Two is one major result of this intent because he sees in Egypt a wide pool of evidence for the 'fullest of wonders' (*pleistathōmasia*, 2.35), and his curiosity and catholic interests are never more on show than in this extended *logos*. The marvels he wants to share with his audience are diverse, to put it mildly: 'miracles, fulfilled dreams, portents and prophecies, extraordinary adventures, sudden reversals of situations, moral virtues of the good old days, heroism on the battlefield, gruesome tortures, stratagems, trickeries, witticisms: in short, the products of the irrational and of intelligence'.[1] Egypt for Herodotus, and for many Greeks, was not dissimilar to the way Japan is still sometimes presented in the contemporary world – an enigma and fascinating for this reason – and likewise Egypt, the land of the Sphinx (of which Herodotus makes no mention), is alluring because of its perceived strangeness; its otherness.[2]

Egypt was known to the Greek world for centuries before Herodotus. Homer and Solon were said to have made visits there and Herodotus was not the first to write about a country that Greek merchants had been doing business with since the seventh century and which had a trading centre for that purpose at the town of Naucratis in the Nile Delta (2.178–9). Greek mercenaries were busy in Egypt from around the same time, hired by Psammetichus to aid his seizure of the throne (2.152–4). Later, in the reign of another king in the early sixth century, Greek mercenaries travelled far south in an invasion of Nubia and left some graffiti on a leg of a colossal statue of Ramesses at Abu Simbel. A few years earlier, another king paid Greeks to design ships to help fight a Phoenician navy and Herodotus reports how Egyptian kings made dedications to Greek sanctuaries and how one royal married a Greek (2.180–2).

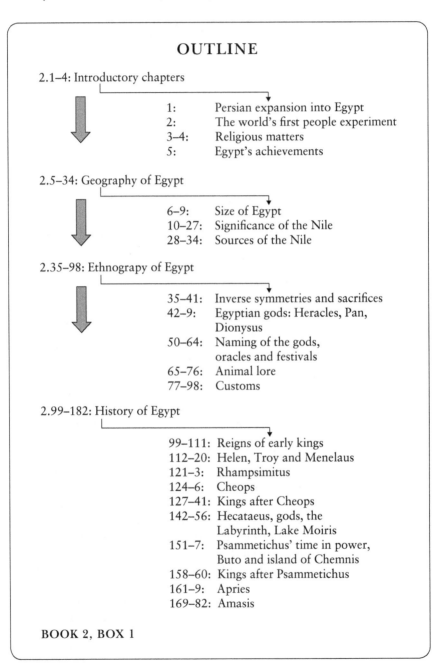

OUTLINE

2.1–4: Introductory chapters

1:	Persian expansion into Egypt
2:	The world's first people experiment
3–4:	Religious matters
5:	Egypt's achievements

2.5–34: Geography of Egypt

6–9:	Size of Egypt
10–27:	Significance of the Nile
28–34:	Sources of the Nile

2.35–98: Ethnograpy of Egypt

35–41:	Inverse symmetries and sacrifices
42–9:	Egyptian gods: Heracles, Pan, Dionysus
50–64:	Naming of the gods, oracles and festivals
65–76:	Animal lore
77–98:	Customs

2.99–182: History of Egypt

99–111:	Reigns of early kings
112–20:	Helen, Troy and Menelaus
121–3:	Rhampsimitus
124–6:	Cheops
127–41:	Kings after Cheops
142–56:	Hecataeus, gods, the Labyrinth, Lake Moiris
151–7:	Psammetichus' time in power, Buto and island of Chemnis
158–60:	Kings after Psammetichus
161–9:	Apries
169–82:	Amasis

BOOK 2, BOX 1

Thales of Miletus wrote about the Nile and around 500 the geographer Hecataeus of Miletus travelled as far south in the country as Thebes and in this way provided Herodotus, it is alleged by some, with material for what became the second book of the *Histories*. What Hecataeus wrote would have been known to Herodotus (he makes one explicit reference to him) and it is possible, as will be seen, that in one place Herodotus is consciously alluding to Hecataeus and scoffing at what he says about the inundation of the Nile.[3]

Herodotus gives many instances of practices and beliefs that he sees as having spread from Egypt to the Greek world, often based on the inference that because Egyptian civilization has such an ancient lineage it must have influenced younger cultures like the Hellenic one. Allied to his respect for the antiquity of Egyptian civilization is an emollient attitude to how Egyptians conduct their lives and, as a negative corollary to this, what also emerges is a combative approach on his part towards those Greek accounts that would denigrate aspects of Egyptian society.

Introducing Egypt (2.1–4)

The first sentence of Book Two follows on from what drew Book One to a close, the death of the Persian king Cyrus. He is succeeded by his son Cambyses who gathers an army that includes Greeks to attack the land of Egypt (2.1), the idea for such a campaign going back to Cyrus (1.153). Military matters, however, are not pursued by Herodotus and they serve more as a trigger for looking into myriad aspects of Egyptian life, beginning with an investigation conducted by Psammetichus to ascertain the identity of the first people to exist (2.2). Herodotus is less interested in the result than in the research methods of the experiment, carefully noting the control procedures and Psammetichus' insistence that he witness for himself the first words uttered by the quarantined children who were brought up without hearing any human speech. Herodotus notes the Egyptians' willingness to accept a result that undermines their self-belief as the world's first people and he dismisses Greek accounts of Psammetichus cutting out the tongues of the women who reared the children. That there is an affinity here with a fellow inquirer seems to be underlined for readers who learn next (2.3) how Herodotus sets out to satisfy his own intellectual curiosity by visiting temples in Egypt (Christ 2013: 233).[4] Herodotus states his credentials as an historian, travelling in person to cross-check sources, while demarcating a boundary between legitimate inquiry and matters of theology (2.3). He does, however, acknowledge his interest in the names Egyptians give to their deities and he goes on to make the surprising claim that having twelve gods, each with their own appellation, is an idea which the Greeks borrowed from them (2.4). He will have a lot more to say about the names of gods but insists on neutrality when it comes to religious affairs because he is firmly of the opinion that some matters are not within the scope of *historie*. Notwithstanding this caveat and without discoursing on the nature of the gods or the beliefs underpinning the worship of them, it turns out there is plenty of scope for looking at aspects of Egyptian religion. As well as the names of gods (*ounomata*), areas like divination and metempsychosis will be touched on as well as communication between gods and man (oracles and portents) and he is comfortable describing festivals, iconography, methods of sacrifice, temple decorum and sacred animals. His statement of reticence (2.3, see pp. 47–8) becomes less of a constraint than it might seem even though he expresses similar reservations elsewhere in his Egyptian *logos* (see Box 2).

Authorial remarks are a narratological characteristic of the Egyptian *logos* and more first-person statements are to be found here than in any other book of the *Histories*. At times Herodotus almost becomes a character in the story he is telling and he wants his audience to know that, by asking questions, listening to answers and stating his sources, he takes little for granted (see Box 3).

HERODOTUS' RETICENCE ABOUT RELIGIOUS MATTERS (2.1–98)

'Now, for the stories which I heard about the gods, I am not desirous to relate them' (3)

'So much I say of this matter; may no god or hero be displeased with me therefore!' (45)

'the image of Pan is made as among the Greeks with the head and legs of a goat; not that he is deemed to be in truth such, or unlike to other gods; but why they so present him I have no wish to say' (46)

'The Egyptians have an account of the reason why they sacrifice swine at this festival, yet abominate them at others; I know it, but it is not fitting that I should relate it' (47)

'I should be brought to speak of matters of divinity, of which I am especially unwilling to treat' (65)

'I have said enough concerning creatures that are sacred' (76)

'the most perfect manner of embalming belongs, they say, to One whose name it were profane for me to speak in treating of such matters' (86)

BOOK 2, BOX 2

EGYPT: SOURCES AND VERIFICATION (2.1–98)

Introductory chapters (2.1–4)

'I heard also other things at Memphis ... and I visited Thebes too and Heliopolis for this very purpose' (3)

Geography of Egypt (2.5–34)

'their greatest breadth from east to west, as I learnt, is a two months' journey' (8)

'for I have seen that Egypt projects itself into the sea' (12)

'Moeris was not yet nine hundred years dead when I heard this from the priests' (13)

'I hold rather that the Egyptians did not come into being with the making of the Delta' (15)

'My opinion ... is attested by the answer which ... I heard to have been given by the oracle of Ammon' (18)

'Concerning its nature, neither from the priests nor from any others could I learn anything ... I wished to know, and asked' (19)

'of which there are two that I would not even mention, save to show only what they are' (20)

'needs no reproof; for I know of no river of Ocean' (23)

'I must now set forth what I myself think about these obscure matters' (24)

'I am persuaded therefore that the sun is the cause of these matters' (26)

'none that conversed with me, neither Egyptian nor Libyan, nor Greek, professed to know them' (28)

'from no other man could I learn anything ... But this much I learnt by the farthest inquiry that I could make, by my own travel and sight as far as the city of Elephantine' (29)

'But this I heard from certain men of Cyrene' (32)

'and as I guess, reasoning as to things unknown from visible signs' (33)

'Concerning its course I have told all that I could learn by inquiry [*historeunta*]' (34)

Ethnograpy of Egypt (2.35–98)

'Concerning Heracles, I heard it said that he was one of the twelve gods' (43)

'wishing to get clear knowledge ... I took ship to Tyre ... Then I went to Thasos' (44)

'For I am assured by inquiry that they came from foreign parts' (50)

'this I know, for I was told at Dodona' (52)

'When I asked them how it was that they could speak with so certain knowledge' (54)

'That, then, I heard from the Theban priersts and what follows is told by the prophetesses of Dodona' (55)

'I hold this proved, because the Egyptian ceremonies are manifestly very ancient, and the Greeks are of late origin' (58)

'it is called the phoenix. I myself have never seen it' (73)

'the most careful of all men to preserve the memory of the past and none whom I questioned have so many chronicles' (77)

'Not far from the town of Buto, there is a place in Arabia to which I went to learn about the winged serpents' (75)

'When I asked why Perseus appeared to them alone' (91)

Methodological qualification

'These Egyptian stories are for the use of whosover believes such tales: for myself, it is my rule throughout this history that I record whatever is told me as I have heard it' (2.123)

BOOK 2, BOX 3

Geography of Egypt (2.5–34)

The interest Herodotus shows in conducting research through experimentation is revealed in his mention of a hypothetical test that would establish beyond doubt that Egypt's soil is directly attributable to the Nile (2.5). Using his own (correct) knowledge of how accumulated silt built up the land around places like Troy and Ephesus, he blends reason with imagination to envisage how, were the Nile capable of overflowing into the Red Sea, it would over a period of 10,000–20,000 years fill it in and reshape world geography (2.11). This is a remarkable and legitimately founded act of speculation and cannot but impress the reader.[5] Herodotus' sustained engagement with the topic of the Nile escalates into a disagreement with the view of Ionian Greeks whose map of the world would restrict Egypt's geographical identity to that of the river alone. He rests his case on a de facto truth: 'Egypt is all that country which is inhabited by Egyptians, even as Cilicia and Assyria are the countries inhabited by Cilicians and Assyrians severally' (2.17).[6]

A polemical stance towards the way some Greeks claim to understand Egypt continues when he considers some of their theories as to why the Nile, inversing what would be expected, floods in the summer months (2.20–3). One theory is that i) the river is prevented from reaching the sea by summer winds from the Mediterranean; another claims ii) it is due to the waters of the Ocean which circulate around the whole world[7]; yet another iii) attributes the cause to melting snow as the river flows from its source. Herodotus' refutation is sharp with its logic: i) is a *reductio ad absurdum*: the Nile floods when there are no winds and other rivers facing the same winds don't flood; ii) is unverifiable and therefore irrefutable because there is no evidence that the Ocean exists;[8] iii) the Nile originates in the hottest of places where, based on four pieces of evidence, there is no snow. While Herodotus does not put across his own theory with equal clarity (2.24–5), it does in places possess more scientific credibility than those he rejects (Lloyd 2007: 256).

Herodotus is fascinated by the Nile and although his curiosity about the river's origins cannot be completely satisfied (2.28) he does give credence to an outlandish tale he carefully traces back third-hand to an Ammonian king, Etearchus (2.32–3). A small number of 'reckless young' (*paidashybristas*) Nasamonians ventured further west into the Sahara than anyone previously, until captured by pygmy wizards and taken to their city where a great river with crocodiles flowed by from west to east. The Nasamonians had only sought to show off amongst themselves but Etearchus is an inquirer like Herodotus: he is curious about strange lands, questions a source of information and draws a viable conclusion. As if stimulated by Etearchus's reasoning, Herodotus engages in a piece of guesswork of his own, drawing an elaborate parallel between the respective courses of the Danube and the Nile (Christ 2013: 222–3). The analogy, which seems bizarre to modern readers, coheres with his abiding sense of symmetry in nature (Hartog 2013: 248–9; Gould 1989: 89–90).

Ethnography of Egypt

Inverse symmetries and sacrifices (2.35–41)

There is nothing oblique about an Egypt versus rest of mankind polarity in Herodotus' ethnographic account, but it is not something peculiar to him as an individual. In Sophocles' *Oedipus at Colonus*, Oedipus turns to Egypt as an analogy for what he sees as the odd way his sons, compared to his daughters, behave:

> Those two [his sons] are like in everything
> to the ways of Egypt,
> both in their nature and in how they live.
> For in that country the men sit within doors
> working at the loom, while the wives go out
> to get the daily bread.[9]

While Sophocles is content with one example, Herodotus lists nearly twenty ways (2.35–6) in which an inverse symmetry exists between the ways of the Egyptians and those of everyone else,[10] though by everyone else he is often referring to the Greeks and this emerges in his description of how Egyptians conduct their sacrifices. The emphasis here is not on theology or iconography but on aspects of the ritual that are foreign to the Greek tradition of sacrifice, an approach that reflects the importance of cult and ritual practices in Greek religion. If the animal to be sacrificed in Egypt is a bull, there are strict procedures for ascertaining its purity (2.38) and the severest possible penalty, death, is ordained for anyone sacrificing one that has not been certified as clean.[11] The certification process is conducted by a priest who wraps papyrus around the bull's horns before marking it with the stamp of his ring. Herodotus goes on to describe what happens to the bull's head (2.39), a practice not just alien to Hellenic sacrificial practices but insulting to Greeks by making them a useful depository for unwanted, curse-laden bulls' heads: 'The Greeks become a figurative cesspool for animal parts that have undergone a scapegoating ritual' (Hashhozheva 2006: 93; and see p. 24).

Egyptian gods: Heracles, Pan and Dionysus (2.42–9)

Herodotus provides different Egyptian and Greek names for the same gods: Zeus is called Amon; Dionysus is called Osiris (2.42); and more equivalent names will be given later. Herodotus relates what he has heard as to why some Egyptians regard rams as sacred before moving on to tackle the vexing issue of Heracles and his twin identity as a Greek hero and an Egyptian god (2.43–5). Herodotus, always respectful of Egypt's long history, reports how Heracles is a particularly ancient god for Egyptians and, given that he can find no evidence in Egypt of the Greek culture-hero with the same name, is confident – 'I have indeed many proofs' (2.43) – that the Greeks derived the name of their Heracles, the son of Amphitryon, from that country. Not content with his inquiries on this matter within Egypt, Herodotus declares how he sought clarification by taking a ship to Tyre in Phoenicia because he has heard of an especially holy temple to Heracles in that city. In Tyre he is informed that the temple there is a very ancient one, long predating any birth of a son to Amphitryon. He rebuts the possibility that the name of Heracles originated in Greece because Egyptians have no knowledge of Poseidon (god of the sea) or Castor and Pollux (patrons of sailors) and yet if seafarers had brought the name from Greece they would surely have brought these other names as well. He is confident in his conclusion that he has 'discovered by inquiry' (2.44) that Heracles is an ancient god.[12] The Greeks, it follows, are being logical when they worship two distinct figures with the same name, one of whom is the Greek-born son of Amphitryon while the other is an ancient Egyptian divinity. He concludes (2.45) by apologizing to gods and heroes, presumably for subjecting to investigation – an account 'peppered with his most scientific vocabulary of proof and evidence' (Harrison 2003a: 239) – a religious matter best left alone.

In the same chapter (2.45) Herodotus gives two reasons for ridiculing the Greek tale that Heracles came to Egypt and only escaped being the victim of a human sacrifice there by slaughtering all his foes.[13] On ethnographic grounds he finds it ridiculous that the Egyptian national character (*phusis*) and its customs (*nomoi*) could ever countenance such a sacrifice; at a common-sense level he scoffs at the idea that one man could kill everyone around him.[14] These three chapters (2.43–5) are testimony to Herodotus as an Egypt-friendly investigative journalist, far from disinterested, indefatigable in the pursuit of a puzzle deemed worthy of solving. His participatory role within the story – questioning, listening, fact-finding, travelling, drawing conclusions – is as interesting as the data he collects, and what is also noticeable is his dismissive attitude towards Greeks. There are, he alleges, 'many ill-considered tales' told by Greeks, and their tale (*muthos*) about Heracles is 'very foolish' (2.45), using *muthos* to indicate a story that lacks credibility.[15]

The god Pan is briefly mentioned but in a confused manner, saying that images of him are painted and carved in the same way for both Egyptians and Greeks but then adding that such a theriomorphic depiction – the god having the animal form of a goat – is a misleading representation for Egyptians (2.46). Herodotus declines to say more on the iconography of Pan and maintains this tone of prudence by refusing to explain why pigs are considered unclean and yet at one special time of the year are sacrificed in a very precise manner and then eaten. The reluctance to say more on such matters follows from his earlier declaration that he will avoid discussing theological issues (2.3). He is interested, however, in conveying information about religious practices and this is clear from his account of the rites of Dionysus (2.48–9). He credits Melampus with having introduced the cult into Greece from the far older civilization of Egypt, allowing for differences in their respective practices but regarding them as not significant enough to override an essential similarity that points to a single source. The Greek custom is to carry phalli during processions whereas in Egypt large puppets, with phalli which are manipulated by strings, are carried by women behind a flute player. Some details point to differences but the underlying similarity is what matters.

The naming of gods, Dodona and festivals (2.50–64)

Herodotus returns to the claim, first made in 2.4, that the naming of the Greek gods was the product of cultural diffusion from Egypt, adding that he has been told this by Egyptians and he believes it himself to be the case (2.50). He is careful to allow for exceptions to the rule, accepting Poseidon's origins in Libya and the names of some Greek gods and the ithyphallic images of Hermes originating with the non-Egyptian Pelasgians,[16] but the foundational role of Egypt in the naming of the Greek gods is paramount. Given, though, that it was earlier noted how Egypt and Greece have different names for the same gods (2.42) it cannot be a phonetic equivalence that Herodotus has in mind. He could mean that cultural transmission brought to Greece a nomenclature for gods where previously there was none, gradually replacing as the object of worship an indistinct plurality with a system of names, identities and attributes for individual divinities. This accords with the remarkable historical reconstruction that Herodotus offers, covering a timescale that stretches back to an epoch when the indigenous inhabitants of Greece, the so-called Pelasgians, possessed a collective sense of the divine without differentiating individual deities: 'The Pelasgians meant by "gods" those who put everything in its place and kept it there' (2.52; Blanco translation).[17] Then, 'after a long while', they learnt names for most of the gods from Egypt, seeking authorization from the oracle at Dodona to use them, and in this way a system of names was passed on to the Greeks who later came to inhabit their land. The names of gods eventually came to be associated with qualities and personal identities, but the temporal canvas was extremely broad and this is duly taken into account: 'Where each of the gods came from, whether they have all always existed, what they look like – these things were unknown to the Greeks until only yesterday, so to speak, or the day before' (2.53; Blanco translation). Herodotus reckons that, some four centuries before his time, Homer and Hesiod were composing their epic poetry and it is to their work that is owed the existing genealogies of the gods, what they look like and their associated rites.

Greek religion functioned without a codified creed or a revealed holy text and what Herodotus says here about epic poetry is important. Ritual practices were the form in which Greeks experienced an awareness of a plurality of powers beyond their comprehension, polymorphic forces of an ineffable nature that could be appealed to, pacified and appeased, and these did not require or provide any particular knowledge about particular divinities or their interrelationships. Gould reasons[18] that this gap was filled by the tradition of epic narrative poetry that allowed for material about the divine to develop into a coherent ideology and iconography. If Herodotus is saying something like this in 2.53 then, as a Greek ethnographer, he is displaying an extraordinary willingness and capacity to step back from his own culture and attempt to objectively contextualize a chief characteristic of its religion by framing it within a historical time frame that includes a vitally determining influence from a far older, non-Greek civilization.

The very ancient oracle of Zeus at Dodona, situated in a remote mountain location in north-west Greece, has its earliest mention in the *Iliad* (16.233ff.), in an invocation by Achilles; in the *Odyssey* there is the first mention of a talking oak tree at Dodona (14.327–8, 19.296–7). According to the sources Herodotus consults, this oracle and another one in Libya were founded at the same time by Egyptians. He hears of two parallel but incompatible versions of how this occurred, one involving a pair of priestesses and the other a pair of black doves, and offers a rationalization which would harmonize the two myths (2.54–7). Herodotus' reasoning, which allows for the role of an oak tree without treating it as sacred or as a source for the god's words, endorses the view that the oracle's origins lay in Egypt but he stresses his diligence in interrogating his sources. The priests at Thebes are asked to provide grounds for thinking their account to be true while the alternative account given in Dodona is accorded an equal degree of respect – though this for Herodotus entails neither account being necessarily accepted as historically accurate – by recording the names of the three priestesses who proffer it as the truth, adding how their version is supported by all the other Dodonians at the shrine.[19]

Before some remarks on Egyptian festivals, Herodotus gives more instances of Greek religious practices – divination and other rites – that he thinks must have originated in Egypt. Chronological precedence, he make explicit, is the basis of his reasoning: 'I hold this proved, because the Egyptian ceremonies are manifestly very ancient, and the Greeks are of late origin' (2.58).

The account provided of six Egyptian festivals and pilgrimages (2.59–63), written as it is before Hellenistic and Roman times, is fairly unique and with all of it relating to Lower Egypt this is consistent with most of Herodotus' material on the country, supporting a common view that his travels in the country were confined to that particular region. The more pictorial details relate to what happens at Papremis, where the staged fights have no equivalent in Hellenic culture, and the Boubastis festival which brings to mind scenes from a Breughel painting: 'a veritable Bakhtinian carnival of communal celebration and excess' (Rutherford 2005: 143–4).

Animal lore (2.65–76)

Religion serves as a bridge in 2.65 to introduce information on animals in Egypt and, from a Greek perspective, to highlight the peculiar attitude of the human population towards them. The earlier inhibition about discussing theology (2.3) is returned to at the beginning of 2.65 but this will not forbid Herodotus from observing how animals are held sacred. Piety underlies their reverent attitude towards animals but Herodotus' interest in the fauna is a mixture of zoological curiosity and a populist desire to appeal to his Greek audience with evidence from the natural world of Egypt's unique wonders. Comparisons are often made with familiar animals, presumably to help Greeks visualize the form of creatures that will be new to them: Egyptian wolves are compared with foxes (2.67); crocodiles have eyes like a pig's and their eggs are similar in size to geese's (2.68); the phoenix looks like an eagle (2.73); and the ibis is compared with a crane and a hen (2.76). Scientific observations like these need to be set alongside others that exaggerate: crocodiles may grow up to 6 metres but not to 17 cubits (9 metres), and hippopotamuses, possessing neither manes or an equine bellow, are not as horse-like as the Greek name for them (*hippoi hoi potamioi*, 'horses from a river') might suggest (2.71). Sometimes Herodotus finds his credulity stretched – expressing disbelief in the story of the phoenix but not denying the bird's existence – while at other times he stretches the credulity of modern readers, as with his account of the winged serpents killed by ibises.[20]

The behaviour of and attitude to cats receives special attention and there is a mention of felines being brought to Boubastis for embalming and burial (2.67), though nothing is said to suggest the practice there of mummifying animals on the wholesale level indicated by excavations of its animal cemeteries.[21] A fascination with the idea that animals could act in ways that suggest rational, goal-directed behaviour is illustrated by the way male cats are seen to sexually exploit the female's love of offspring by kidnapping their kittens (2.66). A more bizarre example is provided by the phoenix and its trial-and-error method of determining how to safely transport its parent's corpse (2.73). Munson summarizes her surprise at these challenges to species boundaries, remarking, 'But here is a developed society where the most cultured and pious of all people worship animals and where animals enact those same elementary impulses that among human beings translate into *nomos*' (Munson 2001a: 95–60).

Customs (2.77–97)

The customs covered in these chapters are divided into those of Egyptians living in arable areas (2.77–91) and those who inhabit the marshy region around the Delta (2.92–8). Various aspects of life are looked at, including diet, social habits, clothing, divination practices, medicine, marriage customs, mortuary customs, coping with mosquitoes, boat-building and sailing. The celebration of the Greek hero Perseus with Greek-style competitive games is a rare exception to the rule that, generally, Egyptians do not like to borrow customs from other lands (2.91); if such conservatism is an expression of national pride it is consistent with their endeavour to scrupulously maintain records of their past. Learned men (*hoi logioi*), a term first employed in 1.1 when referring to Persian chroniclers, are in Egypt worthy of the superlative (*logiōtatoi*): 'the most careful of all men to preserve the memory of the past, and none whom I have questioned have so many chronicles' (2.77). Herodotus' respect is manifest.[22]

The custom at dinner and drinking parties of carrying around a coffin with a wooden image of a corpse as a reminder of mortality may seem morbid but apparently 'is compatible with Egyptian attitudes and archaeological evidence and is entirely credible' (Lloyd 2007: 292–3). Throughout the *Histories*, there is an interest in burial customs and those of the Egyptians receive detailed attention (2.85–90). The technical description of mummification (2.86–9), not just how it was carried out but noting the tripartite pricing system offered by embalmers, is justified because it is another example, an extraordinary one, from a land 'fullest of wonders' (*pleistathōmasia*, 2.35). The account, nonetheless, avoids sensationalism, and the genuine interest Herodotus displays in mummification techniques is evidence of a scientific attitude that continues with culinary, botanical and zoological observations on the customs of those who live in the Delta region (2.92–4).

Herodotus' characteristic interest with the way Egyptian cultural life differentiates itself from Greek habits takes a back seat with the observation that a particular song, the Linus, is common to Greece, Egypt, Phoenicia and Cyprus. He cannot explain how Egyptians got their name for a song so familiar to Greeks – 'I am in wonder' (*apothōmazein me*), he says (2.79) – and, resisting succumbing to cultural hyperdiffusionism, he does not claim it as another instance of a far older civilization bequeathing a practice to the Greeks. Munson views this instance as also running counter to the pre-Socratic commonplace that customs (*nomoi*) are merely conventions when put alongside fundamental differences in nature (*phusis*). For here, with the Linus song, any simple opposition of *nomos* and *phusis* is complicated by a cultural similarity that cuts across different sets of people, suggesting that custom and nature are implicated with one another (Munson 2001a: 99–100).

History of Egypt

The account of Egypt's history falls into two periods: the kings from Min to Sethos (2.99–142) and the Saite kings from Psammetichus to Amasis (2.147–82). The Saite period, named after the city of Sais which during this time was the kings' capital, covers the last dynasty to rule before the Persian conquest of the country in 525. The historical value of Herodotus' accounts of the two periods is assessed very differently: the first section is seen to consist mostly of 'sensationalist Egyptian stories seriously contaminated by Greek material' while the second section is more valuable as 'our only consecutive account of Egyptian history between 664 and 525 ... the bedrock on which all modern work on the period is based' (Lloyd 1999: 444). The first part in particular has been on the receiving end of hostile criticism – 'partial, chronologically preposterous'[23] – including as it does fictitious material, dates going askew, rulers not found on any king lists and corrupted names of real kings. Fornara's complaint is that Herodotus 'narrates the actions of the more memorable Pharaohs without any evident direction. The monuments of their rule ... are calculated to impress and entertain. It is striking that there is no hint of that vision of humanity defining his work as a whole ... even the thoroughly bad Cheops (124ff.) points no moral lesson' (Fornara 1971: 20–1). This is a harsh judgement given that the issue of what makes a good or just ruler does emerge: Pheros is impious and vindictive (2.111); Mycerinus is just (2.129) but wilfully refuses to accept the inevitable (2.133); Apries is a poor leader and provokes dissent (2.162); Rhampsinitus is magnanimous (2.121) and Proteus shows himself to be an exemplary host whose conduct puts the Greek Menelaus to shame (2.115).

Taking the two parts as a whole, a solid outline of pharaonic history is outlined (see Box 4) and due allowance needs to be given for the reliance on oral traditions, especially when the earliest period of Egyptian history is being covered. Something is known about the very first king, Min, and little is said of his 330 successors who are not deemed noteworthy (2.101), but with more recent rulers the historical picture becomes more clearly defined – a chronological contour in keeping with the 'floating gap' that characterizes oral traditions.[24]

Early kings and the Helen *logos* (2.99–120)

Herodotus begins his account of Egypt's history with a historiographical statement (see p. 16), a declaration that henceforth he will be relying largely on local sources (2.99). He makes frequent reference to temple priests as his source of information,[25] having earlier accorded them respect for their record-keeping (2.77), and begins with whom they say was the first king of Egypt, Min. Of the 330 rulers that come after Min, the queen Nitocris is singled out for the tale of her suicidal act of revenge before a lengthy

EGYPTIAN KINGS

Fictitious or false names are in italics; corrupted names of probably or possibly real rulers are underlined.

Archaic (Early Dynastic) Period: *c.* 3000–2686

99:     Min

Old Kingdom (including First Intermediate Period): 2686–2055

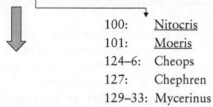

100:     Nitocris
101:     Moeris
124–6:   Cheops
127:     Chephren
129–33: Mycerinus

Middle Kingdom (including Second Intermediate Period) 2055–1550

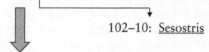

102–10: Sesostris

New Kingdom : 1550–664

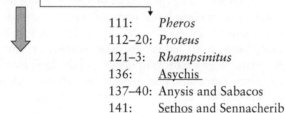

111:     *Pheros*
112–20: *Proteus*
121–3:   *Rhampsinitus*
136:     Asychis
137–40: Anysis and Sabacos
141:     Sethos and Sennacherib

Late Kingdom: 664–332

151–7:   Psammetichus
158–9:   Necos
160:     Psammis
161–3:   Apries
169–82: Amasis

BOOK 2, BOX 4

account is given of the reign of Sesostris. His extensive conquests, historically unfounded, begin with an invasion of Arabia before extending to most of Asia and parts of Europe (2.102–6, 110), and nationalist sentiments may well have encouraged such a fanciful claim (Lloyd 2007: 313–14).

Herodotus detects a racial link between Egyptians and Colchians on the basis of their skin colour and hair type (2.104), with his word *melagkhroes* variously translated as 'dark-skinned' (Godley, Waterfield and Mensch), 'tawny' (Blanco), 'swarthy' (Holland) – only Sélincourt uses 'black'. Lloyd (2007: 315) denies that *melagkhroes* means black and ignores an earlier passage (2.57) where the black colour of the doves is taken as evidence that they came from Egypt. The gloss by How and Wells in their 1912 commentary accepts that Herodotus writes about the Egyptians and Colchians as black but regard it as an 'exaggeration' because he was confused by seeing black slaves in Memphis.[26]

The folkloric tale of Pheros (2.111) has such a blatantly male perspective as to invite laughter were it not for the punishment meted out to the women who failed to restore the king's sight. Quite different is the account of how Helen, the wife of Menelaus, resided in Egypt while the Greeks thought she was in Troy and purposelessly besieged the city for ten years. It is a story that captures the interest of Herodotus and modern readers alike. Questions concerning the likely pedigree for such an alternative history continue to exercise scholars and not least because of the way the case is claimed to rest on Egyptian sources even though it is shaped in ways that are clearly Herodotean. The word 'truth' (*alētheia*), used sparingly by Herodotus in his work, is employed when endorsing the claim that the Trojans must have told the Greeks that Helen was not in their city (2.120).[27]

The claim that Helen was in Egypt instead of Troy was not an outlandish or mischievous invention on Herodotus' part and, unlike Euripides, he makes no mention of a phantom Helen.[28] According to Herodotus, Paris (called Alexander in Herodotus; both names are used in Homer) and Helen are driven by winds to land near a temple in Egypt and the king is informed that a *xenos* (a stranger but a potential guest-friend) has arrived, adding that this person, a Trojan, seduced the wife of his *xenos* (guest-friend) in Greece. Paris is ordered to appear before Proteus and the outraged king tells Paris that were he not a *xenos* arriving by misfortune in his country vengeance would be exacted on behalf of his Greek host whose wife and possessions were stolen from him. Proteus decides he will impound the plunder and look after Helen for Menelaus, 'the Greek stranger' (*tō Hellēni xeinō*, 2.115), until such time as he returns and claims what is rightfully his. Paris is given the opportunity to save his own life if he leaves Egypt within three days. Proteus, his stance rendered in direct speech,[29] not only follows impeccably the protocols of guest-friendship (*xenia*) but demonstrates his ability to empathize with Menelaus for the violation he has suffered by having his hospitality thrown back in his face by the self-serving Paris. In telling this tale Herodotus becomes the narrator of a tale, one that includes himself as an investigator in

Egypt, brocaded with many of the characteristics of the short story genre (see Box 5). There are a limited number of characters, all of whom contribute to a plot that unfolds with a fleetness of foot. As with many of the best short stories, the ending is unexpected and leaves the reader reflecting on events and the narration. In this case, one is left wondering about the two main characters whose voices, thoughts or feelings never find expression. Paris and Helen are absolutely central to the story but they are silent characters and the reader can only speculate about how Helen might have told the story.

PROTEUS: A SHORT STORY (2.112–20)

Characters:

Helen of Troy: the wife of Menelaus of Sparta
Paris: son of the king of Troy
servants of Paris
Thonis: a local official at a mouth of the Nile in Egypt
Proteus: the king of Egypt
Herodotus: a Greek investigative reporter in Egypt
priests in Memphis
Menelaus: the ruler of Sparta
local Egyptians

Locations:

A mouth of the Nile where a temple of Heracles offers refuge to servants
The city of Memphis where the king resides

Scenes and narrative voices:

Servants of Paris revealing the story of Paris and Helen
Thonis messaging Proteus about Paris and Helen arriving in Egypt
The detention of Paris, his ships and goods and Helen
Proteus questioning Paris and his servants
Admonishment of Paris, seizure of his goods and his expulsion from Egypt
The narrator discussing Helen's role in Homer's *Iliad* and *Odyssey*
Herodotus questioning priests in Memphis

BOOK 2, BOX 5

The moral concept of *xenia* in the story of Helen is seen as crucial in understanding the meaning behind Herodotus' explanation for the fall of Troy. He first argues on grounds of reasonable likelihood that if Helen had been taken there then, faced with a Greek army besieging his city, the father of Paris and king of Troy, Priam, would have given her up sooner or later.[30] There was too much at stake and too high a price to pay by refusing to do so. It follows that Priam must have told the Greeks that Helen was not in his city – presumably he could have proved she was not there – and yet he was not believed and the siege continued until Troy fell and all was lost. This seems inexplicable and thus, Herodotus concludes, 'since they did not have Helen there to give back, and since the Greeks would not believe them although they spoke the truth [*tēn alētheiēn*] I am convinced and declare, the powers above [*tou daimoniou*][31] ordained that the utter destruction of Troy should prove in the sight of all men that the gods do greatly punish great wrongdoing. This is my own belief and thus I declare it' (2.120). Although it is not explicitly stated, the 'wrongdoing' can only be attributed to the gross violation by Paris of *xenia*, a transgression for which his city is destroyed.[32] Elaborating on this interpretation, Vandiver makes the point that this explanation, consonant as it is with the divinely endorsed moral universe of Homer's epic, contrasts strongly with the Persian account at the start of the *Histories* that reduces Helen's abduction to a bit part in a trivial tit-for-tat exchange of women (1.1–5): 'Wise men do not make a fuss about such abductions, say the Persian *logioi*; divinity decreed that Troy must fall to show that great wrongdoings encounter great punishments, says Herodotus' (Vandiver 2012: 151).

There is a mordant twist to the *xenia* theme with the tale of what took place when Menelaus arrives in Egypt after the fall of Troy. He is 'very hospitably entertained' (*xeiniōn entēse megalōn*), reunited with Helen, and his possessions that Paris had stolen are returned to him – but he repays such kindness by sacrificing two local children in an attempt to speed up his departure which was being delayed by poor weather (2.119). This not only brings to mind the sacrifice by Agamemnon (the brother of Menelaus) of his daughter Iphigenia when the Greek fleet was delayed from sailing to Troy but it also presents a violent abuse of *xenia* far more repugnant than that displayed by the behaviour of Paris. The contrast between the civic goodness of hospitable Egyptians and the arrogance of abusive foreigners, Greek and Trojan, is writ large and serves as another instance of Herodotus' encomium to Egyptian civilization. The Hellenic concept of *xenia* is seen to be alive and well in Egyptian culture, preciously so when it is being blatantly and barbarically ignored by others, and the demonstration of this in the Helen *logos* reinforces the earlier rebuttal by Herodotus of what he regards as a scurrilous Greek slander. The tale that Heracles was going to be the victim of a human sacrifice by Egyptians was rejected as demonstrably false (see p. 97) and the Helen story strengthens this rejection by having Menelaus guilty of the very outrage some prejudiced Greeks would attribute to Egyptians.

In his adherence to *xenia*'s moral code Proteus exemplifies a virtue that harks back to the heroic age of Homer,[33] but Herodotus also presents him as an investigator who, like himself, seeks to establish the facts of a case.[34] Thonis, the official who arrests Paris when he lands at a mouth of the Nile, awaits the king's decision whether to let him sail away or impound his vessel, but Proteus avoids making a hasty judgement (2.114). Like Psammetichus (2.1) and Periander (1.23–4), he proceeds judiciously and in doing so can be seen to be exemplifying the methods of inquiry employed by Herodotus himself and by some of the priests he questions in the course of his research. He asks them about Troy: 'they gave me the following answer, saying that they knew it by inquiry [*historiēsi*] from what Menelaus himself had said' (2.118). They know about Menelaus sacrificing Egyptian children: 'The priests told me that they had learnt some of this tale by inquiry [*historiēsi*], but that they spoke with exact knowledge of what had happened in their own country' (2.119).

Rhampsinitus, pyramid builders and chronology (2.121–46)

The tale of Rhampsinitus and the consummate cunning of the anonymous thief (2.121–2) shares with the Helen *logos* a literary dimension that makes it a short story in its own right; unlike the other tale, though, this one would not be out of place in a Grimm-like collection of folk tales. Herodotus claims he heard the story from temple priests but its scurrility might indicate a demotic source, Egyptian or Greek or some combination of both, with roots in folklore. The happy-ever-after ending, details like the shaving off of one half of the guards' beards (also found in the Bible, 2 Samuel 10.4) and the king's visit to the Underworld all suggest a tradition of storytelling with origins outside the precincts of a temple.[35]

Rhampsinitus is succeeded by Cheops, his Egyptian name Khnum Khufu (*c.* 2596 to 2573), the first of the pyramid builders of the IV Dynasty to whom Herodotus devotes attention. Suitably impressed by his construction project, the Great Pyramid of Giza, Cheops' claim to fame is spiced up by an anecdote alleging he set up his daughter in a brothel to help cover buildings costs (2.126). A more elaborate mix of seriousness and sex emerges with the reign of Mycerinus and his relationship with his daughter, and this account (2.129–33) includes a folkloric element in the form of an oracle prophesying the king's death. Herodotus relates how the pyramid of Menkaura (Mycerinus is his Hellenized name), the smallest of the three pyramids at Giza, is attributed by some Greeks to the famous Greek courtesan Rhodopis (2.134–5), but he forthrightly dismisses this for historical and financial reasons. With the support of archaeological evidence, however, he does give credence to Rhodopis' self-memorial at Delphi.

The Nubians, called Ethiopians by Herodotus, ruled Egypt for a period of around fifty years and Sabacos (2.137, 139) was the Nubian king Shabaka who consolidated control over the country around 714 and ruled until 702 (Török 2014: 73–80). Sabacos is represented as an exemplary king, virtuous to the point of relinquishing power rather than face the possibility of acting unethically, and the purity of Ethiopian rulers is returned to in Book Three (see pp. 114–15). Herodotus goes on to say how later a priest became King Sethos (the Hellenized name for Shabaka's successor, Shabataka,) and that he fought off the 'Arabians' (Assyrians) who were defeated by an invasion of mice (2.141). The Assyrian king Sennarcherib did come into conflict with Shabataka, the Nubian king ruling Egypt, but the calamity suffered at the teeth of mice 'probably took the form of an epidemic of typhoid or cholera' (Lloyd 2007: 343).[36]

In his account of the first 331 kings, from Min to Moeris, only a very small number are considered worthy of mention. By contrast, forty chapters (2.102–42) are devoted to the eleven kings that came after these and the chronology assumes an equivalence between each generation of kings and those of the high priests. Using a reasonably accurate rule-of-thumb of three generations to a century, it is reckoned that the time period comes to over 10,000 years (2.142). He relates how when the geographer-historian Hecataeus was in Thebes he could trace his own genealogy back sixteen generations to a god, but that the Egyptian priests rejected this as implausible given their records of human history stretching back ten millennia without any god (2.143). It was only before the first king Min that gods walked the earth and this is bad news for the genealogies beloved by Greek aristocrats who traced their lineages back to a god or hero. Herodotus drolly mentions how he did not recite his own genealogy and this could be taken as disingenuous, a tongue-in-cheek remark at the expense of Hecataeus.[37] It has been speculated that Herodotus 'infers' that this is what happened to Hecataeus, based on him having somewhere stated his sixteen-generation genealogy and a visit to Thebes, allowing enjoyment to be had by scorning his inadequate knowledge of Egyptian history (Fowler 2006: 36). What is certain is that Herodotus' attention and his imagination is seized by the verifiable vastness of Egypt's temporal spectrum; he sees for himself the 341 statues of high priests that cover the period up to the reign of Sethos (the extra three that make a total of 344 up to the present time cover the kings after Sethos) and he is impressed by the way temple priests have recorded their past. He mentions how they kept their king list on a roll of papyrus (2.100 and 145) and this, along with the statues, are material evidence. They are like the *erga* that he draws attention to in his preface, evidence that counters the relatively ephemeral nature of oral memories.[38]

Herodotus is fascinated by the measurement of time by Egyptian priests and the bearing this has on chronology in the Greek world.[39] His dates are sometimes questionable, especially as regards Proteus, and the dating in 2.13 for the transition from King Moeris to Sesostris is 300 years earlier than what would be the case if calculated on the basis of three generations to a century. Difficulties are caused for Herodotus because he wants to tie in, first, Greek traditions about Heracles with Sesostris and, second, the Trojan War with the reign of Proteus. In 2.145–6 he returns to the subject of Heracles (2.42–50) and states that he must be the son of mortals who named him after an Egyptian god.

The Labyrinth and the Saite kings (2.147–78)

A methodological change is announced as Herodotus moves on to the labyrinth and then the first of the Saite rulers, Psammetichus. His previous reliance on Egyptians sources will be supplemented: 'I will now relate what is recorded alike by Egyptians and foreigners to have happened in that land, and I will add thereto something of what I myself have seen' (2.147). Psammetichus ruled from 663 to 609 and Herodotus states the exact number of years for his and his Saite successors' periods of kingship. Contact between Greece and Egypt increases during the Saite period, with all four rulers employing Greek mercenaries and with Amasis cultivating relations with the tyrant of Samos (2.182), wanting support from his navy against the threat from Persia. The role of Greek mercenaries helps explain the many references to military exploits: Psammetichus conducts the longest known siege (2.157); Necos builds triremes and uses them against the Syrians (2.159); Psammetichus invades Ethiopia (Nubia), an expedition that took place in 593/2, and his son Apries battles in Phoenicia (2.161); and Amasis faces the Persians.

Before turning to Psammetichus, Herodotus is driven to exclaim over the magnificence of the labyrinth finding its splendour 'too great for words' (*logou mezō*, 2.148). He sees the upper chambers, he hears about the lower chambers and he walks 'from court to apartment and from apartment to colonnade, from colonnade again to more chambers and then into yet more courts' (2.148). What he sees is a wonder (*thoma*) – in his preface his stated intention is to preserve 'great and marvellous [*thomasta*] deeds' – and the word is used again in the next chapter to describe Lake Moeris that stands beside it. Soon he is describing the shrine of Leto at Buto as the most marvellous (*thōma megiston*, 2.155) and repeats the claim in the first sentence of the following chapter. Then there is the floating island of Chemmis (2.156) that he has heard about and although he has never seen it move he is amazed (*tethēpa*, its only use in the *Histories*) if it does indeed float.[40]

Astonishing instances of phenomena like these, real and hypothetical, serve as his justification for such a lengthy excursus on a subject that digresses from the main narrative that began Book Two, the Persians preparing to invade Egypt, and which will get back on track with Book Three: 'Concerning Egypt I will speak at length because nowhere are there so many marvellous things, nor in the world beside are there to be seen so many works [*erga*] of unspeakable greatness' (2.35). Herodotus is overwhelmed by Egypt and his tremendous respect for the country's civilization is encapsulated in an offbeat aside. He is writing about the construction of a canal in the reign of Necos and mentions by the way how Egyptians refer to those who do not speak their language as 'barbarians' (2.157). It is an odd remark given how Herodotus would be aware of his readers' knowledge that this is how Greeks demarcate themselves from those whose speech is not Greek. The paradox is that while Egyptians differentiate themselves from people like the Greeks because they do not speak their language, the Greeks employ exactly the same principle to other people like the Egyptians: 'No Hellenocentrism here' (Gruen 2011: 76).

Book Three: Cambyses, Samos and Darius

Introduction

Book Three begins where the first chapter of Book Two left off, with Cambyses' decision to invade Egypt, and launches into the monarch's reasons for attacking Amasis. Whereas the Egypt *logo* was broadly historical and ethnographic in its subject matter, the focus now is more political and devoted to a shorter timescale than anything that has come before. Book One covered thirty years while Book Two widened the scope considerably, leapfrogging millennia on occasion. Now time is telescoped into a period of less than a decade, covering i) the reign of Cambyses (529–22), ii) a short interregnum when two brothers claim the Persian throne, leading to a conspiracy against them, and iii) the accession of Darius and the first years of his reign. This is the chronological backbone of Book Three and while it seems neat and easy to follow, the reader has to contend with being abruptly led down a digressive channel formed by one lengthy stream (3.39–60) and two shorter ones (3.120–8 and 3.139–49). The digression deals with Polycrates, tyrant of the Greek island of Samos, and within this Samian *logos* there are shifts in time. They cannot be compared to the temporal shifts of Book One but readers may still occasionally need to reorient themselves to the controlling sequence of events (see Box 1).

Within both the main story and the Samian *logos* there is a host of individuals who play their parts in what is just one act in the larger drama of Persian history. They enter a scene, perform their roles and suffer vicissitudes before exiting and leaving the stage to the main players. The brief appearances of some of these minor characters, like their equivalents in Shakespeare, belie the force of the impressions they leave in their wake. Their fates, the natures of which range from the incredulous to the macabre, unfold in a series of anecdotes about personal gratitudes and grievances that transcend the public and political arena, that animate the text. In addition, contributing yet another layer of interest to the multifaceted Book Three, time is found for ethnographic material about Persia – adding to what was

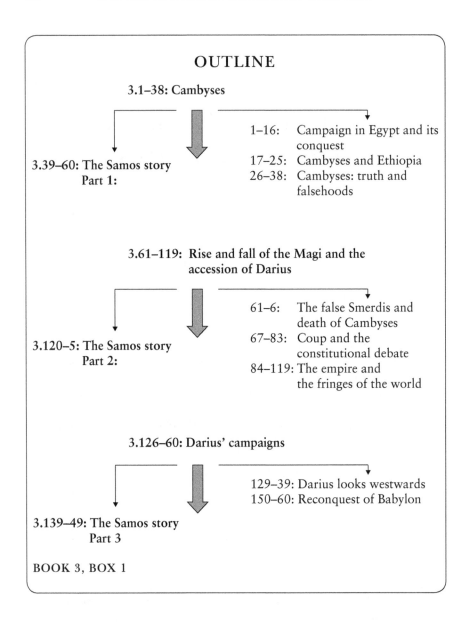

OUTLINE

3.1–38: Cambyses

3.39–60: The Samos story
Part 1:

1–16:   Campaign in Egypt and its
        conquest
17–25: Cambyses and Ethiopia
26–38: Cambyses: truth and
        falsehoods

3.61–119: Rise and fall of the Magi and the
          accession of Darius

3.120–5: The Samos story
Part 2:

61–6:   The false Smerdis and
        death of Cambyses
67–83: Coup and the
        constitutional debate
84–119: The empire and
        the fringes of the world

3.126–60: Darius' campaigns

129–39: Darius looks westwards
150–60: Reconquest of Babylon

3.139–49: The Samos story
Part 3

BOOK 3, BOX 1

said on this subject in Book One (1.131–40) – and places that lie on and beyond the edges of the known world.

Cambyses' campaign in Egypt (3.1–16)

Various causes are given for Cambyses' desire to conquer Egypt and none of them seem historically credible explanations. The first relates to an act of deception practised on Cambyses after he had asked the Egyptian ruler Amasis for his daughter as a concubine but was sent Nitetis instead, the daughter of the king before Amasis. The second cause is a part cause of the first one: Cambyses is initially persuaded to ask for the king's daughter by an Egyptian eye doctor who, resentful at been forced to work for Cambyses, wants to provoke a war. A third account has Nitetis as the concubine of Cyrus (and mother of Cambyses) provoking his wife's annoyance and making the ten-year-old Cambyses vow to one day 'turn all Egypt upside down' (3.3). What these different aetiologies confirm is Herodotus' predilection for the personal element when explaining why things happen the way they do, and this invites the criticism that he fails to go beyond the level of personal motivation when accounting for major political decisions and events. It is worth bearing in mind, however, that Herodotus' familiarity with a world 'dominated by ruling families and elites and by despotic kings surrounded by a closed circle of kinsmen' is far greater than our own and the reader is probably being given the 'true feel of what men said, of how contemporaries perceived' important events (Gould 1989: 67).

The attention paid to personal factors in Cambyses' motives may point to some matrimonial or/and dynastic dispute, originating from sources with different agendas, but the inclusion of traditional motifs like the duplicitous swapping of women – found in the Bible where Jacob is deceived into thinking Rachel has been given to him as wife when her father has exchanged her for another of his daughters (Genesis 29) – also suggests a fictional dimension. Little can be said with any certainty because nearly all that is known about the reign of Cambyses comes from Herodotus. He says that the Persian king was continuing the expansionist policy of his father but, for a modern landmark study of Persian history, to state that Egypt was invaded because the country was the only remaining power of importance in the Near East does not add a lot to saying that the invasion took place (Briant 2002: 51).[1] The *Cambridge Ancient History* has recourse to imagining the thoughts of Cambyses on the eve of his invasion and his contemplation of what may happen if he succeeds – 'Will our children and grandchildren start worshipping dog-headed gods and eating crocodiles?' – the justification being that it is no more fanciful than Herodotus' account (Boardman et al. 1988: 254–5).[2]

After Cyrus conquered Babylon, it may well have become clear to Amasis that conflict with Persia was looming and that potential Greek allies were worth courting; something implied by his friendly and generous attitude towards Greeks (2.178 and 2.182). He does not live to see his country defeated and his successor, Psammetichus III, rules for less than a year before becoming a prisoner of the Persians. Herodotus does not provide any details of the battle between Persian and Egyptian forces, or what part if any was played by naval forces, preferring to dwell on the barbaric revenge by the Greek and Carian mercenaries for the defection of Phanes (3.11) and the wonder (*thoma*, 3.12) of the two sets of skulls on the battlefield.[3]

An intriguing concern with language and truth has been traced in Book Three (Bernadette 1969: 70–50), beginning with the way Cambyses' resolve to attack Egypt is a consequence of the words spoken to him by Nitetis. By revealing the untruth – she is not the daughter of Amasis that has been royally solicited – Cambyses becomes wrathful and determines to depose the man who tried to trick him. The spoken word, not material or political considerations, instigates the invasion of Egypt. Another case where utterance is of vital importance arises with the Arabians. A Greek defector from Amasis' army, Phanes, advises the Persians to seek permission from the Arabian king to reach Egypt by way of the desert (3.4–7). Cambyses makes the request, the Arabians pledge their permission and a short digression highlights the crucial role of pledges in their culture. Once their word is given no other guarantee is necessary (3.8).[4] At another extreme, bereavement is seen to transcend language when words cannot adequately express the painful truth of having lost something absolutely precious. Following the conquest of Egypt, Cambyses torments the captured king, Psammetichus III, by forcing him to witness his daughter's humiliation and his son being led to execution. The grief of the deposed king at these sights can only be expressed by silence and it is only when he sees an old companion reduced to beggary can his sorrow be put into words (3.14).[5]

The visit of Cambyses to Saïs (3.16) is confirmed by an inscription of a statue, now in the Vatican, of Udjahorresnet, a high-ranking Egyptian priest, but it undermines the historical truth of what Herodotus reports about the dishonouring of the corpse of Amasis. The inscription records Cambyses cleansing the temple, restoring its clergy and upholding its traditions in a way that is not consistent with the anti-Persian tone of this chapter (Asheri 2007c: 414).

Cambyses and Ethiopia (3.17–25)

Of the three campaigns mentioned as being undertaken by Cambyses after his conquest of Egypt, the one in Ethiopia (Nubia) receives the most attention and it develops the idea of a place on the periphery of the known world, though one fondly free of most human imperfections.[6] There is a mythical quality to the paradisiacal land of the Ethiopians – in Homer the country is a favoured destination for Olympian gods[7] – and while Cambyses wants to conquer the place he also wants to establish the truth, if any, about the existence there of a legendary, beneficent Table of the Sun (3.18).[8] His spies, the Fish-eaters who speak the Ethiopian language, arrive in the country bearing gifts but the ruler discerns the true motive concealed behind their diplomacy.[9] He admonishes the Persian king for his unethical foreign policy and delivers some heuristic advice – seconding Gyges' moral aphorism that 'one must look at one's own' (1.8) and adding a political dimension to its truth (3.21) – before examining the gifts intended to impress him.[10] The concern with alterity that is so characteristic of Herodotus' anthropological inquiries takes a negative form here, listing what Ethiopians do not practise: dying garments, valorizing gold, using perfume, harvesting wheat to make bread. Humour has its place when the king, asking about life expectancy and learning how wheat is fertilized, replies that 'he was not surprised that their lives were so short if they ate manure' (3.22). Cultivating grapes, on the other hand, meets with approval and seems not to infringe the Ethiopians' deep organicism. Such is their prelapsarian state, with nature bountifully providing their needs, it seems surprising that they would need fetters of any kind, even if, like the ones shown to the envoys (3.23), they are made of gold.[11]

What angers Cambyses to the point of immediately launching an incursive force is hearing about the rejection of his blandishments in the report of his spies and the anti-imperialist message of the Ethiopian king. It is *words* and what they represent that send him into a violent frenzy (3.25): the rebuff of the purple cloak as an emblem of imperial command and of the necklace and bracelets as fetters, symbols of slavery. The Ethiopian ruler has seen through his ruse, the Persian monarch falsely presenting himself as a friend (*philos*) and guest (*xenos*) when really he would abuse the protocols of guest-friendship (as Paris did in Sparta and Menelaus in Egypt). In terms of the language and truth nexus mentioned earlier, Cambyses is affronted by having the falsity of his own words exposed by the Ethiopian king and he reacts to this with what, bearing in mind his previous mindfulness in preparing for an invasion by first dispatching spies, is irrational haste. Playing a psychological card, one might speculate that Cambyses' discomfort is related to his Persian education and a childhood which drilled home the importance of honesty and the message that there is nothing more disgraceful than telling lies (1.137–8).

A small *logos* in its own right, the tale of the 'long-lived Ethiopians' (3.17) 'mixes a Greek traditional utopia with information of varying value gathered in Egypt from Greek-speaking informers, tendentiously hostile to Cambyses'.[12] Such a view seems reasonable as elements like the strong bow that cannot easily be drawn (3.21) carries a Homeric echo (*Odyssey*, 19: 577–8) and the Ethiopians as naturally noble-minded has come up earlier.[13] The historicity of the Ethiopian campaign is questionable (Briant 2002: 55) and the sceptical Fehling dismisses the possibility of any source, Greek or Egyptian, outside of Herodotus himself (Fehling 1989: 191ff.). Notwithstanding, this should not diminish the significance of the Ethiopian *logos* within the political world of the *Histories*. The failure of Cambyses to add Ethiopia to his empire adumbrates in a masterly way the moral and metaphysical landscape which later Persian kings will move across in their abortive invasions of lands not rightfully their own. There may be miraculous spring water, extraordinary life expectancy and glass-like coffins in this African territory but the tale is more than a beguiling utopian idyll. The insatiable impulse of a powerful empire to extend and impose its will on smaller countries ends in the direst of circumstances and compels Cambyses to give up his ill-prepared campaign. The Ethiopians may be lacking in military might and influence but they possess qualities that make them morally superior to rulers like Cambyses, and this *logos* earns its place in Herodotus' history of the perils and errors of the imperialist drive. The Ethiopian king speaks truth to power and his words are the message of the *Histories*, spoken earlier by the Massagetae queen – 'Cease, and be king of your own country' (1.206) – and it will be heard again when the Persians attempt to conquer the Greeks (7.18).

Cambyses: truth and falsehood (3.26–38)

Cambyses in his cruel treatment of Psammetichus III wishes 'to make a trial [*diepeirato*] of his spirit' (3.14)[14] and the odd mixture of inquiry, sadism and compassion that he displays prepares the way for a portrait of a man whose mental instability descends into a series of irrational acts that convinces Herodotus the man is insane (see Box 2). There is clearly a huge bias against Cambyses in the stories of his increasing madness and a negative view of the man is repeated in writers for centuries after Herodotus. What is ignored in this tradition of traducement is the fact that Cambyses builds up a Persian navy and also competently mounts a successful invasion of Egypt and it is possible that Herodotus was misled by some of the stories he heard. The account, for example, of his burying alive twelve noble Persians (3.35) is open to another interpretation: 'If we reject the "moralizing" explanation of the behavior of Cambyses ("cruelty," "madness"), we may surmise that he was actually taking reprisals against the great families that had expressed opposition to some of his decrees' (Briant 2002: 97). Moreover, in addition to the inscription on the statue in the Vatican that was mentioned above, there is also archaeological evidence that presents him positively. An epitaph for the Apis calf entombed at the time of Cambyses has been found and, along with the inscription on the sarcophagus, the indication is that the ruler followed all the funeral proprieties in accordance with Egyptian traditions. This and other hieroglyphic evidence supports the view of modern historians that Cambyses is misrepresented by Herodotus, due possibly to partisan sources in Egypt aggrieved by his interference with temple matters (Briant 2002: 57–61; Asheri 2007c: 427–8, 433–4).[15]

The concern with language and truth that has been noted above feeds into a broader intellectual *donnée*, 'the metaphysical and moral conflict between falsehood and truth' (Asheri 2007c: 391) that can be seen as the leitmotif of Book Three. The opening inquiry into the reason for the invasion of Egypt exposes a series of falsehoods – Cambyses is disguising the truth of his desire for a concubine; the eye-doctor is concealing the truth of his desire for revenge; Amasis lies when he sends someone else's daughter as his own – and a single truth spoken by a woman. This serves as an overture to a succession of events that draw further attention to issues of truth and

CAMBYSES' DESCENT INTO MADNESS

3.14:   Cruelly tests the endurance of the captured Psammetichus

3.16:   Opens the tomb of Amasis, has the corpse dishonoured and, contrary to Persian and Egyptian customs, orders it to be burnt

3.25:   Orders the burning of an oracle of Zeus

3.27:   Accuses nobility in Memphis of lying about the Apis festival and executes them

3.29:   Stabs the Apis calf and orders the priests to be whipped

3.30:   The cupbearer Prexaspes ordered to murder the king's brother

3.31:   Commits incest by marrying one of his sisters, whom he kills, and then marries another of his sisters

3.35:   Kills the son of Prexaspes in front of him and has twelve Persian nobles buried alive for a minor offence

3.36:   Orders the death of the servants who pleased him by not following his order to have Croesus killed

3.37:   Opens coffins in Memphis, mocks images in two temples

BOOK 3, BOX 2

lies and in ways that are curious, not least because they are bound up with Cambyses' descent into madness and then his recovery at the point of dying. Jealousy of his brother Smerdis helps him believe in the truth of his dream foretelling that one day a Smerdis would be king and on the basis of this he orders his trusted Prexaspes to commit murder (3.30). His lawyers say they can find no law (*nomos*) permitting him to marry his sister but they do find a law which allows a ruler of Persia to do whatever he likes (3.31), not a barefaced lie but the kind of legal chicanery that skirts around the truth. The priests who are questioned about the Apis festival tell the truth and are executed and when Cambyses stabs the Apis calf he claims to be showing the truth behind the supposed sacredness of the animal. Croesus, whom we last see 'as an ineffectual courtier dancing attendance on a mad king'

(Dewald 2012: 84), tries to tell him some truths and almost dies for his effort. When Cambyses kills the son of Prexaspes in a crazy test designed to establish if Persians are lying it seems that he can no longer distinguish between what is true and what is false.

Cambyses' disregard of other people's dearly held beliefs and customs becomes sacrilegious when he burns cult images from a temple (3.37) and it helps convince Herodotus that the man has lost his reason. Addressing his audience directly, Herodotus remarks how every culture values its own *nomoi* and he proceeds to describe the ethnographic experiment that Darius carried out. Greeks who cremate their dead could no more eat the corpses of their fathers than a certain Indian community, who happen to practise just such a custom, could burn their own dead. The response of the Indians to cremation is visceral – 'they cried out in horror and told him not to say such appalling things' (3.38, Waterfield translation), using a verb, *euphēmeein*, meaning here 'to keep a religious silence' (Liddell and Scott). The sense of a taboo attached to the thought of even giving expression to such a practice, paralleled by the adamant refusal of the Greeks to ever countenance necrophagy, helps justify describing the experiment as a form of 'cultural torture' (Hashhozheva 2016: 90). It confirms for Herodotus that 'custom is king of all' (*nomon pantōn basilea*) and the obligation this confers on people to respect, and not like Cambyses to mock, the deeply held beliefs of others.

It might seem that Herodotus is subscribing to the idea that what is considered right or wrong, morally true or false, is always culturally relative; the logical corollary being that there are no objective truths. In this regard, Darius' experiment and Herodotus' summation are sometimes referred to in general accounts and discussions of cultural and ethical relativism,[16] but they usually fail to take into account the context in which they appear. Herodotus is giving his reaction to tales of blatant violations of religious habits and beliefs and the outrage he feels is a consequence of recognizing the importance of deeply held values. The power of tradition and convention is not something to be treated lightly and Cambyses' belligerent dismissal of belief in the Apis calf invites retribution because he has transgressed an important boundary by mocking and abusing religious customs. What is not being said is that all cultural values are equally valid; Herodotus, indeed, has been seen to express value judgments about particular customs. He praises the marriage auctions of the Babylonians (1.196) while objecting to their practice of having women wait at a temple to offer their bodies to strangers (1.199). What is being said in 3.38 is that any perspective on another culture is influenced by one's own customs – cultural chauvinism, not cultural relativism, is a universal, belonging to all ethnicities – and that therefore it is sensible to show tolerance.[17]

The idea that Herodotus might be giving credence to cultural relativism could suggest a Sophist influence but a less contentious and more convincing example of the impact of the contemporary intellectual climate is evident in his statement that there is plenty of evidence (*tekmēria*) to support people's belief in the correctness of their own cultural values (3.38). The word *tekmēria* is used by writers of rhetoric, science and medicine, though not in identical ways, and Herodotus employs the term in a manner that helps establish his authority and legitimize his way of writing about the past.[18]

The Samos story (part 1): Polycrates and Periander (3.39–60)

The story of Cambyses and his increasingly bizarre conduct looks to be heading towards a conclusion when the narrative flow is abruptly broken by a lengthy *logos* about Polycrates, the tyrant of Samos. It starts, as the first sentence of 3.39 indicates, with a Spartan assault on Samos that is temporally aligned with Cambyses' attack on Egypt. What follows is an account of Polycrates' exceptionally good fortune and how his friendship with Amasis came to an end, before explaining how a group of exiled Samians and Corinth are also involved in the Spartan attack (see Box 3).

Resentments and reciprocities play an important part in the events leading up to the attempt to depose Polycrates from his position as tyrant of Samos. Two possible reasons are provided for Sparta's involvement: revenge for an alleged theft of gifts or the repaying of a debt of gratitude (3.47). The gifts in question (one of which, intended for Croesus, has been mentioned in 1.70) refer back to events that took place a quarter of a century earlier but the Spartans have not forgotten and Herodotus sees nothing implausible in their desire to seek revenge in what Gould identifies as an act of negative reciprocity.[19] Corinth's involvement is due to the memory of how Samos had once interfered with a plan of its ruler, Periander,[20] to punish Corcyra, a

---

THE SAMIAN *LOGOS*: PART 1

3.39–43: Polycrates' good fortune and the story of his ring

3.44–6:   Exiled Samians and Sparta

3.47–9:   Reasons for Spartan and Corinthian enmity towards Samos
          ↓
          3.50–3: Periander and Lycophron

3.54–6:   The battle for Samos

3.60:   The three wonders of Samos

BOOK 3, BOX 3

Corinthian colony (3.48). Periander's plan had been to expel and punish a group of Corcyrean boys and his motivation for doing so unfolds at a leisurely pace in a story nested within the *logos*. This mini-story ends with the killing of Lycophron, the estranged son of Periander, and the desire of his father to seek revenge on the Corcyreans responsible for his death. The breakdown in colonizer–colonized relations between Corinth and Corcyra is mirrored in the personal breakdown between Periander and his son Lycophron – the political and the personal 'stand in metonymic relationship to one another'[21] – but the parallel is hardly noticed by the reader who is drawn away from the public world of city states and into a compelling tale of family strife that uses direct speech. As the story draws to an end with a personal resolution of sorts in the offing, the political world suddenly intrudes with brute force and Lycophron is slain to prevent his father setting foot on Corcyra.[22]

After this convoluted detour into the past, Herodotus says he has devoted a lot of time to Samos because three of the greatest (*megista*) engineering achievements in the Greek world are to be found there – a tunnel dug through a hillside, a breakwater constructed in the harbour and an especially large temple – but this does not seem a convincing reason for the unearthing of political relations between the island, Sparta and Corinth and the deeply troublesome relations within Periander's family.[23]

The false Smerdis and death of Cambyses (3.61–6)

The text now resumes the story that was temporarily halted at 3.38 and it covers the circumstances that lead to the death of Cambyses, the important consequence of which will be the eventual accession of Darius as a new king of Persia. The account provided by Herodotus would seem to possess historical validity because the events he refers to are also recorded in a trilingual inscription, carved on a rock near the Iranian village of Bisitun and discovered in 1836. The inscription is an announcement by Darius and, though different names are used (Gaumata is the name of the false Smerdis), it tells of Cambyses secretly killing his brother and how sometime later the throne was seized by a pretender claiming to be the dead brother. The inscription proclaims Darius as the legitimate Achaemenid ruler and records how he was able to restore the kingship. The Bisitun inscription, however, is a piece of self-propaganda by Darius – he ordered its text to be proclaimed throughout the empire (Briant 2002:100) – and it may be that the false Smerdis was a fabrication by him to cover up what was his seizure of power and his killing of the true Smerdis.[24]

Questions of truth and falsehood are dramatically played out in Herodotus' account when an impostor with a physical resemblance to the true but deceased Smerdis (apart, that is, from the minor drawback of lacking ears, 3.69) seizes the throne along with his brother. The two usurpers are the Magi, priests of a tribal group of Median descent, and Cambyses suspects the involvement of Prexaspes until the plain-speaking herald of the false Smerdis indicates where the truth lies (3.63). The awareness that there are two people bearing the name of Smerdis prompts Cambyses into remembering the dream, about a Smerdis being king, that had led to him to order the murder of his brother.[25] It is his realization of the truth behind the dream – the impostor on the throne really does have the name Smerdis – that causes him to leap into his saddle and suffer the wound to his thigh that will kill him. The sense that fate is catching up with the monarch is reinforced by the oracle that had predicted he would die in Ecbatana, though not the town of that name in Media, where he thought he would die of old age, but the name of the place where he has suffered the fatal wound to his thigh. As in the story of Atys and Adrastus in Book One, it is in the attempt to avoid fate that brings about its enactment.[26] The sense of inevitability that attaches itself to Cambyses' end is something that he comes to terms with himself as he lies dying. He gathers together a group of Persian nobles, telling them how he had arranged for the assassination of his brother in the mistaken belief that he could control the future: 'for it is not in the power of human nature to run away from what is to be' (3.65). This need not be read as full-blooded predestination but it is a recognition that an individual's choice of action will not always have the intended consequences or will have results that could never have been foreseen. For the ancient world as much as for ours, there is a mystery to the way events sometimes unfold and the nature of the individual's responsibility for their outcome. What concerns Herodotus is causation and while Cambyses chose to have his brother killed and bears responsibility for this, his action is also seen to take place within a world where some notion of a cosmic order does not seem wildly out of place. It is both right and inevitable that he should injure himself in the very place where he outrageously injured the Apis calf.

The tragic note in Cambyses' emotional last speech suggests a possible influence from Greek drama;[27] it also points forward and across millennia to *Macbeth* and that play's dramatization of an individual's tragic downfall. Like Cambyses, Macbeth starts from a position of security but succumbs to a temptation, arising from a prophecy, that leads to murdering someone close to him. Cambyses and Macbeth each descend into a state of moral degradation, ruefully coming to accept that their own death is imminent. A prophecy (a second one in the case of Macbeth) that they seek to disprove through murder is going to be realized in a way they never foresee. Cambyses' dying words do not reach the tragic profundity of Macbeth's 'tomorrow and tomorrow' speech but both men give expression to what for each of them is an important truth about life.

There are numerous occasions in Herodotus where in the course of telling a story a phrase indicating that something 'had to be' occurs, as when the dying Cambyses admits that he 'mistook altogether what was to be' (3.65).[28] When Polycrates tells Amasis how the ring he had tried to throw away was returned to him in the stomach of a fish, Amasis realizes that a run of such outstandingly good fortune can only end badly. He brings their relationship to an end because 'he perceived that no man could save another from what was going to happen' (3.43). Gould (1989: 73–8) shows how such phrases hark back to Homer's storytelling and have less to do with destiny than with a narrator's tool box, a way of shaping or pointing towards what is going to take place or underlining a pivotal moment in a story. Polycrates cannot always enjoy good fortune and Cambyses cannot escape forever the consequences of his insolence, not because of the gods' envy or divine retribution but because this is what human experience suggests will be the case.

The coup and Constitutional Debate (3.67–83)

Luck (*tuchē*) is by definition uncertain and Darius enjoys some good luck that helps him become king. The clever and resourceful Otanes suspects the false Smerdis and with the help of his daughter is able to prove his doubts are well founded (3.68–9).[29] Aspathines and Gobryas are also suspicious (3.70) and Darius joins them and others (he is the last to do so), making a group of seven conspirators, with Darius urging immediate action against the Magi. Pragmatically – and hypocritically if Persian custom does distain lying (1.136) – he observes that liars and non-liars 'aim at the same end' (their own advantage) and advises to 'let lies be told where they are needful' when it comes to gaining power (3.72). At the same time – 'by coincidence' (*kata suntukhiēn*) – the false Smerdis and his brother think they have persuaded Prexaspes to make a public announcement endorsing their rule (3.74). Prexaspes double-crosses them, choosing instead to tell the truth in his announcement and before committing suicide urges Persians to depose the impostors: 'thus honourably ended Prexaspes' honourable life' (3.75). Darius and his supporters are unaware at first of this development and, having decided to go ahead with their plan, they gain entrance to the palace and succeed in their coup.

The Constitutional Debate has probably more exercised the minds of those writing about it than those of its participants,[30] assuming there was an actual debate among Persians as to what form of government it would be best to establish after the coup. A lot of the discussion and differences relating to interpretations of the Debate revolves around whether it could ever have taken place in sixth-century Persia. For some scholars, the language and concepts of the Debate are seen as so typically Greek as to outlaw the possibility that it could have taken place in quintessentially despotic Persia (therefore Herodotus must have manufactured it). Yet the preposterousness of thinking the Persians could have had such a debate is anticipated by Herodotus – 'sentiments were uttered which to some Greeks seem incredible but there is no doubt that they were spoken' (3.80) – and he returns to defending its authenticity later in the *Histories*. In Book Six he points out that the Persians did establish democracies in Greek Ionia in 493 and that this will amaze Greeks who cannot imagine that democracy was discussed in the Constitutional Debate some thirty years earlier (6.43). Such a defence does not convince commentators who point to the fact there was no functioning democracy anywhere in the world at the time of the Debate and that what Herodotus presents as being discussed by Persians belongs firmly in the stable of fifth-century Greek political philosophy.[31] Perhaps Herodotus is aware of the doubtful historicity of the Debate but cannot resist making a dig at the political chauvinism of Greeks and wants to make the point that political debate could take place outside of the Hellenic world.

The kind of interpretative position that takes a less than dogmatic point of view is to be found in Ostwald's *Nomos and the Beginning of The Athenian Democracy* (1969: 178–9). While rejecting the idea that the Debate was lifted from a Sophist text, allowance is made for the influence of a Sophistic political discourse that Herodotus might have experienced at Athens or Thurii. What is deemed equally allowable is the possibility that the Persians who engineered the coup did have a political discussion about the best form for their new state and that they considered monarchy, oligarchy and democracy.[32] Herodotus could have had a Persian or Asiatic Greek source for such a discussion, and his firm belief that a constitutional debate did take place suggests a non-Greek source for at least the substrate of a Persian debate, shaping the information he received into a form and vocabulary familiar to Greek intellectual deliberations about the ideal constitution. What is undeniable is that Herodotus' keen interest in the dynamics of political systems, something which would have appealed to his Greek audience, is very much on display here. This interest is noticeable in the story of Deioces and the emergence of a Median state (1.96–101)[33] and in the account of Peisistratus (1.59–60), which is also about choosing the best form of government at a time of crisis; with the Constitutional Debate this concern has matured into 'the earliest piece of developed political theory in all western literature' (Cartledge 1993: 93–4).

Otanes speaks for democracy (although he does not use this word) because it will avoid the perils of autocracy. He reminds his audience of the wanton insolence of Cambyses (*Kambuseō hubrin*) and of the Magi (*Magou hubrios*), repeating the word *hybris* twice more in his speech (3.80) and using the word *phthonos* (ill will, jealousy) four times. A sole ruler, he remonstrates, will be corrupted by the exercise of absolute power and override the virtue of majority rule which stands for 'equality before the law' (*isonomiēn*). Megabyzus, arguing for oligarchy (3.81), does not disagree with what Otanes says about the dangers of autocracy but rejects a system of rule by the many, seeing it as a recipe for disaster because it invites mob rule by ignorant people. Counselling caution he calls for rule by the few, a small number of the best men (which includes himself). The tripartite typology of political systems is completed by Darius arguing for the virtues of monarchy because it avoids the drawbacks of democracy and oligarchy. He capitalizes on the conservative instinct to preserve what is good about the past, 'ancestral customs' and the 'freedom' that was obtained for Persia not by the many or the few but by one ruler. Darius has the territorial integrity of the country in mind but all three speakers share a concern with some notion of freedom (*eleutherie*).

There is a neat pattern to the Debate in the way the three positions circle around one another: Otanes highlights the pitfalls of autocracy, Megabyzus those of democracy and Darius those of oligarchy; Megabyzus agrees with Otanes about the drawbacks to autocracy, Darius agrees with Megabyzus about the problem with democracy but Otanes cannot agree with either of them. Megabyzus does not, or chooses not to, anticipate the criticisms of oligarchy that Darius will make while Darius fails to address the objections to autocracy that Otanes outlines. Otanes does not allow for the criticism of democracy that Megabyzus will make. All seven of the conspirators, employing the principle of majority rule that Otanes proposed, have a say over which system to adopt and Otanes duly withdraws from any consideration of himself for the autocratic system of government that they vote to adopt by a slender majority.

The empire and the fringes of the world (3.84–119)

After the highly theoretical nature of the debate, the story switches its attention to practical matters and the ruse whereby Darius secures for himself the kingship (3.85–7). There follows eight chapters (3.89–96) listing satrapies established by Darius after his accession to the throne and the taxes paid by each of them. The source and the accuracy of the information cannot be known for sure and while there could have been a Persian document recording the information there is also evidence of a Greek influence. The listing of the provinces begins with Ionia in the far west of the Persian Empire, which would be natural from a Greek view of the world but not from that of bureaucrats at the Persian administrative capital in Susa. It has also been thought possible that the list has been imaginatively created, in the spirit of Homer's catalogue of ships in the *Iliad*, although there are some similarities between Herodotus' information and lists recorded on monuments (Asheri 2007c: 479–81). The numerical calculations in 3.95 do not strictly add up but the overall impression they create is that of a powerful empire with a highly organized fiscal administration. The imperial reach extends to the furthest perimeters of the known world and together with the satrapies the revenue comes not just in the form of silver. There are payments and donations of eunuchs, children, white horses, grain, ebony logs, elephant tusks, frankincense and gold dust. Gold comes from India and this provides an opportunity for the picturesque tale about gathering the gold and escaping on camelback from the fox-size ants that menacingly chase the collectors (3.102, 105).[34]

At the fringes of the world, differences from Greek cultural norms are at their greatest and, as the eastern extremity of the known world, India is a land where alien habits prevail (3.98–106). Instead of the formalities of Greek funerals, cannibalism of the old and ill is practised; in place of a settled agriculture people eat raw meat and fish, others avoid all meat and eat a wild cereal; lacking sexual modesty, copulation takes place in public. As well as wildly different *nomoi* there are disparities in nature: climate is affected by the land being so close to where the sun rises; wildlife is bigger, camels are anatomically peculiar; wool comes from trees (cotton).

History takes a back seat in the Indian ethnographic excursus and there are more 'hairyoddities'[35] to relate about the land of Arabia (3.107–13). Winged snakes were mentioned earlier (2.75) while the cinnamon-collecting birds complement the gold-digging ants for their uniqueness and utility for humans. Arabia is another fringe of the known world and a picture of the earth's outermost regions is completed with the mention of Ethiopia to the south-west (3.114) and the western margins of Europe (3.115). These chapters are an example of Herodotus' use of ring composition,[36] beginning with the observation that at the world's end there are unusual phenomena (3.106) and concluding with a very similar remark (3.116). Peculiarities of all sorts attract his attention, cultural curiosities being mirrored by zoological extremes, but underlying the strangeness he discerns a regulatory and providential natural order governed by a teleological economy (3.108–9).[37] Hares, lions and snakes are adduced as examples, with a remarkable capacity for vengeance on the part of the snake that punishes the mother for her crime of having killed the father by biting through its neck during insemination: 'as though a miniature *Oresteia* were played out in the snake world with each new generation of young' (Romm 2006: 183).

The return from the bizarreness of the empire's fringes to the business of running it occurs via an account which is intriguing when looked at alongside the chapter that follows it, of how revenue accrues to the imperial coffers by means of an exploitative water policy (3.117). A mountain-locked plateau fed by rivers through five gorges is dammed and sluice gates built to control the supply of water (there is no evidence of such a place existing). The men and their wives of a local tribe have to petition the king (Darius is not mentioned by name) to allow water onto their land and they pay dearly for it. What comes next (3.118) is the story of Intaphernes, one of the seven conspirators who deposed the Magi, and Darius' order for his execution and all of his male relatives. Darius, relenting when the wife of Intaphernes begs for mercy, allows her to save one member of her family and she surprises him by asking for the life of her brother not one of her sons.[38] At one level this probably relates to political turmoil and dissent following the accession of Darius but from a narratological perspective the story can be matched with the previous one about damming the gorges. There are structural homologies to the tales, with both depending on the absolute power of a monarch who requires supplication at his palace by those who are at the mercy of his authority. Also, the five sluice gates parallel the five remaining conspirators (one of the seven has died and Otanes withdrew any claim on the throne). Griffiths (2001a: 173–7), pointing out these symmetries, reads 3.117 as a coded parable for 3.118, with Herodotus having heard the story of the dammed plateau but failing to see its coded connection to the Intaphernes tale.

The Samos story (part 2): the death of Polycrates (3.120–8)

The first part of the Samian *logos* ended with the failure of the attempt to remove Polycrates from power and the aftermath of the Spartan withdrawal (3.56–9). The story now resumes with the stratagem that leads to the untimely death of Polycrates at the hands of Oroetes and then the way in which the killer meets his own death at the hands of Bagaeus, the agent sent by Darius for that purpose. Herodotus is moved by the unworthy manner of Polycrates' death, unwilling to go into details, and praises him (3.125) even though earlier the tyrant has been associated with fratricide and piracy (3.39) and what might be called an early version of rendition (3.44). The level of detail in these chapters, which extends to the dramatic intervention of the daughter and her willingness to remain unmarried rather than lose her father (3.124), suggests patriotic Samian sources for the information that is provided. Oroetes is a link between Samos and Darius, although an explanation for his entrapment and murder of Polycrates is an enigma for the narrator: 'for though he had received no hurt by deed or word from Polycrates of Samos, nor had even seen him, he formed the desire of seizing and killing him' (3.120). Samian stories of why Oroetes felt so aggrieved – 'anyone may believe whichever he pleases' (3.122) – do not carry much weight for Herodotus and, as with Coleridge's puzzlement over Iago, Oroetes' behaviour remains at the level of 'motiveless malignity'.

Polycrates is not lured to his death out of greed; Oroetes is able to use the promise of riches because he knows money is needed for the expansion of Samian hegemony through naval power. Herodotus adds how Polycrates was the first of what 'can be called the human race' (*tēs de anthrōpēiēs legomenēs geneēs*) to plan such a thalassocracy (3.122). Minos of Crete and anyone earlier, he says, are to be excluded because they belong to the other side of a line dividing historical time from the mythological, from the known to the unknown.[39] His point is methodological and epistemological, harking back to and confirming the principle announced at the start of the *Histories*: he will put aside various abduction stories and look instead to what can be known for sure about the past (1.5).

Darius' campaigns and the Samos story (part 3) (3.129–60)

Returning to Persia, a story unfolds about a Greek physician who administers invaluable treatment first to Darius and then to his wife Atossa. It is a tale with an oriental flavour, indicating Persian oral sources or recourse to stereotypes of the Persian court: palace bedroom secrets, eunuchs, a harem scene, fabulous riches that makes a slave wealthy just by picking up what spills over from cups of gold (3.129–38).

Democedes, the physician, being rewarded by Darius for mending his dislocated ankle with a gift of 'two pairs of golden fetters', makes a witty remark about being doubly punished for his medical assistance (3.130). His joke is similar to the Ethiopian king's jest, after being gifted golden bracelets by the Persian king, that his people have far stronger chains (3.22, see p. 115).

Democedes is keen to return home and uses his new found position of favour to engineer a Persian reconnaissance mission to Greece and a place for him on it, a scheme that succeeds in facilitating his escape. Democedes separates himself from the mission in Italy with the help of a local king and makes it home to his own city-state, Croton, a Greek colony in southern Italy. The story continues when his Persian minders arrive in Croton looking for him, issuing threats that are ignored, but eventually they return to Persia without Democedes. The final part of the story, about the individual Gillus who assists the Persians on their homeward journey, raises the prospect of Darius attacking Greece, a possibility Gillus successfully works to avoid. The conclusion to the story of the Persian intelligence assignment is a matter-of-fact statement but one that registers a significant moment: 'these were the first Persians to come to Greece from Asia and doing so on a spying mission' (3.138).

In hindsight, the end of the Democedes story at 3.138 and the beginning of the chapter that follows mark are significant in the geopolitical history of the region: Darius has shown a willingness to consider an invasion of Greece (3.134) and he does attack and conquer the Greek island of Samos. Yet these two important developments in Persia – Greece relations are not connected – the spying mission is forgotten about and the motive for seizing Samos arises from a personal matter that has nothing to do with the doctor and Atossa's promptings to her husband about Greece – and this may be due to the provenance of the Democedes tale. Historians accept the likelihood of there being a renowned Greek doctor who travelled widely, as far as Persia, but the biography that reaches Herodotus, bearing hallmarks of traditional Eastern Mediterranean folk tales, is more likely to be a popular, romanticized one.[40] It bears remarkable resemblance to the biblical story of Joseph (Genesis 37–50): family antagonism separates the hero from his family and from his country but he enjoys good fortune before adversity leads to imprisonment; eventually the hero extricates himself and uses his talents to help a powerful ruler whose gratitude leads to eventual prosperity and a return home.

The personal matter that leads to the attack on Samos forms the third and final part of the Samos story (3.139–49). Syloson, the exiled brother of Polycrates, had happened to be in Egypt when Darius was there merely as one of Cambyses' guards and his gift to him of a red cloak is repaid when the guard becomes the king. Syloson requests the return of Samos, without bloodshed, and Darius consents by dispatching Otanes. The reader needs to be alert to follow the twists and turns of what unfolds: new individuals become involved (Maeandrius and his heady brother Charilaos) and a series of unexpected reversals characterize the plot and the characters. Syloson's desire for a bloodless invasion is turned on its head when Otanes, who opposed autocracy in the Constitutional Debate because power corrupts, uses his authority to unleash a near genocide and later establishes a monarchy on the island (3.147, 149). Maeandrius, who sought to implement the democracy that Otanes had once advocated, is rudely repulsed by his fellow citizens – 'They had, it would seem, no desire for freedom' (3.143) – and becomes a tyrant (3.143) before escaping to Sparta. He is later expelled from the city because his wealth is seen as likely to corrupt Sparta's citizens.[41]

Book Three concludes with a rebellion in Babylon which, after a long and unsuccessful siege by Persian forces, is finally crushed after the intervention of the ultra-loyal Zopyrus (3.150–60). No explanation for the revolt is forthcoming and the interest for the reader is focused on the gruesome nature of what takes place: a Babylonians slaughter of women and Zopyrus' excessive and uncalled for devotion to the line of duty. The Bisitun inscription refers to two revolts in Babylonia but Herodotus' account has a fictional quality, with infiltrator in disguise being a familiar literary topos found in Homer and Sophocles (Asheri 2007: 523–4). Historical reality is reasserted at the end of the account when, looking ahead to the looming conflict between Persia and Greece, it is mentioned how the grandson of Zopyrus deserted from the Persians to Athens (3.160).[42]

Compared to Book One, which anchors itself around Croesus and Cyrus, and Book Two, which securely focuses on all matters Egyptian, Book Three is history on a roller coaster. Its beginning is stable enough, dealing with Cambyses' campaigns and his increasingly erratic behaviour, but by the end the reader could be reeling from the succession of mini-tales featuring intrigues, hostilities and plots involving a host of men and women. The motives of the various individuals are mixed, with resentments and revenge being of prime importance but also at play are private and family reasons as well as political idealism and political greed (see Book 3, Box 4). Herodotus

MIXED MOTIVES

revenge, resentment

Cambyses against Amasis (3.1, 2)
Exiled Samian nobility against
Polycrates (3.44)
Corinthians against Samos (3.48)
Periander against Corcyra (3.49)
Procles against Periander (3.50)
Aeginetans against Samos (3.59)
Oroetes against Polycrates (3.121)
Otanes' massacre on Samos (3.147)

debt of gratitude

Spartans helping exiled Samians (3.47)
Darius paying back Democedes (3.130)
Atossa paying back Democedes (3.133)
Darius paying back Syloson (3.139–40)

private reason

Periander and Lycophron (3.52–3)
Oroetes taunted by Mitrobates (3.120)
Democedes and Croton (3.129–38)
Syloson and Samos (3.139)
Zopyrus' devotion to his king (3.154)

public reason

Political ambition of the false Smerdis
and his brother (3.61)
Withdrawal by Otanes of his candidacy (3.83)
Desire for power by Darius (3.85)
Suspicion of a plot by Darius (3.119)
Political idealism of Maeandrius (3.142)
Patriotism of Charilaus (3.145)

BOOK 3, BOX 4

holds together his canvas of characters by situating them within a geopolitical frame of Persian history where a butterfly effect is seen to be at work: Darius first considers invading Greece because Atossa had an abscess on her breast and wanted to show gratitude to the physician who successfully treated it; Persian military intervention in the Greek world begins with Darius being gifted a fine cloak when he was employed by the king as a guard. As with the different explanations given for Cambyses' motive in invading Egypt (see pp. 112–13), ad hominem factors are important to Herodotus in explaining how events unfold in the way they do.

Book Four: Darius, Scythia and Libya

Scythia and Darius

The compositional shape of Book Four is not, compared to other parts of the *Histories*, the most reader-friendly even though there are three broad divisions to the text: Darius and Scythia; the foundation of Cyrene on the Libyan coast; and, via a Persian campaign in the country, the ethnography of Libya (see Box 1).

Darius' revengeful intention to invade Scythia is mentioned in the first chapter and returned to at the end of the fourth chapter but then the text digresses into a lengthy account of Scythian geography and ethnography and the subject of Darius' expedition does not reappear until 4.83. The campaign itself (4.83–144) is divided into two parts, divided by chapters with more geographical information (4.99–101) and, overlapping with this interlude, chapters dealing with a council of the Scythians and ethnographic reports on their neighbours (4.102–20).

Book Two started with Psammetichus setting out to conquer Egypt and this led into Egyptian ethnography; Book Four begins with Darius' plan to attack Scythia and this leads to descriptions of the Scythian way of life. However, the Scythian accounts are somewhat disjointed when compared to the compact divisions of Book Two, and the writing jumps around between geography and ethnography.

A part of an explanation for the untidiness is the fact that Herodotus is dealing with what for him is a vaguer geography – the relatively unexplored steppes between the Danube and the Don – and a far less clearly known human landscape.[1] Unlike the Egyptian *logos*, there are infrequent references to first-hand observations and this suggests that he did not travel extensively in the region. His claim to have visited places in and around Olbia, an important trading post founded by colonists from Miletus in the seventh century, tends to be given the benefit of the doubt by scholars[2] and he does provide measurements for distances around and including the Black Sea (4.85–6). His statement about the extent of a severely cold climate (4.28) is

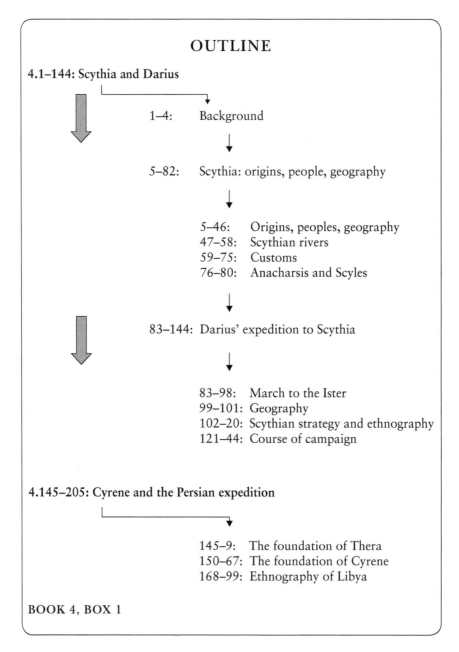

OUTLINE

4.1–144: Scythia and Darius

1–4:   Background

5–82:   Scythia: origins, people, geography

    5–46:   Origins, peoples, geography
    47–58:   Scythian rivers
    59–75:   Customs
    76–80:   Anacharsis and Scyles

83–144: Darius' expedition to Scythia

    83–98:   March to the Ister
    99–101:   Geography
    102–20:   Scythian strategy and ethnography
    121–44:   Course of campaign

4.145–205: Cyrene and the Persian expedition

    145–9:   The foundation of Thera
    150–67:   The foundation of Cyrene
    168–99:   Ethnography of Libya

BOOK 4, BOX 1

a misleading generalization about what is now Ukraine and southern Russia, indicating that he may have been misled by hearing exaggerated tales of cold spells in winter. At another point (4.81), he acknowledges his own uncertainty about knowing how one could arrive at an accurate population count given the lack of a clear sense of what constitutes Scythia. Nonetheless, he feels reasonably sure the number must be very large based on his own visual observation (*opsis*) of the gigantic bowl that one of their kings apparently used to arrive at an empirically verifiable total. The bowl becomes a synecdoche, a part of the whole that stands for the huge mass of Scythians. Herodotus' deduction is part of a 'strategy of authentication' that invites his readers 'to register woolly vagueness as impressive cliometric precision' (Greenblatt 1992: 125).[3]

An added complication is that Herodotus is trying to particularize the Scythians at a time when the term could be used loosely for a wide area of land relatively unknown to the Greek world. He wants to distinguish those he calls the Royal Scythians (4.20) from other Scythians (4.22, 4.56–7) and from those who share Scythian customs despite cultivating crops in the manner of non-nomadic farmers (4.17–8). There are times when the reader struggles, as Herodotus does himself, to make sense of the geography in relation to the ethnic groups (4.17–27, 4.47–58, 4.99–117). It remains unclear, for instance, whether those he called the Royal Scythians are just a politically dominant group or a people with an ethnic-cultural identity of their own.

A helpful essay by West discusses possible sources for Herodotus' information, the archaeological evidence for some of what is said and an overview of what is known or can be attributed to the steppe culture, nomadic and agricultural, of the Scythians. She concludes that Herodotus was grappling with unreliable information he had accrued from hearsay and this, along with the language barrier, means it is impossible to 'trace the extent to which he himself tacitly rationalized (or exaggerated) the improbable or supplied links between data which were in reality unconnected or connected in quite a different way' (West 2002: 456). Readers will benefit by consulting maps when following the expositions on Scythia's geography and useful ones are available (Asheri 2007: 546–7, 550–1, 552; and Strassler: 2007); though it has been concluded that Herodotus' 'orientation is confused and his conception of Scythia can hardly be reconciled with our maps' (West 2002: 441).

Hartog's *The Mirror of Herodotus*, first published in French in 1980 and with an English translation appearing eight years later, remains a highly influential study of the depiction of Scythians in Book Four. For Hartog, Scythians constitute the exemplary Other and by looking at them the Greeks were looking at themselves, as if in a mirror, because of the cultural codes they employed to describe the land and its people. The Scythians are an imaginary Other, an intellectual construction of the Greek mind, a people who live not only in a space far from their own – to the north of the Black

Sea, beyond the limit of Greek colonies in that part of the world – but in a space conceived of as absolutely different: a space lacking familiar features like cities or temples, a marginal land where Prometheus was chained as a punishment, a border zone where *oikoumenē* (inhabited earth) rubs shoulders with uninhabited desert. Herodotus positions Scythia on the boundary with *erēmoi* (empty spaces), an anomalous and liminal space where the Other is a nomad. Hartog's structuralist approach can at times be rigidly grid-bound, eliding the way Herodotus complicates binary oppositions and inversions. He does offer rewarding readings of particular passages and some of these will be highlighted in what follows but there is a possible drawback to his approach which is implicit in the title of the first part of his book: 'The Imaginary Scythians: Space, Power and Nomadism'. Hartog is not saying that the portrayal of the Scythians is fictional but there is the suggestion that Herodotus is presenting a cerebral construct, underpinned by a particular form of a 'structural dualism' that has been seen as part of the ancient Greeks' cultural DNA (Cartledge 1993:16). If, metaphorically speaking, there is something 'imaginary' about the depiction of the Scythians – a delineation shaped by intellectual polarities (Greek/Other; settled/nomadic; autochthonous space/alien space) – it lends itself to a possible depreciation of Herodotus as a historian seeking accurate information about a foreign people in favour of viewing him as a structuralist in search of a well-designed paradigm.[4]

Background (4.1–4)

The revenge that Darius seeks in his invasion of Scythia refers back to the earlier invasion of Media by Scythia, first mentioned in 1.103–6. As with Book Two, the narrative in Book Four begins with an unusual anecdote designed to catch the attention of the author's audience, though there are contenders for the story's most alarming component: a revolt by slaves, illicit sexual relations between slaves and non-slaves or, and this comes first in the telling, the savage practice of blinding slaves and the linking of this with the peculiar nature of their milking task.

The tale of blinded slaves and what awaits the Scythian men when they finally return home from Media is a strange one. The sons of the blinded slaves only flee when confronted by whips, not swords; it is not physical superiority that defeats them but visual signifiers of their inferior status, something they have imbued from their fathers. What Althusser called 'ideological interpellation', the social process whereby individuals recognize the symbolic identity conferred on them by society's dominant ideology, is here brought to life in the moment when the sons of the slaves flee at the sight of the whips. The scene is equivalent to Althusser's own example of a policeman calling out in the street to someone and a person recognizing the call and turning around, a moment that sees that person's transformation into a subject, produced in this case by a discourse and practice of the law.

The individual, carrying within themselves an ideological identity which has 'interpellated' their subjectivity, is produced by social forces within the situation and not by some inner sense of autonomous selfhood (Althusser 1971: 173–83).

The reason why the Scythians traditionally blind their slaves is linked to the use they make of them for milking their horses. It is not explicitly stated why slaves needed to be deprived of their sight; presumably the nomadic way of life could make it easy for them to escape and as they are not needed for other agricultural tasks blinding them does not come at a cost to their masters.[5]

Scythia: origins, people, geography (4.5–58)

Different accounts are given for the origins of the Scythians and the first of these concerns the three sons of Targitaus, the ur-Scythian, and the golden implements that fall from the sky but which burst into flames when the two older sons try to approach them. This does not happen for the youngest son and, intuitively recognizing a semiotic significance to the quenching of the flames, his siblings automatically accept him as their king. The Scythians say this took place one thousand years ago, confirming their status as the youngest race of people (4.5) and registering the first of a number of diametrical differences between Scythia and Egypt (one of earth's oldest people, 2.2).[6] The fact that the golden implements falling from the sky include a plough and a yoke points ahead to the distinction that will be made between Scythia's nomads and the territory's settled agriculturalists (4.17–18).

A different account of Scythia's origins is given by Greek colonists on the shores of the Black Sea, one that features Hercules and a snake-woman but also involving one of three sons who is possessed of an unusual ability which singles him out as king (4.8–10). Herodotus prefers a third account of the origins, one lacking folklore ingredients, that had Scythians inadvertently occupying what at the time was Cimmerian territory and staying there to make it their own land when Cimmerian chiefs couldn't agree on how best to deal with the incursion. In support of this account, Herodotus can point to material evidence as well as the likelihood that it was in the pursuit of Cimmerians that brought Scythians into Median land, thus bringing about Darius' wish for revenge (4.11–12).

Herodotus handles the three accounts of Scythia's origins with a methodological prudence that is characteristic of his approach to myth and its role in a community's sense of identity. He rejects the truth value of the legend of Targitaus – 'for my part I do not believe the tale, but it is told' (4.5) – but not summarily. He respects the Scythians' belief that the gold that supposedly fell from the sky is sacred by describing uncritically the festival that arises from it (4.7). The second account, featuring Heracles and a snake-woman, is told in detail but in the style of an entertaining fairy tale that lies beyond the purview of a serious historian. By contrast, the third account can be backed up with hard evidence and is clearly the most creditable but the evidence is left to speak for itself with the modest remark that it is 'the tradition that I myself do especially incline' (4.11).

It is clear from 4.13 that the Scythians exist on the periphery of the known world, pushed out by the semi-mythical Issedones who inhabit land to the south of the Arimaspians. Herodotus indicated earlier his disbelief in the existence of the one-eyed Arimaspians (3.116) and he probably also doubts tales of gold-guarding griffins said to live to the north of them. The work of Aristeas, an earlier writer who claimed to have visited the Issedones, is acknowledged but Herodotus draws a methodological line in the sand between hearsay and reliable reports by eyewitnesses (4.16). He will report what he has been able to establish 'as far as is possible' (*epi makrotaton*) but acknowledges that he is operating in an epistemological grey area, stressing how little is known for sure about regions beyond Scythia. With this important qualification in mind, he sets out what he has been able to ascertain for himself about the relationship between Scythian geography and the ethnic groups (4.17–27). After a short discussion on climate and a little digression on why mules cannot be bred in Elis, which he confesses is the kind of curiosity he cannot help but find himself addressing (4.30), he concludes in ring composition – 'Thus I conclude my remarks on what are said to be the most remote regions' (4.31) – only to add a postscript (4.32–6) on the Hyperboreans who are supposed to dwell further north than anyone (in what is now Kazakhstan). While a note of scepticism or just uncertainty on the topic of the Hyperboreans is detectable, Herodotus is sanguine about relating what he has heard about them.[7]

Talk of the Hyperboreans triggers an uncharacteristically personal remark about what makes the author of the *Histories* laugh: over-schematizing maps of the world that 'draw the world as round as if fashioned by compasses, encircled by the river of Ocean, and Asia and Europe of a like bigness' (4.36).[8] What follows is a geographical outline of Asia and the various groups that live there, as far east as India but beyond which 'no one can say what it is like there' (4.37–40). He is astonished that cartographers represent Libya, Asia and Europe as being of equal size (4.41) and proceeds to deal with each continent in turn, beginning with Africa (which the Greeks called Libya). He provides two accounts of circumnavigating the continent, both undertaken on the orders of kings,[9] only one of which was successful (4.42–3), and neither expedition attempts to explore the interior though there is a sighting of 'tiny people wearing clothes made of palm leaves'. While exploration of the continent of Asia is also credited to the dictates of a king, Darius (4.44),[10] Herodotus can say very little about Europe because it has not been properly explored (4.45). If Herodotus had drawn his own map of the world in order to correct the errors of previous cartographers it would have shared a feature of our antique maps by showing large areas marked as 'Unknown' or 'Here be dragons'.

At this point there appears to be a turn towards ethnographic matters, highlighting the significance of the Scythians' nomadic way of life – the spatial indeterminacy of their lifestyle makes them invincible (4.46) – only for the narrative to revert to geographical concerns and in particular the rivers which divide up the land.[11] It helps a little to know that the Ister, Tyras, Hypanis, Borysthenes and Tanais are, respectively, the modern Danube, Dniester, Bug, Dnieper and Don but the surfeit of named smaller rivers presents a perplexing challenge for readers (4.47–58). Herodotus expressed earlier his dissatisfaction with existing world maps because he saw them as simplistic and empirically vague (4.36, see above) and it seems he prefers a less static approach to representing the known world, one that takes into account the contingency and change he highlighted at the beginning of his work (1.5). An alternative is to describe the world as experienced by a traveller journeying on the ground, a hodological approach that baulks at the panoptic endeavour to provide a bird's-eye visual perspective: 'Herodotus folds the *graphein* of cartography into the *graphein* of language in an attempt to embed its visual element within an exclusively verbal account' (Purves 2010: 128). This may be the case, and a clear demonstration of this unfolds in Book Five,[12] but sometimes – as with the chapters on Scythia's rivers – the topographical information becomes verbally top-heavy and the reader is in danger of becoming lost amidst a barrage of words.

Scythian customs (4.59–80)

Characteristically, in his account of Scythian religious customs, Herodotus is as interested in ritual practices and the names given to divinities as he is indifferent to theological beliefs and concerns of a spiritual nature. As usual, he has no hesitation in equating the names of foreign gods with Greek ones (4.59) and is unbothered by the assertion that the Scythians' most important deity is Hestia, goddess of the hearth and matters domestic, a seemingly unlikely choice for a people not given to living in fixed abodes.[13] Always interested in comparing methods of sacrifice, Herodotus follows the approach used when describing Persian and Egyptian customs (1.132, 2.38–40) and takes care to note departures from Greek ritual practices (4.60–2). Scythians do not use fire or pour libations, the animal to be sacrificed is not consecrated (no scattering of barley-grains or sprinkling of lustral water), is killed by strangling (not by cutting its throat and therefore, unlike a Greek sacrifice, no collecting of the blood to pour onto the altar and surrounding earth) and the meat is boiled in a pot using the bones as fuel (not roasted on a spit over a fire).

When sacrificing to Ares, selected prisoners of war are also sacrificed and on these occasions wine is poured over their heads and their throats cut. Herodotus notes the Scythian penchant for scalping enemies, preserving their skin and skulls (and those of relatives they fall out with) and drinking their blood (4.64–4–5). Hartog (1988: 157–72) discusses the head-hunting and blood-drinking in terms of Scythian 'otherness', contrasting these customs with those of Greeks and showing, for example, how wine has a value for Scythians that sets them at odds with the civilized world. Each province in Scythia holds an annual event which rewards with wine those who have killed enemies while dishonouring those who have not killed by withholding the drink (4.66). Wine takes on the symbolic value of the blood that is drunk when a Scythian kills his first enemy whereas, in the *Histories*, wine for Greeks, Lydians and Persians is a marker of culture and sophistication.[14]

The Enareis, first mentioned in 1.105[15] where their androgyny is attributed to Scythians who despoiled a temple to Aphrodite in Palestine, are returned to here in the context of the prevalence of soothsayers in the country. In chapter 22 of *Airs, Waters, Places*, a text thought to have been written by a contemporary of Herodotus, a follower of Hippocrates, their androgynous nature is traced back to the excessive amount of time Scythians spend on horseback and the side effect of a treatment for this which causes impotence: 'they put on women's clothes in the belief that they have lost their manhood. And so they act like women, and join the women in doing women's work' (Blanco's translation 2013: 454). In an illuminating article on Scythian ethnography, Chiasson (2001: 41–69) notes how anthropologists have discerned parallels between the Enareis and transvestite shamans in traditional societies and he also discusses the divergence between the Herodotean and Hippocratic accounts of the Scythians.

The account of Scythian funerals (4.71–5) begins with the information that kings are buried in territory where the Borysthenes ceases to be navigable, a 40-day journey up the river (4.53). The location marks a peripheral zone beyond which nothing is known, somewhere not placed in or around a centre and thus an excentric point that befits a nomadic culture where there is no civic centre, no agora, 'an undifferentiated space with no fixed point of reference' (Hartog 2008: 140). Again, in the spirit of nomadism and in contrast to Greek custom, the king's body is taken around in a wagon to different places (a practice that extends to non-royal funerals). The king's body has been mummified but mourners mutilate theirs and for Hartog the self-scarring is a form of communication, part of a collective act of commemoration, a degradation of the body as opposed to the waxed, wholesome-smelling flesh of the king (1988: 146–7). A wandering people are brought together, united as 'they all build a great barrow of earth, vying zealously with one another to make this as great as may be' (4.71).

Suitably impressed by the scale and grandeur of royal funerals, Herodotus' account is best remembered for his graphic description of what occurs on the first anniversary of a king's death. Cutting the wheels of the wagon in half and using them as supports, the preserved corpses of fifty servants are impaled as ghostly riders on the gutted bodies of fifty horses that are suspended above the ground and placed in a circle around the grave of the king (4.73). Archaeological evidence suggests that such macabre cavalcades may be more than the exaggerated tales of a collective memory (Dewald 2008: 652; Corcella 2007: 632; West 2002: 452–3), while Hartog offers a pleasing anthropological epitaph: 'It is the end of all the travelling; the nomadism is over. In life the king was a mobile center; in death he becomes a fixed but "excentric" center of a ring which is itself immobile' (1988: 148).

The smoking of cannabis is described as part of Scythian funerals (4.75); the recreational use of the plant has been mentioned earlier in relation to the Massagetae (1.202). Herodotus seems unaware that if intoxication is the objective then the flower buds and not the seeds would be thrown on the hot coals as the most desirable part of the plant. Finds of hemp-smoking paraphernalia in excavated graves of Scythians support what Herodotus reports, with used hemp-burning kits found alongside tools and weapons, suggesting the practice was a part of everyday life.[16]

The account of Scythian culture comes to an end with the dark side of ethnocentrism: two stories about bohemian individuals, Anacharsis and Scyles, who pay with their lives for adopting foreign customs (4.76–9). Anacharsis is informed on after being seen conducting Greek rites in a wood and is consequently killed by the king; Scyles, who knew Greek from his mother and liked the Hellenic way of life, is executed for performing Bacchic rites. Hartog's reading (1988: 62–84) traces a structural coding at work in both these stories that warns of the danger awaiting those who contravene their culture's codes of behaviour. The parallel between Anacharsis and Scyles, both of whom are killed by their own brothers, springs from the way each of them step outside their culture's comfort zone: Anacharsis belongs to Scythian royalty but leaves his country and travels widely before returning home; Scyles, a bilingual Scythian king with a Greek mother, travels to Olbia (founded by Greek colonists), leaving his army on the outskirts while he accesses Greek space, 'entering within the walls and shutting the gates would doff his Scythian apparel and don a Greek dress' (4.78). Anacharsis finds his illicit shelter within a wood: 'he hid himself in the country called Woodland (which is beside the Race of Achilles, and is all overgrown with every kind of wood)' (4.76). Though screened by trees and walls, each of them is spied upon and Hartog detects in Herodotus' prose the impersonal voice of a culture that decrees they be punished for their transgressions. The end of chapter 77 – 'be this as it may, the man [Anacharsis] was put to death as has been recounted' – and the beginning of chapter 79 – 'But when the time came that evil should befall him [Scyles], this was the cause of it' – bespeak an inescapable destiny that awaits those who ignore cultural borders. They are killed by their brothers, loyal representatives of Scythian *nomoi*, with a finality that betokens the severity of their crimes. In the case of Anacharsis all memory of the man is erased from Scythian consciousness (4.76), while Scyles, immediately upon being handed over by the Thracians on a bank of the Ister, is beheaded by the side of the river (4.80).

Darius' expedition to Scythia

A Persian army is leaving Asia and crossing into Europe with hostile intent– the first recorded intercontinental military campaign of its kind – but Herodotus does not make capital of the fact. This may partly be due to Scythia's location on the edge of the known continent, its isolated position bracketing it off from mainstream Europe. Perhaps for the same reason, Herodotus does not highlight correspondences (see n. 19) between the independently-minded Scythians pluckily resisting the might of Darius and the way that free-spirited Greeks will stand up to the imperial might of an autocratic Persia.

The story of Darius' expedition (see Box 3), interrupted by digressions that return to geographical matters (4.99–101) and ethnographic concerns (4.103–17), singles out particular episodes that are of interest to Herodotus, and one of these, the bridge built across the Ister, is especially significant because it introduces the Ionians and their position as Greek colonies under the rule of Persia.

The march to the Ister (4.83–98)

The challenging of territorial boundaries by crossing rivers are usually significant moments in the *Histories*. When Cyrus decides to attack the Massagetae the decisive moment comes with the crossing of the Araxes, a movement made on the advice of Croesus (1.207–8) who in his own military campaign had crossed a river, the Halys, into Persian land (1.75–6). Both Cyrus and Croesus are defeated after crossing rivers, as Xerxes will be after

DARIUS' EXPEDITION TO SCYTHIA (4.83–144)

4.83–98:   March to the Ister from Asia

4.99–101:   Geography (part 3): the four-sided
                     shape of Scythia

4.102, 118–20:   Scythian strategy

4.103–17:   Ethnography of non-Scythian neighbours

4.121–42:   The Scythian campaign

4.143–4:   Megabazus in Thrace

BOOK 4, BOX 3

his building of a bridge between Asia and Europe (an act often interpreted as an instance of hubristic individuality challenging the inviolability of nature), but Darius is feeling optimistic when he crosses into Europe and sets up two marble pillars to commemorate the event. The stelae are placed on the European side,[17] suggesting the importance that crossing the Bosporus has for Darius, but he cannot know it marks the start of a campaign that will also end in failure. Rather than draw attention to this fact, Herodotus focuses on the ingenuity of the bridge's architect.

The bridge that is built across the Bosporus is the work of Mandrocles of Samos – the island that has been singled out for its engineering achievements (3.60) – and the reader may sense that Herodotus shares the admiration of Darius for an outstanding technical achievement. As with the creation of the lake of Moeris (2.149), the diversion of the Euphrates by the Babylonian queen Nitocris (1.185) or of the Nile under the first king of Egypt (2.99), drawing attention to the building of the bridge across the Bosporus fulfils the resolve, announced in the proem of the *Histories*, to record for posterity human achievements.

When Darius reaches the Ister another bridge is constructed but this time it is not the engineering aspect that comes to the fore. Before this, however, there is the curious account of Salmoxis, described in the same chapter first as a *daimon*, an undefined supernatural power, and then a god (*theos*) (4.94). The way the Thracian Getae communicate with Salmoxis is described but Herodotus also relates how local Greeks regard him as a mere mortal but a wily one who had known Pythagoras and was able to trick the 'simple-witted' Thracians into believing he had returned from the dead and knew about a paradisal afterlife awaiting them (4.95). Herodotus delivers his own point of view on a matter of religion with a characteristic blend of caution and scepticism plus a touch of frustration at not knowing enough to deliver a more nuanced judgement: 'For myself, I neither disbelieve not fully believe the tale about Salmoxis and his underground chamber; but I think that he lived many years before Pythagoras; and whether there was a man called Salmoxis, or this be a name among the Getae for a God of their country, I have done with him' (4.96).[18]

Having defeated the Getae, Darius reaches the Ister and legendary elements now enter the narrative: a conversation with a soldier that proves to be pivotal and sixty knots on a leather strap which, if they are ever all untied by the Ionians left to guard the bridge built over the Ister, will precipitate a crucial decision.

Scythian strategy and potential allies (4.102–20)

After a short digression on the shape of Scythia (4.99–101) the reader learns of the attempt to build a coalition to hold back the Persians, a partnership that if it were implemented would include the ferociously hostile Tauri. From talk of military strategy the text segues into ethnography of a mildly fabulous kind, briefly describing tribes with outré and very un-Greek lifestyles. Aspects of the Tauri's bloodthirsty behaviour find their way into Euripides' *Iphigenia among the Taurians*, the most prominent of which is their tradition of sacrificing shipwrecked sailors. Hall, in *Inventing the Barbarian: Greek Self-Definition through Tragedy*, reading Euripides as 'enormously indebted to the historian' regards it as 'most likely that the poet's barbarous Taurian society constitutes a dramatic bringing to life of chapters in Herodotus, and therefore new to tragedy' (Hall 1989: 112)

The brutally masculine Tauri 'live by plundering and war' (4.103), making the Agathyrsi who are sketched in the chapter that follows effeminate by comparison, the 'most delicate' (*habrotatoi*) of men who like wearing gold (*khrusophoroi*). They share women in the expectation that such sexual licence will help the Agathyrsi regard each other as kin and encourage a friendly cohesiveness. Next come the Neuri, their werewolf proclivities not taken seriously by Herodotus, and then a race of cannibals (4.106) who remain on the far side of the boundary between human and animal, living without any notion of justice (*dikē*) or law (*nomos*).

Having ventured to report on very alien cultures, dubious about the veracity of some of his material, Herodotus is more confident when describing and distinguishing between the Budini and the Geloni (4.108–9). The Geloni have left the coastal trading posts established by Greek colonists and migrated inland to territory inhabited by the nomadic Budini. In the town of Gelonus there are Hellenic temples and altars and here, at the extreme edge of Greek colonization, a hybrid Greek-Scythian language is spoken by tillers of the soil. They are called Budini by other Greeks, prompting Herodotus, keenly appreciative of the fractal nature of what being a Greek may entail, to add 'But this is wrong' (4.109).

There follows another story of cross-cultural interaction, featuring Amazons who kill their Greek captors and escape into Scythian territory (4.110–17). This eventually leads to the foundation of a new community as a result of marriage with Scythian men who leave their homeland to live with the Amazons. The origins of the Sauromatae contrasts sharply with an earlier foundation account that also featured gender reciprocity (4.8–10). That tale had elements of magical realism – the mighty Heracles and a snake-woman, the challenge of bending a bow that can only be met by the youngest of three sons, a girdle with a golden cup – but this one is an anecdote of courtship and civilized courtesy between sexes and across cultures. The Amazons are equal partners in a successful negotiation between people of different backgrounds and a rare instance in Herodotus of a story with a happy ending. Reversing the role of Greek women with their dowries, it is Scythian husbands who bring their goods to their new homes and their wives are not confined to an inferior status: 'they go hunting with their men or without them; they go to war and wear the same clothes as the men' (4.116). Unlike their stereotypical representation in art and literature,[19] these warrior women are not depicted as a threat to men and society but as considerate players in an interesting cultural formation arising from unusual circumstances and based on mutual respect. Mayor, in *The Amazons: Lives and Legends of Warrior Women in the Ancient World* (2014: 52–6), comments on Herodotus' use of the word *ektilosanto*, in the last sentence of 4.113. The word means 'to tame', a rare use of a word that in Homer and Pindar is usually applied to animals and pets, and the sense here is that through sex the Amazons become compliant. Herodotus may be using the word ironically, given how the women negotiate the terms of their life with the men and live with them as equals.[20]

At 4.118 the text returns to the narrative point reached at 4.102, with the call for a regional conference in the wake of the Persian advance; opinion is divided and five of the eight tribes, blaming the Scythians for provoking the Persians, refuse to join an alliance.[21] Consequently, the Scythians resolve on a scorched earth policy and the adoption of guerrilla warfare tactics, using the three tribes that do support them.[22]

The Scythian campaign (4.121–44)

Darius' hapless campaign against the Scythians is mostly spent traversing enemy territory in a futile cat-and-mouse chase: from the Ister (Danube) eastwards to the Tanais (Don) before heading northwards only to eventually loop back into Scythia, having built forts and crossed rivers along the way (4.122–4). He then follows the enemy into the land of those tribes who refused to join an alliance only to again return to where he started (4.125).

Frustrated by these tactics, Darius sends a message to the Scythian king who defiantly replies with a declaration of his people's resolve to resist subjection to a foreign state (4.126–7). The Persians are confused by the Scythians' tactics (4.128–32) and the dramatic pace of events is increased by a change of scene and an interruption to the main narrative (4.133), occasioned by following up on the Scythians' dispatch of a contingent to the Ionians guarding the Persians' escape route back across the Ister (4.128). The Scythians, fondly as it transpires, believe the Ionian leaders will be keen to throw off the yoke of Persian rule: 'Ionians, we are come to bring you freedom' (4.133). Morally scrupulous – or diplomatically astute – they invite the Ionians to fulfil their agreement with Darius, and stay in position. The Ionians seem ready to follow their order to sail for home if Darius fails to return within the agreed time, heightening the growing sense that the Persians are at peril if they remain in Scythia.

At this point the sixty days have not yet passed but it is unlikely that Darius' expedition across thousands of kilometres could have been undertaken within that time scale. This raises doubts about the nature of the sources and the credibility of Herodotus' account. Corcella in his commentary judges it 'impossible that Darius covered such an enormous distance and managed to cross the great rivers of the region', detects inconsistencies between the account and earlier statements about Scythia's geography and questions to what extent information provided for the course of the campaign was checked. He concludes that Herodotus relied to a large extent on unreliable Scythian sources and elaborated on them in order to provide a credible account (2007: 561–5, 653–4).

The Scythian campaign is to some extent portrayed as a struggle between a valiant, tough and intelligent people determined to resist a militarily stronger imperialist force by adopting guerrilla tactics to good effect. The defenders are successful when the enemy, finally coming to realize it cannot win, beats a hasty retreat. A twentieth century parallel would be aspects of the American invasion of and defeat in Vietnam, while within the *Histories* there are echoes of Cyrus' campaign against the Massagetae and Cambyses' attempt to conquer the Ethiopians. What is not made explicit but is prefigured in a tale of a freedom-loving people resisting the oppressive might of a tyrant is, of course, the invasion of Greece by Persia.[23] The question that remains is to what extent the account provided by Herodotus can be trusted and, if he is relying on possibly biased Scythian sources, what can be known for sure about the conduct of and the reason for Darius' campaign: 'we cannot know whether he really wanted to subject all the nomads north of his empire or whether, as some have suggested, he just planned a demonstrative action in order to consolidate the borders of the empire' (Corcella 2007: 565).

Putting to one side to what extent it is based on actual events, what comes across vividly in the telling of Darius' campaign in Scythia is the way the Persian king roams across the land in geographic and cognitive disarray.

As Hartog puts it, when the Persians cross the Ister they enter 'a different kind of space the manner of whose organization totally baffles them' (1998: 59). The Scythians have a strategy based on guerrilla warfare and they know why and where they are leading their enemy; while Darius challenges them to fight a conventional battle he demands that they 'cease wandering' (*pausamenos planes*, 4.126). The Scythians have a firm grasp of their coordinates while the Persians feel they are rambling every which way. Darius, not just flummoxed by a geography that puzzles him, goes cognitively astray in the face of a mentality he cannot comprehend. He can only conceive of warfare in his traditional manner and he admonishes the Scythian king for not thinking in the same way. Idanthyrsus tries to explain: 'I have never fled for fear of any man, nor do I now flee from you; this that I have done is no new thing or other than my practice in peace' (4.127).[24] When the Scythian king sends Darius a mouse, a frog, a bird and five arrows, the Persians think they are the gifts of earth and water that would be expected as tokens of submission and only Gobryas is able to suggest an alternative interpretation (4.131–2).

The difficulty Darius has in comprehending his enemy reaches its nadir at the very point where he thinks a pitched battle will finally be fought. The two armies face each other only for a hare to disrupt the Scythian formation which then breaks rank and scatters in pursuit of the animal. It is a comic moment but also one of poetic clarity; the indifference of the Scythians to Darius crystallizes the nature of his difficulty – dealing with an enemy beyond his ken – and he accepts the need to leave the country and return home (4.134–5). The Persian retreat is described with narrative verve, the Scythians now pursuing a human not animal quarry and reaching the Ister before their foe.

When, after the expiry of sixty days and with the Ionians still in position guarding the bridge, the Scythians can only surmise that 'fear has kept you here . . . [but] we will inflict such a defeat on your master that he will never again lead his army against any nation' (4.136). The debate between the Ionian tyrants at the Ister bridge (4.137) is personalized: Miltiades (an Athenian who will feature later at the battle of Marathon, 6.103–4) initially garners approval with his proposal that they depart with a view to liberating Ionia but Histiaeus wins the day with his argument for expediency and self-interest. The word 'democracy' appears for the first time in the *Histories*, used by Histiaeus to point out what sort of governments Ionians will prefer – 'to live in a democracy' (*dēmokratesthai*) – if they were ever to have a say in their own affairs.[25] Having set about dismantling only one end of the bridge, the tyrants exploit the Scythians' naive belief that their love of freedom is a universal value: 'we are taking down the bridge and will spare no effort to regain our freedom' (4.139).

The ironic twist that concludes the story of the campaign arises from the Persians having to retrace their route in order to find the bridge because of their unfamiliarity with the territory. The Scythians, not accounting for this and knowing their own space, search for their enemy in places the Persians should have been if they had known where to find water and grass for their horses. It is a suitable end to a campaign characterized by misunderstanding.

Darius leaves Megabazus behind in Thrace while he returns to Persia and Herodotus wants his audience to remember Megabazus because the general will reappear at the start of Book Five in a continuation of a narrative that comes to a temporary halt at 4.144. Two moments record the importance of Megabazus and as well as helping to lodge him in the reader's mind they also associate his existence with the Greek world. The first such moment (4.143) is an 'immortal memory' (*athanaton mnēmēn*), referring to a remark by Megabazus disparaging the Greeks of Chalcedon (on the Asian side of the Bosporus) for choosing to settle there when they could have chosen Byzantium on the other side of the Bosporus. The second moment is an anecdote about Darius being asked what he would wish to have as many of as the number of seeds of the pomegranate he is about to eat. Darius answers by saying – and this is before a conquest of Greece is on the Persian agenda – he would 'rather have that number of men like Megabazus than make all Hellas subject to him' (4.143). The scathing judgement of the Scythians on the Ionians – as free men they are the most cowardly and craven of men but as slaves they are the most faithful and least likely to run away (4.142) – suggests the unlikelihood of them ever rebelling against Persian rule.[26] Histiaeus, the tyrant of Miletus who persuades the Ionians to change their mind and keep open the bridge for Darius' retreating army (4.137), is another individual who plays a part in the events of Book Five.

Following two chapters about Darius returning home, leaving Megabazus behind to subdue the Thracians, attention turns to Libya.

Cyrene and the Persian expedition

Just as the Persian expedition against Scythia was briefly mentioned at the start of Book Four but not returned to until some eighty chapters later, so here the expedition against Libya is confined to one sentence (4.145) before being put aside; it is briefly resurrected many chapters later (4.167)[27] and finally returned to for a short spell at the end of the book (4.200–5). It is clearly not the focus of interest in the chapters that make up the remainder of Book Four whereas the foundation of the Greek colony of Cyrene in Libya very much is. Given the nature of what is coming next in the *Histories*, with the conflict between Persia and Greece taking shape and precipitating a fateful encounter, it might seem surprising that more is not made of their first military clash.

Imperial Persia appears to have expansionist ambitions, seeking to subdue Libya and using as an excuse for its invasion the wish to aid the mother of Cyrene's king (4.167). It needs to be remembered that Cyrene had earlier been under Persian authority, something made clear at 3.13 and 4.165, and an argument can be made for suspecting that Herodotus is the one making excuses, using a very limited Persian expedition designed to reaffirm Cyrenean compliance as his pretext for weaving in material he had previously collected on Libyan ethnography (Corcella 2007: 568–9, 694). An argument like this harks back to Jacoby's contention that Herodotus the ethnographer came before Herodotus the historian and only at a later stage did he conceive of bringing all his material together and expanding on it under one overarching theme (see p. 30).

That Herodotus and his readers had a keen interest in and a familiarity with genealogies is a strong impression a modern reader receives from the Cyrene foundation stories. The intricacy of the family networks and the related criss-cross of maritime journeys are handled with what his audience probably appreciated as deftness and while this makes it knotty for today's readers the result is a fascinating insight into the importance of family and other social connections in the Greek world. Modern technology may have made the world a smaller place but the ancient Mediterranean world was always small, a pond in Plato's famous simile around which the Greeks lived like frogs.[28] Some of these frogs knew one another and about each other through colonization, kinship, myth and political affiliations, resulting in a rhizome-like network rooted in a social and political soil. A cartographic rendering of this network would bring out the jigsaw of voyages up and down and from one side to the other of the Mediterranean but it could not so easily visualize the social nature of a different kind of geography, a mapping of spatial relationships shaped by cultural and political topologies. A people's sense of space and routes across it is inseparable from their experiences and perspectives and cannot be equated with coordinates registering the relative locations of particular places and sea routes between them.[29] A map showing the places mentioned in relation to the foundation of Cyrene would need to be overlaid by cognitive and affective networks shaped in varying degrees by genealogical and geopolitical aspects, ones which are transmitted by Herodotus in the form of mini-narratives.[30] The first of these relates to a group of people arriving in Sparta from the island of Lemnos in the north-east of the Aegean (4.145–6).

The foundation of Thera (4.145–9)

The Minyans who set up a camp on Mount Targetus near Sparta are descendants, 'children of the children' (*paidōn paides*), of the legendary Argonauts and they have 'come to their fathers' land (*hēkein es tous pateras*), claiming a right to settle there (4.145). Having journeyed from Lemnos, their destination is not chosen at random and they are received sympathetically after the Spartans learn of their ancient lineage. The Minyans' choice of destination and their initially positive reception in Sparta arises from another expedition set in a mythical past, that of the Jason and the Argonauts who sailed from Greece to the shores of the Black Sea in search of the Golden Fleece. The Spartans hold dear the memory of royal half-brothers, Castor and Pollux (Polydeuces), who had sailed with Jason from their own city and the recollection is the basis for their hosting of strangers.[31]

Fractiousness on the part of the Minyans comes to make them deeply unwelcome in Sparta and when an attempt to execute them is foiled they are offered a place on a colonizing expedition being led by Theras to Calliste (4.146–8), an island that will become known as Thera after its colonization. Like the Minyans, Theras has a dormant, myth-based connection to the place in which he wishes to settle. Theras' genealogy, the subject matter of chapter 147, stretches back to the legendary founder of Thebes, Cadmus, who had spent time on Calliste and left kinsmen on the island.[32] Theras, a descendent of Polynices (the son of Oedipus), is well connected in other ways and was the regent of Sparta before his nephews became the state's first double kings. His genealogical history and the story of the Minyans is presented as background information to the main story of how a Greek colony came to be established in Libya.

The foundation of Cyrene and its kings (4.150–67)

Foundation stories can be crucially important for a colonial community seeking to establish a corporate identity, helping to form a social glue that lends continuity and coherence to the body politic. A new colony has only its links with the mother city to help build a story but, at a critical time when political conflict undermines any collective sense of identity, different social memories may come into play.

Herodotus is aware of more than one account of the foundation of Cyrene and he draws on Spartan, Therean and Cyrenean traditions. The first version (4.150–3), concentrating on the role of Therans in establishing the colony of Cyrene, features a number of sea crossings: from Thera to Delphi and Crete, voyages to Platea off Libya by a Cretan fisherman and then two trips by Therans, first in an advance party and then as the main body of carefully chosen colonizers. A sub-narrative tells of another journey from Samos in the eastern Aegean to Egypt by a merchant who is blown off course towards the Libyan coast and then on to the western limit of the Mediterranean. The second version (4.154–8) makes Battus the centre of attention and his fable-like biography, which features a cruel stepmother, a narrow escape from death thanks to a 'Mr Right',[33] and the urgings of an oracle, serves to emphasize the royal line that he establishes while at the same time demoting Cyrene's links to Thera and its maritime links. Cyrenean royalty would have had an interest in promoting its Battiad lineage (the city was ruled by Battiads until the middle of the fifth century), asserting their independence at the expense of a colonial aristocracy that identified itself by relating to the mother city: ergo, two traditions and two versions of the past.

The inquiry (*historie*) of Herodotus into Cyrene's history brings out the importance of foundation stories and the way they can be contested by different groups within a colony seeking to establish a sense of identity. It seems likely that there was no single, consolidated tradition uniformly shared by the Cyrenean community about their city's foundation or, at best, there was once a collective tradition but consisting of a set of loosely bound stories amenable to being modified or edited to suit different agendas and horizons of expectations. Herodotus' *historie* has him collecting different strands of legends and memories of the colony's foundation and, from a cluster of narrative voices, uncovering different constructs of the past.[34] A consideration of these local traditions, including a comparison of Pindar's fourth and fifth *Pythians* (written in 462 for Arcesilaus IV, a descendant of Battus I) with Herodotus' two accounts, is to be found in an essay by Giangiulio (2001), 'Constructing the Past: Colonial Traditions and the Writing of History. The Case of Cyrene'. Giangiulio, looking at the kind of oral and possibly written material that Herodotus and Pindar could draw on, positions Herodotus' writing after the political demise of the Battiad monarchy (unlike Pindar) and being receptive to a mixture of narratives about the colony's history.[35]

Herodotus does not claim to have visited Cyrene but his sources enable him to present an outline of the Battiad kings (Box 4) down to the intervention of Aryandes, the Persian satrap in Egypt (4.166). The story of what happens after Aryandes dispatches an army is delayed until chapter 200, interrupted by information of an ethnological kind, and it resumes with the siege and capture of Barca. In this story Cyrene does not take part in the vengeful plotting of Pheretime, suggesting a source for this account from within the city's aristocracy that was opposed to Arcesilaus III. The aristocrats 'painted Pheretime in dark colours as a bloodthirsty monster, and were happy to consider her horrible death as the just punishment for her tyrannical excesses' (Corcella 2007: 569) – which is how Book Four comes to an end. Herodotus makes a generalization, inferring from the manner of her death that as an avatar of revenge Pheretime took upon herself a divine prerogative and that such culpability arouses the punitive anger of the gods. (4.205).

HISTORY OF CYRENE (4.159–67)

Battus I and Arcesilaus I (159)

- The colony falters, with no increase in size

Battus II (159)

- Other Greeks invited to join the colony
- Egyptian army, supporting local Libyans robbed of their land, defeated by Cyreneans

Arcesilaus II (160)

- Disaffected brothers found new colony at Barca
- King seeks revenge, is defeated and killed

Battus III (161)

- Demonax from mainland reorganizes the colony

Arcesilaus III (162–7)

- King rejects Demonax and is exiled to Samos
- Pheretime, the king's mother, flees to Cyrus
- King returns to Cyrene and seeks revenge
- Some of the rebels escape to Thera
- King killed in Barca where he fled to escape an oracle's warning
- Pheretime flees to Egypt seeking Persian help
- Persian force seeks to subdue Libya under pretext of aiding Pheretime

BOOK 4, BOX 4

Ethnography of Libya (4.168–99)

Coming after the ethnographic material on Persia, Egypt and Scythia, the approach to writing about the customs and lifestyles of Libya's many tribes is not startlingly different. Starting from the border with Egypt, the commentary systematically covers coastal regions to the west (4.168–80) before moving to a description of an inland stretch of land and the people who dwell there (4.181–5). There is then a return to the point reached in chapter 180 and the account covers the coastal people who live to the west of Lake Triton and some aspects of the country's nomads. As with Scythia, the fringes of Libya form a boundary between the known and the unknown and little is known about the Sahara and its vast extent (4.185).

Herodotus usually likes to note unusual sexual practices, ways of conducting a sacrifice and, more generally, instances of the bizarre and wonderful that a punning James Joyce labelled 'hairyoddities' and 'horodities'.[36] Libya is not an exception in this regard: there are the Garamantes who avoid all contact with other humans and possess no weapons (4.174);[37] a tribe where kudos accrues to women with numerous lovers (4.176); people with no names (4.184); and 'dog-headed men and the headless that have eyes in their breasts, as the Libyans say' (4.191).

The emphasis Herodotus gives to the diffusion of customs and traditions from one culture to another, especially so between Egypt and Greece,[38] is also evident here. In the case of the Adyrmachidae, who dress like other Libyans but follow Egyptian usages in most other respects, this is none too surprising because they live close to Egypt (4.168). Similarly, the Asbystae who dwell to the south of Cyrene have adopted many of the customs of the Greek colony and, it is noted, the Asbystae are the keenest of all the Libyan tribes when it comes to driving four-horse chariots (4.170). At Greek sporting competitions the four-horse chariot race, introduced to the Olympic Games in 680, was the most prestigious event and Pindar wrote more odes for winners of these events than for any other sport. Surprisingly, Herodotus claims that Greeks learnt how to drive four-horse chariots from the Libyans and in the same chapter (4.189) he gives another instance of such diffusionism, asserting that 'the robe and aegis of the images of the Athene' was adopted by the Greeks from Libyan dress.

Book Five: The Ionian revolt – causes and outbreak

Before the Ionian revolt

The kernel of Book Five consist of the events leading up to the outbreak of the Ionian revolt against Persian rule, which spreads to the Hellespont in the north and Cyprus in the south, and the involvement of Athens. This, though, given the number of digressions and diversions that will be encountered, is a highly inadequate summary of what awaits the reader of Book Five. These detours deal mostly but not always with individual players and political and military background material but to say that Herodotus takes a roundabout route is a polite way of warning readers about the likelihood of sometimes losing the way. Herodotus is aware of the danger and some signposts are provided at 5.55 (the start of the longest digression) and at 5.62 (returning to the start of the long digression) and then at 5.65 (the start of the rest of the long digression),[1] but there are other excursions that are not flagged up (Box 1).

The content of Book Five denotes a narrative and thematic break from the Libya *logos* that has gone before (4.145–205), although Darius' European campaign which occupies the opening chapters was flagged up in Book Four (4.144). The geographical location moves well away from North Africa – from one westward limit of Persian rule to another – starting with land on the European side of the Hellespont before moving south to where the Persian Empire reaches the shores of the eastern Aegean. Crossings between Asia and Europe using bridges and boats, which began with the Scythian campaign in Book Four, now become a significant part of the narrative and will reach a climax when Persia decides to invade Greece (see Box 2).[2]

The stories in this book, in the middle of the *Histories,* unfold in borderlands, crossroads between Europe and Asia where Greek colonies had been founded in the past. The Ionians, the 'great middle men of Greek civilization' (Emlyn-Jones 1980: 7), built their cities and developed their politics along the lines of other Greek colonies but aspects of their

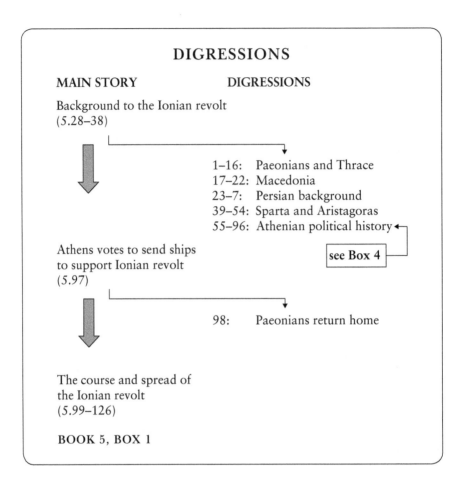

DIGRESSIONS

MAIN STORY   **DIGRESSIONS**

Background to the Ionian revolt
(5.28–38)

1–16:   Paeonians and Thrace
17–22: Macedonia
23–7:   Persian background
39–54: Sparta and Aristagoras
55–96: Athenian political history

Athens votes to send ships
to support Ionian revolt
(5.97)

see Box 4

98:     Paeonians return home

The course and spread of
the Ionian revolt
(5.99–126)

BOOK 5, BOX 1

culture – pottery style, cult and burial practices – indicate a receptiveness to Achaemenid and Anatolian influences, with factions within the *poleis* looking to the east as well as the west for affiliations that would buttress their authority.[3] The beginnings of the Ionian revolt feature in a collection of articles looking at different ways geographic space is represented in t he ancient world, principally in the *Histories* (Barker et al. 2016). In one of the articles, network diagrams of spatial relationships in Book Five show Miletus as the place of pivotal importance; it becomes the bridge between Europe and Asia 'more so than the actual bridge of the Hellespont' (Bouzarovski and Barker 2016: 172). That this is not immediately evident in the reading of Book Five is partly because of the way the story unfolds through the actions of individuals, especially Aristagoras and Artaphernes.

CROSSINGS BETWEEN ASIA AND EUROPE

4.89:   Darius crosses Bosporus – the start of the
                  Scythian campaign

4.143, 5.11:   Darius crosses the Hellespont – remembers debt of
                  thanks to Coes (4.97) and Histiaeus (4.137)

5.12:   Paeonian brothers follow Darius – planning to
                  become tyrants

5.23:   Megabazus crosses the Hellespont – escorting the
                  displaced Paeonians

5.34:   Megabates crosses the Aegean – hoping to capture
                  islands for Persia

5.97:   Athenians vote to dispatch ships to Ionia –
                  'beginning of troubles for Greeks and barbarians alike'

BOOK 5, BOX 2

Book Five, being largely concerned with the course of historical and political matters at the expense of inquiries bearing on ethnography and geography, signals a clear change of emphasis in the *Histories*. Such a change can be taken as part of a more general fault line that divides the *Histories* into two parts, the first of which looks to the history of the East and the contours of Persian power – a non-Greek arena which attracts Herodotus' interest in the social and cultural make-up of a community– while the second part maintains a focus on the course of events when Persia sets about conquering the Greek world (Rutherford 2012: 23). The first part began with Herodotus turning to Lydia and its king, 'whom I myself know [*ton de oida autos*] to have been the first to wrong the Greeks' (1.5), and this led to accounts of Persia and its campaigns. As the background to these campaigns, perspectives on the cultures of those that succumbed to or resisted Persia were incorporated into the accounts of the first four books. Book Five, if viewed as the start of the second half of the *Histories*, can also be seen as beginning with background material appropriate to its subject: how Ionia came to revolt and the advances made to Sparta and Athens for military assistance. In this way, the reader learns of the Naxos affair and follows digressions on the earlier history of Athens and Sparta in order to appreciate their roles in the events that unfolded.

When Book One gets underway with the story of Croesus, his conquest of Greek Ionia is mentioned early on (1.6, 1.26,) and the compulsion on Ionians to pay tribute marks a significant moment: before this, 'all Greeks were free' (*pantes Hellēnes ēesan eleutheroi*). Ionian subjection continues when Croesus is defeated by Cyrus and the Persians take over his former territory (1.169). Now, in Book Five, Ionia revolts against foreign rule.

Persian campaigns in Europe (5.1–27)

After the failure of the Scythian campaign Darius returns to Sardis and leaves Megabazus in Thrace with orders to subjugate the local population (4.144 and 5.2). Book Five starts at this point and, after a short interlude dealing with Thracian customs (5.3–10), what follows is a curious digression about two Perinthian brothers and Persian dealings with Macedonia. While these chapters (see Box 3) are a little puzzling, because most of them are not essential to what will become the main narrative – unfolding the background to the Ionian revolt – the book's very first sentence does flag up the issue of local autonomy versus Persian power: Perinthus is a Greek colony and the Perinthians are 'unwilling to be Darius' subjects' (5.1).

It is the opening tale of how the Perinthians suffer defeat at the hands of the Paeonians that may strike readers as odd and inconsequential. There is a peremptory oracular order and a strange threefold duel involving men, horses and dogs which leads to a premature celebration by the Perinthians and a somewhat silly interpretation of this by the Paeonians. Bringing Thracian Paeonians into the picture could be a narrative device that prepares the way for the antics of the aspirational brothers and the mass deportation of Paeonians that their plotting precipitates (5.12–15) but this will not diminish many readers' sense of incredulity at a tale based around an etymological pun. In their joy at winning the first two of three duels, the Greek Perinthians sing a *paeon* (a song of thanksgiving, hence the English 'paean') and the Paeonians, who presumably do not speak Greek, take it as a reference to themselves – 'This is surely the fulfilment of the prophecy; now it is time for us to act' (5.1) – and thus a fulfilment of the oracle's condition for launching an attack. No comment is made on this unusual course of events though there is a hint of kledonomancy – a branch of divination that invests seemingly insignificant words with an oracular or uncanny aura – and a reminder of Herodotus' interest in lucky- and ominous-sounding names.[4] The author may well just be entertaining his Greek audience with an amusing and contrived tale as a warm-up to his Thracian *logos*.[5] The tale of Psammetichus' language experiment (2.2), also based around an improbable use of words, may be performing a similar function in introducing the Egypt *logos*.

BEFORE THE IONIAN REVOLT (5.1–38)

5.1–10: Thrace

1–2:	Megabazus in Thrace; the Perinthian paeon
3–10:	Ethnography of Thrace

5.11–16: Darius in Sardis

11:	Darius remembers Ceos and Histaieus
12–13:	Darius meets the Paeonian brothers and their sister
14–16:	The consequences for the Paeonians

5.17–22: Dinner party in Macedonia

17–21:	Amyntas' dinner party
22:	Alexander's Greek ethnicity

5.23–7: Darius gives orders and departs for Susa

23:	Megabazus counsels Darius
24–5:	Darius summons Histiaeus and appoints Otanes
26–7:	Otanes' campaign

5.28–34: The Naxos affair

28–9:	Naxos, Miletus and Parian Peacemakers
30–2:	Aristagoras and Artaphranes plot
33:	Aristagoras and Megabates quarrel
34:	Collapse of the plot

5.35–8: Start of the Ionian revolt

35–6:	Plotting the revolt
37–8:	Starting the revolt

BOOK 5, BOX 3

The chapters dealing with Thracian customs (5.3–10), constituting the shortest ethnographic *logos* in the *Histories*, begin with the statement that these people make up the biggest nation in the world apart from Indians.[6] It may seem surprising, then, that little is said about them and what is conveyed about their manner of life does not unduly stress their alterity.[7] When compared to the ethnographic depictions of the Egyptians or the Scythians, the portrayal of the Thracians cannot command the exotic appeal of the Other and this may be partly explained by a degree of familiarity by Greeks, through colonization and trade, with ethnic groups inhabiting the north Aegean and coastal regions of the Black Sea. The Thracians' 'most notable customs' are cursorily listed (5.6) – young women are sexually free until purchased for marriage from their parents; tattooing is socially prestigious; and warriors are more honoured than farmers – and little of this is shockingly remarkable. Sexual permissiveness accorded to unmarried women is an inversion of the Greek norm but it has been earlier noted as an aspect of Lydian life (1.93), while the lauding of martial values above those of agriculturalists suggests Thracians are not too unlike Greeks in this respect. Not uncharacteristically, Herodotus is drawn to *terra incognita* that lies beyond the familiar and even though the land to the north of Thrace is described as 'empty' (*erēmos*) he becomes relatively animated when conveying what he knows about the solitary Sigynnae. They claim to be of Median origin, with territory that apparently stretches as far as the Adriatic, but the improbability of this is tempered by his awareness that 'anything is possible in the long ages of time' (5.9). As Mensch observes in her translation of the *Histories*, these words could serve as an epigraph for the entirety of Herodotus' work.[8]

Following this brief ethnographical foray, the narrative goes back to the time in Book Four when Darius, having left Megabazus in Thrace (4.143), returns to Sardis. The account of how he then rewards two of his men and what happens thereafter (5.11–22) has been shown to be bound up with issues of power and the control of resources, matters that thread their way throughout the *Histories* (Osborne 2007). Darius remembers Coes for his advice to keep open an escape route from Scythia (4.97) and, when Coes is offered a reward, asks to be made tyrant of Mytilene in the north Aegean. Histiaeus, rewarded for being equally valuable (4.137), is already the tyrant of Miletus in Ionia and he asks for a power base in a resource-rich quarter of Thrace close to Macedonia. The tale that comes next concerns the two Paeonian brothers who also hope to be rewarded with a position of power, as tyrants of their own city, if their ploy to impress Darius is successful. Their attractive, multi-tasking sister does make an impact on the Persian king but not with the consequence desired by her brothers; instead, he orders the forced movement of the Paeonians to Asia because their industriousness 'was not in the manner of the Persians or Lydians or any of the peoples of Asia' (5.12). Such a talent is a resource not to be wasted.[9]

Most of the Paeonians are defeated by the Persians because their will to resist is crushed when their empty towns are seized and only those whose dwellings on a lake protect them from capture manage to avoid being deported to Asia. Their lacustrine lifestyle (5.16) is described with details of a self-sufficient economy and child-friendly homes in a way that suggests an almost idyllic existence, a far cry from the calculations of wannabe tyrant brothers and, what will now follow, a drink- and sex-fuelled dinner party in Macedonia (5.17–22).

Megabazus continues on his westward advance into Europe and messengers are dispatched to Amyntas, king of Macedonia, with the symbolic demand for submission – earth and water – to Persian authority. The *logos* that follows is open to different levels of interpretation which do not always complement one another, chiefly because the seemingly dominant theme – Macedonian rejection of Persian hegemony – finds expression in an ambivalent tale where submission and self-determination are not always clearly separated. On the face of it the story is a piece of pro-Macedonian propaganda, designed to accommodate a move from acquiescence to autonomy on the part of the country's rulers, played out in a narrative where the political symbolism is obvious.[10] Amyntas' biddable behaviour at the party represents a willingness to comply with Persian demands whereas his son's defiance, cast in the form of a gentlemanly desire to protect female virtue, symbolizes a Macedonian resolve to resist foreign rule. The eventful dinner party has a theatricality that makes for a good story, with the increasingly lascivious intentions of the Persian emissaries defeated by some clever cross-dressing and concealed daggers. Alexander's stratagem, however, leads to his strategic bribe and a gift of his sister to the general leading the Persian search party (5.21). His willingness to barter a woman in order to cover up multiple murders is as morally unwholesome as the behaviour of the lustful dinner guests and, at the level of geopolitical symbolism, may represent a degree of accommodation to a foreign power that could be construed as falling not too far short of a Persian–Macedonian alliance.

When Megabazus returns to Asia, having organized the forced movement of Paeonians, Darius takes heed of his warning about granting Histiaeus a power base in Thrace. The sensible warning is about material resources being made available to a 'clever and cunning Greek' – forests for building ships and mines for silver (5.23) – but it has an unforeseen and most ironic consequence. Histiaeus will be motivated to provoke an Ionian rebellion (5.35) because of what amounts to his house arrest in Susa, but this detention only comes about because of the warning by Megabazus. He thus brings about the very kind of situation he sought to avoid, a Greek malcontent stirring up trouble for the empire.

The letter that Darius writes to Histiaeus confirms a suggestion about Darius' competence as a ruler that emerged in the earlier tale about the Paeonian brothers. The Persian king is not gullible, he keeps their sister under observation (5.12) and after questioning her brothers concludes that such industriousness would be a valuable resource and not one to let wither on the vine in Thrace. Now, demonstrating his ability to listen to and act on advice, he writes another letter (occasioned by the addressee of his first letter) and follows Megabazus' recommendation to 'bring Histiaeus to you by gentle means' (5.23). He is invited to Susa with flattering talk of 'great matters' to discuss (5.24) but it seems clear that he has no intention of allowing his Greek 'guest' to ever return home.

The Naxos affair and Ionian revolt (5.28–38)

What becomes clear from Herodotus' presentation of the Ionian revolt[11] is that a negative and cynical view of the rebellion emerges, especially when compared to the coming story of the Persian Wars. The difference that is bound to emerge between oral traditions of successful resistance by Greeks acting in cooperating against Persia and those traditions that tell of defeat offers a plausible explanation for why Herodotus' sources for the Ionian revolt result in a markedly unheroic tale of ambitious and perfidious individuals. In defeat 'memory is fragmented into individual episodes of folly, treachery or heroism; self-justification and accusation become primary reasons for remembrance' (Murray 1988: 471).

The people of the twelve Ionian cities on the Asian coast (1.142) do not figure as communities with a consistently common purpose; no motive, ideology or rhetoric associated with a fight for freedom is coupled with the cause of the revolt – unlike the Perinthians who 'fought like brave men for their liberty'(5.10). Instead, the Ionians are seen as passive victims of past and present misfortunes: 'trouble began to come on the Ionians from Naxos and Miletus once more' (5.28). A commitment to emancipation does emerge as the Ionian revolt gets underway but the well-intentioned Parian peacemakers who in the past brought an end to factional fighting in Miletus (5.28–9) make a transparent contrast with the self-seeking and rich oligarchs of Naxos who solicit aid from the equally self-seeking Aristagoras. The 'trouble' that afflicts the Ionians comes from cliques composed of members of elite families bound by ties of *xenia* (guest-friendship) and political interest. The puppet tyrant of Miletus, Aristagoras, is a son-in-law and nephew of Histiaeus, a Greek in the pay of the Persians, and the general Megabates who is dispatched to aid the Naxian 'men of substance' (5.30) is a cousin of Darius and his brother Artaphernes. The daughter of Megabates, Herodotus notes, will allegedly marry a power-hungry Spartan: 'all Greeks in love with power are in bed with Persians, one way or another' (Munson 2007: 157).

Aristagoras easily persuades Artaphernes to dispatch a fleet to Naxos, an island halfway between Ionia and Greece, offering as further bait other islands in the Cyclades as well as Euboea (which he falsely says is as large as Cyprus). He stresses the contiguity of the islands, saying Naxos is 'near to'

Ionia when in fact it is halfway between the Greek mainland and the Aegean littoral in Asia Minor, translating this into the ease of conquering them and stressing the material rewards that will follow (5.31). Aristagoras and Artaphernes are not unlike the Paeonian brothers, cunning in their intentions but clownish when it comes to the execution of their plans. The Naxos affair becomes a debacle and ends in acrimony (5.33) and however hard it may be to accept as historical fact the ludicrous sequence of reported incidents (5.33–6) it points to a felt absence of dignity and nobility of purpose amongst those involved.[12]

Aristagoras plans the Ionian revolt to protect himself when he receives the tattooed message from Susa.[13] Histiaeus, former ruler of Miletus, enjoyed the backing of Persia and the value of this support was stated when there had been an opportunity to maroon Darius and his army in Scythia. He argued that without Persian backing his city and others 'would be sure to choose democracy in preference to despotism' (4.137). Now, in a blatant volte face, he seeks to exploit those democratic impulses by provoking an Ionian rebellion in the expectation that Darius will then order him back to Ionia to deal with the situation (5.37).

Herodotus has been criticized for personalizing the causes of the Ionian revolt, reducing its origins to personal plots and intrigues at the expense of social, economic and geopolitical factors affecting the situation.[14] There may be some justification to this but it is also true that an authentic insight into how the revolt was perceived and understood at the time is being provided in Book Five and that what has to be taken into account is that Herodotus writes about the causes of the revolt in a way that is different but not intrinsically inferior to how some modern historians might approach the same topic. The way Herodotus follows up on the roles of individuals indicates a considered and measured understanding of causation, one where individuals act on the basis of personal agendas while unaware of larger configurations that take shape around the causes and consequences of what they do.[15] Consequences are unforeseen in Herodotus' world because contingencies come into play and there are a couple of these in the events leading up to the Ionian revolt: if the captain Scylax had not forgotten to post a watch then his guest-friend (*xenos*) Megabates would not have fallen out with Aristagoras and enabled the Naxians to thwart the Persians (5.33–4); if the tattooed messenger had not arrived when he did, Aristagoras might not have carried through what was in his mind (5.35–6).

Sparta and Aristagoras (5.39–54)

The narrative of the Ionian revolt continues with Aristagoras travelling in the hope of enlisting a powerful ally but what follows at 5.39 is a digression that deals with Sparta's political history, one that links back to Book One where there was a similar digression about the city (1.65–70) when Croesus was making his inquiries about Greek states.[16] On both occasions an envoy from the East arrives seeking support in hostilities against Persia; on the first occasion the digression explains how, thanks to the lawgiver Lycurgus, Sparta achieves *eunomiē* (good political order) and emerges successfully from a difficult period with neighbouring states. (This, it will be seen, is analogous to a similar development that unfolds in a parallel digression that is about to come regarding Athenian political history.)

Book Five's detour into Sparta history begins with a problem facing its royal line, there being first a lack of heirs and then a surplus, and the accession of Cleomenes leading to his indignant half-brother Dorieus setting off on a colonizing mission (5.39–42). This occasions an involved story with two versions, appealing to connoisseurs of the byzantine, concluding with a metanarrative statement by a seemingly indifferent Herodotus – 'the master of the unadjudicated alternative' (Hornblower 2004: 99) – leaving it to his naratees to referee: 'you may adopt whichever view seems to deserve most credence' (5.45).[17] Herodotus also points to a counterfactual, for if Dorieus had not departed in a huff he would have become king of Sparta (5.48), something that could have changed the course of history.

It is not just Herodotus' interest in how matters of geography affect geopolitical matters that comes into play with Aristagoras' appeal to Cleomenes (5.49). How he goes about trying to persuade the Spartan king has been seen to embody a historiography that contrasts with Herodotus' own method of inquiry while at the same time revealing a similarity of approach (Branscome 2010). Aristagoras is duplicitous in underemphasizing the extent and military capability of the Persian Empire but in his description he moves in a geographically orderly manner, westwards from Ionia towards the Persian capital of Susa, in a way that is not dissimilar to how Herodotus proceeds in his account of the Libyan tribes (beginning in 4.168). Here there is also an orderly progression, moving westwards from Egypt, and a similar vocabulary about lands and people being 'next to' each other.

Aristagoras' sales pitch comes complete with a visual aid, a world map engraved on a bronze plate (a *pinax*), something of a novelty for Herodotus' audience to have featured in a narrative, especially one relating an encounter between a Spartan and an Ionian,[18] and probably even more uncommon – a wonder (*thoma*) even – for Cleomenes to behold. The meeting, however, is not the first to take place between an Ionian and Spartans. After the conquest of Lydia by Cyrus left the Ionians feeling pregnable (1.141), they sent Pythermus to Sparta asking for assistance and despite making a long speech (*elege polla*) in fine purple clothes his request is turned down (1.152). When Polycrates was ruler of Samos he exiled his political opponents and they turned to Sparta as a potential ally and also spoke at length (*elegon polla*) and, despite a second shorter address with the aid of a sack, were equally unsuccessful (3.46). There is a third encounter when, in the turmoil following the death of Polycrates, Meandrius travels to Sparta hoping for military support and instead of making a long speech tries to win over Cleomenes with gifts of gold and silver cups; he too is rebuffed (3.148).

Aristagoras, the tyrant who earlier convinced Artaphernes to conquer the Cyclades for Persia, begins with flattering and hypocritical rhetoric about protecting the freedom of 'Ionian kinsmen' of Spartans and follows this up with a dismissal of Persian fighters as leather-trousered, turban-headed wimps.[19] He then turns to his map to deliver his clinching argument about the material rewards for toppling the Persian Empire. Territories indicated on the map are in proximity to one another, the word for 'next to' (*ekhomai*) is used four times, as if travel from one region to another is effortless (a ploy he used earlier (5.31) when persuading Artaphernes to capture the Cyclades and Euboea). The landscape is defined not by its geographical features but by its riches, offering consumer therapy of a luxurious kind: 'gold first, and silver too and bronze, richly embroidered garments, beasts of burden and slaves' (5.49). The price tag – a three-month journey – does not appear in this synchronic shopping catalogue which starts with the Ionians and ends in the Persians capital and the king's treasuries (*hoi thēsauroi*).[20]

Aristagoras' interviews with Cleomenes are told by Herodotus with keen regard for visual and narrative drama afforded by the occasions. Direct speech is used for the first encounter, punctuated by the author at a theatrical moment when the audience is prompted to imagine Aristagoras revealing his world map – 'showing as he spoke the map of the earth' – and referring to it as he covers the ground between Sardis and Susa. He uses pronouns relying on a context of pointing – '*here* are the Ionians . . . *here* the Lydians . . . you see the Phrygians *here*' – and these deictic words invite not just Cleomenes but the wider audience of readers or listeners to follow a journey that audaciously culminates in the hubristic claim that when Susa's treasuries are expropriated 'you need not fear to challenge Zeus for riches' (5.49). When the journey time is revealed in the second interview, Aristagoras' ekphrastic endeavour – to vividly bring to life a graphic representation – flounders and, upon further importuning and attempted bribery, collapses with the intervention of a child and the silent departure of Cleomenes to another room of his house.[21]

What follows (5.52–4) is a different way of representing geographic space, not by way of a visual aid but by using words to describe a journey undertaken on the ground, the kind of hodological account observed in the description of Scythia's rivers.[22] Cleomenes' rejection of an expedition that would involve three months of travelling was made after first hearing Aristagoras' description of the journey because that account abstracted the physical nature of such a trip while highlighting the material benefits of conquest. Herodotus' account of the journey does the opposite, ignoring the potential for personal enrichment and concentrating on measurable distances in parasangs, half-parasangs and furlongs. Exactness is emphasized, with three days added to the total journey time to cover travelling from the Ionian coast to Aristagoras' starting point of Sardis for the trip he tried to tempt

Cleomenes into undertaking. Now the journey is broken down into stages and attention is given to the difficulties in crossing between lands that lie next to one another: at the River Halys there is a 'great fortress' and gates through which it is an 'absolute necessity' (*pasa anagkē*) to pass; in Matienian land four rivers 'must needs be' (*pasa anagkē*) crossed by ferries.

The differences between a cartographic representation of space as employed by Aristagoras and the experiential one offered by Herodotus has appealed to scholars seeking to examine different spatial models in the *Histories*. For some, there is a marked contrast between the visual space in a cartographic representation, producing a timeless synoptic view of the world, and the virtual space of a textual representation that does not iron out topographical features and difficulties in traversing the terrain. Such a dichotomy, and the related championing of a hodological mode at the expense of a cartographic one, is resisted by other readings that draw attention to how the two accounts use similar geographical styles of writing, albeit for different purposes.[23]

Athenian history (5.55–96)

Aristagoras' visit to Sparta afforded the occasion for a digression concerning that city's political history and his trip afterwards to Athens also affords an excursus, though a far lengthier one, that looks back to earlier political difficulties in the Athenian *polis*. It carries on from events covered in a parenthesis in Book One (1.59–65) about how Peisistratus became tyrant of Athens, and concludes in Book Five with the fall of the Peisistratids and the gain for Athens of *isēgoriē* (equality, freedom of speech), analogous to Sparta having emerged from its past period of trouble with *eunomiē* (good political order).

Some chapters within the digression into Athens' past are minor detours of their own and while the first two of these – the family origins of the tyrannicides and how the alphabet came to be used in Greece (5.57–61) – are not obviously relevant to the Ionian revolt, their subject matter and treatment are hallmarks of Herodotus. There is an abiding interest in *Histories* with questions of kinship and lineage, and looking into the foundations of the Greek alphabet is consonant with the principled intention, announced in the proem, of 'showing-forth' the 'inquiry of Herodotus of Halicarnassus'. The investigator's eyewitness evidence – 'I myself have seen' the Cadmean inscriptions (5.59) – is very much characteristic of how the author goes about fulfilling his announced objective and an interesting example of how he uses inscriptions to throw light on a very distant period, supposedly predating the Trojan War, when little of any oral tradition has survived or carries much value (Thomas 1989: 90). Another instance of Herodotus' liking for embedding portions of his text is the loop within the digression that begins at 5.55 with the information that the tyrant Hipparchus was

ATHENIAN HISTORY (5.55–96)

Tyrants rule Athens (5.55–6) (continuing from 1.59–64)

- Family of tyrannicides (5.57)
- Origins of Greek alphabet (5.58–61)

End of tyrants' rule (5.62–5)

Cleisthenes' reforms (5.66–9)

- Grandfather of Cleistehenes in Sicyon (5.67–8)

Cleisthenes versus Isagoras (5.70–3)

- Alcmaeonids as the Accursed (5.71)
- Cleomenes' failure (5.72)
- Envoys to the Persians (5.73)

Spartans, Boeotians and Chalcidians attack Athens (5.74–8)

- Benefit of democracy to Athens (5.78)

Thebans ask Aegina for help in attacking Athens (5.79–89)

- Origins of hostility between Aeginetans and Athens (5.82–7)
- Athens prepares to attack Aeginetans (5.89)

Spartans seek to restore Hippias as tyrant of Athens (5.90–3)

- Speech by Socles about tyrants of Corinth (5.92)

Hippias in Sigeum (5.94–6)

BOOK 5, BOX 4

assassinated: the loop delves into origins of the Greek alphabet at 5.58 before returning at 5.62 to the point reached at 5.56. Having reached this point, the reader learns what happened after the assassination of Hipparchus at a Panathenaic procession. The loop completed, the main digression about Athens' past continues with background information that will lead to the context for understanding why, some thirty-five chapters later, Athens responds to the visit of Aristagoras in the way it does.

The large number of chapters making up this digression do not unfold in a linear chronological pattern, and the various forays into the past that constitute much of the text can make it difficult to follow on a first reading. Herodotus, always aware of the roundabout routes he is making, employs verbal markers to alert the reader to the beginnings and ends of many of the chronological detours (see Box 4).[24] What emerges from these chapters as a whole is the sense of Greek poleis divided ethnically, culturally and politically.

Athens: end of tyranny and Cleisthenes (5.62–9)

How Athens came to be under the rule of tyrants was covered in Book One's digression into Athenian history (1.59–65) and the story of how it came to an end after thirty-six years (*c.* 546–510) is told in 5.62–5. That the expulsion of the Peisistratids is seen as a definitive moment is stated in the first sentence of 5.66 and Herodotus signposts his intention to cover the 'noteworthy things' that happened to Athenians 'once they had been freed', before returning to the Ionian revolt at the point where he left it in 5.38. The freedom that came to Athens depended, however, on the help of a Spartan army and an element of pure luck when the children of the Peisistratids were captured and there is an almost wistful looking back to the noble ancestry of the tyrant's family that nuances any simplistic tyranny-versus-freedom polarity (5.65).[25] The sense of a more complex politics at work gains traction when, after the expulsion, faction fighting between aristocratic Athenian families leads to Cleisthenes instituting reforms as a way of gaining leverage in his struggle against Isagoras (5.66).

Another digression embedded within a digression occupies 5.67–8 with an account of how Cleisthenes of Athens imitated the method of his grandfather, Cleisthenes of Sicyon (a city in the northern Peloponnese). It is an odd episode because while it is a typical instance of analepsis, marked off by ring composition with the opening sentences of 5.67 and 5.69, the point of this lengthy flashback is not clear other than as an explanatory factor in Cleisthenes' institutional reforms in Athens. As such it is not especially revealing and leaves untouched important questions about the motive and purpose of the constitutional changes brought about by Cleisthenes. The story about Cleisthenes of Sicyon indicates that aristocratic family traditions, the Alcmaeonid in this instance, provided Herodotus with sources of information but he also mentions the dishonourable behaviour of the Alcmaeonids in bribing the Delphic oracle in order to enlist the support of the Spartans in removing the Peisistratids, an incident family tradition would seek to erase from memory. There is also evidence of anti-aristocratic traditions that downplay Cleisthenes' part at the expense of collective action by the people of the city, a tradition which looks instead to an Athenian political consciousness rooted in a broader citizenship, that of the demos.[26]

Cleisthenes' reforms created political machinery that undermines the hegemony previously exercised by aristocratic families in Athens and in doing so he is credited with a pivotal role in the emergence of Greek democracy. Each citizen became a member of a deme, a territorial unit which formed the basis for the tribes which Herodotus refers to in 5.69, and these demes formed the basis of the political and military organization of the polis.

Athens: Cleomenes, Isagoras and Hippias (5.70–96)

These chapters cover an intense period of political activity in Athens, beginning with Isagoras using his guest-friendship (*xenos*) with the Spartan king to help bring about the expulsion of Cleisthenes, his political rival, and the families who supported him (5.70–2). Resistance comes when there is an attempt to dissolve the Council, a body that had been established or modified as part of Cleisthenes' reforms, and this results in a seizure of the Acropolis by Isagoras and his Spartan supporters. When Cleomenes approaches the sanctuary on the Acropolis the priestess tries to bar him from entering, her grounds for exclusion being that he is no Dorian. His claim to be Achaean recalls the Alcmaeonid family genealogy that goes back to the Achaean Heracles[27] but Herodotus' remark about how he 'took no heed to the word of omen' (*kledon*) is bound up with the information provided earlier about Dorieus, the half-brother of Cleomenes, who failed to become the king of Sparta (5.42). There is a play on words – 'unlawful for a Dorian/Dorieus to enter' and 'I am no Dorian/Dorieus' – which echoes the earlier suggestion of kledonomancy when the Perinthians sing a *paeon* and the non-Greek Paeonians take this as a reference to themselves (5.1, see above).

Although the families supporting Cleisthenes are in exile, 'the rest of the Athenians' are of one mind (*ta auta phronēsantes*) in besieging the Acropolis (5.72). Cleomenes is forced to depart and Cleisthenes and the exiled families are recalled to Athens. Fearing Spartan reprisals, envoys are dispatched to form an alliance with Persia but severely censured on their return for submitting to Persian authority (5.73, see below).[28] Herodotus' account of the political tumult in Athens has been variously interpreted, with some reading it as the portrayal of infighting between aristocratic families who are willing to draw Sparta into their internal affairs and one leader, Cleisthenes, successfully promising democratic measures to gain the upper hand. From this point of view, it is aristocrats on the Council who, to threaten Isagoras and his supporters when they retreat to the Acropolis, use 'the rest of the Athenians', people who had previously tolerated tyranny under the Peisistratids and lack a civic consciousness of democracy. From a different perspective, Herodotus is seen to be describing part of a democratic revolution and in 5.72 uses a phrase 'of one mind' to signal a new political consciousness in the polity.[29] It may well be that both points of view are at play in these chapters but ultimately what is important in a reading of the text is Herodotus' concern with the consequences of the change in Athens' form of government. The purpose is not to provide a detailed account of the political manoeuvrings and motives behind the events but to show how 'Athens, which had before been great, grew now yet greater when rid of her despots' (5.66). It is easy to forget that these chapters are providing background material to what is the main subject matter, the Ionian revolt and Aristagoras' need to secure a powerful Greek ally.

What comes across in these chapters is not just the intensity of the political turmoil in Athens resulting from its intra-*polis* class and factional antagonisms but a sense of disaffected Greeks vying with one another and, as a result of inter-*polis* antagonisms, prepared to draw in the Persians. At one point, as noted, the symbolic offering of earth and water is made to the Persian king by an Athenian delegation (5.73) and they will not be the only Greeks willing to involve the eastern superpower.

Cleomenes does plan to avenge his expulsion from Athens and the city faces an array of enemies – Spartans, Boeotians and Chalcidians – but survives the challenges in various military engagements (5.74–7). With a rhetorical flourish, Herodotus confidently links Athens' strength on the field of battle with its democratic form of government; the benefit of *isēgoriē* (equality, freedom of speech) is that it brings out the best in everyone (5.78). Democracy is not being championed as the most ethically laudable system of government but there is an assertion that freedom is better than despotism. Under the rule of autocrats Athens was militarily no better than its neighbours but when citizens were freed 'each one was zealous to achieve for himself'; acting self-interestedly but in unison 'they were far and away the first of all' (5.78).[30] They need the kind of strength that is built on unity because the Boeotians are looking for a way to harm Athens.

Thebes, the chief city in Boeotia, is persuaded by an interpretation of a Delphic oracle to enlist the aid of Aegina, an island off the coast of Attica whose citizens have been on bad terms with Athens for half a century. The complicated account of the origins of this hostility (5.82–7) is an extraordinary and sometimes bewildering piece of narrative about four *poleis* – Athens, Epidaurus, Aegina and Argos – which embroils itself in tales of cult statues and broken promises. Aegina steals the statues from Epidaurus and doesn't give a hoot for the agreement with Athens that entailed making annual religious offerings, though they dutifully worship the statues with sacrifices and special choruses. The religious aspect takes on a supernatural quality when an attempt is made to rope the statues and drag them away: one account has the men go mad and kill each other while in another version the statues miraculously drop to their knees while being hauled away and remain in that position for evermore.[31] For Gould, the narrative is notable for conveying 'so eerily the awesome and uncanny nature of the obligations of the gift' (2001: 298–9), a prime example of the importance attached to ties of obligation arising from the giving of gifts and the dire consequences that can attend a breach in the reciprocity that is expected.[32] For Polinskaya (2010: 66–7), aligning this story with the earlier one about the transference of Orestes' bones (1.66–8), illustrates the criterion of ownership in Greek religious thought and practice: gods are not 'abstract free agents: they were tied to specific locations and specific communities' (61).

The unfortunate end of the sole survivor of the Athenian rescue mission is a notable instance of women acting together, one of the five types of active women identified by Dewald in the *Histories* (2013b: 157–74). A family resemblance is found with misogynous folk tales where demented women attack an innocent man, transformed here to an outbreak of communal grief-induced rage and resulting in an odd 'punishment' that forces females to change their style of dress (5.87).

This delving into the past to explain a long-standing enmity between Aegina and Athens has been interpreted as a digression that offers an insight into the nature of historical change, specifically a shift in agency towards the human and away from the cosmic and the divine. Epidaurus finds a solution to its crisis by erecting statues to Damia and Auxesia – 'divine wrath and resolution' (Haubold 2007: 233) – whereas for the Aeginetans it is human initiative that leads to the stealing of the statues. They do observe religious propriety by setting up a new cult around the statues but it is one with a social structure, ten male leaders (*choregoi*) of choruses of women that lampoon only other women. A similar kind of contrast is traced between the way Athenians attribute the failure of their rescue mission to divine intervention, an otherwise inexplicable outbreak of mass madness and a clap of thunder precipitating it, and the Aeginetans who point to the material support of an Argive force. The contrast gravitates towards a gender distinction: a female chorus under male *choregoi* in Aegina but autonomous female agency in Athens when the sole survivor returns home. Male Athenians find his death 'more dreadful' (*deinoteron*) than the loss of all his companions (5.88) and given that *deinoteron* can also mean 'more powerful' or 'more important' the women's decisive act, described as a 'deed' (*ergon*), becomes a constituent of history in the way the proem declared 'deeds' (*erga*) to be. 'Their "deed" inaugurates a new era, aptly characterized by its protagonists' "new clothes"' (Haubold 2007: 242).

Haubold's interpretation avoids being too programmatic and it succeeds in orchestrating the Aegina–Athens tale from a curious tangential duo into the symphonic sound of Herodotus the historian working intuitively with different modes of historical change.

Fixing a chronology for the origin of the Aegina–Athens enmity is difficult but this does not diminish its explanatory force for the historic nature of bad feeling between the two states. The tales fit a pattern, seen as characteristic of Herodotus, which traces acts of revenge and retaliation as a replacement for the chronological links which are missing from an account of events in the distant past. The 'floating gap' that has been identified in oral traditions is replaced by a set of explanations which do not require chronological exactitude for a community's memory of its past.[33]

The Spartans, alarmed at Athens' growing power, attempt to restore the tyrant Hippias as the autocratic ruler in Athens and call on their allies for assistance (5.91). Opposition to such intervention is expressed in a speech by Socles and wins general approval, leaving Hippias to return to Sigeum, on the Asian coast near Troy, where he lobbies Artaphernes for Persian support (5.92–6). Socles' speech, the longest in the *Histories*,[34] is not what might be expected for an address to an audience of military-minded men considering regime change. The lofty tone and the hyperbolic imagery of his opening remark hardly prepares for the storytelling speech that follows, one that features a smiling baby, a complaining ghost with a riddle, necrophilia, a message-laden walk through a wheat field and the stripping naked of women. Athenian democratic *polis* traditions have been identified as a likely source for a speech that could be seen as a championing of democracy (Forsdyke 2002: 542–5),[35] but the reader is still left wondering about a discursive cocktail that mixes political partisanship and historical references with fairy-tale motifs and mythical elements.[36] Some of the fabulous parts have been met with in earlier stories – the baby saved from death is found in the infancy of Cyrus (1.108), the phrase 'divine chance' (*theiē tuchē*) that occasions the infant's smile (some translations elide the providential nature of this moment) also describes Sylosson's spontaneous gift of his cloak to the young Darius (3.139), and Thrasybulus' talent for secret messaging echoes Histiaeus' use of a tattoo.[37] If the speech is an encomium to democracy and a critique of autocracy, it contrasts with the theoretical analysis of these forms of government in the Constitutional Debate, imbuing the lapidary expression of autocracy's perils in 3.80 with real life examples from Corinthian history.[38] Socles' argument is about deeds not discourse and abjures the conjectural: 'if you had experience of it, as we do, you would be able to offer sager advice that you do now' (5.92). The narrative of events concerning Cypselus and Periander are part of an embroidered storyline about the two tyrants that threads its way through the *Histories*, going back to Book One when the location of Gyges' dedicatory offerings at Delphi is linked to Cypselus (1.14).[39]

The anecdotal element to Socles' address has not held back political readings that attribute to Herodotus a tone of irony by way of a silent juxtaposing of historical moments. The Corinthian speech advocating non-intervention in Athenian affairs (referring to a tyranny that dates back to the mid-seventh century) is set in the last years of the sixth century while Herodotus' audience in the 430s would be well aware of the contemporary state of Corinthian–Athenian hostility. Such foreshadowing, laced with a strong dose of irony, is detected in the words of Hippias in 5.93.[40]

The consequences of Socles' successful speech lead to a turning point in relations between Persia and the Greek world. Hippias persuades Artaphernes to take his side and the refusal of Athens to countenance a return to autocratic rule makes war with Persia inevitable (5.96). At this crucial moment, Aristagoras arrives in Athens to make a case for assisting the Ionians in their revolt.

The Ionian revolt (5.97–126)

The story continues from the point that had been reached some forty chapters earlier (5.55) and it now maintains a more straightforward trajectory through to the end of Book Five.[41]

Aristagoras' arrival in Athens is timely, Athenian–Persian relations having reached a low ebb, and the Assembly votes to dispatch twenty ships to assist the Ionians (5.97). There is apparently little discussion over the matter – no direct speech is provided – and the brevity of Herodotus' account contrasts strongly with the protracted decision-making process when Aristagoras visited Sparta.[42] Two sentences at the end of 5.97 attract attention: the one about it being 'easier to deceive [*diaballein*] many than one' could be a barbed observation on the nature of democracy but could just as likely be taken as a playful remark designed to amuse;[43] there is less uncertainty about the likelihood of the final comment, about the ships being 'the beginning of troubles' (*arkhē kakōn*) for Greeks and barbarians, carrying a Homeric import. In the *Iliad* (5.63) the ships that carried Helen away to Troy are described as *arkhkakoi* for the Trojans, and another 'beginning of trouble' (*kakou ... pelen arkhē*), in anticipation of the death of Patroclus, is noted later in the epic (11.604).[44] The Homeric resonance gives a hugely fateful significance to the Athenians' vote to send ships: by motivating Darius to seek revenge it can be viewed as a starting point for the Persian Wars and, even if there are other factors that help make a Persian invasion inevitable, it marks a decisive moment that puts the coming East–West conflict on a par with the Trojan War.

The opening moves in the Ionian revolt are not propitious: Aristagoras is not acting out of regard for the Paeonians when he instigates their journey home and the accidental engulfing of Sardis in flames leads to a situation which results in the Ionians retreating back to the coast under cover of darkness (5.98–101). The Persians then move against the Ionians and defeat them in battle and while the Athenians are considering their options Darius pledges to punish them for supporting the rebels. Cyprus joins the revolt but Onesilus the leader is killed in battle and the Persians gain the upper hand, not only regaining Cyprus but defeating the Ionians who had sailed there in support. In other battles the Carians, who had also joined the revolt (5.108–20), are defeated. There are further military engagements between Persian forces and those in revolt and Book Five draws to a close with the death of Aristagoras in Thrace (5.121–6), the region of the Greek world where Book Five opened.

Athenian involvement in the Ionian revolt has been of short duration: they send twenty ships, disembarking at Ephesus and joining the Ionian rebels, and contribute to the attack on Sardis before withdrawing back to the coast with the rebels. When the pursuing Persians inflict a defeat on the Ionians at Ephesus the Athenians have a change of heart and sail for home, ignoring the pleas of Aristagoras and leaving the Ionians to fend for themselves (5.102–3). No explanation is offered as to why they abruptly reverse their foreign policy but from Darius' point of view they have done enough to warrant revenge, having joined in the attack on Sardis which resulted in the burning of a temple dedicated to the native goddess Cybele.

Darius, it is reported, on learning that the Ionians had outside help in their attack on Sardis has to inquire as to who these Athenians are, before making a vow of revenge and ordering his servants to repeat to him three times a day, 'Master, remember the Athenians' (5.105). Something similar occurred during the reign of Cyrus when Sparta sent an embassy to the Persian king forbidding him to harm any Greek city since they would not tolerate it; Cyrus has to ask who these Spartans are that dare to issue such a command (1.153). Along the same lines, when Athens had once sent ambassadors to Artaphernes, ruler of Sardis, asking for Persian assistance in their conflict with Sparta, the Persian satrap had to ask who these Athenians were and in what part of the world they lived (5.73). As Garland observes (2017: 15), such a pattern suggests a literary trope 'perhaps intended to indicate ill-judged Persian contempt for the Greeks'; Herodotus' Greek audiences may have enjoyed what they read as self-deprecation.

Book Six: The Ionian revolt – defeat and aftermath

Introduction

Whether the division of the *Histories* into nine books is the work of Herodotus himself or not,[1] the passage from Book Five to Six has a marked continuity while at the same time signalling a notable change in the story of the revolt. Book Five ends with the death of Aristagoras and this is mentioned at the start of the next book before it continues to unfold the course of events in the Ionian revolt. The story of the revolt which began with the Naxos affair (5.28) will not end until well into Book Six (6.32) but whereas Book Five deals with events leading up to the revolt and its outbreak the spotlight now is on the defeat of the Ionians and the consequences for them and the wider Greek world (see Box 1).

Matters touching on the religious, accommodating a variety of narrative moments, constitute a complex topos of their own in Books Five and Six. While oracles are frequently mentioned in the *Histories* and the one directed to the Paeonians at the start of Book Five is not unusual, kneeling statues frozen in time and related phenomena of a supernatural kind are bizarre by comparison (5.82–7).[2] The seriousness with which religious beliefs and practices are generally regarded is not to be doubted yet the accidental burning of the sanctuary of a local goddess in Sardis (5.101–2), with severe consequences for future Persian–Greek relations, comes close to being reduced to a tit-for-tat excuse by the Persians for putting Greek temples to the flame. In other cases, it is not always clear what Herodotus thinks about moments where the narrative register points to another dimension in the order of phenomenal reality: an explanation utilizing idioms of the divine would seem obvious but he often proceeds with caution and reticence in reporting such events. There are a number of incidents in Book Six, attached to the breaking of oaths, ignoring the inviolability of sanctuaries and committing acts of sacrilege by violating divine ground, where Herodotus does not dwell unduly on the impiety of what is done – which would be akin to superfluously describing a camel when Greeks are familiar with its

OUTLINE

6.1–33: Failure of the Ionian revolt

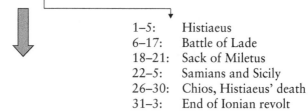

1–5:	Histiaeus
6–17:	Battle of Lade
18–21:	Sack of Miletus
22–5:	Samians and Sicily
26–30:	Chios, Histiaeus' death
31–3:	End of Ionian revolt

6.34–48: After the Ionian revolt

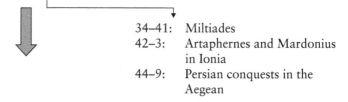

34–41:	Miltiades
42–3:	Artaphernes and Mardonius in Ionia
44–9:	Persian conquests in the Aegean

6.49–93: Sparta, Aegina and Athens

See Box 3

6.95–140: The Marathon campaign

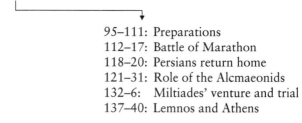

95–111:	Preparations
112–17:	Battle of Marathon
118–20:	Persians return home
121–31:	Role of the Alcmaeonids
132–6:	Miltiades' venture and trial
137–40:	Lemnos and Athens

BOOK 6, BOX 1

appearance (3.103) – because he accepts the common Greek view that infringements of a religious nature will bring forth a divine response of the punitive kind. This is allied to a belief that some transgressive acts provoke the gods into exacting *tisis* (requital), an idea that in the *Histories* first finds hesitant expression with the possibility that Croesus suffers because he believes himself to be blessed (1.34), reinforced later by the assertion that Helen's presence in Egypt throughout the Trojan War was part of a divine plan to punish the Trojans (2.120) and confirmed in the case of Pheretime's horrific death (4.205).[3] Instances of transgressive behaviour that populate Book Six, especially in relation to the swearing of oaths, bear out the punitive role of the gods as a basic cause of reversals in human fortune.

There are some digressions in Book Six, about Samian exiles in Sicily, the island of Chios, the family of Miltiades in the Chersonese, but the reader is soon returned to the story of the failure of the Ionian revolt and its consequences. Overall, there is a tighter grip on the temporal sequence of events and narrative signposts are provided at times: 'The Persian fleet wintered at Miletus and putting out to sea in the next year' (6.31); 'All this had happened three years before ...' (6.40); 'In this year no further deed of enmity was done by the Persians ...' (6.42); 'But at the beginning of spring' (6.43); 'In the next year after this ...' (6.46). A consequence of the Ionian revolt's failure is the expedition mounted by Darius under new command, culminating in the Battle of Marathon, and this is reported in a strict chronological manner.

Failure of the Ionian revolt (6.1–33)

More biographical information is provided about Histiaeus than any other individual in the *Histories* and the first five chapters add to what the reader already knows about the life of this intriguing Greek (see Box 2). Having departed from Susa (5.106), after falsely swearing to the gods of Darius' royal family, he is unnerved by Artaphernes' knowledge of his plotting and escapes from a difficult situation by decamping under cover of darkness. He flees to Chios but thwarted again, this time by the betrayal of Hermippus the messenger to his Persian contacts, he tries returning to Miletus. Having little to show for his time there, other than a wound in his thigh, he moves on to Lesbos from where he sails to Byzantium and becomes a buccaneer. His roles are multifarious – 'tyrant, founder of cities, courtier, King's Adviser, instigator of revolt, potential leader, privateer' (Murray 1988: 486) – but it is only possible to speculate about the nature of an apparently mercurial and guileful character who constantly changes in response to circumstances. What degree of consistency can be attached to his motives is difficult to pin down and Herodotus is likely to be drawing on different sources, some portraying him as a folk tale hero of sorts and others presenting him as untrustworthy and unprincipled. It has been doubted if his conversation with Artaphernes (6.2) ever took place, or that he conducted secret

HISTIAEUS' BIOGRAPHY

4.137–8:   Opposes Miltiades on the Ister bridge and saves Darius
            from being stranded in Scythian territory

5.11:   Rewarded by Darius with permission to found a new
            city, Myrcinus, in Thrace

5.23–4:   Recalled by Darius to Sardis and then Susa

5.35:   Plots revolt in Ionia and sends tattooed message to
            Aristagoras

5.106–7:   Swears an oath and tricks Darius into letting him return
            to Ionia on the pretext of dealing with the revolt

6.1–5:   Hurries from Sardis to Chios, contacts Persian
            dissidents and tries to return to Miletus; travels to
            Lesbos and sails on to Byzantium

6.26–7:   Reacts to fall of Miletus by departing Byzantium and
            conquering Chios

6.28–30:   Returns to Lesbos, is captured by Persians and
            executed by Artaphernes

BOOK 6, BOX 2

discussions with Persian dissidents (6.4), and perhaps there is a plan to help the Ionian rebels when he sails to Byzantium (Cawkwell 2005: 233–6). The Lesbians have provided him with eight triremes and presumably they accompany him in these warships to Byzantium on some understanding that this will support their opposition to the Persians. Histiaeus' intentions remain opaque and the historical inferences that can be drawn from Herodotus' account of his activities are hedged with uncertainty.[4]

While Histiaeus is busy trying to survive, the narrative of the Ionian revolt continues.[5] The Persians are mounting a land-and-sea assault on Miletus and this time the Milesians will not be as successful in resisting as they had once been against the Lydians (1.17–21). They now face an international force from Phoenicia, Cyprus, Cilicia and Egypt and, in the autumn of 494, a decisive naval battle takes place outside their city at the small island of Lade (6.6–17). When the Samians withdraw 119 triremes from the battle, leaving 234 vessels to face a Persian navy of 600, the defeat of Miletus is inevitable. It brings to an end a remarkable period of Greek history centred on an intellectual revolution in Ionia and its domination of trade in the Mediterranean and the Aegean. The defeat of its impressive navies at Lade represents 'the end of the archaic period more definitely than any other political event' (Murray 1988: 490).

Up until now, by linking the causes of the Ionian revolt with the machinations of the tyrants Aristagoras and Histiaeus and greedy Persians like Artaphernes, Herodotus has avoided applying any heroic gloss to his telling of the story. When it comes to relating the preparations for the Battle of Lade, the tone changes: the Ionians are defiant in the face of ultimatums delivered by their erstwhile tyrants (6.10) and Dionysus of Phocaea steps up to announce what is at stake. Borrowing the metaphor used by Nestor to embolden Diomedes against the enemy in the *Iliad* (10.173–6), he addressed the assembled Ionians: 'Our cause stands on the very razor-edge of decision whether we be freemen or slaves' (6.11). Nestor on the field of battle outside Troy issues a summons to act boldly in the face of an imminent and deadly attack – the Trojans are on the verge of driving them into the sea – and for Dionysus the stark choice between freedom or slavery (*eleutheroisiē ē douloisi*), in the full knowledge of what a Persian victory will bring down on them, has an equally existential force. The Homeric allusion may be a rhetorical device on the part of Dionysus but by raising the ideology of freedom he ennobles the Ionian cause; his address harks back to the appeal made by Aristagoras to the Spartan king (5.49), but on this occasion there is no taint of hypocrisy attached to the speaker's words. Dionysus is not an ex-tyrant and, as Histiaeus made plain at the Ister bridge (4.137) and later in conversation with Darius (5.106), the Ionians' desire for freedom is genuine and long-lasting. Their valour in the cause of freedom was on display when first resisting the Persians under Cyrus (1.109) and Aristagoras' ploy of replacing the Ionian tyrannies with democracies (5.37) indicates popular support for autonomy and an egalitarian system of government. Herodotus, though, is not going to eulogize the Ionians at the expense of other truths: they buckle after one week of disciplined battle training (6.12) and after the battle they abuse one another with accusations of cowardice.[6]

The typically convoluted mini-narrative of the Samians in Sicily (6.22–4) is a bleakly political version of guests being invited to a party where they not only trash the place but occupy what is a very attractive residence, expelling the homeowners. It gets worse: called on for assistance, their neighbours turn out to be far from helpful and aid the squatters instead, in return for half of the house contents, before suggesting the homeowners be all killed.[7] The Samians come to Sicily as stalwart upholders of the cause of freedom, which they saw being reneged on by their generals at the Battle of Lade, but arriving on the island they collude with two tyrants and end up treating their Zanclaean hosts in a way that is not too different to the Persian handling of the defeated Milesians. They do spare the lives of the 300 leading citizens of Zancle but this refusal to shed blood is on a par with Darius' treatment of captured Milesians (6.20). The behaviour of the Samians calls into question the sincerity of their initial motive for sailing away from their own island but Herodotus does not comment on this and only concludes the story by remarking how the 'beautiful city' (*polin kallistn*) of Zancle came into their possession without difficulty (6.24). This could be wryly ironic or a sad reflection on the way their honourable motive in leaving Samos was corrupted by the untimely intervention of Anaxilaus, a tyrant who seized an opportunity offered by the Zanclaeans happening to be absent from their city just when the Samians arrived.[8]

Chios fights valiantly but suffers at the Battle of Lade, staying behind after the Samians and Lesbians desert, only to face another misfortune afterwards when Histiaeus conquers the island: 'One can imagine old men on Chios 30-odd years later saying to Herodotus: one disaster, then another . . .' (Scott 2005: 158). Before these events, two accidents occurred – an outbreak of plague and the collapse of a school roof – and these are reported as warnings of an impending disaster: 'It likes to foretell when a great misfortune is about to happen to a city or a people' (6.27).The subject of the verb 'likes' is not given in the Greek but that it is the divine order is shortly confirmed after detailing the two accidents: 'These signs had been shown to them by a god [*hos theos*]'.[9] History is not seen to operate like a pinball machine, moments in time randomly ricocheting off one another, and while Herodotus is well aware that many religious practices are a matter of custom (*nomos*) and relative to the society observing them but he wants to express his sense of there being traceable patterns in the way events unfold; the vocabulary of the divine is a way of satisfying the hermeneutic temptation, the need for cognitive mapping of a metaphysical matrix beneath the level of mere doxa.

After bringing the biography of Histiaeus to a close (6.28–30) there are chapters on the mopping-up operations by the military forces of Persia; the definitive end of the revolt comes with the statement that the Ionians had now been reduced to slavery for the third time (6.33), referring to their conquest first by Croesus and then by Cyrus after his defeat of Lydia.[10] The mention of the Chersonese (the Gallipoli peninsula) as one of the regions being subdued initiates a short digression which brings Miltiades, the Athenian who counselled against the Persians at the Ister bridge (4.137), back into the picture.

After the Ionian revolt (6.34–48)

The folkloristic element in the tales favourable to the older Miltiades (6.34–7) suggests family traditions as the source, but these traditions are unlikely to account for what is relayed about his descendant with the same name. It is possible there was a dispute over the tyranny passing to the younger Miltiades after the death of his brother Stesagoras who became tyrant after the demise of their uncle. The storyline's vector wobbles a little with the flashback to earlier trouble with the Scythians (6.40) but quickly resumes its course and, returning to the chronological framework, Darius' generosity to the captured son of the younger Miltiades is recounted (6.41). This incident recalls earlier instances of the king's grace: his treatment of the embalmed head of Histiaeus (6.30) and his conduct towards the captured Milesians (6.20). Any such mercifulness is absent from the handling of Ionian citizens by Persian commanders who are seen following oriental practices by having boys castrated and girls made concubines (6.32). At the same time, ameliorative political and economic measures are introduced (6.42).

The following spring brings the appointment of Mardonius, the son of one of the original seven conspirators (3.70), as Darius' commander. The establishment of democracies in Ionia that follows is pointedly used to refer for the second time to the Constitutional Debate and its promotion of democracy. On the first occasion Herodotus acknowledges that many will find it fanciful that such a debate could have occurred but he insists it did (3.80). Now, in dialogue with his Greek audience about the likelihood of Persians ever discussing democracy, he supports his assertion with what he regards as firm evidence: after the revolt Mardonius deposes Ionian tyrannies and replaces them with democracies and, therefore, democracy could indeed have been entertained thirty years earlier by Persians (6.43). This kind of argument, described by Luraghi as using an 'analogy' rather than reaching for sources to defend the authenticity of a position (2001:142–3), has been seen as illustrative of a major difference between Herodotus and modern historians. There is an analogy of sorts being drawn – before the revolt democracy was a theoretical possibility just as afterwards it becomes a practicality that is implemented – but perhaps not so much as a knockdown argument and more as a demonstration of how the Persians can prove surprising.

The main purpose of Mardonius' expedition is military, not just the subjection of Athens and Eretria for their role in the revolt and the burning of a sanctuary in Sardis but also to take 'as many of the Greek cities as they could' (6.44). The Ionian revolt has been completely crushed but if, as seems likely, Darius has always harboured a plan for the westward expansion of his empire – going back to the reconnaissance mission of Democedes (3.135) – Ionian resistance to his rule has delayed his imperial ambitions for over five years. The European Greek cities now have to decide whether they accept Persian suzerainty or join together, fight the assaultive power of a common enemy and plan for a better outcome than that which befell the Ionians.

Sparta, Aegina and Athens (6.49–94)

Aegina's willingness to submit to Persia causes consternation in Athens, due to the proximity of the island and its long-standing enmity towards Athens (5.83–9), and an appeal is sent to Sparta for Panhellenic assistance. This is the cue for a digression on the dysfunctional state of the present Spartan kingship via its genealogy, ethnicity and some ethnographic aspects of the people (see Box 3).

SPARTA, AEGINA AND ATHENS (6.49–93)

6:49: Athens turns to Sparta for support against Aegina

6.50–65: Cleomenes and Demaratus

6.56–60: Sparta: ethnography

6.61–72: Cleomenes deposes Demaratus

6.73–84: Cleomenes' enmity with Aegina and his death

6.85–6: Leotychides in Athens and story of Glaucus

6.87–93: Athens–Aegina enmity

BOOK 6, BOX 3

Herodotus is no Greek chauvinist and that he seeks to interrogate the nature of Hellenic identity is implicit in what he says on the subject of Spartan ethnicity. It emerges from tracing the mixed lineage of the two royal houses of Sparta, though this involves the reader making connections between what is said in Book Six and information from earlier parts of the *Histories*. The basic ethnic difference between Dorians and Ionians (referring to a people not the geographical region, Ionia) is set out when the non-Greek-speaking Pelasgians, ancestors of the (Ionian) Athenians, are first mentioned in Book One (1.56–8). The equivalent role of a barbarian ingredient in the Dorian genetic make-up is the Spartan descent from Perseus, the great-grandfather of Heracles.[11] Perseus is regarded by the Egyptians as one of their own (2.91) and Herodotus now endorses this claim (6.53). Perseus is Achaean – thus allowing Cleomenes to claim he is not Dorian when seizing the Acropolis (5.72) – and his granddaughter, Alcmene, is the mother of Heracles.

The Spartans themselves trace their presence in the Peloponnese to Arisodemus who marries Argeia and whose twin sons, Eurystheus and Procles, form their two royal houses. The brother of Argeia is Theras whose story is told in the account of Cyrene, and these two are descended from the royal line of Thebes, whose founder was the Phoenician Cadmus (4.147). Mixing the ethnic pot still further, Herodotus adds the Persians' assertion that Perseus was an Assyrian (6.53–4); all part of what comes across as a highly polemical stance on the ethnic origins of the Spartans and genealogies involving Heracles, Perseus, Phoenicians, Dorians and Achaeans.[12] Amidst the complexity it is noteworthy that in referring to the Dorian king lists Herodotus makes a methodological point when he explains that he will stop at Perseus (said to be the son of Zeus) because, unlike Heracles, he has no known mortal father.[13]

The folk tale about the twin sons and the origins of the feud-prone dual kingship (6.52) is part of a digression into Spartan affairs that reads in places like one of the ethnographic surveys that populate earlier books of the *Histories*. Such surveys characteristically include material on funeral practices, and the conduct of Spartans when one of their kings die is described as if a barbarian tribe inhabited the Greek state; similarities with Persian and Egyptian customs are explicitly recorded (5.58–60).

At 6.61 the narrative returns to the feuding between Cleomenes and Demaratus that was raised at 6.51 and although the quarrelling is probably related to the political question of how Sparta will respond to the Persian threat it is played out through a complex family drama. It begins with a background story about the infancy of the wife of Ariston's friend and introduces the possibility of the semi-divine Helen manifesting herself and ensuring a baby grows up to become the most beautiful woman in Sparta.[14] The encounter between the nurse and an unknown stranger is reported in a tone of neutral respect, clearly pointing to something occult, but the non-committal attitude is carefully maintained and suggests a lack of firm belief by Herodotus in a tale of a miraculous intervention. At the same time, he likes a good story that will interest his audience and it is included perhaps for this reason. Ariston achieves his wish to obtain a third wife (6.62) by means of what is described as a 'trick' but it only becomes one because oath-taking is taken so seriously; his friend feels he has no choice – he is 'compelled' (*anagkazomenos*) by his oath to hand over whatever possession of his is requested.[15] In an earlier story, Democedes asks the wife of Darius for a similarly open-ended oath but he is careful to offer an assurance that he will not ask for anything that might compromise her (3.133). Demaratus makes no such promise to his friend and is free to exploit the situation in an unfair but not impermissible way. Oaths are crucial in the execution and aftermath of Cleomenes' stratagem for removing the man who shares the kingship with him. This strategy relies on his kinsman Leotychides declaring under oath that Demaratus has no right to reign in Sparta and producing witnesses who heard Demaratus himself state his own negative oath that the son born to his third wife could not be his own. Given the seriousness of the dispute, the oracle at Delphi is consulted and this leads to Cleomenes' interference in priestly matters.

Some forty oaths are recorded in the *Histories* and they have been divided into three types: those relating to ethnic customs, to treaties between states and thirdly, like those here, oaths sworn by individuals in 'crises of credibility' (Lateiner 2012: 158).[16] Some of those belonging to this third category, like Histiaeus' oath to Darius 'by the gods of your kingship' (5.106), are blatantly ignored while in the case of Ariston a conscious act of deception is at work. No judgement is expressed in either of these cases: perhaps Histiaeus' behaviour is seen as excusable on the grounds that the gods are Persian and not Greek and that this neutralizes his obligation while, in the second case, Ariston is dishonest but not culpable for using the unconditionality of an oath's obligation to obtain what he wants. His duplicity is allowable in so far as the terms of the oath are not broken and a parallel is found in the conduct of the Persian commander Amasis when he swore to uphold an oath with the Barcaeans 'as long as the ground beneath our feet stands firm' (4.201). Having made the oath on planks of wood that covered a wide trench – a situation known to him but not to the other party – they could be later dismantled and thus allow him to ignore what had been promised without breaking the terms on which the treaty was agreed. Herodotus likes to recount tall stories bearing on the wily behaviour of individuals and when it involves playing with sworn oaths a dash of piquancy is added to tales of their ingenuity.[17]

After Demaratus is forced from office, his story has an unsettling sequel when he is mocked at a festival by the vengeful man who has taken his place as king and he leaves for home in shame after covering his head with a cloth, a telling non-verbal gesture. The sanctity of what follows is underlined by his sacrifice of an ox to Zeus and the enforcement of his mother's participation by placing the entrails in her hands and asking her to solemnly confirm his paternal origins. His uncertainty and suspicion find poignant expression in a first-person plea for the truth but his mother's admission that she herself cannot be sure who the father is cannot assuage his anguish and he chooses to become an exile. His difficulties continue and a man who was once an athletic hero in Sparta only finds refuge as a guest of the Persian king (6.70).[18] The man who deposed him will fare little better and he too will end his days as an exile, banished for bribery and his house will be razed to the ground (6.71–2). Herodotus provides this glimpse into the future before returning to the eventful life of Cleomenes. He binds Arcadians to oaths of unconditional support, wishing to have some of the leading citizens swear by the Styx, the river of Hades, where it flows above the ground in the city of Nonacris in the Peloponnese. Although he returns to Sparta, a descent into madness quickly follows and he suffers a gruesome death (6.75). In his madness, Cleomenes has been described as 'a sort of mirror-image of the Persian Cambyses' and an Oriental quality has been discerned in the court stories of Leotychides and Demaratus (Pelling 2013: 365). This is seen as part of the positioning of Sparta as anomalous, a cultural oddity – hence the ethnographic approach noted above – and a political one as well given that kingships were anachronistic in most of fifth-century Greece.

Different possible explanations for the madness that seizes Cleomenes are provided, all but one of them identifying it as a punishment from the divine (6.75–84). Herodotus says the majority of Greeks trace the king's insanity to his bribery of the Pythian priestess, described in 6.66, but that Athenians connect it with his destruction of a sacred grove when he invaded Eleusis (a campaign described in 5.74–5 but with no mention there of the grove). The Argives have their own explanation, involving the execution by Cleomenes of some of their men and the burning down of their sacred grove, while the Spartans themselves attribute his madness to his drinking of undiluted wine. Herodotus gives his own opinion, regarding the Spartan king's fate as a punishment for his treatment of Demaratus. The chapters dealing with Cleomenes' impious behaviour also cover his misreading of an oracle that predicted he would conquer Argos – his 'conquering' only amounts to the burning of the grove of Argos – and they lead into a curious consequence of his death when ambassadors from Aegina turn up in Sparta.

The Aeginetans want the return of their citizens who were taken to Athens as hostages by Cleomenes and Leotychides, something mentioned in 6.73, but when they go to Athens with Leotychides to reclaim them the Athenians are not willing to hand them over. What follows is a peculiar anecdote, told by the Spartan king as a parable, about a man called Glaucus who is trusted with money but reneges on his agreement to return it. He consults the oracle at Delphi, asking whether he could commit perjury by swearing on oath that he had never received the money and then keep it for himself.[19] He receives an intimidating warning about the 'child of Oath', a frightening creature without a name, hands or feet who will relentlessly pursue the oath-breaker and exterminate his entire family. Such a spectre has an ancient pedigree – he is rendered here with particular force as an avenging power to be avoided at all costs[20] – and is adamantly unmoved by Glaucus' immediate change of heart and plea of forgiveness for even asking the question of the oracle. The money is returned but the offence stands as a sort of thought crime and the terrifying price has to be paid by the wrongdoer: 'There is at this day no descendant of Glaucus, nor any household that bears Glaucus' name.' It is as if he never existed. Yet the singularity of the story's menacing tone is matched only by its inability in persuading the Athenians to release the Aeginetan hostages. Athens is not minded to help a neighbouring state with whom relations have been strained for a long time and, having made no oath to Aegina regarding the return of the hostages, is able to use the excuse that its deal was made with two Spartan kings and cannot be unmade with just one of them.

The outcome of Leotychides' presentation, the collapse of its performative power, is not the only unusual aspect of this incident. There is impropriety in Leotychides saying anything about the sanctity of oaths given his dubious role in Cleomenes' stratagem for removing Demaratus from the kingship. He swears under oath that Demaratus is not the son of Ariston for two selfish reasons: he will be made king in his place and he is disgruntled with the man who managed to marry the woman he had intended to make his wife (6.65). There is also the irony of having Leotychides quote the Pythia at Delphi to support his case when he himself owes his position as king to Cleomenes having previously corrupted a Pythia (6.66). A political purpose has been detected in Leotychides' storytelling speech, seeing it not just as an address to Athens – advising them not to prevaricate with excuses when asked to return what is not theirs to keep – but also a criticism of Aegina for trying to have it both ways, first by being willing to accept Leotychides from Sparta in exchange for the hostages (6.85) and then happily making him their ally in Athens.[21] There may be at some level a political message in the speech, the second of only two speeches in Herodotus that functions as a narrative (the other one is Socles' in 5.92),[22] but it possesses a strange mix of ingredients – the macabre, the ironic, the medley of motives – that leaves the reader puzzled and curious.[23]

The long-standing enmity between Athens and Aegina (5.80–1, 89–90), the undercurrent in Leotychides' enforced mission to Athens, breaks out into violence in the chapters that follow his speech about Glaucus. The eventual fate of the hostages held in Athens is never mentioned but the Aeginetan assault on the delegates to the festival at Sunium and the events that follow (6.87–93) are presumably a consequence of the Athenians' refusal to release the hostages. When a prisoner being led to execution on Aegina escapes and claims sanctuary by taking hold of one of the door handles in the porch of a temple, his hands are sacrilegiously chopped off before he is dragged away. This brings pollution (*agos*) to those who committed the deed and expiation is only possible by expelling them from the island.

The Marathon campaign (6.94–140)

The main narrative resumes with a series of reminders: Darius' desire for revenge (5.105), the pro-Persian Hippias, son of Peisistratus (5.96), and the failure of Mardonius' expedition at Athos (6.45). New commanders are appointed and the second expeditionary force to Greece takes a different route, stopping first at the island of Naxos and then Delos, before landing on the mainland at Marathon. As with the Ionian revolt, the course of the Marathon campaign is well covered by historians of the ancient world and the present emphasis is more on aspects of Herodotus' account than the historical events themselves.[24]

The inauspiciousness of the earthquake occurring on Delos shortly after the Persian expedition sets sail is unmistakeable: there is first the pivotal geographical location of the island, a maritime crossing point in the middle of the Aegean between Asia and Europe[25] and second the uniqueness of the event, personally emphasized by Herodotus and endorsed by an oracular utterance. The earthquake is seen as a portent (6.98), the shaking of the island 'stands by synecdoche for the shaking of the Greek world' (Thomas 2016: 41), like the 'great signs' (sēmēia megala) that came to the Chians before their disasters (6.27). Thucydides will refer to Delos' earth tremor and its uniqueness (2.8) as a putative sign of divine origin but only in the context of the Peloponnesian War; for Herodotus its semiotic significance is broader, encompassing the Persian Wars and the internecine warfare of Greek states, and has a temporal weighting: more misfortunes befalling Greece in the three generations covered by Darius, his son Xerxes and his grandson Artaxerxes than in the twenty generations before the three-king period.

The Persians land at Marathon, guided by Hippias the son of Peisistratus, and one of the ten generals commanding the forces waiting for them is Miltiades. When the history of his family, the Philaids, was first provided (6.34–41) Herodotus promised he would explain later how Miltiades' father, Cimon, died (6.39). The promise is now fulfilled (6.103) and by showing how he was murdered by the Peisistratids the antagonism between the two families is seen to be acting itself out on a geopolitical platform that subsumes the personal as part of a larger public conflict. Miltiades is credited with persuading Callimachus to cast his decisive vote in favour of engaging the enemy at Marathon and he does so by evoking a stark choice between slavery and freedom and emphasizing the existential nature of what is at stake, just as Dionysus of Phocaea did before the Battle of Lade (6.11). He also holds out a prospect of fame and glory to Callimachus as the man who saves his city. Significance has been attached to another aspect of Miltiades' language, the way he claims that if Athens is successful in protecting its freedom it could become the 'first of Greek cities' (6.109). When Herodotus reflected on how isēgoriē brought benefits to Athens (see p. 168), he did so in terms of military supremacy and pointed out how once the rule of tyrants was removed Athenians became 'the first of all'. In both cases, it is argued, freedom for Athens is linked with an increase in military power and the ability to assert itself over other cities (Baragwanath 2008: 196–7).

That the coming battle is going to be momentous is underlined by the epiphanic encounter between the long-distance runner Philippides and the god Pan. Hornblower (2002: 381) reads the meeting as an example of Herodotus' tendency to use indirect speech when a particular divinity is said to play a role in an historical event, part of his general reticence when dealing with religious matters. The experience Philippides has on the road to Sparta is described using his own words, and Herodotus remarks how it becomes a 'story the Athenians believed to be true' (6.105). It is not reported how Pan fulfilled his promise to help the Athenians, which may also be a reflection of Herodotus' reserve on such matters, so the reader is left wondering if he did so by spreading panic (*panikos*) among the Persians on the field of battle.[26]

A discussion of the specific historical issues arising in Herodotus' account of the Battle of Marathon is found in Scott (2005: 597–629): the Athenian response to the imminent Persian landing (6.103), the Spartan delay in assisting Athens (6.106), the role of Hippias (6.107), the disposition of Athenian and Persian forces and the battle itself (6.111–13), and events after the battle (6.115–16).[27]

The Battle of Marathon took place within living memory for older contemporaries of Herodotus and he would have heard informal tales of the engagement from local communities, anecdotes that were already gathering a patina of the strange and wonderful. One example, referred to as a *thōma* (wonder), is the story of Epizelus and the apparition which in the midst of the battle rendered him blind, a huge armed figure whose beard cast a shadow over his shield and who passed him by but killed the man at his side. Herodotus does not claim to have witnessed a first-hand account by Epizelus but he does say, twice, that he has heard about the Athenian soldier relating his experience: 'I heard that he told the tale ... Such was the tale Epizelus told, as I heard' (6.117). What is conveyed is an authentic sense of Herodotus listening to local, bona fide sources of information and reporting what he hears without recourse to embellishment.

After the land battle at Marathon, on the east coast of the peninsula of Attica, the Persian fleet sails around the peninsula's southern tip, Sunium, in the expectation of landing on the west coast and seizing Athens before their enemy has time to return home on land. The rumour is reported that the Alcmaeonids were a fifth column and that using a shield they flashed a message to the Persian fleet as it sailed around Sunium (6.115). An accusation of treason against a notable aristocratic Athenian family like the Alcmaeonids is a controversial matter but Herodotus says no more on the topic at this stage and his narrative continues with other material. The Persian fleet does not land, sailing for home instead, but this is followed by a time switch back to the battle itself and the blinding of Epizelus, then forward to post-battle incidents (Datis returning a stolen statue to Delos and the treatment of the captured Eretrians back in Susa) before returning to a moment before the battle (the dispatch of a message to Sparta and their late arrival in Athens). Five chapters are occupied with these concerns (6.116–20) before the allegation of Alcmaeonid collusion with Persia is taken up again with a personal declaration by the narrator dismissing any such possibility of treason. What follows is a robust apologia for the family and its anti-tyrant credentials before the text changes tone and delves into a not always commendable history of the Alcmaeonids (6.121–31).

Herodotus' treatment of the Alcmaeonids has attracted critical attention from historians seeking to pin down his position and the lack of agreement among them is related to an interesting literary observation. To begin with, there is a narrative delay between the first mention of the family's traitorous behaviour and a response to the accusation five chapters later. Baragwanath turns to Iser's reader-response theory,[28] noting how the reader's attention is first engaged by bringing up the contentious allegation but then held in suspense until the topic is resumed with a vigorous rebuttal of the charge. The narrative voice in 6.21, which sturdily rejects as an incredible wonder (*thoma*) any likelihood of an Alcmaeonid conspiracy, is seen as an ironic projection by Herodotus, a virtual author who should not be mistaken for the author of the *Histories*. The virtual author is akin to the unreliable storyteller found in nineteenth-century fiction – the paradigm is Nelly Dean in *Wuthering Heights* – a persona adopted by the supreme narrator in order to provoke and steer readers into an engagement with the text.[29] The necessary background for appreciating this approach to the presentation of the Alcmaeonids is to be found by putting together the jigsaw of information on the family that is scattered across the *Histories* (see Box 4). What takes shape when this information is put together is a disjunction between, on the one hand, an explicit defence of the Alcmaeonids and, on the other, a family chronicle that is so far from creditable as to introduce ambiguity into any overall judgement of the Alcmaeonids. It does not amount to a paradox but the tenor of some of the stories from family history, when allied to particular historical circumstances, does create a space for wondering if the stalwart defender of 6.121–3 and the author are one and the same.

The problem of interpretation arises from the broad and the particular contexts that question the sound assertion that the Alcmaeonids are 'tyrant-haters' (*misoturannoi*), exiled for their opposition to the Peisistratids and to be applauded for their meritorious role in eventually freeing Athens (6.121–2). Herodotus has already pointed to the concordat between an Alcmaeonid and the Peisistratid tyrants (1.59–60), as well as family ties with the tyrant Cleisthenes of Sicyon (5.66–9). Then there is the possibility, though never more than this, that Cleisthenes the Athenian might have been involved in an approach to the Persians (5.72–3) and the fact that at one stage he had bribed a Pythia at Delphi to doctor the oracle's advice (5.63–5). It is hardly an unblemished record, even if the burden of the Accursed (5.71) is lifted

THE ALCMAEONIDS

5.71: An Alcmaeonid murders an Athenian, Cyclon, who had taken refuge in a sanctuary on the Acropolis, and the family becomes known as the Accursed (mid-seventh century).

6.125: An Alcmaeonid, Alcmeon, is rewarded by Croesus with great wealth (first half of sixth century).

1.59–60: Megacles, son of Alcmeon, first opposes the Athenian tyrant Peisistratus but then joins forces to help restore his rule on condition that the tyrant marries his daughter (sixth century).

6.126–30: Cleisthenes, wealthy tyrant of Sicyon, arranges his daughter's wedding to Megacles (marrying for the second time) and their son is named Cleisthenes (sixth century).

1.61: Peisistratus avoids having procreative sex with his Alcmaeonid wife because of the family curse and falls out with Megacles (sixth century).

5.62: The Alcmaeonids, banished by the Peisistratids, conspire to depose Hippias, son of Peisistratus, as tyrant of Athens (late sixth century).

5.63–5: Cleisthenes the Athenian bribes the priestess at Delphi to facilitate the deposing of Hippias by enlisting the aid of Sparta (late sixth century).

5.66–9: Cleisthenes introduces political reforms in Athens, inspired in part by his grandfather, Cleisthenes, tyrant of Sicyon (late sixth century).

5.72–3: Cleisthenes' political enemies have the support of Sparta and, to counteract this, an approach is made to the Persians – the implication being that Cleisthenes supported this contact with Persia (end of sixth century).

6.115: The Alcmaeonids are suspected of passing a secret message to the Persian fleet after the Battle of Marathon (early fifth century).

6.136: Miltiades, the victor of Marathon, is prosecuted by Xanthippus who is married to a niece of Cleisthenes (early fifth century).

6. 131: The son of Xanthippus and his wife is Pericles (early fifth century).

BOOK 6, BOX 4

from the family's shoulders on the grounds that it happened a very long time ago,[30] and for a brief moment the possibility that the family are quislings is seriously entertained before being formally dismissed for the last time (6.124).

The ambience of the two stories that follow, relating to the early history of the Alcmaeonids, however, manages to reintroduce uncertainty about the family's good name. Alcmeon's greed-fuelled antics in the treasury of a Lydian king, stuffing purposefully baggy trousers and oversized boots with gold, showering his hair with gold dust and cramming his mouth with the precious element, is amusing and unedifying in equal measure (6.125). The next generation of the family sees the son of Alcmeon, Megacles, being gifted a lucrative marriage opportunity and the patronage of a wealthy tyrant but only because he lacks the chutzpah and cavalier wit of the suitor Hippocleides (6.126–30). The lion dream of Pericles' mother carries its own ambivalence for, while it seems to be complimentary, the lion is also an emblem of royal, autocratic power and this allows for irony in the telling of the dream.

Baragwanath's use of Iser's reader-response theory is an attempt to deal with a perceived inconsistency in Herodotus' treatment of the Alcmaeonids in the *Histories* as a whole. She posits the voice of 6.121–3 as being like the unreliable narrator in nineteenth-century novels because it allows for Herodotus to be seen as being in strategic control of his material, challenging readers to question their own judgements. At the other end of the interpretive pole, Herodotus may be read as sincere in his defence in 6.121–3 before he cheerfully changes tack by adopting a different discourse in 6.125–30, one marked by folk humour and burlesque. Coming at these chapters from this point of view, Munson concludes that Herodotus 'dances away ... the question of what the truth is in the old controversy of the shield at Marathon' (2001a: 259–65).[31]

Miltiades, the victor of Marathon, is put on trial for the failure of a get-rich-scheme he proposed to the Athenians and the account of this entrepreneurial venture, an expedition to Paros, segues into another historical topic. This other topic is the expulsion of the Pelasgians from Lemnos, which is brought up by way of Miltiades' defenders referring to his earlier conquest of Lemnos as proof of his public services to Athens. All this is the subject matter of the concluding chapters of Book Six (6.132–40) and they cover a dense and fascinating multitude of themes, ranging from issues of ethnicity to attitudes to Athens, land ownership, the objectivization of women and the role of curses and oracles.

With the two conflicting accounts of why Athens expelled the Pelasgians from Attica, the ethnic status of these elusive people is once more raised. The Pelasgians are first mentioned in 1.57 as pre-Greek inhabitants of Attica from whom the Athenians are apparently descended and they are again mentioned in 2.52 as the people in Greece who learn the names of the gods from Egypt. The Pelasgians exiled to Lemnos, however, would appear to be ethnically distinct from the Athenians who expel them from Attica with no qualms, either because they unjustly want their land, as Hecataeus is referenced as saying, or because they are justly responding to Pelasgian sexual assaults and a plot to attack Athens (6.137).[32] Throughout the *Histories*, the Pelasgians never get to appear in their own right or speak for themselves and this is again the case when their expulsion from Lemnos is being discussed. Miscegenation and hybridization lurk in the background but is never made explicit: 'it seems that in the case of the Pelasgians he [Herodotus] wished to emphasize a breach of memory – or, in other words, that for some reason he was not willing to admit that the Pelasgians of his own day were true descendants of the ancient Pelasgian' (Luraghi 2001: 159–60).[33]

Herodotus says he will not adjudicate on the motivation behind the expulsion, claiming he can only report what he has been told, but Athenian probity has been put under a spotlight when Miltiades promises Athens great riches if they would supply him with ships and they agree with alacrity (6.132). He is put on trial for deception (but court proceedings seem unlikely if he had returned with the promised riches) and, in keeping with the pecuniary nature of the story, he is punished with a huge fine.[34] He escapes the death penalty, it would seem, because his defenders were able to point to his earlier conquest of Lemnos, a material benefit to Athens that in a way compensates for his failure to enrich Athens by seizing Paros (6.136). Athenian avarice was displayed earlier when Delphi had told the Pelasgians they could only make amends for their wrongdoing by submitting to Athenian wishes, resulting in a demand for ownership of the island and its material resources (6.139).[35]

Women become more than pawns in a male conflict when the group who are kidnapped and forced to conceive on Lemnos bring up their children with fidelity to their Athenian identity (6.138). This act of cultural resistance recalls the Carian women who, finding themselves in a similar position, determined to pass on to their children a refusal to share meals with their husbands or call them by name (1.146). The Ionian husbands of the Carian women manage to live with this but the men of Lemnos, seized with fear for the possible consequences of the female insubordination they face, conduct a savage act of mass murder. This in turn brings about a response from the divine, with Lemnos and its women becoming barren, a curse which is only lifted when they turn in desperation to the oracle at Delphi. Book Six ends with a narrative return to Miltiades and his capture of Lemnos for Athens and on one level this wraps up the preceding material and prepares the ground for the ongoing and paramount *logos* of Persian expansionism and the fate of Greece. At another, more metaphysical level the curse of sterility that afflicts Lemnos is the last of the many occasions in Book Six where a sense of an order higher than the human has made itself felt. Usually, as in this instance, it arises from transgressive behaviour and the consequences of impiety that point to a divine, regulative force at work in the universe (see Box 5).

IMPIETIES, EPIPHANIES, CURSES AND DIVINE MESSAGES

6.19:   Oracle foretelling the fate of Miletus

6.27:   Signs for the Chians of impending disasters

6.34:   Oracle for the Dolonai to receive as a colonist the first man to offer them hospitality after leaving Delphi

6.61:   Possible manifestation of the semi-divine Helen of Troy

6.75:   Three impieties of Cleomenes

6.78:   Unfavourable omen deters Cleomenes from crossing River Strymon

6.82:   Cleomenes claims omens tell him Argos will not be captured

6.86:   Oracle rebukes Glaucus for breaking an oath and foretells destruction for the family of perjurers

6.91:   Gross impiety by wealthy Aeginetans and a curse which they can never expiate

6.96:   Datis burns temples on Naxos and (6.101) Eretria

6.98:   Earthquake on Delos a likely warning from the divine of impending misfortunes

6.105:   Pan appears to Philippides

6.118:   Datis has a dream which leads to discovery of statue stolen from Delos

6.134:   Miltiades on Paros violates sanctuary and suffers a wound (from which he dies)

6.139:   Curse of sterility on Lemnos for murder of Athenian women and their children

BOOK 6, BOX 5

Book Seven: The road to Thermopylae

Introduction

The story of events that lead to Thermopylae begins formally when the first chapter of Book Seven states Darius' resolve to mount a full-scale, land and sea military expedition with the objective of conquering Greece. The possibility of such an endeavour can be traced back to an earlier period in the king's reign when, as a consequence of his and his wife's indebtedness to the Greek doctor Democedes, a reconnaissance mission to the country was set in motion as a preparatory step in Greece's conquest (see Box 2). That mission came to nothing but notice had been served that the European continent was in the sights of Persia's expansionist ambitions. The invasion of Scythia became the first Persian incursion into Europe and, though not related, the assistance given by Athens and Eretria to the Ionian revolt provided a pretext for a second acquisitive move westwards, this time an attack on Greece. It was rebuffed on the plain of Marathon but is now renewed by Darius with redoubled vigour and determination as a consequence of that setback.[1]

There is no single cause for the war between Persia and Greece but the advance of Persian power, its impulse to exert dominion over other states and extend its hegemony has been an overarching theme in the *Histories*. It might be better to call it an undertow given how, until Book Six, the textual surface has been mostly filled by Herodotus' interest in describing the cultures of those countries that have succumbed to or being threatened by Persian military might. What has often been put into the background is the nature and intentions of the superpower that, with occasional stumbling blocks mounted by the Ethiopians, the Massagetae and Scythians, is steadily increasing its material resources and political influence to a level unmatched by any previous empire (see Box 3). Greece remains to be conquered and as there is no need to provide an ethnographic survey – Sparta being an exception (6.56–60) – the narrative remains focused on the developing East–West showdown. The spatial meanderings that were a concomitant of the earlier ethnographic forays come to an end as the geography, under a

OUTLINE

7.1–19: Debates and dreams

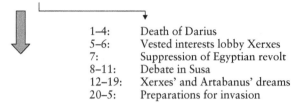

1–4:	Death of Darius
5–6:	Vested interests lobby Xerxes
7:	Suppression of Egyptian revolt
8–11:	Debate in Susa
12–19:	Xerxes' and Artabanus' dreams
20–5:	Preparations for invasion

7.26–56: Reaching and crossing the Hellespont

See Box 4

7.57–131: Hellespont to Thermopylae by land

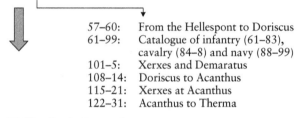

57–60:	From the Hellespont to Doriscus
61–99:	Catalogue of infantry (61–83), cavalry (84–8) and navy (88–99)
101–5:	Xerxes and Demaratus
108–14:	Doriscus to Acanthus
115–21:	Xerxes at Acanthus
122–31:	Acanthus to Therma

7.132–77: The Greeks Respond

133–7:	Sparta and the Persian heralds
139–44:	Athens and the oracles
145–52:	Spies in Asia; embassy to Argos
153–6:	Background to Gelon of Sicily
157–71:	Embassies to Gelon (153–67), Corcyrea (168) and Crete (169–71)
172–7:	Political and military manoeuvres in Thessaly

7.178– 239: Thermopylae

178–95:	Persian navy and storm
196–201:	Persian army takes up its position for battle
202–9:	Greek forces
210–33:	Battle of Thermopylae
234–7:	Xerxes' post-battle strategy
238–9:	Mistreatment of Leonidas' corpse and Demaratus' secret letter

BOOK 7, BOX 1

THE ROAD TO THERMOPYLAE

3.134–7: Darius, persuaded by Atossa to conquer Greece, orders a spying mission which proves unsuccessful when Democedes, whose machinations were behind Atossa's entreaties, escapes.

3.139–41: Starting as a personal favour to Syloson, the Greek island of Samos is attacked and conquered by Darius.

4.83–9: A bridge is built across the Bosporus and Darius crosses into Europe on a military campaign to conquer Scythia.

5.12–14: The ploy of two Paeonians to become tyrants results in the forced transportation of most of their people to Asia.

5.97: Aristagoras wins over the Athenians with talk of Asia's wealth and the ease of conquest.

5.101–2: Athenian and Eretrian forces sack the non-Greek city of Sardis and burn a sanctuary there in the course of supporting the Ionian revolt against Persia. Darius vows vengeance (5.105).

6.33: The Chersonese, the European side of the Hellespont, is conquered by Persia's Phoenician fleet after the failure of the Ionian revolt.

6.43–9: Persian forces under Mardonius cross the Hellespont and demand submission from Greek states. Aegina is one of those that acquiesce.

6.94: Darius plans an expeditionary force against Athens and Eretria.

7.1: Darius determines a full-scale invasion of Greece.

BOOK 7, BOX 2

teleological imperative, unfalteringly follows the course of Persian land and sea forces as they make their way towards northern Greece.

A foretaste of what is to come has been provided in the lead-up to and description of the Battle of Marathon but that encounter was not decisive and Greece remains more threatened that ever in the face of Darius' determination

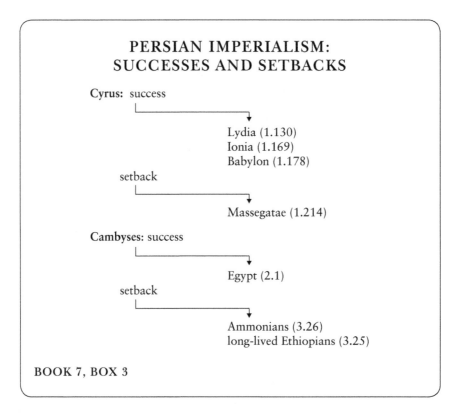

PERSIAN IMPERIALISM:
SUCCESSES AND SETBACKS

Cyrus: success

Lydia (1.130)
Ionia (1.169)
Babylon (1.178)

setback

Massegatae (1.214)

Cambyses: success

Egypt (2.1)

setback

Ammonians (3.26)
long-lived Ethiopians (3.25)

BOOK 7, BOX 3

to subjugate it. This is the state of affairs in the opening chapter of Book Seven but there is a substantial delay in the story before the next battle is fought, with the pause in action carrying its own dramatic weight by focusing on the whys and wherefores of attacking Greece. The death of Darius is mentioned in 7.4 and Herodotus draws out and dramatizes the importance of the decision-making process by placing Darius' successor at a crossroads in his life and letting lobbyists with divergent opinions speak for themselves. The debate in Susa has Homeric precedents[2] and the overall effect is to create the sense of a new beginning, as if everything in the *Histories* has been leading up to this ground-breaking moment that is so pregnant with consequences.

Book Seven does not have the temporal shifts and lengthy digressions that characterize the two preceding books and once the discussions in Susa are completed the narrative maintains a steady course that culminates in the Battle of Thermopylae. Time is still found for short digressions, arising from localities passed on Xerxes' itinerary, and there are reminders of a divine awareness of the unfolding events. The metaphysical predispositions that in Book Six found expression in accounts of *tisis* (retribution) from an implacable, unnameable agency that takes affront at immoderate behaviour (see Book 6, Box 5, p. 191), maintain a presence in the narrative, though not to the same degree. What now comes to the fore is not sacrilegious behaviour provoking a divine reaction but the likeliness of human arrogance falling victim to chance (*tuchē*) because of the way an excess of pride precludes the prudence that should be the sensible response to life's inherent unpredictability. Attributing the unexpected to 'the god' (*to theion*) – never identified as an anthropomorphic being – becomes a way of moralizing the feeling that the overly self-important do not always deserve to succeed and this is one aspect of the philosophical reflections on the nature of human experience that characterize Book Seven.

Debates and dreams (7.1–19)

The debate at Susa and the apparitions that appear to Xerxes and Artabanus combine to produce a complex picture of vested interests, decisions made, unmade and made again, arguments for and against invasion and the burden of history weighing down on Xerxes. A jigsaw of pressure, persuasion and the power of dreams finally bring Xerxes and Artabanus together in an ambitious plan to bridge the Hellespont and conquer Greece (see Box 4).

DECISIONS, DEBATES AND DREAMS

7.5–8:	Vested interests pressurize Xerxes into changing his mind and agreeing to invade Greece.
7.8:	Xerxes announces his reasons for invading Greece.
7.9:	Mardonius endorses the reasoning.
7.10–12:	Artabanus disagrees and urges caution; Xerxes angrily confirms his decision to invade; Xerxes changes his mind and ignores the first apparition in his sleep.
7.13:	Xerxes announces his change of mind.
7.14:	Apparition appears for second time.
7.15:	Xerxes seeks to test the divinity of the apparition.
7.16:	Artabanus reiterates the case for caution and thinks the apparition is not of divine origin.
7.17:	Apparition appears to Artabanus.
7.18:	Artabanus, convinced of the apparition's divinity, changes his mind and supports the invasion.

BOOK 7, BOX 4

Herodotus is concerned with questions of motivation and he is willing to give his own interpretations of the facts. Xerxes claims the throne after the death of his father, though not being Darius' eldest son there is ground for disputing his accession. The exiled Greek, Demaratus, supports him with the argument that being the eldest son born during the king's reign trumps any claim by an older son born before Darius became king. No authorial comment is made – perhaps because his audience needs no reminder – of the irony of having a Spartan king who was deposed over an issue of legitimacy advise another king on royal succession. Herodotus adds only an *aperçu* about Darius' 'all-powerful' widow, Atossa, a remark that coheres with the earlier mention of the queen's influence when she sweet-talked her husband into turning his attention to a conquest of Greece (3.134).[3]

Xerxes does not at first accept an inheritance from his father to subjugate Greece – initially he is more concerned with putting down the rebellion in Egypt – but he is lobbied by Persian and Greek interests and oracular support is conveniently supplied by a purveyor of oracles, Onomacritus. The king is under pressure and, Herodotus reports, 'over time' (*khronō*) Mardonius works upon Xerxes and succeeds in changing his mind (7.6). This success is confirmed when the king announces his decision to an assembly of nobles and repeats Mardonius' arguments as the rationale for mounting an invasion. His address has been analysed using a narratological approach that looks at the 'anachronical' structure of the episode (see p. 35, and de Jong 2013: 273–81). This is seen by de Jong as a way of accounting for the textual cohesion of the debate and an example of the value of a narratological perspective in reading Herodotus. The anacronies also highlight the different ways in which the three speakers use the past: Xerxes offers a retroactive redemption of past wrong – the burning at Sardis and defeat at Marathon – while Mardonius presents a version of the past that fails to match what Herodotus has already reported about it. Artabanus, using a record of the past that accords more closely with Herodotus', uses it as evidence for his fears for the future.[4]

In his first address, Xerxes give three analeptic reasons for his decision: revenge for the temple burning in Sardis, a bellicose expansionism that goes back to Cyrus and bitter memories of defeat at Marathon (7.8). His recall of Cyrus, Cambyses and Darius gives parity to his Persian listeners and to Herodotus' narratees: reminding one audience of their own past, the other of the preceding books of the *Histories* and both a sense of the weight of history bearing down on the present. Xerxes' proleptic announcement to bridge the Hellespont, which readers know will take place, also looks back to one of the oracles provided by Onomacritus. The king's conviction of divine justification fuels an extravagant design for a future that goes well beyond merely punishing two Greek states. Aristagoras' map of the world collapsed space in a way that alarmed the home-loving Spartan king but Xerxes, as an architect of imperialism, proclaims with pride his own intention to do likewise: 'we shall make the borders of Persian territory and the firmament of heaven to be the same . . . I will make all to be one country' (7.8). The speech has been interpreted along the lines of a psychological profile of Xerxes, with talk of a 'psychologically credible depiction of his increasing levels of emotion',[5] but such a reading may be less convincing than one that sees Herodotus outlining a hubristic vision of empire that regards expansion as a systemic component of the monarchic Persian state.

Mardonius' reply to this announcement begins smarmily and becomes a spin on recent history, glossing over Marathon and making the first expedition against the Greeks seem like a victory (7.9). In spite of the reader's mistrust of Mardonius' ability to tell the truth, it is he who comments judiciously on the Greeks' inability to stop fighting each other and observes that, as they speak the same language, they should settle disputes by heralds and messengers. Such sentiments are not entirely in character – though this is the man who had the nous to introduce democracy to the defeated Ionians (6.43) – and it is tempting, both here and in what the next speaker will say, to detect the ventriloquial voice of Herodotus. Artabanus, disputing Mardonius' interpretation of the past and concurring with Herodotus' account in a way that brings him close to sounding like an alter ego of the author, delivers some home truths wrapped in conventional Greek ideas about the human condition (7.10). He uses an 'internal repeating analepsis' (de Jong 2013: 280), referring to the failed expedition against the Scythians that has already been narrated by Herodotus (4.125–40), and a prolepsis to correctly describe what will happen if the Hellespont is bridged.[6] Artabanus' advice to be cautious is couched in traditional terms and he warns his king to be careful because 'the god suffers pride [*phroneein mega*] in none but himself', the literal translation of *phroneein mega* being 'to think big'. His reminder to his nephew that the gods resent mortal displays of excessive self-assurance is familiar to Greek thought; in Sophocles' *Ajax*, the seer Calchas is worried about Ajax for just this reason – 'lives that are grown too proud' will 'fall on grave difficulties sent from the gods' (758–61) – and Artabanus provides an example that bears directly on the subject of the debate when he points to the way 'a large army is destroyed by a small one, when the god in his envy [*phthonos*] casts fear or lightening upon it' (7.10). Solon makes a similar remark about haughtiness and *phthonos* in conversation with Croesus (1.32) but the Greek term, like that of *hybris* which Artabanus will also use shortly, has no one-word translation in English: 'it has elements of envy, ill-will, self-protectiveness, and begrudgement' (Mikalson 2003: 39). It is best to read Herodotus here as giving voice to age-old Greek ideas about human experience and the way that *phthonos*, as Lloyd-Jones outlines it, 'originates in the primitive fear that one's life is always open to the possibility of being endangered by the spite of a supernatural being'.[7] The gnomic language of Artabanus is giving expression to the kind of generalized and proverbial truth that functions in a narrative as a way of bringing an audience into a recognizable sphere of shared meaning.[8]

The debate at Susa may have begun in a way familiar to Greek deliberations on matters of policy but a principled difference between 'open' discussions in Persia and Greece emerges after Artabanus' contribution. Xerxes' immediate and furious reaction is to order his expulsion from the expeditionary force and his sequestration at home with women. After a period of reflection, Xerxes comes to change his mind and he rescinds the decision to invade Greece. This policy reversal comes after dismissing his first dream of a 'tall and goodly man' standing over him and warning him to abide by his decision (7.12). What causes Xerxes to change his mind again is the reappearance of the apparition (*opsis*) and the result of his test, – having Artabanus dress in royal robes and sit on the throne before sleeping in Xerxes' bed, comparable to Croesus' testing of the oracles (1.46) – that has his nephew experiencing the same *opsis*. Artabanus, who had argued that a divine agency could not be deceived in this manner, is convinced by the way the figure in his dream knows full well it is not Xerxes to whom he is appearing. Oddly, while Artabanus has come across until now as a reliable reporter, he misreads the dream by assuming it guarantees the destruction of Greece (7.18). The double-layered irony is that Persia and not Greece will be the victim (bringing to mind Croesus' misreading of the oracle about the consequence of his plan to attack another country) and that this is just what Artabanus warned Xerxes would be the result if he went ahead with his plan to invade and attack the Greeks. What makes this tale of a dreamlike and apparently god-sent instruction so curious, however, is not its irony but the mystery of why it is delivered.[9] A comparison with Zeus' false dream to Agamemnon in the second book of the *Iliad*, persuading Agamemnon that he can capture Troy by launching a full-scale assault, might suggest the figure in Xerxes' dream is a deceiver luring the king with false hope of victory but it is only Artabanus who is deceived and he does this to himself.

The dream figure urges Xerxes in no uncertain terms to carry on with his projected invasion and Artabanus is severely admonished for trying to dissuade him, threatened with having his eyes burnt out for interfering with 'that which must be' (7.17). The cautionary Artabanus is being rational when he places an attack on Greece in the context of earlier failed campaigns against the Massagetae, Ethiopians and Scythians (7.18), but there is equally little that is irrational in his acceptance that a higher power is overruling his thinking and insisting on the pursuit of a questionable invasion. It seems that destiny decrees Persia must, irrespective of Xerxes' willingness to cancel his invasion plan, go ahead and attack Greece; put like this, it is hardly fair to level accusations of hubris against the Persian king for pursuing a foreign policy under divine duress. Countering this is the fact that Xerxes entertains an ambitious and sweeping vision of world conquest before his dream and the apparition can be seen as responding to this original presumption of the king by forbidding a change to what he had intended to accomplish. Xerxes thought he should be an agent of Persia's manifest destiny to expand through conquest but his and his country's fate is to fail in such an endeavour;

divinely sanctioned doom awaits him, as it must. He tells his nobles that he is aligning himself with Persian *nomos* (7.8), translated as 'custom' or 'law' and carrying both senses here: 'As I learn from our eldest, we have never yet remained at peace ever since Cyrus deposed Astyages and we won this our lordship from the Medes. It is the will of heaven.' Such a perspective on the past is immanent to Persia's perception of itself and Xerxes' projected war has its origin, goal and raison d'être in this *nomos*. Aware that war has always been an intrinsic part of the Persian way of life, Xerxes positions himself within this tradition and the apparition is forcefully endorsing such a stance; the dream is an 'apotheosis of the Persian *nomos* of imperial expansion' (Scullion 2006: 197) and, as Evans put it nearly half a century earlier when making the same point, the dream is telling the truth to Xerxes because if he abandons the invasion campaign he will also be abandoning the *nomoi* of Persia, customs which created a great empire (Evans: 1961).[10] If Xerxes ignores the imperial imperative, the dream warns him, his status as a great ruler in the tradition of his forefathers will be brought low in as short a period of time as it took for him to attain the kingship (7.14). This could refer to the succession quarrel after the death of Darius and the intervention of Atossa and Demaratus on his behalf (7.2–3), a reminder to Xerxes that his disputed kingship needs to be firmly asserted with a show of action in the tradition of past kings. Herodotus presents a man who because of different but interrelated circumstances is under enormous pressure to adopt the course of action he does.[11]

There is a similarity between Xerxes deciding not to invade Greece and the predicament Glaucus finds himself in when he changes his mind and determines to return the money he was entrusted to keep safe.[12] In both cases a change of heart comes too late; Glaucus and Xerxes have little choice but to bear the consequences of an original transgressive audaciousness: Glaucus contemplating a false oath and Xerxes intending world domination and personal glory. Another similarity has been noted – 'We are close here to the world of *Macbeth*' (Griffin 2006: 50) – for just as the witches give voice to and encourage an ambition that already lies deep within Macbeth, the apparition, likewise, impels Xerxes to act on a desire he attempts to disavow.[13]

A moral temper to the original decision of Xerxes to invade Greece is very pronounced when Artabanus, accepting that he has to go along with the test of the seemingly divine apparition, explains why he was perturbed by the king's judgement. There was a choice, he says, and it was the one 'tending to the increase of pride [*hybris*]', a choice that showed 'how evil a thing it is to teach the heart continual desire of more than it has', that to his dismay was chosen by Xerxes.[14] The term *hybris*, looked at earlier because of the way it has been used to describe Croesus (see p. 74), is employed here without a religious connotation, in keeping with nearly all uses of the word in Herodotus.[15] Artabanus is making a judgemental statement about the limits to imperial ambition and his disappointment that the king has allowed himself to be swayed by a grandiose prospect of supreme power.

Reaching and crossing the Hellespont
(7.20–56)

The first stage of the march comes to an end at Sardis, with Xerxes and his army spending the winter there before setting off in spring for the second stage that will bring them to the Hellespont. The narrative of the journey is interspersed with an account of the canal-building at Athos and, where Xerxes is presumably also not present but overseeing and intervening when the first constructions collapse, the building of two bridges over the Hellespont (see Box 5).[16] It helps the reader following the journey of the Persian expedition to consult maps.[17]

The prefatory chapters (7.20–21) announcing the importance and magnitude of what will occupy the remaining books of the *Histories* bear two points of comparison with Herodotus' proem. The Homeric echoes that can be heard in the proem are displaced by a deprecatory remark in 7.20 about the comparative slightness of the expedition to Troy but, by way of similarity between the two prefaces, there is a common concern with the

---

REACHING AND CROSSING
THE HELLESPONT

7.20–1: The scale of the invasion campaign

↓

7.22–4: The Athos canal project

7.25:   Logistics of bridge-building at the Hellespont

7.26–32: Xerxes marches to Sardis, meeting Pythius en route

↓

7.33–6: Bridge-building at the Hellespont

7.37–43: Xerxes, rejecting the plea of Pythius, marches from Sardis to Troy

7.44–5: Xerxes, reaching the Hellespont, reviews his army and cries

7.46–52: Conversation between Xerxes and Artabanus

7.55–6: Crossing the Hellespont by Xerxes and his army

BOOK 7, BOX 5

epistemological difference between accounts of the remote past and more recent history. Herodotus does not know the actual size of the forces that travelled to Troy but the scale of the Persian campaign can be quantified, just as the Persian versions of Io, Europa, Medea, and Helen are unreliable when put alongside the sure knowledge that Croesus was the first Asian to attack Greeks. The ground for such demarcations is temporal: Troy and the likes of Io belong to a far distant past, a known unknown; what happened to Croesus goes back a few generations and is recoverable through oral tradition; the Persian campaign of 480 dates back only some fifty years and there are still some living eyewitnesses plus many of their children who remember the first-hand accounts they heard. Not surprisingly, then, the chronicle of Xerxes' expedition has a density of empirical information unlike anything that has gone before; but the story of the expedition, before and after the crossing of the Hellespont, will not exclude anecdotes, talk of portents and wondrous deeds.

Xerxes' professionalism and his dedicated approach to the challenge of invading Greece is evidenced by his hands-on role in the work of the quartermasters, personally considering the logistics involved and the best sites for supply depots (7.21). He seeks to avoid the mishap that led to Mardonius' fleet being shipwrecked off Mount Athos by having a 2-km-long canal dug for the passage of his ships (7.22–3), and Herodotus carefully records its construction as if to deliver on his intention, declared in the proem, to record 'great and wondrous deeds' (*erga megala te kai thōmasta*). Baragwanath reads the Athos chapters as balancing two focalizations (another narratological term introduced by Genette, to indicate the perspective through which a narrative is presented), one of which is Xerxes.[18] The king is haunted, in the full sense of the word, by the thought that he will be orphaned by the history of Persia's glorious past if he does not emulate the great exploits of his ancestors, and the Athos canal is one product of such an anxiety. There is an obligation, arising from Persian *nomos*, to gain some kudos by demonstrating his aptitude for notable achievements. Herodotus also says, 'as far as I judge by conjecture' (7.24), that Xerxes' reason for building a canal was one of *megalophrosunē* and when this is understood as meaning pride – the word is translated by Waterfield as 'a sense of grandiosity and arrogance' – we have a Greek perspective that views the construction as indicative of the king's inclination for excessive showmanship. Judging the building of the canal as a gratuitous exercise is endorsed when Herodotus points out that the sea journey around the tip of the peninsula could have been avoided by dragging the ships across on land, supporting the feeling that self-aggrandisement, not engineering necessity arising from safety concerns, could be what motivates Xerxes. With two contrasting ways of accounting for the canal project, the text's equivocation hangs on the understanding given to *megalophrosunē*: 'pride', 'towering ambition' or, when the focalization is Persian and not Greek, 'greatness of mind', 'pride in his magnificence', 'relish for magnificence'.[19] The word, as will be seen, will be used in an unambiguously positive way about Xerxes (7.136) but the ambivalence that is maintained here reflects the shifting impressions of Xerxes that continue to emerge as the expedition approaches and prepares to cross the Hellespont into Europe.[20]

The suggestion of nobility on Xerxes' part arising from his genial encounter with Pythius (7.28–9) will be severely qualified when they next meet, but at this stage it encourages the kind of affirmative impression of the king that attaches itself to his appreciation of a beautiful plane-tree (7.31). When a storm sweeps away the first two bridges constructed across the Hellespont, the king's proclivity for violent behaviour reveals another side to his character. He orders the execution of the bridges' engineers and, accompanied by insults and threats, the whipping of the sea and throwing of fetters into the water to symbolize its enslavement, possibly even an attempt to brand the sea. The scene is a memorable one, attaining iconic status as a signature of human arrogance and, some two millennia later, Milton works it into a simile for the labour of the two infernal engineers who build a bridge over Chaos to enslave humanity.[21] Persian kings have built bridges before in pursuit of imperial conquest – Cyrus over the Araxes (1.205) and Darius over the Bosporus and the Ister (4.88–9) – but a more pertinent precedent is Cyrus' punishment of the Gyndes after his sacred white horses drowned in it (1.189–90).

In Aeschylus' *Persians*, a drama that could have influenced Herodotus, the ghost of Darius is summoned from the Underworld and, castigating his son for challenging the gods' mastery of nature, the bridging of the Hellespont with chains is recalled as evidence of Xerxes' impiety towards Poseidon, the god of the sea (744–50).[22] The ethical and religious nexus of *Persians* is cast in the language of *hybris* and *atē* (ruin) and the contravention of a boundary between the human and the divine that invites retribution, but it is premature to read such terms wholesale into Xerxes crossing of the Hellespont. Interfering with nature to exert control is not, per se, an impious affront to the gods for Herodotus and nothing sacrilegious is suggested when Darius crosses the Bosporus (4.87–8). Herodotus describes a lake built by Egyptians in a desert (2.149) and a dam constructed by Persians with no hint of disapproval (3.117) and the detailed explanation of how the second set of two bridges over the Hellespont serves to mark it as an engineering feat worthy of admiration.[23] Herodotus strongly disapproves of Xerxes when, using *barbarous* for the only time in a pejorative way (7.35), he describes the king's abuse of the water as 'barbaric and reckless' (*barbara te kai atasthala*) but, unlike the occasion when Pheros angrily threw his spear into the Nile (2.111), there is no intimation of divine retribution. Croesus, it is supposed, suffered nemesis (*ek theou nemesis*, 1.34) for his self-regarding smugness but while this is not being suggested here there is something hubristic about Xerxes' overconfidence and 'thinking big' at the Hellespont.[24] He wants to gaze down on his entire army and navy, thinking well-being can be quantified (as Croesus did (1.30) by the contents of his treasury) while also emulating a Persian tradition (4.85), but Xerxes' tears at the brevity of life (7.46) and Artabanus' contribution to this moment of philosophical reflection unexpectedly evokes the wisdom of Solon.[25] The sudden transition from self-satisfaction to sober melancholy creates for the reader a remarkably arresting and reflective interlude between the commotion of the regatta Xerxes has been watching and the hustle and bustle of the imminent crossing of the Hellespont.

In their conversation, Xerxes and Artabanus dwell on the strangeness of life: it unpredictably but inevitably mixes good moments with a share of misfortunes that have to be endured, resulting in the feeling that we enjoy only 'a taste of life's sweetness' before becoming subject to the divine envy (*phthonos*) already referred to in the debate (7.10). Trepidation besets Artabanus for this reason and Xerxes offers reassurance with equally sound reasoning about the need to take some risks when the alternative is to chance nothing and achieve nothing. He again positions himself with a pattern shaped by history and uses his predecessors' successes to counter his uncle's caution (7.50). The conversation's philosophical sensibility is characteristically Greek and Herodotean, harking back to Solon and Croesus (1.32) and Polycrates (3.40–3),[26] but the focus on human vulnerability, the fragility of happiness and life's paradoxical blend of joy and tears is authentic and moving enough to invest it with a universal value of cognitive and emotional interest.[27]

At a psychological level, Xerxes' sudden mood swing from pleasure at watching the regatta to pain at sensing the ephemeral nature of life is consonant with a possible lack of stability in his mental make-up indicated by other aspects of his behaviour. He changes his mind three times over whether to invade Greece, moves from appreciating a plane-tree for its beauty to punishing the sea for acting unjustly towards him and, most spectacularly of all, undergoes a Jekyll-and-Hyde-style transformation from gracious friend of Pythius to savage executioner of the man's son (7.27–9, 38–40). What appears as troubling about Xerxes' conduct is not just the change in his attitude towards Pythius but the difference between a man who can reason with himself and others, as shown in the debate and conversations with Artabanus, and someone whose anger can explode into the kind of gratuitous and sadistic violence that characterized Cambyses in his treatment of Prexaspes (3.34–5). Baragwanath (2008: 269–78) offers an understanding, resolving some of the difficulty in forming an opinion of Xerxes' character, by drawing attention to the reciprocal social bond that underpins the king's first meeting with Pythius. The feeding of his army and an offer of financial assistance is warmly reciprocated by Xerxes when he extends guest-friendship (*xenia*) to his host and cordially acknowledges the social intent behind Pythius' offer to hand over the entirety of his cash wealth by refusing it and giving him some money instead. The formality of the moment is registered in Xerxes' language: 'Therefore, in return for this, I give you these gifts of honour [*gerea*]' and they part company as guest-friends (7.29). Pythius breaks their bond with his special pleading and Xerxes, with his own sons participating in the invasion, feels personally betrayed by the selfish 'shamelessness' of his former host (7.39). He sees the punishment he metes out as commensurate with the injury he has received by having his guest-friendship bond violated in such an outrageous manner while, at the same time, making clear to his own army that desertion and disloyalty will not be tolerated.

Baragwanath's approach looks at the story in terms of a Greek social ecosystem and while convincing in many respects it does not seem an adequate explanation for the ritualistic nature of the murder of Pythius' son. Acts of excessive violence as punishment are not in themselves that unusual – Darius has already provided an example when Oeobazus asked for one of his sons to be exempted from military duty (4.84) and a reference has been made to Athenians nailing someone alive to a plank (7.33) – but there is a particular context to this case which might offer a clue to what has been missing from the story's hermeneutic horizon. As Xerxes is leading his army out of Sardis a solar eclipse occurs and, while he is reassured by his priests' benign interpretation of the phenomenon, it worries Pythius and motivates his request to the king (7.37–8). Evidence of a Hittite ritual practice, involving the march of an army through the space of a dismembered human body, could be linked through cross-cultural diffusion with a Persian purificatory rite which Xerxes performed (Rollinger 2000). The solar eclipse could be a contributory factor and rituals are observed when the Hellespont is being crossed (7.54). It may be that Herodotus heard an account of Xerxes' purificatory ritual and, not fully understanding it, framed it for his audience within a recognizable setting of a violation of guest-friendship and stereotypical exaggerations of a despotic Persian ruler.[28] Herodotus admits to a degree of incomprehension, admitting that he finds it difficult to choose between the reasons for Xerxes throwing a silver cup, a golden bowl and a sword: they could be offerings to the sun or an act of repentance for his earlier flogging of the Hellespont.

The departure from Sardis is marked by the Persians with a degree of theatrical formality that emphasizes the importance of the moment (7.40). Supplies for the army travel at the front and are followed by a huge army that leaves a gap of open space before a body of 1,000 horsemen, the same number of spearmen and selected troops make their appearance. A set of ten caparisoned horses follow, then a sacred eight-horsed chariot with the driver holding the reins as he walks behind the steeds. All this is the prelude to the royal chariot with Xerxes and his charioteer standing beside him. The soldiers in front of the king have their spears pointing downwards while those after him carry their spears pointing up; some spears are topped with golden pomegranates, others with silver ones or apples instead.

Darius crossed this stretch of the sea on his return home after the failed Scythian campaign, leaving Megabazus to conquer the area (4.143–4). In subduing the Ionian revolt, the Hellespont was again subject to Persian power (5.117, 6.33) and now Xerxes is in the same region with the intention of completing the historical mission initiated by his father and endorsed by the obligations of a Persian *nomos* that was first articulated in the *Histories* by Atossa when, instigated ironically by a Greek, she successfully persuaded her husband to set his sights on Greece (3.134).

Hellespont to Thermopylae (7.57–131)

At Doriscus, on the northern shore of the Aegean where the Persian fleet also pauses, Xerxes, having assumed the imperialist mandate in accordance with Persian *nomos*, wants to record the significance of what is happening. He orders his army to be counted[29] and then reviews it for himself by riding in a chariot with a scribe to take down information that the king gathers by questioning his soldiers; the same procedure is followed for his fleet (7.100). 'Xerxes becomes a *histor* [inquirer] like Herodotus' (Grethlein: 2009a: 267).

Detailed information concerning Persian land and sea forces is provided (7.61–99), recalling the equally lengthy description in the *Iliad* describing all the Greek forces at Troy (2.494–760). Herodotus begins with the origins of the Persians and a folk genealogy that derives their name from Perses, a son of Perseus whose father was Zeus and whose mother, Danaë, was impregnated by the god after appearing to her as a shower of gold (7.61). An odd consequence of this is a distant kinship with the Spartans who also claim to be descended from Perseus (6.53, see p. 181), and it is soon made clear that the Persians are very aware of a genealogical relation to some Greeks.

The ethnographic and fashion-show flavour to the catalogue of the polyglot Persian army, with aspects of clothing and weapons described in detail, becomes a verbal tour de force that invites the reader to visualize the multicultural variety of forms on show. We see the turbaned Cissians, the helmets of twisted bronze on the Assyrians, tapered caps on the heads of the Sacae, Indians dressed in cotton and carrying cane bows and arrows tipped with iron, cloaked Caspians, Sarangae in knee-high boots. The Ethiopians of Africa are wrapped in leopard and lion skins and their arrows tipped with sharpened stones while the Asian Ethiopians wear on their heads the scalps of horses with the ears standing upright and the manes serving as crests. The Thracians wear fox-skin caps and fawn-skin shoes and the Sagartains, noted for their reliance on just daggers and lassoes, pale into visual insignificance alongside the Persians with an abundance of gold in their display of multicoloured garments and with body armour that looks like fish scales as they march carrying shields, spears and bows. The words of a local man, observing the army just after it crosses the water and crying out in astonishment that Zeus has changed his name to Xerxes (7.56), are the ancient world's equivalent of Hegel's when he glimpses Napoleon on the eve of the Battle of Jena: 'I have seen the Emperor – this world-soul – riding out from the city on reconnaissance. It is indeed a wonderful sensation to see such an individual who ... astride a horse, reaches out over the world, and masters it' (1984: 114).

Herodotus also provides information on ethnic origins and it is not just the Persians who have an eponymous link to famed individuals of the distant past: the Medes are named after Medea (7.62), Lydians after Lydus (7.74), Cilicians after Celix (7.91), Ionians after Ion (7.94). The Phrygians and Thracians have changed their names as a result of migration (7.73, 75) and attention is also paid to colonization (7.74, 90, 95) when detailing the different groups of people in the Persian army. Herodotus is always far more interested in ethnic hybridity and fluidity than notions of aboriginal purity and here also he is seen characteristically observing cultural similarities: the Phrygians, for example, equip themselves 'very like the Paphlagonians but with small differences' (7.73).

The names of various commanders are given but it is Artemisia (7.99) who is singled out for special attention, becoming a 'wonder' (*thoma*) for Herodotus before he goes on to describe her courage and resolution as 'manly' (*andrēiēs*). If the adjective is taken as a straightforward description of stereotypical 'masculine' prowess it might suggest a similarity between Artemisia and Tomyris, the fierce Massagetae queen who fills a wineskin with human blood and contemptuously plunges into it the head of Cyrus (1.214). *Andrēiēs*, however, is being used here with a studied refinement that goes beyond a simple inversion of a male–female divide. The widow of the ruler of Halicarnassus, Artemisia has taken over her husband's position but as a woman she has no obligation to join in person the Persian fleet and does so voluntarily. This emphasis on the free exercise of will mark her out as more Hellenic than Persian, befitting someone with a Greek name and Greek descent, yet she is a trusted confidant of Xerxes and provider to him of the 'best opinions' (*gnōmas aristas*). To cap it all, she commands only five ships out of more than a thousand but they are rated the second-best contingent in the entire fleet. In the events that are to follow, the singularity of her character will emerge in new and surprising ways that distinguish her not only from Tomyris but also from other prominent women like Candaules' wife, Nitocris, Atossa and Pheretime.

Xerxes asks another non-Persian on his side, Demaratus, if battle is inevitable or whether, as he himself is inclined to believe, surrender by the Greeks without fighting is more likely. Their conversation circles around a nurture/nature antithesis (*nomos/physis*) with Demaratus remarking how a quality of excellence (*aretē*) has been cultivated from the harsh nature of Greece's physical environment. Hard work and social cohesion has kept poverty at bay (7.102)[30] and, for the Spartans at least, their social conditioning will not allow them to back down even if outnumbered in a battle (7.104). Custom (*nomos*), he says, is their master (*despotēs*), echoing a judgement that Herodotus himself has made (3.38).[31] A laughing Xerxes is relaxed and considerate, confident that the numerical size of his army will prove to be a more decisive factor, but laughter in Herodotus is usually a warning that a character has lost his sense of vulnerability.[32]

At 7.105 the journey of the Persian expedition continues on its way from Doriscus, the place reached in 7.59, only for there to be a unusual chronological hiccup for two chapters (7.106–7) with an account of events after Persia's defeat. Herodotus is drawn to the tale of Boges, even though it refers to a siege that took place in 476–5 (the final year of the *Histories* is 479), and the way in which he died. As so often happens in the *Histories*, the significance of a moment or of a minor character crystallizes when the motif into which it fits is recognized. Boges' leap into the fire can be placed alongside Arion's leap from the pirate ship (1.24) and Prexaspes' leap from a tower (3.75); three individuals whose freedom of action is severely curtailed by circumstances but for whom the exercise of their own agency is paramount. Prexaspes can live by accepting the terms he is offered and Boges can save himself by surrendering to the Athenians but in these extreme circumstances their sense of integrity and honour is more important than self-preservation, and suicide becomes a preferable option. They prepare for death under their own terms, assuming their fate, and comport themselves accordingly: Arion by playing and singing, Prexaspes by his speech and Boges by sacrificing his family and throwing his gold and silver into the river.

The uneventful nature of the journey from Doriscus to the River Strymon, passing though territory already under Persian control (5.1–2, 6.43–5), is matched by the leisurely pace of Herodotus' commentary. He records some topographic and toponymic information, a few details about some of the Thracian tribes and mentions an oracle in the mountains with a priestess as in Delphi but otherwise unremarkable. It is indifferently noted how, bridging the river at a town called Nine Ways, they bury alive nine unfortunate children of the area. At the town of Acanthus, just north of the Athos peninsula, Xerxes pauses before continuing westwards towards Therma (Thessaloniki) in Macedonia where the fleet will meet up with the army.[33] The Acanthians are rewarded for their support of the Athos project and the funeral of Artachaies, who directed the canal-building, distresses Xerxes. Information is given about the costs imposed on Greek cities in providing meals for the army that march their way, bankrupting some in the process and occasioning Megacreon's acerbic remark that the gods should be thanked that the Persians only require feeding once a day (7.120).

In Therma, Xerxes is impressed by the mountain scenery and puts some time aside for a sailing excursion with his fleet to view the Peneus as it flows into the sea; seeing it, he is overcome 'with wonder' (*en thōmati*) and asks if it would be possible to have the course of the river diverted (7.128). Background information follows, noting that Thessaly, surrounded by mountains, was once a giant lake but an earthquake created a massive gorge that became an outlet for the river and turned the lake into dry land (7.129). Surmising that if the river was dammed Thessaly could again be flooded, the king concludes that this is why the Thessalians submitted to the Persians and that they were wise to do so (7.130). Xerxes is again seen as *histor* (inquirer) but not a disinterested one and in this way he fits into the 'meta-historical dimension' of Herodotus' representation of investigative royals that throws light on his own practice as a historian (Christ 2013: 212, 225–6).

The Greeks respond (7.132–77)

The narrative now goes back in time (and occasionally forward) to cover events that take place in Greece while the expeditionary force is making its way from Persia. The first journey of heralds to Greek cities to demand earth and water as tokens of submission to Persian sovereignty takes place in the aftermath of the Ionian revolt (6.48) and the second occasion during Xerxes' winter stay in Sardis before setting off for the Hellespont (7.32). On the second occasion it is said that no further heralds were sent to Athens or Sparta and the reason for this, a violation of the heralds' diplomatic immunity that amounts to impiety (7.133), is now made clear. Xerxes' lenient treatment of Sperthias and Bulis, the volunteers prepared to die for their city's killing of the Persian heralds, is described as *megalophrosunē* (7.136) – usually taken to mean 'magnanimous' – the word that when used earlier has been seen to carry a negative connotation (7.24, see above). Herodotus accepts that the violations of Sparta and Athens will meet with divine punishment and, while uncertain what form this takes for the Athenians, he feels sure it can be discerned in what happened to the children of Sperthias and Bulis (7.137).[34] The story of these children requires a chronological jump to the year 430, the second year of the Peloponnesian War, but the narrative returns after this prolepsis to the reception given by various Greek cities, excluding Athens and Sparta, to the ultimatum that the arrival of Persian heralds represents.[35] This leads to Herodotus stating that were it not for the Athenians the whole of Greece would inevitably have been conquered by the Persians (7.139).[36]

He begins by acknowledging that his opinion (*gnome*) will not be pleasing to many but 'by necessity' (*anagkaiē*) he must say what 'seems to me to be the truth' (*moi phainetai einai alēthes*, 7.139).[37] Herodotus, rarely shy in giving his opinion on non-religious topics, does not usually invoke the concept of 'truth' (*alētheia*) and, although his statement is qualified by 'it seems to me' (*moi phainetai*), there can be little doubt, given the way he continues, that he takes his belief to be justified. Herodotus the historian is speaking when he develops a detailed counterfactual argument that leads to a confident assertion, by way of a proof more than analysis, that Greece was saved from enslavement by the Athenians; reaching again for the notion of *alētheia*, he states unequivocally that his conclusion 'hits the truth'.[38] Athenians, he says, have a choice and by deciding to remain free they inspired other cities to do likewise and, moreover, Athens stood firm against the pessimistic Delphi oracles (7.139–40). By framing the city's achievement in terms of a choice, a phrasing also used by Dionysus in the Ionian revolt (6.11) and by Miltiades before Marathon (6.109), the importance of autonomy and agency is emphasized; the Athenians could have chosen otherwise and the exercise of their freedom of will adds to the value of their accomplishment.[39]

What follows Herodotus' encomium to Athens are a series of historical accounts dealing with how various Greek cities respond to the imminent Persian threat, starting optimistically with a congress of those prepared to join in an alliance of resistance, the sending of spies to Asia and the dispatch of emissaries to Sicily, Corcyra and Crete in the hope of securing more allies (7.145). The spies are captured but Xerxes' leniency shows him to be clever and calculating (7.146–8). An embassy is also sent to the Argives and they seem prepared to join the alliance, despite negative oracular advice and enmity with Sparta, and negotiate terms, unsuccessfully as it turns out, with Spartan envoys. This, though, is only their version and most other Greeks have heard 'another story' (allos logos) that the Persians made entreaties to Argos on the basis of a historic kinship that goes back to Perses (7.61) and that their negotiations with the Spartans were just an excuse to disguise their wish not to fight the Persians (7.148–51). Herodotus refuses to be drawn on these rival versions and adds an aphorism of his own about how people disproportionately assess their personal misfortunes (oikēia kaka) because they are ignorant of the weight of problems afflicting other people. Herodotus, aware of what Argos suffered in its war with Sparta and how this might have affected the situation, does not feel the Argives should be singled out for criticism. Faced with competing versions of Argive behaviour, he comes close to a plague-on-both-your-houses attitude with the statement that he may be obliged to record what people say but not to always believe them (7.152). For good measure he adds as a prolepsis a third version: it was Argos, out of desperation to survive after what they already suffered at the hands of Sparta, who invited the Persians to invade Greece.[40]

Herodotus goes on to report how Gelon in Sicily, the Corcyreans and the Cretans respond to the idea of joining the anti-Persian alliance, making clear their disunity and dissembling (7.153–71). Excuses, arguments, appeals to a mythic past[41] and shows of self-righteousness jostle for attention as chances for joint action slip away. Herodotus holds backs from an explicit condemnation of the fence-sitting tactics being deployed but with the Corcyreans he shows just how minded some cities were to avoid committing themselves by using direct speech to report what they would have said had the Persians been victorious.[42]

When the diplomatic missions are dealt with the main narrative returns to the congress mentioned at 7.145; Thessaly's response and the first military movements of Greek forces are covered,[43] with the Greeks abandoning their first position at Tempe and making the momentous decision to confront the Persian army at the pass of Thermopylae (7.172–7).

Thermopylae (7.178–239)

Xerxes, having spent four years preparing for a conquest of Greece, has arrived in the north of the country after bridging the Hellespont and marching across Thrace, 'compelling all that he met to join his expedition' (7.106). Historians question the huge numbers given for the size of the Persian army and navy (7.184) but do not doubt the seriously large size of the expedition – the largest the world has seen, says Herodotus (7.20) – and that the confrontation mounted by the Greeks at Thermopylae was remarkable and crucial in inspiring continued resistance to the invaders.

The war narrative in the first half of Book Seven has found time for extraneous material, from details about lions attacking the army's camels on the march to Therma (7.125) to an excursion by Xerxes to view the gorge of the Peneus (7.128–30), but attention will now focus on topography relevant to the battle scene, the disposition of military forces, key political and social factors, decisions made and the course of the four-day battle. Oracles have been consulted by the Athenians (7.140–4), Argives (7.148), Cretans (7.169), Delphians (7.178) and Spartans (7.220), and battle plans discussed (7.177) before the first encounter takes the form of a naval skirmish (7.179–83) and the loss of three Greek ships. Consternation among the main fleet at Artemisium leads to a manoeuvre by the Greeks that makes one historian distrust Herodotus' grasp of events.[44]

Before the battle in the Thermopylae pass is described, Herodotus focuses on Xerxes' incomprehension at the Spartans' insouciance and their valedictory behaviour: his spies tell him they are exercising and combing their long (explained in 1.86) hair, knowing the battle about to commence is one they cannot win, and Demaratus' explanation only baffles him (7.209). A reliance on numerical advantage, noted in Book One as a cultural disposition of the Persians (1.136), underpins Xerxes' shock-and-awe battle plan and he waits four days in expectation that the enemy will withdraw. Enraged by his enemy's unwillingness to flee, Xerxes orders an engagement and sends in his Mede and Cissian contingents.

Herodotus' account of what happens next bears testimony to the vow in his proem to remember the past and preserve for posterity 'the great and marvellous' deeds (*erga*) of Greeks and non-Greeks. Events leading up to the battle have already produced notable achievements, not just the engineering of a bridge across the Hellespont for the world's largest military expedition but also the crucially important role of Athens in inspiring resistance and saving Greece (7.139). With Thermopylae, the greatness of the battle is attributable to the courage of individual Spartans and Herodotus consciously fulfils his chosen role as a memorialist seeking to preserve a record of a past that, like everything subject to the erasing power of time, will otherwise inevitably fade away into oblivion.

Many Medes fall on the first day of the battle and while their courage is recorded it is also remarked that while there were many of them 'there were

THE BATTLE OF THERMOPYLAE

210–12:   The first three days of the battle

213–18:   Mountain path behind the pass at Thermopylae

219–22:   Leonidas orders his allies to withdraw; oracle predicting either the fall of Sparta or the death of a Spartan king

223–35:   The final battle

226–33:   Remembering the dead and the survivors

234–8:   Xerxes and Demaratus convers

239:       Demaratus' letter announcing Xerxes' expedition

BOOK 7, BOX 6

few men' (7.210). Day two sees them replaced by the Immortals, reputedly the best Persian soldiers (7.83), but they fare no better and are outwitted by the Spartan manoeuvre of appearing to run away only to wheel round and surprise the enemy. Day three proves equally unrewarding for the Persians and they are forced to withdraw once more, only to be saved by Ephialtes' willingness to show them a path across the mountains to the other side of the pass. The news that the Persians have outflanked them confirms for the Greeks what their seer tells them at dawn and in the council that follows there is an alarming lack of unity (7.219). Herodotus voices his opinion that Leonidas saves the lives of his allies by ordering them to leave, leaving only Spartans, Thespians and some Theban hostages. Achieving by his sacrifice the task that Herodotus sets himself in the opening statement of the *Histories*, Leonidas attains 'glory' (*kleos*) for himself and ensures the 'good fortune' (*eudaimonie*) of Sparta will not be wiped away and lost forever.[45] In this way the words of the oracle are also fulfilled (7.220).[46]

The last hours of fighting are described with a simple but effective economy: the Persian conscripts are literally whipped into action and die alongside the Thespians and Spartans who Homerically beat back their enemies four times for the corpse of Leonidas.[47] In place of epic similes, though, clipped facts and the reasons for them are straightforwardly recorded; in 7.223 the explanatory 'for' (*gar*) is used on five occasions: 'for he had been directed by Ephialtes . . .'; 'for the descent from the mountain . . .'; 'for they had been holding the wall . . .'; 'for the leaders whipped them . . .'; 'for knowing death was looming . . .'. The power of the battle narrative is inseparable from the writing style and certain memorable moments that Herodotus records: the Spartans exercising and grooming themselves as if preparing for a scene for which they have been handed the final script (7.208), Dieneces' death-defying *bon mot* (7.226) and the speech act that names Ephialtes: 'on him I here fix the guilt' (7.214). The other reference to naming – Herodotus laying claim to knowing the names of all 300 (7.224) – is not dissimilar to the sublimity that Yeats in 'Easter, 1916' attaches to individual surnames. For Herodotus, as for the Irish poet, the quotidian (here the exercising and arranging of hair) is transformed into something moving and ennobling.[48]

After the battle there is a discussion between Xerxes and Demaratus, with Achaemenes decisively intervening to influence strategy and the king affirming his trust in Demaratus (7.234–7). This is the third conversation between Demaratus and Xerxes regarding the martial nature of the Spartans but this one (7.234–5) signals a marked progression from the previous two (7.101–4, 7.209): previously, Xerxes has been dismissive of the Spartans but now he acknowledges the correctness of Demaratus' assessment. Book Seven concludes with Xerxes' mutilation of Leonidas' corpse and a story about Demaratus sending a secret message to the Spartans warning them of the impending invasion.[49]

Book Eight: Showdown at Salamis

Artemisium and retreat (8.1–39)

Book Seven concludes with a self-sacrificing stand at Thermopylae in defence of Greece; Book Eight begins with a reminder that divisions between Greek states are a threat to the unity that will be necessary if viable resistance to the Persian invasion is to be maintained. The disunity and inter-state bickering that could undermine Panhellenic solidarity, which emerged when diplomatic missions visited Gelon in Sicily, the Corcyreans and the Cretans in the hope of forging an anti-Persian alliance (7.153–71), now resurface with the thorny issue of who is to lead the Greek fleet at Artemisium.

An analepsis reveals that both Athens and Sparta are contenders for leadership of the fleet but that the other allies insist on Sparta being given overall command, though whether their motive is dislike of Athens or respect for Spartan military prowess is not clarified. Athens, in accepting Spartan hegemony, would seem to be acting selflessly by recognizing the paramount importance of a united front, and the authorial voice concurs with an observation about the corrosive harm of internal strife. The Athenians waive their claim and, in Sélincourt's translation, continue to do so 'for as long as Greece desperately needed their help' (8.3). But the apparently authorial endorsement then qualifies itself by way of a prolepsis that suggests Athens was only ever interested in its own needs and masqueraded behind a show of Panhellenic unity. Looking forward to events after the defeat of Persian forces on Greek soil, 'the Athenians used the arrogance [*hybris*] of Pausanias [the Spartan supreme commander] as an excuse to deprive the Lacedaemonians of command' (8.3). In the light of this, Sélincourt's wording could be questioned and if it was reordered, making the Athenians the subject of the clause, it would read 'for as long as the Athenians needed their [the allies'] help'. Most modern translations – Blanco, Holland, Mensch, Waterfield – favour a wording along these lines, with the implication that Athens accepted Spartan leadership only because the alternative was to invite defeat by the Persians.[1] If Herodotus is

OUTLINE

8.1–39: Artemisium and retreat

1–18:	Sea battle at Artemisium
19–23:	Themistocles' post-battle tactic
24–6:	Xerxes after the battle
27–33:	Thessaly–Phocis feud
34–9:	Persians advance towards Athens and attempt to plunder Delphi

8:40–83: Before Salamis

40–1:	Attica abandoned
42–9:	Greeks at Salamis
50–5:	Persians reach Athens
56–64:	Greeks debate at Salamis
65:	divine dust-cloud
66–77:	Persians prepare for battle
78–83:	Greeks prepare for battle

8.84–96: Battle of Salamis

8.97–144: After Salamis

97–103:	Xerxes, Mardonius and Artemisia in conversation
104–6:	Hermotimus' revenge
107–25:	Xerxes retreats and Greeks debate their response
126–9:	Artabazus rejoins Mardonius
130–9:	Military moves in spring of 479
140–4:	Speeches by Alexander and Spartans; Athens' replies

BOOK 8, BOX 1

questioning the integrity of Athens' display of nobility in relinquishing her claim to leadership of the fleet, he nonetheless brackets off the city's suspected duplicity in deciding not to contest the matter of leadership. The observation, that civil war is as much worse than a war against a common enemy as war itself is worse than peace, is an ethical statement about the intrinsic worth of Athens' choice. It carries a moral conviction which is similar to what Herodotus attributes to Croesus in his conversation with Cyrus: 'No man is so foolish as to choose war instead of peace: in peace, sons bury their fathers; in war, fathers bury their sons' (1.87).

Book Eight does not follow on in strict chronological order from the end of Book Seven but goes back to a few days before Xerxes orders his troops to engage with the enemy at Thermopylae (7.210). The Persian plan is to simultaneously achieve victory on land and at sea, breaking through the pass at Thermopylae while at the same time trapping the enemy's fleet in the narrow strait between the mainland and the island of Euboea. The Greeks stationed at Artemisium in the north of Euboea, having good reason to feel imperilled and tempted to avoid open battle with a much larger fleet, are persuaded by the Athenian Themistocles not to retreat but stand firm. Themistocles is first introduced in Book Seven at a tense moment when two oracles from Delphi are being discussed in Athens (7.140–3). The first oracle is alarming, advising Athenians to flee to the 'ends of the earth', while the second one refers to a 'wall of wood' that will save the city. This could be referring to ships and thus signalling the importance of a naval defence but the oracle also associates the island of Salamis, near Athens, with disaster and this, contrariwise, could indicate a defeat at sea. Themistocles successfully argues that because the oracle refers to 'blessed' Salamis any calamity close to the island will be suffered by Persia, not Athens, and therefore the city should prepare for a battle at sea.[2] Herodotus adds that Themistocles' earlier advice to his city, to use a newfound source of wealth to build up a navy instead of sharing the proceeds amongst themselves, was also a crucial intervention (7.144).

Book Eight develops and nuances the characterization of Themistocles by describing the role he plays before the Battle of Artemisium. As long as a Greek force remains in position at Thermopylae it is strategically desirable for a naval presence to be maintained at Euboea, deterring the Persian fleet from moving south and outflanking the Greek army. The Euboeans, primarily concerned for their own safety and wanting the Greek fleet to remain long enough for them to flee to safety, privately offer a substantial bribe to Themistocles for this reason. He disposes of less than a quarter of the bribe to convince two other Greek commanders to stay and fight, allowing them to think the funds originate with Athens, and is able to pocket the rest of the money for himself. Herodotus' account of how Themistocles deftly manages to satisfy the Euboeans, maintain a unified Greek naval defence and discreetly secure a handsome profit for himself (8.5) carries no suggestion of moral disapproval. Indeed, given the ingrained Greek respect for *mētis* (cunning intelligence), what might be ethically questionable for a modern readership could well have impressed Herodotus' audience as laudably shrewd behaviour and worthy of the Homeric hero, Odysseus, the very embodiment of *mētis*.[3]

Xerxes orders a detachment of 200 ships from his fleet to sail down the east coast of Euboea, around its southern tip and up the other side, blocking the Greek fleet if it tries to retreat into the strait on the west side of the island (8.7). A storm wrecks this plan, which a Greek diver had already given them notice of after deserting from Persian service. A preliminary skirmish between the main fleets (8.9–11) boosts Greek morale and helps them stand up well to the numerically superior Persian fleet when the Battle of Artemisium gets under way (8.16–18). Herodotus aligns the three days of the sea battle with the three days of fighting at Thermopylae (8.15) and although he attributes the storm to a divine sense of fair play (8.13) his account of the sea battle itself offers a rational analysis of how the gargantuan size of the Persian navy proved advantageous for the Greeks.[4]

When news arrives of the Persian breakthrough at Thermopylae the Greek fleet loses no time in retreating southwards but the ever resourceful Themistocles finds time to sow what he hopes will be a seed of dissension in the ranks of the Ionians fighting on Persia's side (8.22). Such aptitude for clever, quick thinking is a defining characteristic of Themistocles and further examples will emerge in the course of the events unfolding but for the present it offers a sharp contrast with an attempt on Xerxes' part, taking place at the same time, to create an advantage for himself. The numerical scale of his losses at Thermopylae was a costly price for victory and to disguise the fact while also making the best of the situation he orders the secret burying of most of his own dead, leaving a relatively few scattered around the scene of the battle. This leaves a greater number of Greek corpses exposed to view and he has them heaped together in one pile before inviting his sailors to visit the scene. They are not so easily duped by what they see and the failure of Xerxes' inept subterfuge invites mockery (8.24–5). For Herodotus, a deceit can be appreciated if, like the telling of a good joke, it is well executed and there are a number of occasions in the *Histories* where a cleverly designed and successful stratagem speaks for itself and incurs no rebuke from the narrator. One was devised by the Persian general Amasis who, unable to capture Barca by conventional means, finally succeeded with a ploy involving a sworn oath.[5] In the field of cunning deception, Themistocles will be seen as a master professional when his ruses are compared to the crude amateurism displayed by Xerxes in his attempt to hoodwink his sailors.

The Thessalians respond to the news about Thermopylae by dispatching a herald to their neighbours, the people of Phocis, the only city in this northern region of Greece who has not thrown in its lot with the Persians. The Persian-friendly rulers of Thessaly, the Aleuadae, played a minor role in Xerxes' decision to mount an expedition against the Greeks (7.6), but the

Thessalians themselves were ardently anti-Persian and had called on their fellow Greeks to make a stand at Tempe. When the allies withdrew further south to Thermopylae, leaving them exposed, the Thessalians felt they could only protect their land by joining forces with the invading enemy (7.172–4). The herald they now send to Phocis is the bearer of blackmail, for unless the Phocians come up with a substantial amount of money the Thessalians will do nothing to prevent the Persians from destroying their land.

As if this is not enough to draw attention to the difficulties of keeping the Greek alliance unified, Herodotus sketches in the history of enmity between the Thessalians and Phocians (8.27–8) to explain what he thinks is the only reason why Phocis did not side with the Persians. Such was their hatred, claims Herodotus, that if the Thessalians had joined the Greek allies then Phocis would have joined forces with the Persians just to spite their old enemy (8.30). Memories of past hostilities leading to mistrust and vengeful manoeuvres pose a constant threat to Panhellenic camaraderie because the Thessalian–Phocian feud is by no means an aberrational feature of Greek life. Xerxes' father, after the Ionian revolt, was the first to send heralds to Greek cities demanding earth and water as tokens of surrender and Athens' neighbour, the island of Aegina, had duly obliged. It was the history of bad feeling between them that made Athens suspect the Aeginetan response was motivated by past enmity and sought only to harm their city (6.49, 5.83–9). The realization that Persia is intent on conquering Greece provides a centripetal impulse that can bring independent Greek *poleis* to support one another and act in unison but this impulse is always in danger of being suppressed and cohesion shattered by a centrifugal force fuelled by inter-state rivalries, wrangling and jealousies. A foretaste of what could happen is seen at Thermopylae when the Greeks realize they are about to be trapped: 'opinion was divided . . . the army split up; some departed and dispersed to their various cities, while others made ready to stand by Leonidas' (7.219).[6]

The main body of the Persian army marches south towards Athens while a smaller division splits off to ransack Delphi and expropriate its renowned treasures (8.35). A remarkable series of miraculous events greets the Persians at Delphi and Herodotus reports them without comment: sacred weapons from the inner shrine mysteriously appear outside, a bolt of thunder causes a rock fall that kills some of the Persians, a battle cry is heard from within the temple and two giant-sized figures pursue the fleeing soldiers. Herodotus says the rock fall could still be seen in his own day, though not that he has seen the evidence for himself, and from a modern historical perspective it is tempting to surmise that the supernatural lore developed in order to explain away Delphi's willingness to come to terms with Persian power before the invasion was repelled. Such a relegation of the role of the magical, however, risks falling into a dualist approach that would demarcate between a propensity for supernatural explanations exhibited in the early books of the *Histories* and a more 'professional' historical understanding that comes to the fore in the final three books.[7] The paranormal events at Delphi have

THE PERSIAN INVASION: OMENS, THE UNCANNY AND THE DIVINE

7.10:   Artabanus warns of divine displeasure with those who 'think big'

7.12–17:   Ghostly visitations to Xerxes and Artabanus warning of the dangers if the plan to invade Greece is abandoned

7.42:   Thunder and bolts of lightning

7.43:   A panic seizes men in the camp at Ilium

7.57:   A portent while wintering in Sardis: a mule gives birth to a foal with male and female genitals

7.37:   After leaving Sardis and setting off for the Hellespont, the army witnesses an eclipse of the sun

7.57:   Having crossed the Hellespont, another portent when a mare gives birth to a hare

8.13:   Herodotus attributes the storm that wrecks the Persian contingent of 200 ships to a supernatural intervention

8.37–8:   Miraculous events at Delphi when a plundering Persian force arrives

8.41:   Food regularly left out for a sacred snake on the Acropolis remains uneaten, taken as a sign that the goddess has departed the temple

8.55:   A burnt olive tree on the Acropolis produces a fresh shoot

8.65:   A sacred Eleusinian procession heading towards Salamis is seen by Dikaios and Demaratus

8.84   At the start of the Battle of Salamis, the spectre of a woman appears and the Greek fleet hears her voice urging them on

8.77:   An oracle speaks of Persia's defeat and divine justice

8.94:   During the Battle of Salamis, the Athenians say a ghostly ship appears to the fleeing Corinthians

8.129:   An unexpected flood, drowning the Persians who profaned a sanctuary at Potidaea, is believed to be the work of Poseidon

BOOK 8, BOX 2

their place in a pattern of uncanny moments that accompany Xerxes' invasion from its very inception (see Box 2) and some of them, as will be seen, have their own complexity.

Before Salamis (8.40–83)

The Battle of Artemisium proves inconclusive – in the naval theatre of war, a draw at best for the Greeks – and inconsequential for the Persian army marching southwards. Confrontations are looming on land and at sea but amongst the Greeks there is no agreement as to where and how these should be conducted. After Artemisium, the Greek fleet heads for the island of Salamis, only a short distance west of Athens, and preparations get underway for the evacuation of citizens from the region. The allied land forces have withdrawn to the Isthmus of Corinth, an eight-kilometre stretch of land that separates the Peloponnese from the rest of mainland Greece, so there is no alternative for the Athenians but to hurriedly abandon their homes and farms (8.40–1).[8] The allied fleet has increased in size, more than compensating for its losses at Artemisium, and a council of war takes place to try and decide on the best course of action.[9]

The council of war is interrupted by news of the Persians having reached Athens and set fire to the Acropolis (8.50–5) and this reinforces the general inclination to withdraw to the Isthmus and defend the Peloponnese. Themistocles is persuaded by an Athenian, Mnesiphilus, of the need to oppose this and he visit Eurybiades, the general in overall command of the allied fleet, to argue the case for staying and confronting the Persian navy at Salamis. In the discussion that follows (8.58–63) Themistocles' proposed tactics are sensible, pointing to the advantage of battling the enemy's fleet in narrow waters where numerical supremacy cannot be put to effective use, and both Thermopylae (7.211) and Artemisium (8.16) bear out the efficacy of his recommendation.

The Persians hold their own council of war (8.67–9) when Xerxes summons his commanders to convene and follow the order of the hierarchically arranged seating plan. Mardonius is appointed to question them for their opinions of the best military course of action to adopt. The orderly Persian convocation contrasts markedly with the animated proceedings of the Greeks[10] whose initial debate breaks up in panic when news is received of the Acropolis being torched (8.56). When it does reassemble it witnesses the trading of verbal hostilities between Themistocles and Adeimantus and while Eurybiades does decide to stay and fight at Salamis he is motivated, says Herodotus, by fear of his navy's plight should the Athenians pull out of the alliance and, as they threaten to do, sail away. He has also been persuaded by what Themistocles has said privately to him, that collective resistance to foreign conquest will dissipate if a united stand is not made at Salamis. Credit for this argument, however, is given to an unknown Athenian, Mnesiphilus, possibly suggesting that Herodotus' information originated from a source hostile to Themistocles.

The likelihood of Greek resistance imploding under certain circumstances is what Artemisia anticipates taking place if the Persians abandon the prospect of a sea battle and maintain their presence in Greece as a military threat. In her argument at the Persian debate Artemisia envisages the collapse of Greek resistance for, now that the Persians are in Greek territory, there is no need to risk a sea battle and in a matter of time, she assures Xerxes, 'you will scatter them and they will flee each to their city' (8.68).[11] Themistocles, in his private conversation with Eurybiades, also spoke of the danger of the Greeks scattering to their own cities (8.57) although in the presence of other Greek commanders he is politic enough not to accuse them of bare self-interest (8.60). Artemisia also displays a command of diplomatic skills in the way she couches her objections to the prevailing view while taking care to praise Xerxes' kingly virtue as 'the best of all men' (8.68). The way her projected scenario parallels one that Themistocles fears – notwithstanding the way they use them to draw opposing conclusions – invites the reader to see them in a similar light: outsiders who are prepared to advocate a course of action that is not supported by their military peers. Even if Themistocles is parroting what Mnesiphilus has said, he is prepared to publicly go against the grain just as Artemisia is willing to express an opinion which the other Persian commanders think is likely to result in her execution.

Artemisia's advice is appreciated by Xerxes who shows himself to be a competent commander-in-chief, considering different options and choosing one for a sound reason (8.69) even though it will fail to deliver the victory he plans for. This side to Xerxes, nuancing earlier negative portrayals of him as an Asian despot who ignores physical and moral boundaries, complements the figure of an individual who has to cope with the institutional pressures that come with supreme rule of an expansionist empire and a slavish mentality prevailing amongst most of those under him. The refusal on Herodotus' part to indulge in a one-dimensional portrait of a barbarian megalomaniac is also revealed when, after setting fire to the Acropolis, he wishes the Athenian exiles in his army to make sacrifices at the burnt temple 'after their manner' (8.54). A similar respect for foreign *nomoi* led him to sacrifice oxen to the Trojan Athena at Troy (7.43) and the apparent piety Xerxes now displays in Athens, coming so soon after he has ordered the destruction of the Acropolis, has Herodotus suggesting remorse over burning the Acropolis as a possible reason for his behaviour (8.54). The other reason, a prompting in a dream to have Athenians offer a sacrifice, could also reflect a guilty conscience or, as has been suggested, serve as a reminder to readers of earlier dreams that pressurized him to attack Greece in the first place: 'Xerxes, after all . . . is a prisoner of fate' (Flory 1987: 76).

As king, Xerxes has dictatorial powers but he convenes a Persian council of war and openly solicits opinions, refusing to censor Artemisia for her unorthodox point of view. Contrasting this with the democratically minded

Greeks throws up a paradox when noting the duplicitous scheming of an autocratically-inclined Themistocles before the Battle of Artemisium.

Xerxes commits his navy to an engagement at Salamis, convinced that his personal observation of the battle scene will ensure a more robust response on the part of his sailors. His army sets out for the Peloponnese where Greeks are desperately building a wall across the Isthmus of Corinth; the states contributing to this joint defence are listed and the point noted that not every Peloponnesian city made an effort to help (8.72–3), a reminder of the discords that have kept important states like Argos out of the anti-Persian alliance[12]. The near panic that threatens to undermine Eurybiades' decision to hold fast the allied fleet at Salamis is convincingly evoked given that the crisis facing the Greeks is an existential one. Thermopylae has proved a glorious failure, Persians have marched through central Greece and into Attica, Athenians are homeless, forced to abandon their city and farms, and it is only a matter of time before the invaders march towards the Peloponnese. There is discontent at the decision to keep the fleet at Salamis and another assembly is held which lays bare the lack of agreement amongst the allies (8.74). The situation leads to Themistocles' stratagem for forcing a sea battle at Salamis (8.75) and the broader context, the desperate urgency afflicting the Greeks' predicament, helps account, at this crucial state of affairs, for the specificity of a prophecy that underpins an authorial statement of belief in oracles (8.77).

Impelled by the empirical proof of the Bacis prophecy, Herodotus uses a double negative to express his conviction as to the truth of the divine utterance and the foolishness of anyone who would dispute it. The Persians, 'in the madness of hope', have sacked Athens and the prediction of a battle – 'bronze upon bronze shall clash' – that will 'redden the sea with blood' only to see Hellas emerge victorious will be borne out by the historical facts. What is noticeable about the prophecy of Bacis is its ethical import: it is 'divine justice' (*dia dikē*) that will put an end to the greed and the insolence of the wanton violence (*hybris*) of the invaders; Zeus, the son of Cronus (*Kronidēs*), will ensure that the Persians are defeated. The vocabulary in the prophecy, strongly religious and philosophical and rooted in highly traditional Greek thinking, can be related to the extremity of a situation that imperils the Greeks' sense of selfhood.[13] Herodotus' empathic engagement with this emotionally-charged historical moment is evident in his endorsement of the truth value accorded to a prophecy which uses the term *hybris*, the second of only two uses of the word in relation to the Persian invasion, in conjunction with the feeling that the natural order to the world (*dikē*) is being overturned.[14] It should be noted, however, that the authenticity of 8.77 has been challenged by editors of Herodotus from Macan in the early twentieth century to Bowie a hundred years later.[15]

Another prophetically-loaded moment, the fresh shoot growing from the burnt olive tree on the Acropolis (8.55), is handled more circumspectly. It is reported as an incidental happening, squeezed in between the occupation of

Athens by Xerxes and those he plans to subdue on the verge of hoisting sail and fleeing back to their homes across Greece. Herodotus does not offer an interpretation of what is seen on the Acropolis and, being focalized through the Athenian exiles ordered by Xerxes to offer a sacrifice on the despoiled and burnt out Acropolis, its significance only shines out in retrospect.[16]

While the Greeks are still wrangling about what is best to do with their fleet, Aristides arrives with the news that Themistocles' secret message to Xerxes has been received in the way he hoped it would: the Persians have blocked any escape from Salamis and a naval battle has become unavoidable for the Greeks.

The Battle of Salamis (8.84–96)

The military course of the Battle of Salamis has been discussed by historians and, because there is also an account of the battle in Aeschylus' drama, *The Persians*, what Herodotus writes can be compared with a second source.[17] As with Thermopylae, Herodotus singles out individuals and events that he considers noteworthy (8.85–96) and Artemisia continues to arrest his interest. The queen of Halicarnassus attracted attention on two previous occasions (7.99, 8.68–9) and her behaviour at Salamis confirms for Herodotus the extraordinary nature of her character. Artemisia's ramming of a ship that is on her side allows her to escape from a pursuing Athenian trireme and although there are different possible motives for ramming the ship there is no doubt about the double advantage it brings her. She escapes with her life because the Athenian ship thinks she must be on the Greek side and she earns admiration from Xerxes who mistakenly thinks she must have rammed an enemy ship. Munson sees a parallel between Artemisia and the pragmatic self-interest of Athens and, though such equivalence may be more than Herodotus intended, the similarity she discerns between Artemisia and Themistocles is intriguing.[18] It has been seen how both of them can envisage the withering away of the Greek alliance – for Artemisia an opportunity for victory; for Themistocles a recipe for certain disaster – and each of them also manage to deceive both sides at Salamis. Artemisia deceives both the pursuing Greek ship and, unintentionally, Xerxes while Themistocles prepares for the battle by deceiving his allies by not telling them that he has tricked Xerxes into thinking the Greek fleet is on the verge of departure.

The Athenian rumour that the Corinthians fled the battle and only returned after the action as the result of a supernatural phenomenon is reported (8.94), but it is puzzling because Herodotus can be seen to be questioning its accuracy by noting how other Greek states testify to the loyalty of the Corinthians. On the other hand, their commander Adeimantus has shown himself to be vehemently opposed to the idea of a battle at Salamis, although this could be part and parcel of an Athenian slander against a city they regarded as unfriendly.

Two messengers reach Susa with news about the outcome of the invasion, one about the capture of Athens and the second about the defeat at sea (8.99), an example of what has been called the 'laughter, tears and wisdom' motif in Herodotus (Flory 1978a): a spell of jubilation suddenly shattered by grief. An earlier instance saw Xerxes' initial gratification at the spectacle of a sailing race abruptly curtailed by a moment of reflection and here the celebratory mood which sees Susa's streets strewn with myrtle is unexpectedly turned to sadness and tears when the second messenger arrives.

Xerxes is minded to return home after the defeat at Salamis and Mardonius asks to be allowed to remain in Greece with an army. The king seeks the advice of Artemisia and their meeting takes place in private, unlike the public debate before the battle where Xerxes rejected her proposed strategy but recognized the value of an independent voice (8.67–9). He trusts her enough to put his sons in her care and that of a dependable eunuch and this allows for the telling of how Hermotimus came to be castrated when he was a child. In adult life he happens to encounter the merchant Panionius, responsible for his condition, and confronts him with his past – 'you made me a nothing instead of a man' (8.106) – before inflicting on him and his sons what he regards as an appropriate payback. The tale of Hermotimus' vengeful act of reciprocity may strike a reader as a non sequitur, a disparity unrelated to the post-Salamis military and political context, but it has been read as an analogy (Gray 2002: 308–9): Hermotimus calls Panionius 'unholy' because of the nature of his trade (8.106) and Themistocles similarly labels Xerxes for his acts of impiety in Greece (8.109); Xerxes and his family are in danger after Salamis and so too are Panionius and his sons. Gray admits that the analogy stops there, for while Hermotimus sees the gods as delivering the violator to him for punishment Xerxes does not suffer in such a personal way, unless the defeat of his invasion is seen as his punishment.

The revenge of Hermotimus harks back to an earlier tale of gruesome requital on the part of Astyages (1.119) as well as anticipating a tale soon to be told which also features a monstrous act of punishment (8.116). It is the unadulterated form of Hermotimus' *tisis* (vengeance) that Herodotus draws attention to in the opening sentence of 8.105, and the purity of its logic underlies his conclusion to the tale: 'Thus retribution – and Hermotimus – overtook Panionius' (8.106).[19] This incomparable act of revenge can be related to the importance of reciprocity in the Greek world – in this case changes of fortune brought about by reciprocal behaviour – and Herodotus' particular interest in wonders and exceptional events (Braund 1998: 165–7).

In tales like this one, Herodotus engages with the extraordinary *form* that supremely dedicated acts of revenge can take and victims suffer wordlessly because their subjective reactions are not what matter. As Strid observes, they are 'not represented as lamenting or complaining' and 'Herodotus himself wastes no words of empathy on them' (2006: 393). For Griffiths, there is no need for the author to say anything given the gross humour behind what he calls the 'situational irony' of a story about someone entrusted with the guardianship of children who has so grotesquely mistreated other young people (2001a: 172). For Hornblower (2003), the tale is not to be taken too literally and, in an intriguingly multi-layered analysis of the story, he looks to the biblical story of Joseph, the history of Chios, the nature of eunuchs in Persia, the identity of Panionius and why the tale occurs at this particular juncture in the *Histories*. Such tales and the different readings they produce raise the question of Herodotus' intentions as a storyteller and such a question will shortly arise again with the story of Xerxes' alternative sea journey back to Asia.

After Salamis (8.97–144)

When the Greeks discuss whether to pursue the Persian fleet from Andros to the Hellespont and prevent their enemy from returning home, Themistocles emerges again as a central and this time more complex figure. He initially argues for chasing the enemy and breaking up their bridge across the Hellespont, but when this policy is rejected by most of the commanders an insouciant Themistocles reverses his position and argues for the opposite course of action (8.108–9). His speech to the Athenians, who still want to pursue the Persians, persuades them to adopt the majority view but in a rare nod to events outside the scope of the *Histories* – an ostracized Themistocles will later flee Greece for the Persian court[20] – Herodotus claims his motive is a wish to ingratiate himself with the Persians in the event that one day he might need their support. To this effect, Themistocles dispatches a secret message to Xerxes assuring him of his success in restraining the Greeks from pursuing him (8.108–10).

Themistocles' Athenian past has been presented in a positive light (7.143–4) and at Artemisium his political and practical skills were put to good use in the defence of Greece. His ruse to keep the allied fleet at Salamis is effective (8.75), preventing a possible collapse of the defensive alliance, and it will be seen how his importance is recognized by other Greeks. The aspersion cast on him by Herodotus could, as noted above with regard to the way an unknown Athenian is credited for recognizing the need to fight at Salamis (8.57), be due to the author's reliance on a hostile source for some of his information.[21] What is not in doubt is the rhetorical skill of Themistocles in persuading the Athenians to relinquish the idea of a pursuit to the Hellespont. He applauds what they have already achieved – saving themselves and 'all of Greece' by repulsing 'this great cloud of men' – while piously acknowledging the help of the gods and concluding in a homely and heartening fashion: 'let us remain in Greece and take care of ourselves and our families' (8.109). It is a polished performance, finely analysed by Baragwanath (2008: 298–322), and the emotional appeal of the speech reaches out to Herodotus' audience, most likely engaging their support for what is a sound and sensible summation of the situation. And yet it is quickly undercut by the cynical observation that his motive is a selfish one. Themistocles, comments Herodotus immediately after the speech (8.110), was 'deceiving' (*dieballe*), using the same verb that Herodotus used after Aristagoras' success in winning over the Athenian assembly – having previously failed to convince the Spartan king – when acerbically noting how 'apparently it is easier to hoodwink (*diaballein*) a crowd than a single person' (5.97). Nonetheless, it seems unfair to bracket Themistocles with Aristagoras or, for that matter, with the Athenian assembly tempted by promises of riches in Persia. It is difficult to reach a conclusive judgement concerning the characterization of Themistocles, a gifted individual who plays a major role in saving Greece, but scholarly reception has not always held back from detecting a negative portrayal or finding his character too contradictory for comfort. In a valuable examination of how and why Themistocles is presented in the way he is, Fornara's riposte to those who feel the need for a more consistent representation is to remark that Herodotus is not interested in portraying him as if he were a hero from a nineteenth-century novel (2013: 327). Herodotus is writing in a cultural climate where wiliness and adroit self-interest are not disdained and for an audience well aware of Themistocles' sensational escape to the Persian court. The abrupt change of mind, once a race to the bridge at the Hellespont has been ruled out, is not so much the behaviour of a hypocrite as a quick-thinking reaction to circumstances and a shrewd ability to make the best out of a situation. Such a reading of Themistocles is not incompatible with the possibility that Herodotus is presenting an Athenian audience with uncomfortable aspects of their own greed and violence, using Themistocles to critically comment on Athens' usurpation of the Delian League for its own imperial purposes (Blösel 2001).

In his speech, Themistocles gives expression to the role of the gods in punishing Xerxes for his sacrilegious behaviour and arrogant presumption that Asia and Europe could be yoked together under one man's arbitrary rule. It is a conventional viewpoint that finds a poetic voice in Aeschylus' *The Persians*[22] and, as noted earlier, Herodotus endorses a similar sentiment when spoken by the oracle of Bacis (8.77). The two contexts, however, are dissimilar, for the oracle is referred to in a highly-charged situation where disagreement amongst the Greeks threaten their survival whereas Themistocles is seeking to mollify the Athenians' desire for revenge by explaining how the gods have terminated Xerxes' ambitions and all is now well.

Andros is besieged by the Athenians and Themistocles comes in again for some hostile reporting when the demand for money from various islands is attributed to his pecuniary greed (8.112). Notwithstanding his earlier pocketing of a bribe (8.5), it had been agreed among the allies that those states who submitted to the Persians would have to pay an indemnity in the form of an offering to Apollo at Delos (7.132). Greek commanders acknowledge their debt to Themistocles, awarding him most of the second

votes (their first votes went to each of themselves) for a prize of valour at the
Battle of Salamis (8.123), and Sparta goes out of its way to honour his
achievement (8.124). Sparta also dispatches a herald to the Persians in
Thessaly demanding reparation for the murder of their king at Thermopylae.
Xerxes' response is to laugh and then point to Mardonius, saying he will
give them the reparation they deserve (8.114). Laughing is nearly always
in Herodotus a sign of something uncongenial in the offing and, with
Mardonius dying at the hands of the Spartans at Plataea, so it is in this case.

Mardonius' choice of troops and Xerxes' journey home to Susa occupy a
number of chapters (8.113–20) but the memorable incident is the account of
a sea journey that Herodotus believes never took place. For Mardonius the
defeat at Salamis is only a contingent failure, something to be remedied by
trying again; for Xerxes, whose desire to immediately return home signifies
a deeper sense of loss, solace is found by leaving behind a proxy subject to
obtain the satisfaction which he has failed to find. The alleged account of
Xerxes' sea journey is regarded by Herodotus as empirically improbable but
this does not deter him from reporting it in remarkable detail (8.118), using
direct speech and pictorial details that bring it alive – the developing storm,
a heaving ship and crowded deck, Persians doing obeisance before hurling
themselves overboard – capping it with an extraordinary response by the
king whose life has been saved. So vivid is the telling of the tale that prosaic
explanations of its purpose seem inadequate: a capricious tyrant, given to
excessive mood swings, characteristically contradictory in his behaviour.[23]
Macan in his commentary on the passage before summarizing the tale's
import impishly asks if the captain wore the crown at his execution: 'The
anecdote illustrates the despot's cowardice and caprice, and the ludicrous
loyalty of his subjects; it is a part of the comic Nemesis, though a trifle grim'
(2013: 546).

The remaining chapters of Book Eight are mostly taken up with military
matters: Mardonius spends the winter in Thessaly and Artabazus, having
escorted Xerxes in safety to the Hellespont, sets out to rejoin him. Along the
way, Artabazus lays siege to two cities in northern Greece that have revolted
against Persian rule but suffers a mishap outside one of them, Potidaea,
when an unexpected flood-tide drowns many of his men. Herodotus accepts
that they have been punished by a god for profaning the sanctuary that
stood outside the town (8.129), recalling what happened at Delphi to the
Persians for their impieties (8.35–9) and Herodotus' earlier statement that
the storms off Euboea were attributable to divine agency.

What remains of the Persian navy gathers at Samos and in the spring
of 479 the Greek fleet comes together at Delos under the command of
Xanthippus, with no reason given for why Themistocles no longer holds
that position. Mardonius consults oracles in the region of Greece where he
is camped and sends an ambassador to Athens (8.133–6). The emissary is
Alexander of Macedon, the man whose first encounter with Persians proved
eventful (5.18–22) and who later advised the Greeks (7.173). Herodotus

now provides an account of how three brothers from Argos in Greece came to rule over the kingdom of Macedonia. Readers today can enjoy a charming story, featuring bread mysteriously doubling in size, a younger son gathering sunlight three times into the folds of his tunic, a life-saving flood and a land where roses each with sixty petals blossom with a fragrance surpassing all others, and appreciate its folk tale elements. For Herodotus, there is also a creditably traceable line of direct descent from the younger son in the tale to the historically real Alexander, ancestor of Alexander the Great, who arrives in Athens on behalf of the Persians. Such a combination of the fabulous with the factual is characteristic of Herodotus' handling of oral traditions and genealogies and he seems not to notice – or if he does, is not bothered by – recurring motifs in local stories he hears. The Macedonian tale, with its singling out of the youngest of the three brothers, bears a family resemblance to the two stories about Scythian royalty: in one, golden objects fall from the sky and the younger brother assumes the kingship (4.5); in the other, only the youngest son can bend the bow of Heracles (4.8–10). The challenge of bending a particularly strong bow featured earlier in the account of the Ethiopian king and his defiant message to the king of Persia (3.21). Another case of a recurring motif occurs just a little earlier in the story of Artabazus and Timoxenus secretly communicating with one another (8.128). Their recourse to arrows, with letters wrapped around the notched ends, shot to prearranged locations is not used elsewhere in the *Histories* but other modes of secreting messages are.[24]

Mardonius' reasons for choosing Alexander as his ambassador and his objectives in doing so, as presented in 8.136, point to a highly analytic approach, though this may be taken more as a reflection of Herodotus' ability to comprehend and summarize a complex situation than of Mardonius' political skills at assessing how best to proceed after Salamis. The concluding sentence of this chapter, a casual suggestion that the oracles mentioned earlier (8.133–6) could have played a part in the deliberations, may carry more weight than the offhand way in which it is delivered. When Alexander does reach Athens he addresses his audience, relaying the words of Xerxes that are nested within the words of Mardonius that are delivered as a speech direct to the Athenians. This is followed up with Alexander's own speech urging his fellow Greeks to accept the offer from the Persians but Athens delays replying until a Spartan delegation, arriving in the knowledge that the Persians are trying to broker a deal, has also been heard. The Spartan response is a mixture of intemperance, blaming the Athenians for causing the trouble in the first place ('none of us desired it'), curtness (dismissing Alexander as a Persian lackey) and solicitude (offering material aid for non-Spartan civilians who have suffered).

What follows is, first, Athens' defiant rejection of Persia's terms and Alexander's entreaties and, second, a high-minded reply to the Spartans declaring why Athenians would never betray the Greek people who 'share the same blood, the same language, the same temples, sacrifices and customs'

(8.144).[25] Athens has stage-managed events for maximum self-kudos by arranging Sparta's presence at the time of Alexander's mission and allowing themselves to be reprimanded before stealing the show with their espousal of Greek solidarity. The Spartan delegates can hardly object to the request for immediate military support, a crucial concern to Athens which now faces a second invasion of their city unless the Persian war machine is confronted in Boeotia.

The Athenians have the high moral ground and, taken with Herodotus' earlier assessment that they played the supremely pivotal role in saving Greece (7.139), the rhetorical register of their two speeches expressing a commitment to freedom and Hellenic solidarity looks to be justified. An issue that arises, however, is to what extent Herodotus is being ironic in reporting, using direct speech, the self-declared stance of Athens in the face of Persian power. At the time when Herodotus is writing, around the third quarter of the fifth century, the prospect of mellow amity between Greek states is at its most unlikely. Athens is exerting imperial power over fellow Greeks and in the search for allies at the beginning of the Peloponnesian War (431) looks to the old enemy Persia. The Greeks are about to enter another war but this time an intra-ethnic conflict of their own making. What the Athenians declare about the identity of Hellenism (*to hellēnikon*), often taken out of context as a definition of how the Greeks viewed themselves, needs to take account of the political and military situation in which the speech is delivered. The victory at Salamis does not guarantee the safety of Athens, the Persian army still poses an existential threat for the city, and military support from Sparta for an unavoidable battle on land is essential. The rousing declaration of a common ethnicity may be wishful thinking, looking to a shared language, religion and culture but omitting intra-Greek political divisions and internecine disputes over territory that undermine talk of solidarity. The speech concludes with a pragmatic appeal for the Spartans to dispatch their army without further delay.[26] None of this, though, robs the two speeches of their power to impress and they possess an immanent grandeur because the future is so uncertain and the chances of a concerted alliance so precarious. What is defined, identified as Hellenism, *comes to be* through the impending threat of being lost. The words of Alexander, urging the striking of a deal, have a persuasive force because Greece is a self-divided collection of quarrelling states and Athens does risk bearing the brunt of Persian aggression on her own. Paradoxically, Alexander's speech generates what it sets out to negate: a Panhellenic Greece – as opposed to what has been called an 'intrahellenic' one (Hall: 1997: xiii) – emerges from its imminent loss.[27]

Irony is present if Herodotus is viewed as commenting to his audience on the politics of his time, exposing hypocrisy or with a purpose 'to educate them, to prepare them for the great challenges present and future'.[28] It is equally possible that nostalgia and regret inform the irony, a wistful nod to the utopian sentiments to which they eloquently give voice. From this perspective, the speeches bear witness to a Panhellenic consciousness that was raised to a new and noble height in the face of the Persian threat while also acknowledging it could not ultimately triumph over the endemic wrangling and territorial jealousies that so clearly existed long before the Persian invasion. Within the textual narrative, a shortcoming that risks scuppering the principle of eternal resistance to the invader will soon come to the surface when the Spartans fail to deliver the military support that Athens so desperately needs.

An important aspect of the story of the Persian invasion which emerges across Book Seven and Book Eight is the tight chronology of decisive moments

---

TIMESCALES FOR XERXES' INVASION

7.20: After **four years** spent preparing troops and the logistics, the march of the Persian army begins.

7.37: After the **winter season** waiting in Sardis, the march continues towards the Hellespont.

8.51: **One month** is spent crossing the Hellespont.

8.51: In **three months,** the Persians march from the European side of the Hellespont to Athens.

8.66: After Thermopylae, within a **few days,** the Persian fleet sails away from the region and reaches the Bay of Phalerum, south of Athens and close to Salamis.

8.71: The Persian fleet departs Phalerum and **the same night** the Persian army under Mardonius sets off for the Peloponnese.

8.113: **A few days** after Salamis, the Persian army marches to Boeotia in central Greece.

8.129: After trying to capture Potidaea for **three months,** Artabazus (who escorted Xerxes back to the Hellespont) sets off to rejoin Mardonius.

8.130: After **the winter of 480/479,** the Persian fleet gathers at Samos.

8.131–3: With **the arrival of spring,** the Greek fleet heads for Delos.

BOOK 8, BOX 3

and movements of the opposing land and sea forces. A concern with carefully recording the sequence of historical events by way of the seasons of each year is a hallmark of Thucydides' account of the Peloponnesian War while Herodotus' *Histories*, by comparison, tends to be loosely associated with a less systematic and more leisurely approach to his subject matter. Such a perceived difference between the two writers is a vestigial echo of what for a long time was a diacritical opposition between Thucydides the 'professional' historian, scientific and meticulous, and Herodotus the 'entertaining' historian, the artful teller of sometimes tall stories. Such a polarization, of course, ignores the different time spans that concern the two historians: a specific period of very recent conflict between Athens and Sparta for Thucydides, an eyewitness, as opposed to a conflict between Greeks and barbarians that for Herodotus has roots stretching back to before the Trojan War. He has to rely on oral traditions passed down through the ages, king lists and genealogies and personal accounts that reach back three generations at most.[29] When it comes to the rise of the Persian Empire, the reigns of the four kings provide a firm temporal grid and by the time of Darius' invasion of Greece a generation that includes Herodotus' parents has elderly representatives alive to recall their memories.

Beginning with the Ionian revolt in 499, Herodotus is able to provide a year-by-year account of events and after Darius' defeat at Marathon in 490 the chronological record refers to shorter and shorter periods of time, from seasons to months, to days and even to hours, and there are more precise temporal references than ever before (see Box 3).

Book Nine: Persia defeated

Hostilities resumed (9.1–27)

Salamis is a victory at sea for the Greeks but the Persian army remains undefeated on land. Xerxes has returned to Asia while Mardonius, after receiving Athens' rejection of peace terms, prepares for their subjugation by military force. Mardonius' desire for victory cannot be assuaged by resorting to the bribery of Greek commanders, as the Thebans suggest (9.2),[1] and Herodotus attributes this to his obstinacy and his wish, using beacons from the high points of islands, to signal Xerxes in Sardis that Athens has been captured (9.3). This is not a belittlement of the man and is consistent with his character as it first emerges in Book Seven with his urging Xerxes to add Greece to the list of many races that Persia has conquered (7.9). After the setback at Salamis, although Mardonius remains confident of ultimate victory he is prepared to die nobly on the battlefield, a price worth paying to prevent the Greeks mocking Persia (8.100). The note of self-dramatization in his make-up could partly be compensation for his own less-than-glorious campaign in Thrace (6.45) and his worry after Salamis that he will be blamed for encouraging Xerxes to invade Greece (8.100). Artemisia shows no willingness to celebrate his renown or his value, telling the king that it matters not if something happens to him while remaining behind in Greece (8.102). If Mardonius can vanquish the Athenians in their own city he will triumphantly redeem himself, win glory for Persia and be justified in rejoicing by having beacons signal his victory across the sea to Asia. The prestige that would accrue to him by signalling Xerxes in such a dramatic manner finds support in the theatrical value that Aeschylus mines in just such a means of communication when, at the start of *Agamemnon*, news of the fall of Troy reaches Argos in this way. Clytemnestra crisply informs the Chorus of the news in stichomythia, dialogue in alternate lines between two characters, before devoting some thirty-five lines to a solo tour de force that poetically describes the triumphant progress of the beacons.[2]

OUTLINE

9.1–27: Hostilities resumed

1–13:	Mardonius occupies Athens, Spartans delay sending support
14–18:	Mardonius in Boeotia
19–25:	Persian cavalry in action and the death of its commander, Masistius
26–7:	Tegeans and Athenians argue

9:28–75: Battle of Plataea

28–32:	The rival armies
33–8:	The seers
39–50:	A waiting game
51–9:	The Greeks move camp and the Persians attack
60–70:	The battle
71–5:	Individuals of renown

9.76–89: Plataea's aftermath

76–85:	Division of the spoils and Pausanias' dinner
86–8:	Retribution for Thebes
89:	Artabazus returns home

9.90–107: Battle of Mycale

90–2:	Samian request for support
93–5:	Story of Euenius
96–7:	Movement of Greek fleet and the Persians
98–101:	The Greeks land and attack
102–7:	Persians defeated and Greeks sail to the Hellespont

9.108–22: After Mycale

108–13:	Xerxes' illicit desires
114–21:	Athenians at the Hellespont, Abydos and Sestos
122:	Cyrus' advice to the Persians

BOOK 9, BOX 1

Apropos the earlier look at how the Athenians' speech to Alexander might be interpreted (8.143, see pp. 230–1), the response to Lycidas' proposal that Murychides' delivery of the same peace terms be given serious consideration indicates in no uncertain terms how the Athenian public feels about the matter (9.5). They not only stone Lycidas to death but the city's women, in what comes across as an act of mob violence that could be deemed hysterical, do the same to the man's wife and children. Herodotus does not comment on this shocking outbreak of communal violence but it points to tensions within the Athenian body politic and an alarming limit to its capacity to tolerate the expression of dissenting opinions.

At the time of Alexander's embassy the Spartans were also addressed and courteously implored to send an army to support a joint military engagement with the Persians in Boeotia, before the enemy invades Attica for a second time. Such help is not immediately forthcoming, leading again to an evacuation to Salamis and the occupation of an empty city by the Persians; the Athenians repeat their request with a hint that an accommodation with the enemy may be necessary (9.6–7). A Spartan army is eventually dispatched, under the command of Pausanias, but it is self-interest that rouses the city into action after it is pointed out that the wall that has been built and fortified across the isthmus will not protect Spartans if Athens strikes a deal and becomes an ally of the Persians (9.9). According to the ambassadors in Sparta, Athens is prepared to accept the Persians' peace proposals (9.11), something previously declared impossible (8.143–4), though declaring such an intention could be their final negotiating ploy in a desperate attempt to shift Spartan recalcitrance. Baragwanath considers this quite likely, though alongside the further possibility that the Athenian messengers and public opinion in Athens (bearing in mind the fate of Lycidas and his family) are not of one mind (2008: 234–7). She also draws attention to the similarity between the unenviable position Athens finds herself in and the one faced earlier by the Thessalians (7.172–4). The people of Thessaly were keenly opposed to Persian hegemony and only changed their allegiance when they felt there was no alternative. Their predicament is now Athens' and it convinces the Persian commander that the city will come to make a similar decision out of the same sense of necessity (9.13). Mardonius gets it wrong; he puts Athens to the torch for the second time and heads back to Thebes to await the Greeks who have not come over to his side.

The force of necessity (ananke) that the Thessalians submit to is material, not fatalistic; the powerful size of the Persian army cannot be defeated by one group of people acting in isolation. This has enabled it to coerce others into submission (7.108) but what Thersander relates to Herodotus – a rare case where the author names his source – is on the face of it a tale about a different kind of ananke. The Persian who shares a couch with Thersander feels certain that his side will be defeated in the coming battle but he is equally sure that there is nothing he can do to change the outcome: 'that which heaven wills, no man can turn aside ... many of us know this yet we obey, constrained by necessity' (9.16). It seems he does not mean the kind of necessity that compels the Thracian tribes to serve as infantry for Xerxes (7.110) but the kind that Amasis recognizes when he hears how Polycrates finds the ring he had deliberately cast away into the sea (3.41). Themistocles mockingly conflates these two kinds of necessity when he tells the Andrians, from whom he is extracting money, that the Athenians have two gods to aid them, Persuasion and Necessity (8.111). Perhaps the anonymous Persian who weeps in his conversation with Thersander also, though without the calculated cynicism of Themistocles, senses the two kinds of *anankē*, intuiting the doomed nature of an invasion that the gods will not allow to succeed but also pragmatically aware that the orders of Mardonius cannot be questioned: 'this is the worst of human sorrows, to have knowledge but be powerless to act', he regretfully concludes (9.16).[3]

When the Spartans and their allies in the Peloponnese arrive in Boeotia they encamp in the foothills of Mount Cithaeron near Plataea. They are reluctant to contest the Persians on the more open ground of the plain which separates them from the River Asopus, on the other side of which Mardonius has stationed his forces. Descending to the plain would invite a full-scale pitched battle but the Greeks are subject nevertheless to cavalry charges by enemy squadrons. In one such foray, a contingent from Megara calls for assistance – 'Sore bestead by the darts and arrows of the enemy, and with no cavalry to aid them, the Megarians required succour' (Bury 1957: 290) – and 300 Athenians come to their assistance. When the Persian cavalry commander Masistius is killed there is a much larger engagement between the entire cavalry and the Athenians. The result is a victory of sorts for the Greeks when, unable to retrieve the corpse of Masistius and suffering losses, the Persian cavalry decides to retreat.

The account of the death of Masistius and the struggle for his body (9.22–3) is uncharacteristically detailed for Herodotus – descriptions of death on the battlefield are something he tends not to dwell on – and it is told from an Athenian vantage point. This suggests an Athenian source for the story, a source keen to draw attention to that city's contribution to the victory at Plataea. The magnitude of Athens' contribution is reinforced by the emphasis on Masistius' heroic qualities: renowned for his good looks and his height, he is not easily killed and only when a soldier targets his eye is the formidable opponent finally slain (and, echoing the killing of Ilioneus by Peneleos, in a Homeric fashion, *Iliad*, 14.475). The sense of loss experienced by the Persians at the loss of their commander (9.24) further underlines the value of the Athenian presence at Plataea.

The withdrawal by the Persian cavalry gives the Greeks confidence to move to lower ground with a better water supply (9.20–5). When it comes to the disposition of the various Greek contingents, however, a dispute arises between the Tegeans and Athenians over who has the most right to hold the remaining prestigious position on the left wing (Sparta holding the right wing).

The contretemps between the Tegeans and Athenians (9.26–7) is revealing for what it suggests about Herodotus' critical awareness of the distance between mythical and historical time (see pp. 18–19), an abiding concern from when it was first raised at the start of the *Histories*, and his respect for the cultural importance that communities attach to mythological material. The two sides disputing the right to take up a high-status battle position use the mythical past to buttress their claims and win the argument and this eristic use of mythology, more characteristic of the later books than the early ones, relates especially to Xerxes' expedition (Bowie: 2012: 278–9). The Tegeans look back to their stand against the Heraclidae, sons of Heracles, led by Hyllus who proposed that their dispute with Peloponnese cities be settled by single combat. It was a Tegean king who took up the challenge and killed Hyllus, winning privileges which include the right of leading one of the wings in any joint Peloponnese enterprise. The Athenians counter this by referring back to their support for the Heraclidae, recovering the bodies of those who fought with Polynices, a son of Oedipus, for control of Thebes, and throw in for good measure their defeat of the Amazons and their contribution to the war with Troy.

In this game of myth-telling one-upmanship, the Athenians have stronger cards to play with given that the Spartans are Heraclids (7.208, 8.114)[4] and, their winning ploy, the verbal contest can be brought to an end by acknowledging its silliness and reminding everyone that their prowess has been validated by facing up to and defeating the enemy at hand. Conveniently forgetting to mention the Plataeans who fought with them at Marathon – 'we alone of all the Greeks met the Persians single-handedly' (9.27) – they rest on their laurels and, with a graciousness that is as diplomatically astute as it may be authentic, ask to be put wherever the Spartans see fit.[5]

The rival mythic-loaded claims are terminated – 'enough about deeds of long ago' – more abruptly but no less decisively than in the opening of the *Histories* (1.5) when a line is drawn between the unverifiable tales of the Persian *logoi* and the historical figure of Croesus (and the making of a similar distinction at 3.122). A recall of the opening chapters is strengthened with the remark about how a brave people of the past may become cowards in the present and vice versa, an echo of the proem's concluding observation that the great and the small can undergo reversals in the course of time.[6]

Battle of Plataea (9.28–75)

Before the battle itself is described, the role of seers in the opposing armies receives attention in a way that is not a feature of the earlier accounts of Marathon, Thermopylae or Salamis.[7] This could be an indication of the importance both sides attach to the coming battle, recognizing it as the decisive moment that will determine the success or failure of the Persian invasion, but this may not be the primary focus of Herodotus' treatment of the seers. Tisamenus, on the Greek side, comes from Elis but along with his brother has the unique claim of being granted Spartan citizenship. The story of how this came about, rather than details of his divinely gifted ability to prophesy, is what attracts Herodotus' interest (9.33). The manner in which he gained Spartan citizenship is compared with the way the legendary Melampus acquired the kingship of half of Argive territory and another one-third for his brother (9.34).[8] The point of the comparison is not clear and one may wonder if it is only for the sake of amplifying the narrative about Tisamenus that the analogy is drawn out at such length.[9] The huge importance that the Spartans attach to Tisamenus stands in its own right as testimony to the desperation felt by the Spartans at the possibility of defeat at Plataea. They have correctly interpreted the significance of the value Delphi accords the seer: he will win five military contests not athletic ones, and his presence on the field of battle is the only way they can feel confident about victory given the numerical advantage enjoyed by the Persians (9.32). The unprecedented price they are prepared to pay for his presence at Plataea is an index of the extremely dire threat posed by the Persian army encamped on the far side of the Asopus river; this has been spelt out for them by Chileus (9.9).

The Persians have their own paid seer, Hegesistratus a Greek, and as with Tisamenus there is a background story to tell. It is a tale of (unspecified) crime and punishment, self-mutilation and escape, embittered hatred and sanctuary in the camp of the enemy (9.37). Hegesistratus cuts off his own foot to escape from the stocks the Spartans have placed him in, pending his execution, and he finds refuge in Persia. His going over to the other side places him in a line of such actants: Hippias (6.107), Demaratus (6.70, 7.3) and Themistocles (8.109).

After eight days of a waiting game, the Persians capture a Greek supply column and continue with their cavalry forays while Mardonius resists the entreaties of Artabazus to withdraw back to Thebes where there are abundant supplies (9.39–41). The Macedonians have been placed opposite the Athenians (9.31) and now their leader Alexander, making his final appearance in the *Histories*, rides across to the Athenian camp with the news that Mardonius has decided to attack (9.44).[10] In response to this, battle lines are reorganized by Pausanias (as with the slaying of Masistius, the reorganization of the Greek battle line at 9.46–8 is another reminder of Athens' valuable contribution to the battle) but by now the Greeks are low on supplies and the source of their water supply has been contaminated by the enemy. A decision is made to withdraw under cover of darkness and move closer to Thebes for fresh water and the replenishment of supplies (9.51). The narrative meanders at times and is not always easy to follow because a lot happens before the battle proper begins.[11] The decision to withdraw at night leads to confusion when some of the Greeks follow their own minds and not the orders given, compounded by the refusal of one commander from the Peloponnese, Amompharetus, to move as it would seem he was running away (9.53). This leads to a protracted argument but eventually Pausanias is joined by Amompharetus; the Athenian contingent also starts moving position but along a different route. The Persian cavalry attacks Pausanias' and Amompharetus' troops and a complacent Mardonius, receiving news of the Athenian departure, thinks a general retreat is taking place and triumphantly gives chase (9.58–9). The last of his recorded words, addressing a group of Thessalians, hark back ironically to Xerxes' riposte to the Spartans that Mardonius will be the one who will make amends to them (8.114). Here he is seen misunderstanding the movement of the Spartan troops and insisting they be relentlessly pursued so that they make amends and suffer the punishment that is due to them (*dikas*, 9.58).

Pausanias sends a message to the Athenians calling for their assistance but they are held back by a contingent of Greeks who are fighting on Persia's side (9.60–1). The Spartan and Tegean hoplites, armoured and bearing spears, battle the Persians on their own and prove superior;[12] Mardonius is killed and his dispirited army withdraw to a fort they have built near Thebes. Persians are slain in the vicinity of a sanctuary of Demeter but, extraordinarily, not a single one is killed within it and Herodotus is prepared to see this as another sign of divine intervention, fitting a pattern traceable throughout the invasion (see Book 8, Box 2, p. 220). The Greeks who had earlier disobeyed orders try to join the fray when they hear that Pausanias is winning but they are cut down by Theban horsemen. The Athenians, impeded by no fault of their own, make a belated contribution.

Individual Greeks are singled out for their bravery but Herodotus has no doubt that the battle was a Spartan victory (9.70–9). The killing of Mardonius is atonement for the death of Leonidas and, augmenting the memory of Thermopylae by way of a memorable numeral, it is remarked how the slayer of the Persian commander, Arimnestus, would also later die leading 300 men against the Messenians (9.64).

The death of Callicrates (9.72) is (like the death of Masistius) an exception to the general character of the way moments of death are reported by Herodotus. Boedeker (2003) draws attention to the way the subjective, emotional experience of the dying character is not usually reported and Strid (2006: 402), refining this by noting the all-important factor for Herodotus of the marvellous, can point to what is exceptional about Callicrates and makes his death an exception to the general rule. The man was not only regarded by everyone in the Greek camp as the most 'beautiful' (*kallistos*) but his regret at dying off the field of battle and, in his mind, not having accomplished a deed worthy of himself is exactly what does endow the end of his life with nobility.

Sophanes does not die at Plataea but he gains the prize for valour and Herodotus provides two accounts of how he distinguishes himself (9.74): the one that would have him on the field of battle dropping an anchor that is tied to his waist so that he couldn't be driven from his position is palpably fictional but an appealing anecdote nonetheless; the other account, that he bore an emblem of an anchor on his shield, is more likely to be true but prosaic by comparison. There may well be tongue-in-cheek humour at work here – a burlesque of Greek battlefield heroism even (Flory 1987: 74) – but not to the extent of discrediting Sophanes' courageous tenacity. His bravery has already been established and his honourable conduct and death at a battle yet to come is recorded with respect (9.75, 6.92).

A more complex use of time than that found in 9.26–7, recalling for a modern audience the opening lines of Eliot's *Four Quartets*,[13] characterizes the information that is provided about Sophanes' home village (9.73). The name of his village in Attica, Decelea, sets off a time journey into the mythic past and the search by the Spartans Castor and Pollux (the Tyndarids) for their sister Helen, abducted by Theseus and hidden somewhere in Attica. The granting of privileges to the Deceleans by Sparta takes Herodotus to a future time that is beyond the temporal remit of the *Histories*, Sparta's invasion and devastation of Attica during the Peloponnesian War which always leaves Decelea untouched.[14]

Plataea's aftermath (9.76–89)

Lampon's suggestion that the corpse of Mardonius be mutilated is described by Herodotus as 'unholy' (9.78), although the idiom of the heroic is heard in Lampon's language. Pausanias, he says, has saved Greece and won greater renown (*kleos*) than any Greek known to men. It remains to magnify his enduring fame and ensure that no foreigner ever again tries what the Persians attempted. Mardonius, persuading Xerxes to invade Greece (7.5), used a similar register and spoke of the king acquiring a good reputation and warning others not to try to imitate Greece by attacking Persia (as happened when Sardis was torched by the Athenians during the Ionian revolt). *Tisis* (vengeance) calls for Mardonius to be treated in the way Leonidas was after his death at Thermopylae (7.238) and by doing so Pausanias will win praise from all of Greece. Remarkably, Pausanias rubbishes the idea unequivocally – it befits only barbarians he replies – and in doing so he rejects the ethos and edifice of a pitiless reciprocity. Interestingly, Herodotus' use of the epic term *kleos* in a battlefield context is restricted to only Thermopylae (7.220) and Plataea.

Pausanias is presented here in a very positive light by Herodotus and another instance of the Spartan's magnanimity is revealed when he is supplicated by a Greek concubine of the Persian Pherandates (9.76). She dresses herself in her finest clothes and jewellery, clasping Pausanias by the knees when she recognizes him directing post-battle matters, and he grants her clemency, especially after learning that she is the daughter of a close guest-friend (*xenos*). Flory (1978: 416) thinks she expects to be executed on the spot – her finery drawing attention to her concubine status – and that she bravely chooses to face the prospect in grand style. This is only an inference: the woman's state of mind is less at issue than the graciousness of the Spartan commander and the way his exemplary behaviour creates a disparity with the earlier allusions pointing to his disreputable life after Plataea.[15] His professionalism is also evidenced in his handling of the considerable Persian valuables that are collected after the battle.

Another side to Pausanias shows itself when he arranges for a luxurious meal to be prepared in the Persian style and presented to the Greek commanders alongside a typically plain Spartan meal. The contrast in the dishes, served on gold and silver tables, speaks for itself but Pausanias is in a humorous mood – this time there may be nothing worrying about the laughter in the scene[16] – and he jokes about the disparity of having the over-pampered Persians coming all the way to Greece to rob his people of their poverty (9.82). This has been seen as a 'delicious hint' of the Pausanias to come (Pelling 2006c:116), the one Herodotus' audience will know about as a man who does come to be tempted by what Persia represents, but it does not follow that Herodotus is here dropping such a hint.[17] The temptation to read more into the text than what is actually there arises again when Artabazus beats a hasty retreat back to Asia with some 40,000 soldiers under his command (9.66). While Alexander's Greek kinship is not denied and his Panhellenism never explicitly challenged, it is possible to detect a subtle questioning of his loyalty by way of a gap in the narrative. Alexander informs his fellow Greeks of Mardonius' intention to attack (9.44–5) but when Artabazus is hotfooting it back to Asia he is not assailed until he reaches Thrace (9.89), passing safely through Macedonia where presumably he could have been harassed. Baragwanath (2008: 320–1) hesitates to endorse such a reading on the grounds that Herodotus is usually able to make plainer his qualifications about particular courses of action; and the same reservation could be applied to Pausanias' dinner.

Battle of Mycale (9.90–107)

Until now, the narrative drive of Book Nine has been devoted to pressing military and political concerns as the Greeks and Persians prepare for and engage with what they know will be a decisive battle. This still seems to be the case when the story returns to the Greek fleet that was last heard of when it arrived in Delos (8.132). Samian messengers arrive on the island requesting assistance against the Persians who still hold sway over islands in the eastern Aegean and Ionia on the Asian coast. The name of one of the messengers, Hegistratos ('leader of men'), is taken as auspicious and the Greek fleet prepares to sail to Samos (9.90–2).[18]

The seer accompanying the Greek fleet is Deiphonus and it is the tale of his father, Euenius, that now interrupts military proceedings (9.93–4) and provides an interlude of the kind that has been largely absent from the narrative for some while. Griffiths, noting how the story of Euenius 'hums and buzzes with the tones and harmonies of Greek traditional beliefs' (1999: 172), goes on to delineate some of what he calls its 'allotropes', family resemblances from the world of folk tales. Foremost is Homer's tale of Polyphemus (*Odyssey*, 9.360–412), featuring a shepherd and his cave, a falling asleep, a blinding and a protective and punitive god. Equally striking, given this other-worldly tale of a totemic flock in far-flung Apollonia, is the cattle of the sun story (*Odyssey*, 12.127–41) that tells of harm to sacred animals incurring the wrath of the gods.[19] What comes across with equal clarity, though, are dissonant notes that make this more than just the reshuffling of the cards in an immanently plural mythical tale. The gods demand justice for the community's blinding of Euenius, their punishment of the man who by falling asleep allowed wolves to enter the cave and kill some of the sacrosanct flock, but they do not object to the dishonest way in which the citizens deal with their responsibility to the divine and to the man they have harmed so grievously. Some archaic notion of justice is at work, with gods insisting on reparation but leaving it entirely to mortals to negotiate a resolution in whatever cunning way they choose. Euenius is enraged when he learns how he has been deceived but unlike Tisamenus and Melampus he is no position to renegotiate. The Apollonians have legally purchased the properties he asked for and, anyway, he is gifted with the power of prophecy, as the oracle promised, and becomes a famous man. Then, just as the narrative is about to return to the main story, a dubitative Herodotus questions whether the Deiphonus accompanying the fleet really is the son of this Euenius (9.95).

The distancing effect created by Herodotus' doubting, a volte-face of sorts appearing as an addendum to a traditional tale, adds to the puzzle of why this story appears where it does, an oasis of *muthos* (myth) in the historically-minded *logos* of Book Nine. Griffiths (1999:180–2) locates its place within the broad ring composition structure of the *Histories*. Just as the Arion and dolphin story (1.24) is sandwiched between historically-grounded attacks on Greek cities by Asian kings, the tale of Euenius finds its position between two equally historical events (the battles of Plataea and Mycale). Herodotus, the fact-bound historian but also the storytelling artisan, juggles with the two different types of discourse that such narrative ambidextrousness requires.

The Persian fleet declines the opportunity for another sea battle and joins the land forces at Mycale on the Asian mainland. The Persians cannot take the loyalty of their Ionian contingents for granted, while the Greeks are buoyed up by the rumour of victory at Plataea and what is taken to be the auspicious sighting of a herald's staff lying on the beach. Herodotus' wager is that there are many such 'signs' (*tekmēria*)[20] of divine intervention 'if' (the judicious use of the conditional here is often not translated) the battles at Plataea and Mycale took place on the same day. He notes another uncanny synchronicity, how both conflicts were fought at sanctuaries of Demeter

(9.101), before reporting how it was later established that the military engagements at Plataea and Mycale did indeed take place on the same day. The argument is carefully reasoned: if the two battles occurred on the same day then this fact is an omen and not a coincidence; the fact is established and therefore an omen has occurred. The other coincidence, the proximity of a sanctuary of Demeter at each place, adds to the certainty of the inference that transforms a contingent truth into a necessary one. Herodotus has earlier expressed his belief in divine omens and there have been a number of occasions where signs of divine involvement have been recorded (see p. 210 and p. 223).[21]

The Battle at Mycale is another victory for the Greeks and it brings to an end the threat represented by Xerxes' invasion of the Greece.[22] The defeat of the Persians also brings to an end their influence in the eastern Aegean and there follows a disagreement between Athens and Sparta about how best to protect the region from the possibility of a future Persian threat. Athens' position is a proprietorial one, seeing as presumptuous the very idea of Sparta having any say in Ionia's future. Samos, Chios and Lesbos are incorporated into the alliance that had been formed to resist Persia (7.145), binding them with pledges 'and oaths to be faithful' (9.106). Herodotus chooses to remain silent as regards any ominous implications in this outcome although he is aware of how Sparta's involvement in the alliance is weakened when reason is later found to remove Pausanias as its leader (8.3). Athens will take over leadership of the alliance (Thucydides, 1.96) and the allies' collected funds will be transferred first to the island of Delos and eventually to Athens. Some readers find in the ending of the *Histories* indications that Herodotus is indeed aware of the dangers of an incipient Athenian imperialism.

The ending of the *Histories*

Three episodes bring Book Nine to a close: Xerxes' infatuations (9.108–13); the siege of Sestos and the crucifixion of Artayctes (9.116–20); and Cyrus' advice to his people (9.122). Due to their placement at the end of the *Histories*, many readings of these episodes address possible roles they might play in bringing closure to Herodotus' work, assuming there is closure. Scholarly opinion has been divided on historical grounds – whether the siege of Sestos is acceptable as a conclusion to the Persian War – and on the aesthetic question as to whether the final episodes of the work constitute an artistically appropriate conclusion to the work as a whole.[23] Over recent years the tendency has been, on the aesthetic front at least, to view the final episodes as part of the work's large-scale ring composition, integrating them with themes and concerns first given voice at the beginning of the *Histories*. This brings closure to the work without ruling out the possibility that the ending also adumbrates the future history of Athens.[24]

Xerxes' infatuations (9.108–13)

The sordid tale of Xerxes' sexual intrigues begins with his infatuation for the wife of his brother Masistes and, after the failure of his attempted seduction, his thinking that by marrying his son to her daughter, Artaynte, his chance of success will improve. Instead, what happens after this marriage is the transfer of his passion from his sister-in-law to her daughter Artaynte; and this time it is reciprocated. In the course of their relationship he gives her a shawl which his own wife Amestris had embroidered for him as a gift and, because Artaynte enjoys wearing it, his wife discovers the affair. She blames the girl's mother, not Artaynte herself, and sets about a cruel revenge. At the king's birthday banquet, when his wife is allowed to ask for a gift which cannot be refused, she demands Masistes' wife as her present. Xerxes reluctantly complies, though fearing the worse, and his wife has the woman sadistically mutilated in a most extreme way. Masistes tries to flee the country, intending revenge against his brother, but he and his sons are all murdered on the orders of Xerxes.

There are correspondences between this episode and the story of Candaules (1.8–13), two tales of death by romance that begin in Sardis. Both Xerxes and Candaules fall in love (sharing the vocabulary of love: *eraō* (9.108) for Xerxcs and *eramai* (1.8) for Candaules) but their sexual desires lead to a conflict with convention (*nomos*): one eastern king is already married and the other would have his wife seen naked by another man.[25] Gyges and Xerxes find themselves with difficult choices: Xerxes must either submit his sister-in-law to his wife's wrath or disgrace himself by refusing what he is obliged to do ('constrained by law', 9.111) while Gyges must either kill his king or face death himself. Xerxes tries to extricate his brother from the calamity he has brought down on him (9.111) and it is only when Masistes plans a revolt that Xerxes feels compelled to have him killed.

The granting of requests that carry the compulsory force of an oath connects Xerxes' promise to Artaynte to fulfil whatever she wishes (9.109) with his earlier assurance to Pythius that he will grant whatever is asked of him (7.38). He fulfils his promise to Pythius, though in a way that no one could have anticipated. Another man, Agetus, also found himself being obliged to grant a wish that could not be refused and in this case the parallel with Xerxes is more striking because he is asked to gift a woman, his own wife, to another man (6.62). Amestris asks for a woman as a gift but, unlike the request made to Agetus, only in order to inflict terrible violence on her. The force of *nomos* that lies behind the obligation to grant Artaynte's request also creates a ring composition effect in the way it connects with Xerxes' acute awareness of the contract he feels he has entered into as king, a contract that demands he carry out the duties and responsibilities of a Persian monarch.[26]

Interestingly, Xerxes makes a point of not using violence. Hermotimus in the pursuit of his brother's wife (9.108) and the Persian king cannot

FEMALE ROYALS EMPOWERED BY VENGEANCE

1.10–12: A Lydian queen, the wife of Candaules, plans the deadly punishment of her husband for allowing another man to see her naked.

1.205–15: Tomyris, a Massagetae queen, defeats Cyrus in battle and in revenge for his killing of her son dips the Persian's severed head in a wineskin of blood, fulfilling her threat to give him his fill of blood just as he gave her son his fill of wine.

2.100: Nitocris, an Egyptian queen, drowns those responsible for the death of her brother.

4.202: Pheretime, a Cyrenaean queen, avenging the death of her son, impales on stakes the men responsible and cuts off the breasts of their wives for display around them.

9. 108–12: Amestris, a Persian queen, orders the mutilation of the woman she blames for her husband giving his lover a gown she had embroidered for him.

BOOK 9, BOX 2

be reduced to the caricature of a lecherous eastern potentate whose lust knows no bounds. Sancisi-Weerdenburg provides a useful corrective in this regard, positioning Xerxes as a man caught in a 'tragic entanglement' (2002: 585–6), due to an obligation of his kingly office that compels him to grant his wife's wish. From this point of view, Xerxes is a character portrayed in a way that can be linked to a popular pattern in traditional stories (like the story of Herodias and John the Baptist in Matthew 14.1–12).[27] Amestris, his wife, can also be situated within a pattern of vengeful queens (see Box 2) and this aspect is another echo of the Candaules story. The wife of Candaules shares with Amestris a capacity for fury that leads to disproportionate violence as well as a chilling self-control in seeking revenge. Seeing Gyges in her bedroom, she says nothing but the next day she calculatingly has loyal members of her household on call before summoning Gyges and issuing her ultimatum. Amestris plots her revenge with equal forethought and malice, waiting for the occasion when she knows Xerxes cannot deny her request.

Artayctes (9.116–20)

After the Battle of Mycale the Athenians who have sailed to the Hellespont decide to remain in the region and exert their control over the city of Sestos close to where Xerxes' bridge had ended. Although on the Greek side of the Hellespont, Sestos is still under the rule of an infamous Persian governor who is known for his gross acts of impiety. He stole treasures from a sanctuary dedicated to Protesilaus, the legendary hero credited as the first Greek to have died at Troy, telling Xerxes it was the house of a Greek who deserved to be punished for attacking Asia. He also used the sacred precinct for sexual activities, a taboo for Hellenes to which Herodotus has previously drawn attention (2.6). The Athenians under their commander Xanthippus besiege Sestos, Artayctes tries to escape but is captured and put to death along with his son. Another Persian who escaped with him, Oeobazus, is captured by Thracians and used as a human sacrifice to their local gods. Oeobazus had stored in Sestos the cables that had been used in the construction of the Persian bridges and they are taken by the Athenians when the city is captured.

The recall of Troy in the Artayctes episode and the associations with Xerxes' invasion, by way of the city's location and the bridges' cables that are stored there, link back to the opening of the *Histories* and the origins of Europe–Asia hostilities. It suggests that the distinction between the distant 'mythical' past and more recent history is by no means absolute for Herodotus. The Persians rebuke the Greeks for being the first to challenge their suzerainty in Asia – by besieging Troy because of what they regard as a hysterical reaction to the taking of Helen – and they see this as a root of the bipolar relations between the two continents (1.4). Xerxes' invasion positions itself within this overarching enmity and Herodotus' genealogy of the intercontinental conflict loops back on itself by coming to an end at the precise place where Europe was artificially joined with Asia (7.33–4) – geographically not very distant from Troy – and with the Athenians sailing back to Greece with the cables of the bridge (9.121). Other expeditions that ignored the division between Europe and Asia are listed by Herodotus but Xerxes' was the mightiest of them all (7.20) and now it is finally over.

The decadent conduct of Artayctes and the manner of his death is considered noteworthy enough to be mentioned on two occasions: when the first bridge is being built across the Hellespont (7.33) and in more detail in Book Nine where Protesilaus is of central significance. Boedeker (2013) identifies two sources for the material on Artayctes and Protesilaus, one Athenian and one local to the Chersonese region, and shows how in places one or the other can be tracked. The Athenian source accounts for information on Xanthippus and the siege of Sestos while the local source is more concerned with the wrongdoings of Protesilaus, a figure in whose semi-divinity the realm of myth coalesces with the power of religion. His Homeric stature as a poignant hero of Troy is indisputable (*Iliad*, 2.700–2), but the potency of his cult status gives particular meaning to the omen that the captured Artayctes recognizes when dried fish are being cooked by one of his guards. The dried fish are *tarikhoi* but the word can also refer to a dead body preserved by embalming (and used as such on numerous occasions for accounts of Egypt in Book Two). When the dried fish leap about as if they are fresh from the sea the omen denotes a live act of communication which is received by the intended recipient: 'it is to me that Protesilaus of Elaeus would signify that though he be dead and dry he has power given to him by the gods to take vengeance on me that wronged him' (9.120).

Artayctes has done wrong by stealing from the sanctuary and committing sacrilege within it; as a Persian governor for Xerxes he is a representative of the Asian power that would rob Greece of its freedom and burn its temples. His capture and execution is a settling of scores on both counts and the prevalence of retributive action for Herodotus carries an ontological charge as well as being a metaphysical and psychological explanation for the whys and wherefores of human behaviour. It is bound up with notions of balances and cycles; the turning of the wheel of life that Croesus talks about to Cyrus (1.207) is often powered by the needs of individuals and states to seek redress. A pattern for this is laid down at the start of the *Histories*: Phoenicians snatch Io from Argos and a balance is restored when Greeks kidnap Europa from Phoenicia, but this equilibrium is upset by Greeks seizing Medea, only to be restored again by Paris taking Helen to Troy. The Trojan War introduces a new cycle, intercontinental conflict, one that concludes with the failure of the Persian invasion of Greece; Protesilaus, from his death in Troy to his metaphorical rebirth at Sestos, is the nexus that turns the conclusion into a cyclical return. The vengeance of Protesilaus has a moral dimension but it is invested with a sense of justice that is experienced as divinely endorsed. This has been repeatedly stressed (2.120 and see Box 2, p. 245) and Artayctes recognizes that it is the gods who give Protesilaus the power to exact his punishment (9.120).

On both occasions when the punishment of Artayctes is mentioned his grisly manner of execution – worthy of a Jacobean tragedy – is specified. The severity of this form of un-Greek punishment may be an indication of the righteous anger of the citizens of Elaeus but this does not make it any less excessive and disproportionate. A comparison may be made with the refusal by Pausanias, on the grounds that it befits only barbarians, to decapitate the corpse of Mardonius and impale it on a stake (9.79). The Athenians have no scruples about nailing Artayctes to a plank and stoning his apparently innocent son to death before his eyes. The murder of sons on account of their fathers' behaviour is associated with Darius (3.118–19, 4.84) and Xerxes (7.39) and for Xanthippus to act in this way could be seen as an acerbic but unspoken observation by Herodotus on the way Athens, its soft power rapidly hardening, is beginning to behave like a Persian tyrant.[28] On the other hand, the Greek Hermotimus felt justified in his extreme punishment of the sons of the man who had castrated him and there is no suggestion of censure by Herodotus; Greek mercenaries in Egypt also butchered the children of a man they wanted to avenge (3.11).

Cyrus' advice (9.122)

A felicitous link, by way of an ancestor of Artayctes, brings the reader back to the rule of Cyrus, the founder of the Persian Empire; again, and for the final time, there is a recall of earlier events in the *Histories*. Artembares suggests to Cyrus that the Persians leave their poor and rugged land and find a new home in richer pastures but Cyrus warns them of the likely consequences: 'soft lands breed soft men; wondrous fruits of the earth and valiant warriors grow not from the same soil' (9.122). Neither of the two men objects to imperialist expansion; Cyrus is saying that if they lose their hardness then they will also lose their freedom and – the last word of the *Histories* – 'become slaves' (*douleuein*).

It may seem that Cyrus was ignoring his own advice when he asked his people which of two experiences they enjoyed the most: a day of manual labour clearing rough ground with their scythes or a day enjoying a marvellous picnic with wine and good food (1.126). On that occasion, however, the options were to either accept the slave's lot of toiling for someone else – the Medes who at that time ruled over the Persians – or fight for their own freedom and gain control of their lives. It is a political choice that he offers (just as his advice to Artembares is political): his people opt for a free life in a rugged land and the Persian Empire grows great and powerful. Matters, though, are not as neat as this for, although Sandanis is able to warn Croesus not to attack the resilient and tough Persians (1.71), by the time of Cambyses they are themselves growing accustomed to the good life to judge by the way the Ethiopians are intended to be impressed by the jewellery and other fine gifts the Persians bring as blandishments (3.20). In the reign of Xerxes, Demaratus is presenting the Greeks as the poor but tough people who will never accept slavery (7.102) and the presumed contrast with Persians re-emerges when Pausanias hosts a typical Spartan meal alongside luxurious Persian dining (9.82). While this points to a downward spiral from 'hard' to 'soft', such a pattern does not categorically define a trajectory for a failing Persian Empire. It has been defeated in Greece and Xerxes' domestic troubles do not bode well for his future – Herodotus' audience will know he is assassinated in a palace coup in 465 – but the empire does not implode. On the battlefield at Plataea the Persians do not lack courage or strength but the Greek hoplites are better armed and trained (9.62).

The last chapter of the *Histories* is open to different interpretations and one view is that Herodotus is suggesting Athens might be heading towards the kind of imperialistic ambitions that saw the rise and fall of the Persian Empire.[29] Cyrus warns that if Persians choose to go down a path that leads to a materially easier life and the prospect of holding sway over other nations then they must be prepared for an unpleasant consequence. A soft life produces 'fine fruits' not 'great warriors' (9.122) and such a trajectory invites a comparison between the tough and hardy Greeks who stood up to and defeated the Persians and the citizens of later generations who grow prosperous as a result of their new-found power. Pausanias, according to Thucydides (1.130), falls prey to the temptation of a soft life and Herodotus is witness to Athenian brutality (9.116–21) that bears comparison with ruthless acts of cruelty by oriental despots.

While accepting the ways in which the final three episodes tie in with central concerns of Herodotus, Dewald (2013a) appreciates the difficulties many readers continue to have with the work's ending. It lacks a formal summarizing statement of the kind that characterizes the work of many conventional histories. The reader may question why it ends, as Dewald puts it, with Cyrus advising his people to 'enjoy the skimpy soil of Persia when we have just spent 800 pages reading that they did not stay there, or stay simple and hardy?' (395). She finds an open-endedness that is related to the work's literary roots in oral narrations and the intrinsic nature of the 'showing-forth' (apodexis) of his 'inquiry' that Herodotus announced was his intention in the very first sentence of the Histories. The success of his historie is a presentation that is necessarily pluralistic and indeterminate because his 800 pages record the inconstancy and uncertainty at the heart of history and human behaviour.

Like the ending of the Iliad, Herodotus' final remarks make plain the dissimilarity between the necessary finitude of the text's narrative and ongoing events set in place by the history recorded in that narrative. At the end of the Iliad, the reader of Homer knows that in time to come Troy will fall and Achilles will die; Herodotus' readers know that after the events recorded in Book Nine Athens will go on to develop an empire of its own. An event referred to at the start of the Histories, Helen's journey from Europe to Asia, has shown itself to be a starting point for, in addition to ten years of war at Troy, a multilayered history that continues to unfold beyond the end point of Herodotus' Histories.

Notes to Commentary

Book One

1   In the *Iliad* (7.91) Hector challenges the best of the Achaeans to fight him, confident in the knowledge that in his victory his glory will not be forgotten. In the *Odyssey* (4.710) Penelope worries that Telemachus will fail to achieve anything by which his name will be remembered.

2   Glory is *kleos* and the Greek for being without glory (*aklea*) employs the privative a.

3   For other Homeric echoes in the proem Pelling 2006a: 81–3.

4   The two purpose clauses also employ a grammatical parallel by way of two neuter nouns that indicate general states when referring to 'human achievements' and 'great and marvellous deeds': things done (*genomena*) and deeds (*erga*).

5   The word *historie* is in the Ionic dialect, as is the whole of the *Histories*, and this was the dialect used by Homer and the Ionian writers of science. Herodotus' home city used the Doric dialect while in the Attic dialect used by Athenians, the standard in modern dictionaries of ancient Greece, *historie* is *historia*.

6   *Apodexis* is translated as 'the showing-forth' in the edition of the *Histories* by Mensch; as 'presented' by Waterfield, 'publication' by Blanco, 'set forth' by Godley, 'displays' by Sélincourt and Holland; 'making public' could also be considered as a helpful translation. The 'showing-forth' (*apodexis*) will include 'the great and marvellous deeds' that have been 'displayed' (*apodekhthenta*) by Greeks and barbarians, a phrasing that uses an aorist in the middle voice (*apodekhthenta*) and a noun (*apodexis*) from the same verb *apodeiknimi* ('to bring forward, display, demonstrate'). The way the word play 'opens the possibility that Herodotus is not just commemorating history: he is creating it' (Moles 1993: 94) is consistent with a reading of the semantics of *apodexis* in the proem (Bakker 2002: 23–7) that stresses involvement by the subject in the act. If the great deeds are not recorded by Herodotus and preserved for posterity they will be erased by time – using the word *exitēla* that means 'losing colour, fading' – like an inscription on a stone monument. Herodotus seeks to prevent this happening, a constructive act on his part that allows 'the great and marvellous deeds' to be fully accomplished for as long as the *Histories* are read. For the related sense that Herodotus' work stands as a monument to be read by the reader, see Bakker 2002: 30–1.

7   In support of the likelihood that Herodotus was an oral performer of his work, Waterfield (2009) points to 'tricks of the trade of an oral performer' while also acknowledging the 'hugely intricate architectural unity' of the *Histories*, concluding that he wrote down 'what he and others had been telling orally and which accordingly retains marked features of oral presentation' (487).

   It has been suggested that the original text of the *Histories* was made up of twenty-eight papyrus rolls, each containing one *logos* suitable for a lecture, before Alexandrian librarians reduced the material to nine books (Wilson: 2015: xi–xii).

8   See p. 21 for the understanding that should be brought to Herodotus' use of cause (*aitiē*).

9   As with Io and Europa, the myth is stripped of sentiment and the aura that could be attached to the voyage of Jason and the Argonauts and their search for the Golden Fleece. They are just Greeks who having completed their other business happen to seize the daughter of the local king. In myth, Medea is the niece of the witch Circe and granddaughter of Helios, the sun. Her magical powers enable Jason to defeat the dragon and escape with the fleece. She cuts off all relations with her family and country and in some versions, to evade her pursuing father, she chops up her young brother and throws his scatted remains on the ground, knowing her father will pause to gather up the pieces. In Euripides' tragedy, *Medea*, she kills her own children in an act of vengeful despair and poisons the woman whom Jason marries in the interests of political expediency.

10   For the spatial dimensions of the geopolitical rupture, see Rood 2010: 45–53.

11   This is Fehling's opinion (1989: 50–7); Griffiths (2006: 137) exclaims: '(as if Persians would have their own variant accounts of Greek legends!)'.

12   In Greek mythology, Io, for example, was loved by Zeus who tried to save her from his wife's suspicions by transforming her into a heifer, but he couldn't stop his wife sending a horsefly to torment her. In her affliction, Io traversed Greece and travelled to the Adriatic, the Black Sea and Asia Minor before arriving in Egypt. Here she is returned to human form and becomes identified with the goddess Isis. For Europa, see Calasso 1994: 1–6. In myth, Paris of Troy was asked to decide who was the most beautiful of the three goddesses – Aphrodite, Hera and Athena – and he chose Aphrodite because she promised to bestow on him the beautiful Helen.

13   For the differences between the various kidnappings, see Rood 2010: 55–8.

14   Drews came to the same conclusion three decades earlier – 'a parody of previous treatments of the subject' – and also sees a didactic purpose, reminding readers 'how sterile was the attempt to distil truth from legends' (1973: 89), while noting how Aristophanes in one of his comedies can be seen to be laughing with Herodotus when he has women snatched in reprisal for a previous kidnapping of a courtesan and all Greece 'set ablaze' (*Acharnians*, 523–9). Henderson (2012: 144–59) also sees a similarity between the attitudes of Herodotus and Aristophanes while Rood (2010: 64–5) sees differences in their accounts as significant. In his analysis of the abductions, Wçowski (2004: 149–55) claims that Herodotus is being humorous not by trying to rationalize what is magical but by quickly passing over it; for Wesselmann (2016:

210–12), the Io story bears a non-parodic allusion to the *Odyssey*'s tale of Eumaios' nurse (15.415–75).

15 Another interpretation is that Herodotus is seeking to denigrate Persian rationalizations of myths, showing 'learned Persians who are contemptuous and dismissive of Greek mythic traditions, concerned to destroy the *kleos* of Greek accounts of events rather than preserve it; thus, the Persians and the Greeks are in conflict even in their understanding of the most remote past and the views of the Persian *logioi* are in direct opposition to Herodotus' stated purpose for writing "so that great and marvellous accomplishments would not lose their glory"' (Vandiver 2012: 152, n. 33).

16 'The start of his *logos* not only introduces his theme of the clash between East and West, but also makes the crucial point that he is not writing about the mythical past. In this way, Croesus is the start of Herodotus' histories and the start of history for Herodotus' (Flower 2013: 128).

17 For a detailed breakdown and analysis of the proem, see Immerwahr 2013a: 163–6.

18 Pelling, seeing an East/West antinomy as a construct that Herodotus destabilizes, finds it pertinent that the *Histories* gets underway with an Oriental ruler and a kingdom that does not easily fit polarizing terms of a Greek–barbarian antithesis: 'Herodotus begins by pressing on the boundaries and blurring them, not by establishing them clearly' (2013: 367). Moreover, the four Lydian kings before Croesus had been attacking Greek cities far earlier (1.15–22) so he, it would seem, was not the first Asian ruler to subdue Greeks. Even if he was the first to impose tributary domination, as opposed to sporadic forays with hostile intent, the fact remains that what holds our attention in Book One are the literary tales rather than a schematic resolve to tell first of the initial overthrow of Greeks by Croesus (1.92) and then, in the *logos* of Cyrus, how they were enslaved 'for the second time' (1.169).

19 For more on genealogies in Book One, see Dewald 2012: 67–74.

20 For surprising ways in which this proverb and the other two (a woman casts off her shame with her clothes and eyes being more trustworthy than ears) operate, see Pelling 2006b: 144–5; for the way the proverbs while seeming to contradict each other clarify two opposing points of view, see Shapiro 2000: 96–9.

21 For the idea that ancient Mediterranean mores view sexual desire (*erōs*) as disruptive, so that when Herodotus begins 'Candaules, then, fell in love (*ērasthē*) with his wife' (1.8) his audience know from the word *erōs* and its 'ominous conjunction' with marriage that 'desperate events were in the offing', see Winkler 1990. For *erōs* as socially disruptive, see also Johnson and Ryan 2005: 1–5.

22 For the likely influence of Attic drama, see Griffin 2006: 50–1.

23 The wife of Candaules feels ashamed (*aiskhuntheisa*, 1.10), using the same word that later will be used by the Greek Democedes when he assures the wife of the Persian king that he will not ask of her anything that will bring shame (3.133). Being motivated by shame of the body is only referred to on these two

occasions in the *Histories* and on both occasions relates to the position of women; see Dominick 2007.

24 Plato, *Republic* 2.359c–360b. On the folkloric dimension, see Hanson 1996 and 2002: 316–27.

25 For the motif of brave individuals facing death with dignity, which will be instanced by the behaviour of other characters in the *Histories*, see Flory 1978b.

26 For the Pelasgian presence in Herodotus, see pp. 189–90 and n. 33.

27 In an interesting essay (Sinos 1993), it is argued that there were 'ritual precedents for a heroic illusion such as Peisistratus created' (1993: 86) and that Herodotus mocks the Athenians for their foolishness in falling for the ruse because of the contrast with what Croesus goes on to learn about Sparta. Lycurgus receives divine sanction from the oracle at Delphi (1.65), in contrast to Peisistratus who manufactures divine approval. The Athenians are aware of the stratagem and freely accept it, wanting to be part of a heroic world conjured for them by Peisistratus.

28 For the way in which another digression into Spartan history, the conflict over Thyreae with Argos (1.82), has been interpreted as a 'failed duel' and a model for Thermopylae in Book Seven, see Dillery 1996: 218–34.

29 This is also the understanding that Stahl (1975) brings to his reading of the Croesus *logos*.

30 In Baccylides' version, for instance, Zeus rescues Croesus on the pyre and Apollo is sent to escort him to the land of the Hyperboreans. Herodotus has Croesus calling to Apollo to rescue him and a rainstorm suddenly dousing the flames, but a causal link is not explicitly stated and the account is qualified by being what 'the Lydians say' (1.87).

31 The visit of Solon from Athens and his dialogue with Croesus fits neatly into such a supposition, the truth of the Athenian sage's remarks being illustrated by the course of Croesus' own life.

32 Tellus is happiest because he consistently enjoys moderate prosperity, escapes the wretchedness that life can bring and dies well; Cleobis and Biton are the second happiest because while they do not live as long they do die well. For the subtle use of 'exceedingly glad' (*perikharēs*) to describe the proud mother of Cleobis and Biton as she prays that they be granted the best possible fate (1.31), see Chiasson 1983.

33 For a discussion of 1.32–4 in these terms – relating it to a later episode about Polycrates (3.40–3) – see Versnel 2011: 179–90.

34 Sometimes, as in the tale of Atys and his other son who was mute until his father was about to be killed by a Persian soldier who hadn't recognized him (1.85), this results in a grim irony: 'the silent, nameless son comes to speak and thereby to save his father's life; the competent son is, by his own eloquence, reduced to the silent anonymity of the grave' (Sebeok and Brady: 1978: 14).

35 For a good introduction to the substantial amount of commentary on the encounter between Solon and Croesus, see Pelling 2006b: 142–55; see also Shapiro 1996.

36 For references to opinions about whether Croesus is guilty or not of *hybris*,
    see Vandiver 2012: 164, n. 74. Much of the difficulty arises from different
    understandings of the term and applying the traditional view of *hybris* to
    Croesus – seeing it as a wilful affront to the gods caused by an arrogant
    disposition to transgress limits imposed on mortals – is soundly rejected by
    Fisher (1979:42–3) and by Gould (1989: 79–80). Fisher argues for a more
    secular understanding of *hybris*, regarding is as 'essentially the serious assault
    on the honour of another' when the intention is to enjoy a sense of superiority
    that it is felt to bring (2002: 1). Put like this, the term belongs to the Greek
    moral, rather than religious, vocabulary. For a commentary on Fisher's view,
    see Cairns 1996.

37 For Xerexes and the use of the term *hybris*, see p. 201.

38 The importance of reciprocating action and the obligations of kinship are seen
    in Croesus' revenge motive in attacking Persia. He seeks to avenge what Cyrus
    has done to his brother-in-law, Astyages, and it emerges later (1.108) that
    Cyrus' motive for attacking Astyages had been to pay him back for attempting
    to have Cyrus killed as an infant.

39 For an elucidating discussion of the scene on the pyre, see Pelling 2006b:
    155–64.

40 For a reading of this story that brings out the way Herodotus creates suspense
    and tension, see de Jong 2013: 281–91.

41 He is keen to repay the debt because Croesus' act of goodness has to be
    redeemed according to a social principle of reciprocity that expects an act of
    generosity to be repaid at an appropriate time. In ancient Greece this is part of
    the grammar of giving and receiving gifts (Gould 2001: 283–303) and in this
    instance Croesus makes it explicit: 'you owe me a return of good service for the
    good which I have done you' (4.41).

42 In Euripides' *Hecuba*, Agamemnon admonishes Polymestor, a king of
    Thrace, for murdering a *xenos* for the sake of gold: *xenoktonia* (killing a
    guest-friend), Agamemnon tells him, 'is something we Greeks consider
    disgraceful' (1247–8).

43 Croesus' defeat partly comes about because Cyrus uses camels against the
    Lydian horses (1.80), the camels becoming 'a synecdoche for the strange
    invader himself' (Munson 2001a: 245).

44 For a scholarly assessment of how Cyrus was represented in the ancient world,
    see Kuhrt 2007: 169–91.

45 Pierre Briant suggests Herodotus is using what he knew of Persian court
    practices 'as a veneer over an entirely imaginary Media' (Briant: 2002: 26).
    This reading of Deioces has been found wanting by Harrison (2011: 33–4)
    who argues that even if it is an account 'suffused' by knowledge of Achaemenid
    court practices, retroactively attributed to Deioces, it does not follow that
    Herodotus constructed it as a fabrication; for the 'invisibility' of the Persian
    monarch to his subjects, see Llewellyn-Jones 2013: 44–8.

46 Although the word tyranny is used (*turannidos*, 1.96), not all translations use
    it – Godley has 'enamoured of sovereignty', Blanco 'in love with power' and
    Holland 'a lust for power' – probably because the Greek term does not entail

the despotic associations that the word now carries. For a discussion of how tyranny is presented in the *Histories*, see Dewald 2003.

47 See p. 138.

48 Similarities include a grisly recognition scene when the victim is presented with the head and feet of whom they have consumed and other shared details are noted by Burkert (1983: 103–9).

49 For an account of Cyrus' childhood that locates it within a purely Persian context, see Lincoln 2007: 34–6.

50 If Astyges had not had the first dream, or had it interpreted differently, he would not have married his daughter to a Persian and without the second dream he would not have ordered Harpagus to kill her child, setting in train the events that led to Harpagus instigating Cyrus' revolt against the Medes.

51 Cyrus emerges as a character with a wicked sense of humour: replying to Astyages' summons with the message that he will be seeing him much sooner than will be liked (1.127); after the defeat of Lydia, when the Ionians and Aeolians try to negotiate with their new rulers, he tells them a traditional story with a moral they find discomforting (1.141); and his facility for acidulous remarks is evidenced in his description of the Greek marketplace as an organized space for the practice of cheating one another and breaking oaths (1.153). At the very end of the *Histories*, the acuity and wisdom of Cyrus is displayed (9.122).

52 A study of the presentation of an Achaemenid imperial list of lands and people is seen to support Herodotus' account of the form of greeting being governed by a sense of the relative distance, socially and geographically, between the two parties. King Darius in the text of his Bisitun inscription gives priority to provinces closest to the imperial centre (Llewellyn-Jones 2013: 75–6, 170). 'The center [Persia] has absolute primacy, and peoples closer to the center take relative precedence over those further out' (Lincoln 2007: 25). A similar kind of political geometry marks the description of Ecbatana, in 1.98–9: the Median capital is surrounded by seven walls that reach a greater height as they approach the centre, the two innermost being coated in silver and gold, with the imperial palace occupying the highest, golden, level.

53 For Herodotus' interest in Persian sacrifice rituals, see Gould: 2013: 190–1.

54 The same Europa who is mentioned in the proem (1.5).

55 Androgeus, a son of Minos, visits Athens and by defeating Aegeus in athletic contests becomes the target of his enmity. Aegeus sends him to Marathon to capture a wild bull and Androgeus dies in the endeavour. An angry Minos makes war on Athens and is only appeased when the city agrees to send seven young men and seven young women to be fed to the Minotaur.

56 The auctions may also be seen as a socialist measure in the way they use profits, accrued here from the sale of the more desirable women, to subsidize those who would otherwise be discarded by free market forces. In another essay, Griffiths (2001a: 165–7) discerns structural homologies, arising from oral storytelling and its potential for adding variants, between the accounts of the marriage auctions, the prostitution custom and the treatment of the sick.

57 The view of Stahl (1975), that Croesus' advice to Cyrus is unwise, is countered by Shapiro (1994: 350–2).

58 For a discussion of Croesus' advice to Cyrus, see Pelling 2006b: 164–72.

59 Lenin's caution against listening to Beethoven's *Appassionata* – it makes you soft and inclined to cuddle your enemies and 'whisper sweet nothings in their ears' when the task at hand demands merciless aggression – distantly recalls what Sandanis says will happen to the Persians if they are conquered by Lydia (www.marxists.org/archive/lukacs/works/xxxx/lenin.htm, accessed 4 December 2017).

Book Two

1 Asheri 2007b: 14–15.

2 For an overview of Herodotus on Egypt, see Harrison 2003b.

3 To what degree Herodotus owes a debt to Hecataeus is a matter of debate: 'As long ago as 1887, it was demonstrated by the German philologist Herman Diels that Herodotus was extensively plagiarizing the work of his illustrious predecessor Hecataeus, especially in the geographical and ethnographic sections of his Egyptian volume. It has consequently been argued that Hecataeus ought to have at least some of the credit for developing the basic intellectual framework that characterized Herodotus and most later Greek authors writing about Egypt' (Shaw 2004: 13).

4 There is no agreement amongst scholars as to how far Herodotus travelled in Egypt and how many of the places he claims to have visited really were seen by him. *Ancient Egypt: A Very Short Introduction* offers a judicious overview: 'His travels in Egypt may have extended as far south as Aswan, but he gives no detailed account of Thebes, concentrating mainly on places in Lower Egypt' (Shaw 2004: 12–13). For a more detailed summary of where he claims to have visited, see Lloyd 2007: 226–7.

5 It puts to shame the temporally-challenged mindset of nineteenth-century Christians who meagrely restricted the time scale between Eden and modernity to a mere 6,000 years (Gould 1989: 87).

6 Herodotus, recognizing the contiguity underlying a tripartite global division, is criticizing Greek geographers who neatly divided the three continents known to them and made the Nile the boundary between Asia and Africa.

7 Hecataeus is known to have been a proponent of this view: Herodotus' long section on the Nile's summer flooding (2.19–26), however, also brings his *Histories* into close connection with later and contemporary thinkers, one of the most striking examples of where he is explicitly engaging in articulate debate with contemporary natural philosophers: 'For while the theory of Thales (unnamed) is rebutted in 2.20 and Hecataeus' in 2.23, it is the theory of Anaxagoras (also unnamed) that the flood derives from melting snow which receives the longest and most careful critique, surely because Anaxagoras' theory, as the newest, was most worth rebutting' (Thomas 2006: 63). It is likely that it also receives the greatest attention because it is the most plausible.

8   It is possible, then, that Herodotus is criticizing Hecataeus for adhering to an archaic geography, a *muthos* that in 2.23 he says 'Homer or some other ancient poet probably invented'.

9   Grene and Lattimore 1991: 94.

10 Their customs are 'completely contrary' (*panta empalin*) to everyone else, 'part of Herodotus' polemic against both the Greeks' sense of being a special nation (even special in the sense of their being the exclusive representatives of normalcy) and the dismissive attitude they affect towards Egypt in particular' (Munson 2001a: 76).

    Lévi-Strauss notes an entry in a book by Basil Hall Chamberlain, *Things Japanese*, entitled 'topsy-turvydom', in which the author explains how 'the Japanese do many things in a way that runs directly counter to European ideas of what is natural and proper'. Examples include reading from right to left, dressmakers threading needles by pushing the eye over the thread and carpenters sawing by pulling the saw towards them (Lévi-Strauss 2016: 21–2).

11 'Egyptian sources neither confirm nor refute these claims. It would be wise to suspect an element of exaggeration; it is more likely that cases of wilful killing of a treasured sacred animal led to summary lynchings and that such incidents were transmuted by classical tradition into a regular legal process' (Lloyd 2007: 262). In August 2016, *India Live Today* reported a case (not unique) of a man killed by Hindu cow vigilantes for transporting cows for slaughter.

12 Gruen (2011: 84) notes how Herodotus is not disparaging Greece or championing Egypt and he does not base his case on the a priori basis of Egypt's greater antiquity.

13 As early as the sixth century King Busiris was stereotyped as regularly sacrificing travellers arriving inadvertently in Egypt.

14 Depictions of Heracles slaying Egyptians was not uncommon with Greek artists and there is, for example, a late sixth-century water jar (illustrated in Cartledge 1998: 46) showing a muscularly naked Heracles trampling underfoot a host of relatively effeminate-looking Egyptians as they scatter in panic before him.

15 This is the only other use by Herodotus of the word *muthos*, see n. 8 above (Baragwanath and Bakker 2012: 110–14).

16 For the Pelasgians, see pp. 189–90.

17 Herodotus employs a (debateable) etymological argument, linking *to theoi* (the gods) to *thentes*, the aorist participle of *tithēmi* (to set in place). The 'gods' for the Pelasgians are those who set the world in place and thus the divine order 'has an explanatory role in history roughly comparable to the role played in our modern sensibility by climate change, the stock market, or the progress of infectious diseases – forces that are very important, but hard to discern at the time of their working' (Baragwanath and Bakker 2012: 78).

18 Gould's essay on Greek religion appears in Munson 2013b: 183–97 and Gould 2001: 359–77

19 Fehling, characteristically questioning the veracity of Herodotus' source citations, is suspicious of the inquiries into how the oracle at Dodona came to be established (Fehling 1989: 65–70). Giving the names of the three priestesses

as 'witnesses', with the unanimous support of others at Dodona, is seen as part of a fabrication covering up the fact that Herodotus never had the conversation with the Theban priests and never travelled to Dodona to establish the alternative version of the myth: 'Egyptians could hardly have known Dodona even existed' (Fehling 1994: 3).

20 Lloyd suggests that different sources of information interacted to produce the winged serpents: i) 'Egyptian iconography which often attributed wings to the cobra goddess Wadjet of Buto'; ii) 'the horned viper's habit of flinging itself through the air to attack its victims'; iii) 'information on the flying lizards of South-East Asia' (Lloyd 2007: 290). Flying serpents are mentioned in the Old Testament (Isaiah 30.6).

21 Though relating to a period half a century after Herodotus, so many deposits of animal mummies were excavated in Bubastis by nineteenth-century archaeologists that the viability of sending them to Europe to manufacture manure was considered. On this and the possibly duplicitous practice by priests at Bubastis, see Rutherford 2005: 144–6.

22 It has been noted (Christ 2013: 218) that the phrase Herodotus uses here to describe his own activity of questioning (*egō es esdiapeiran apikomēn*) was used earlier when describing the investigative method used by Psammetichus (*esdiapeiran . . . apikesthai*, 2.28). The noun in common here, *diapeira*, means 'a trial', indicating a resolve, shared by Psammetichus and Herodotus, not to be hoodwinked. The same noun is used when referring to Croesus' testing of oracles (1.47) and it appears in verb form in 3.14.

23 Waters 1985: 52.

24 See p. 19 and Thomas 2001: 208–9.

25 2.100, 101, 102, 107, 109, 111, 112, 113, 116, 118, 120, 121, 122, 124, 127, 129, 136 and 139.

26 Thomas (1998: 136) does use the word black; for the racial gaze in Herodotus and perhaps in some of his translators and commentators, see Samuels 2015. Volney (1788: 81–3), a French orientalist (1757–1820), in his *Travels through Syria and Egypt, in the years 1783, 1784 and 1785,* may have been the first modern to note the significance of the link Herodotus makes between Egyptians and black people. For Volney in the context of Bernal's *Black Athena: The Afroasiatic Roots of Classical Civilization* (1987), see McConnell 2013: 18–22.

27 Herodotus attributes his account to Egyptian priests and while some scholars believe him (but assume that the Egyptians depended on one or more Greek sources) others flatly refuse to do so ('intrinsically absurd' Fehling 1989: 63) and some feel that the jury has to remain out on the dispute. For references to this scholarly discourse and the extensive literature on the Helen *logos*, see the footnotes in de Jong's close reading, 'The Helen *Logos* and Herodotus' Fingerprint' (2012a: 127–42). Her reading of the *logos* finds indications of Herodotus' crafting of a narrative, whatever its sources, using themes and story patterns characteristic of the *Histories* (principally, the enquiring king and the notion of divine retribution). The voice of Herodotus in pursuit of a historiographical inquiry is also recognized, telling us that the Trojan War was not fought over a beautiful woman but '*because people fail to check a story*'

(de Jong's italics, 142). For the Hellenic flavour of the tale and the quirky use of Homer, see Gruen: 2011: 86–90; see also Bakker 2012: 107–26; Vandiver 2012: 143–66; Fehling 1989: 59–65.

28 Baragwanath and Bakker 2012: 109, n. 6; Euripides' *Helen*, first performed some thirty years after Herodotus, is the best known variant of the alternative tradition of Helen's whereabouts during the Trojan War. Menelaus arrives by accident in Egypt and comes to recognize her – the woman he had thought was Helen was a phantom created by the jealous Athena and Hera – and at the end of the drama he takes flight from the land, reunited at last with his wife who would otherwise have faced the prospect of marrying the lascivious son of the pharaoh. See also Austin 1994.

29 It is the only passage of direct speech in the lengthy account of Egypt's early kings (Bakker 2012: 124).

30 In developing his argument, Herodotus is at odds with what is found in Homer given that Helen's great beauty is seen by some as sufficient reason for holding out against the siege (*Iliad*, 3.156–7) and Priam accepts his son's refusal to hand Helen back to the Greeks when he is advised to do so by a Trojan elder (*Iliad*, 7.372–4).

31 Translations of *tou daimoniou* are broadly in agreement: 'the gods' (Waterfield), 'by the hand of the divine' (Holland), 'providence' (Blanco).

32 The chorus in Aeschylus' *Agamemnon* (ll. 60–2) points to the same idea: 'Zeus lord of host and guest [*xenios*], sends against Alexander the sons of Atreus'.

33 Passages in the *Odyssey* come to mind, like the reception given to Telemachus by Nestor (2.31–50) and the treatment accorded Odysseus by Alcinous (7.155–81).

34 For a reading of Proteus as 'an example of how an inquiry should take place, and as an emblem of the difficult struggle a historian faces in the process of making a multi-layered work of art', see Bakker 2012: 118–26.

35 For folklore and the Rhampsinitus tale, see Griffiths 2001b; Munson 1993; West 2007; Luraghi 2013a: 104.

36 The Assyrians under Sennacherib (705–681) were on their way to Judah, according to biblical accounts (2 Kings 18; 2 Chronicles 32) and corroborated by Assyrian records (Marks 2012: 1762).

37 For a discussion of Herodotus' portrayal of Hecataeus, see West 1991.

38 For Assmann (2011: 57), Herodotus shows how for the Egyptians 'the triviality of history results from the fact that it is manmade'; momentous events occur in the time of the gods and what the Egyptians learn from their annals and king lists is that nothing has changed.

39 See Vannicelli 2001: 222–7.

40 There is a Hecataeus fragment referring to the floating island so it is possible that Herodotus, by making a distinction between what he sees for himself and what he just hears about, is obliquely criticizing him. At the same time, by attributing the claim that it floats to the Egyptians and not Hecataeus, whose work he would have been familiar with, it is very possible that he chooses not to acknowledge a predecessor. For the nature of a possible connection between Herodotus and Hecataeus on Egypt, see West: 1991: 158–9.

Book Three

1　See Harrison 2011: 45–6. Another account is equally vague about motive though the language is more theatrical; 'Cambyses, every bit as ambitious for conquest as his father, would turn his armies not against the impoverished tribesmen who had killed Cyrus but towards a kingdom at the opposite end of his frontiers, rich in gold and gargantuan temples, the one great power still surviving from the old world order, and that the most timeless and celebrated of all. He would wage war on Egypt' (Holland 2005: 22).

2　At the same time, 'His [Herodotus'] account is so important that, whatever his faults, all modern histories of the period are essentially a commentary on him' (Boardman et al. 1988: 285).

3　The motivation behind the soldiers' barbaric revenge on Phanes, 'angry with him for leading a foreign army into Egypt' (3.11), seems hypocritical given that they are mercenaries themselves (Baraganwath 2008: 111–12). For *thoma* in Egypt, see p. 109.

4　There are some forty oaths recorded by Herodotus and this one falls into the first of the three types they have been divided into: ones relating to ethnic customs; elements in political situations and ones sworn by individuals at moments of crisis (Lateiner 2012: 158–69).

5　For Walter Benjamin's use of the Psammetichus tale, see p. 3 and Beasley-Murray 2013: 776–9.

6　For the difference between the historical Ethiopians, who were Egyptianized, and the independent Ethiopians who were not part of any Persian satrapy and subject to an aura of myth, see Asheri 2007c: 415–16.

7　*Iliad* 1:424–4; 23:206. *Odyssey* 1.22; 5.282.

8　Of the two explanations for the Table of the Sun that Herodotus provides (3.18), the first can be seen as a rationalization of the myth that underlies the second explanation, a fable that harks back to Homer and the feasting of the gods in that land (Török 2014: 97).

9　By viewing the golden bracelets as fetters, the Ethiopian king 'lifts the euphemizing veil' on the gift he is given and they become an image of 'the symbolic violence of the Persian king's domination' (Moyer 2006: 240).

10　For a discussion of this exchange of gifts as exemplifying the 'problematics of reciprocity', see Braund 1998: 167–9.

11　The verb used to describe the king's approval of wine (*huperēdomai*, 'to rejoice beyond measure') and an adjective similar in meaning (*perikharēs*, 'exceedingly glad') are each used only once by Herodotus to denote a moderate experience of pleasure; all eleven other uses of the words refer to excessive pleasure of an inappropriate kind. *Huperēdomai*, for example, describes Croesus' premature elation at hearing from the oracle that he will destroy a great empire if he attacks Persia (1.54) and *perikharēs* describes the feeling of the mother of Cleobis and Biton at their pious but fatal accomplishment (1.31). For the uses of these words and the way joy usually prefigures misfortune, see Flory 1978a. The Ethiopian king, exceptionally, is able to laugh (*gelaō*, 3.22) innocently and his great pleasure at learning about wine is not immoderate.

12 This quotation is taken from the useful commentary on 3.19–24 in Asheri
    2007c: 418–23.

13 This was touched on in Book Two (2.137, 139); see p. 108.

14 For the use of *diepeirato*, here and elsewhere (3.16, 31, 35.5), see n. 22,
    p. 259. In his testing of human endurance, customs or moral standards,
    Cambyses is 'a scientist of sorts, a researcher of *nomoi*, and in this capacity
    the foil to the *histor* of the *Histories*' (Munson 2001a: 168); see also,
    Branscome 2013.

15 What also needs to be allowed for is the possibility that a repositioning of
    Cambyses, in the light of alleged misinformation apparently recycled by
    Herodotus, goes too far in the opposite direction and thereby risks explaining
    away instances of the abuse of power by the Persian ruler. Harrison (2011:
    76–80) draws attention to the difficulties of interpreting the available evidence
    and how, for instance, there is a gap of eighteen months in the records between
    the death of one Apis and the birth of a new one – creating a possible space for
    Cambyses' sacrilegious outrage.

16 For example, in an Encyclopaedia Britannica article: www.britannica.com/
    topic/ethical-relativism (accessed 19 November 2017).

17 Redfield (2013: 275–7) discusses 3.38 as an example of Herodotus' interest in
    cultural patterns revealed by anthropology. He sees the practices attributed to
    Greeks and the Callatiae as both creating a cultural meaning by eliminating the
    body, in diametrically opposite ways, by piously preserving and elevating a
    memory of the dead. Herodotus is seen to be alert to the systematic opposition
    discernible in two arbitrary but ultimately similar acts, an insight which
    Redfield sets alongside a revealing passage from Lévi-Strauss's *Tristes
    Tropiques*.

18 For a discussion of the use of *tekmēria* in 3.38 (and 2.104), see Grethlein 2011:
    150–2; for *tekmēria* in Herodotus, see Thomas 1997, Thomas 2000 and West
    1997.

19 Gould 2001: 299–302; for this digression as an example of chronology taking
    second place to explanation, see Thomas 2001: 204.

20 This is the same Periander who featured in the story of Arion and his rescue by
    a dolphin in Book One (1.234).

21 Boedeker 2002: 113.

22 The Corcyreans' killing of Lycophron has been interpreted as a permutation of
    a narrative pattern arising from a religious idea – that of a pollution being
    transferred via a scapegoat from one's own community to the enemy's – taking
    a secularized form as a political or military stratagem (Stern 1991: 309–10).

23 A possible explanation is the biographical tradition that links Herodotus with
    Samos (Asheri 2007c: 437), but Irwin disagrees (2009).

24 For an outline of differing interpretations, and a translation, of the Bisitun
    inscriptions, see Asheri 2007c: 458–9, 528–37. In Gore Vidal's novel *Creation*,
    the wife of Darius (Atossa) knows full well that he has killed the true Smerdis
    and uses her knowledge to force him to marry her: 'You are the usurper,
    Darius, son of Hystaspes; and one word from me to the clans, and all of Persia
    will go into rebellion' (1981: 411).

25 The role of various doubles adds to the aura of folk tale surrounding the story of how Cambyses comes to die, not just two men with the same name but two Ecbatanas and two wounds in the same part of the bodies of the Apis calf and of Cambyses.

26 See p. 44.

27 Sophocles' *Women of Trachis* has been referenced in this respect because of the way the truth of prophecies are realized when it is too late and Heracles comes to understand, through suffering, something about the human condition. See also Finkelbeg 1995.

28 Other instances: 1.8 (Gyges), 2.161 (Apries), 4.79 (Scyles), 5.33 (Naxos), 5.92 (Eetion's son), 6.64 (Demaratus).

29 '[A]n amusing harem story, certainly of Persian origin, and perfectly suited to the ambience of the exotic and fantastic palace of Susa' (Asheri 2007c: 465).

30 For a discussion of the Debate within the *Histories*, see Lateiner 2013 and Barker 2009: 182–8. For the drawing of a comparison between Herodotus' methodology and Thucydides' in the way they use speeches, pointing out that Thucydides draws attention to his own method in 1.22 of *The Peloponnesian War* in a way that has no counterpart in the *Histories*, see Hornblower 2011a: 13.

31 This is argued by Cartledge (1993: 94–5) who thinks the Debate may bear the imprint of Protagoras of Abdera 'who was apparently a democrat and the author of such works entitled "Knockdown Arguments" and "Adversarial Debates" among others'. Protagoras, as represented by Plato at least, is associated with ethical relativism and his Sophistic influence in this area of thought could be seen to have a bearing on the alleged cultural relativism to be found in 3.38 (see p. 118). Another take on the historicity of the Constitutional Debate (Moles 1993: 118–20) argues that one must 'bite the bullet and say either that Herodotus invented the Persian constitutional debate on the basis of Mardonius' selectively conciliatory attitude to democracy in Ionia, or that he invented both items'. See also Thomas 2000: 115–16.

32 It is reasonable to think that the coup of 522 was the cause or effect of a political crisis within the Persian ruling class. The three-year tax break and exemption from military service that was instituted by the false Smerdis (3.67) suggests a policy of pacification that maintained imperial rule but the coup could well have provoked internal dissent amongst the Persian nobility about how best to reorganize the state. 'The essential choice must have been between the continuation of the centralist "tyrannic" government of Cambyses (and Gaumata), and a return to the limited, paternalistic, and idealized monarchy of Cyrus' (Asheri 2007c: 472)

33 See p. 77.

34 Picturesque and quaint but possibly based on the fact that excavation mounds of marmots in parts of the Himalayas contain some gold (Peissel: 1984).

35 James Joyce's wordplay in *Finnegans Wake* (275, n. 5) on Herodotus and his more outlandish examples of foreign customs and forms of life.

36 See p. 8.

37 The explicit reference, in the second sentence of 3.108, to 'divine providence' (*tou theiou hē pronoiē*) is noteworthy for being one of the very few statements about divine activity in Herodotus' own narrative voice.

38 This has been seen as a possible source for the passage in Sophocles' *Antigone* (905–12) where Antigone gives the same reason for burying her brother Polynices; see Ostwald 1991: 143.

39 For the translation and significance of *tēs de anthrōpēiēs legomenēs geneēs*, see Baragwanath and Bakker 2012: 23–6, and Williams 2004: 155–61. Williams picks up on the use of *legomenēs* ('what is called') as symptomatic of an anxiety in Herodotus about distinguishing between the recent past and the time and nature of the very remote past. The term 'what is called' was used earlier when telling of Cambyses' diplomatic-spying mission to Ethiopia and how the emissaries were shown 'what is called the Table of the Sun' (3.23). There is some doubt about its identity and Cambyses is curious and wants to know more (3.18). Here, with Herodotus, the uncertainty arises from a lack of general agreement about establishing boundaries between times when gods walked the earth, when semi-divine figures like Minos existed (he was the son of Zeus and a mortal), and historical times that can be known about for sure. See pp. 18–19.

40 For the idea that the story is a case of identity theft, the historical Democedes being hijacked by a folk tale hero, see Griffiths 1987.

41 For a study of 3.139–49 as a tale of gift-giving and how life can become disastrously messy, bearing out Solon's gnomic observations on the human condition, see Veen 1995.

42 The family of Zopyrus will also mentioned in Book Four (4.43); see p. 265 n. 9.

Book Four

1 For background information on Scythia and the Greek gaze on the relatively unknown people who inhabited the land, see Mayor 2014: 34–7, 38–41.

2 West 2002: 443 and, less sure, Strassler 2007: 752. Herodotus also calls Olbia (north-west of what is now Odessa) the town/trading post of the Borysthenites (4.17, 78, 79). Asheri thinks it likely that he did travel in the region (2007: 553, 555) and may have sailed along the Crimean coast and as far as the Sea of Azov.

3 Armayor (1978: 49–57) is of the opinion that ancient metallurgy would not have allowed for the construction of a bowl as large as the one Herodotus specifies (holding some 20,000 litres, and the same size as Croesus' silver bowl gifted to Delphi (1.51)); see also Fehling 1989: 223 and in response Pritchett 1993: 136–8; Asheri (2007b): 112 and Corcella (2007: 640–1) also comment on the size of the bowl.

4 With this in mind, Hornblower draws attention to two epigraphic finds (2011a: 102–5), one of which features a real-life Scyles. Also, contra Hartog's intellectualizing about Herodotus' fascination with the nomad, see Curthoys and Docker 2006: 27–9. The irony and the hubris for Curthoys and Docker is

that the Persians and Greeks regard themselves as settlers but are always unsettling themselves and others by incessant warfare, colonizing and conquest, while settled indigenous people, who don't build towns or practise agriculture and yet remain steadfastly within their own lands, are regarded as nomads. Greenblatt (1992: 124–8) looks at Herodotus' portrayal of Scythian nomadism in the light of Hartog.

5   This seems to be the indication of the last sentence of 4.2: 'this is the reason for the Scythians blinding all the prisoners they seize; for they are not tillers of the soil but nomads'. For Griffiths (2001a: 168–73), the blinding is a displaced instance of the Greek mindset about punishment suiting the crime, the offence in this case being a wholesale transgression of the master–slave nexus. For Luraghi (2013a: 99), Herodotus may be rationalizing an earlier story that provided an aetiology for the customary treatment of slaves by Scythians.

6   Scythians occupy not vast expanses of time but of space and, while Egypt centres on one river, the Scythian world arises from a multiplicity of rivers (4.47). Redfield (2013: 278–82) lists other differences between the two cultures and develops the opposition between Scythia and Egypt as 'prototypical cases' of 'the hard and soft peoples of the world'. Hard people like the Scythians are severe, uncivil and ferocious while soft Egyptians are more inviting, given to luxury and complex *nomoi*. Hard cultures have a loose political state compared to centralized, tax-gathering soft ones. In the *Histories*, argues Redfield, hard peoples are never conquered by soft ones and when soft peoples are conquered they get their own back by changing the conqueror and leaving them with a self-destructive insatiability.

7   There is a case for not jumping to the conclusion that the existence of the Hyperboreans is being dismissed in 4.32–6. For Romm (1989), Herodotus regards the investigation into them as sui generis, a unique case, and that this is consistent with his empiricist attitude to mythic geography.

8   Twice earlier, the existence of a legendary Ocean has been denied, first in 2.23 – 'The opinion about the Ocean is grounded in obscurity and needs no disproof' – and attributed to Homer 'or some older poet', and then in 4.8 – 'As for the Ocean, the Greeks say that it flows from the sun's rising round the whole world, but they cannot prove that this is so.' As with the putative Tin Islands in the far west of Europe (3.115), there is no empirical evidence that can be called upon.

9   One of these orders, by Darius to Sataspes, involves members of a Persian family that appear on a number of occasions in the *Histories*. The first to appear is Megabyzus (the Elder) and he was one of the seven conspirators who spoke in favour of oligarchy during the Constitutional Debate (3.81). His son, Zopyrus (the Elder), was the self-sacrificing follower of Darius who single-handedly secured the capture of Babylon (3.153–9). His son, Megabyzus (the Younger), is the brother of the woman raped by Sataspes. His punishment, to circumnavigate Lydia, comes after his mother intercedes with her brother Darius and saves him from the death penalty, though only temporarily because Darius has him put to death when he returns from his failed mission. The very end of Book Three tells how Megabyzus (the Younger) fought in Egypt against Athens and how his son, Zopyrus (the Younger), defected from Persia to Athens (3.160).

As has been astutely noticed, it is very possible that Zopyrus (the Younger) was a source of information for the stories about his father (Megabyzus the Younger), the rape of his aunt, his grandfather (Zopyrus the Elder) and great-grandfather (Megabyzus the Elder): 'Everything points to the conclusion that these are events recorded in the traditions of particular great families and collected by Herodotus in the course of his enquiries' (Gould 1989: 23).

10 Fragments from a log of Scylax, a Greek navigator of the late sixth century and from a city under Persian rule, are extant; Hall (2008: 76) sees the influence of the *Odyssey* on the log and it is possible that Homer's epic tale of foreign lands and the strange ways of indigenous people feeds into the Greek audiences' appetite for the kind of ethnographic material Herodotus provides.

11 For a discussion of Herodotus and the Scythian rivers, see Strassler 2007: 756–8.

12 5.52–4, see p. 163.

13 Hartog's not always convincing explanation links Hestia to the royal hearth, the swearing of oaths and the king as representative of the body politic and the centre of a social space for a nomadic people (1988: 119–25). For Herodotus' habit of equating the names of foreign gods with Greek ones, see p. 98.

14 Croesus is advised not to attack the Persians because there is nothing to be gained by conquering an inferior people who wear only leather clothes and drink no wine (1.71). Persians come to appreciate wine (1.126, 133) and for the long-living Ethiopians it is the only gift from Cambyses that they appreciate (3.23).

15 See p. 78.

16 For the use of cannabis in Scythia, see Mayor 2014: 147–51. Mayor concludes, given that the Amazons were Scythians, that 4.75 allowed Herodotus' readers to imagine 'euphoric, naked, glistening Amazons inside their steamy sauna tents, inhaling billowing clouds of hemp smoke, and then languorously applying lotion redolent of cedar and frankincense before retiring to their beds of soft furs' (151); see also West 2002: 450.

17 Corcella 2007: 644: 'They must have stood on the European side of the strait, given that they were reused by the Byzantines' (4.87).

18 For Salmoxis as a distorted version of shamanism seen through a Pythagorean optic, see Hartog 1988: 84–109, and Lateiner 1990: 241–5.

19 Beard (2017: 10) writes of 'feminist energy' being wasted on trying to establish that an Amazon society, ruled by a 'monstrous regiment' of women, was a historical reality: 'Dream on. The hard truth is that the Amazons were a Greek male myth. The basic message was that the only good Amazon was a dead one.' For the representation of the Amazons in the Greek classical world, see Fantham et al. 1994: 128–35

20 For an interpretation of the encounter in terms of a prosperous aggressor (the Scythians) and noble savage (Amazons) motif, see Flory 1987: 109–13. The motif is perceived to be at work throughout the *Histories*: the Persians attacked by Croesus, the Massagetae by Cyrus, the Ethiopians by Cambyses and the Scythians by Darius as variations on the theme, culminating in Xerxes as the prosperous aggressor attacking the Greeks.

21 It might seem a little odd that tribes presented earlier as peculiar or savage
– the lycanthropic Neuri and the lawless cannibals – put forward their case
quite reasonably, arguing that the Persians never harmed them in earlier times
and should not now be attacked without provocation. Their argument,
nonetheless, makes perfect sense within Greek terms of reciprocal action: the
Persians have done them no harm and there is no good reason to start
hostilities whereas the Scythians did invade Persian territory in the past and are
now paying the price (Gould: 1989: 83–5).

22 The Scythians (4.120, 122, 123, 125–8) anticipate by two and a half millennia
what Mao Tse Tung set out in 1937 in *Guerrilla Warfare:* 'When the invader
pierces deep into the heart of the weaker country and occupies her territory in
a cruel and oppressive manner, there is no doubt that conditions of terrain,
climate, and society in general offer obstacles to his progress and may be used
to advantage by those who oppose him. In guerrilla warfare we turn these
advantages to the purpose of resisting and defeating the enemy . . . When
guerrillas engage a stronger enemy, they withdraw when he advances; harass
him when he stops; strike him when he is weary; pursue him when he
withdraws' (www.marxists.org/reference/archive/mao/works/1937/guerrilla-
warfare/ch01.htm, accessed 17 November 2016).

23 There are some correspondences between the invasions of Scythia by Darius
and Greece by Xerxes that will only emerge later. Both of their armies
commence military operations with the building of bridges, both rulers pause
to contemplate at these junctures and Artabanus advises both rulers against
their invasion plans (4.83, 7.38–9). There will also be a parallel to the brutal
response to Oeobazus' request regarding his sons (4.84, 7.38–9).

24 For the symbolic value of the Scythians' 'exemplary ideology of war', see
Munson 2001: 212.

25 The same verb (*dēmokratesthai*) occurs later when Herodotus returns
to the Persians' Constitutional Debate and Otanes' espousal of democracy
(6.43).

26 For a discussion of the complex ways in which the Scythians' withering remark
could be interpreted and how it relates to evaluations of the Ionian revolt in
Books Five and Six, see Irwin and Greenwood 2007: 21–5.

27 In 4.167, Herodotus draws a historiographical distinction between an
ostensible cause and an underlying explanation that is not made explicit
by the agents of an action. Aryandes, the satrap of Egypt, sends an army
westwards into Libya on the grounds of helping Pheretime whose son has
been killed (4.165), but, says Herodotus, this is only a pretext for Aryandes'
desire to conquer Lydia. Thucydides, famously, makes a similar distinction
early in *The Peloponnesian War* (1.23), in a context where he wants to state
and draw attention to his methodology as a historian. Herodotus' stated
method of working, by contrast, emerges less rhetorically, more sporadically
and, as here, dropped into the text at points that he chooses (Hornblower
2011a: 11–13).

28 Plato, *Phaedo* 109b.

29 This is the subject of Tuan's *Space and Place: The Perspective of Experience*
(1977).

30 The idea of spatializing narrative opens a perspective that has been developed by Purves who, noting Peter Brook's observation about how the word 'plot' has a topographical dimension, argues that 'plot's spatial legacy is pervasive in ancient Greek thought, where songs might be conceived as pathways, *logoi* as routes, writing as the movement of oxen turning back and forth across a field with a plough (*boustrophedoni*), narrative as pictures or landscapes, and plots even as living creatures that take up set areas of space' (2010: 15).

31 The twin half-brothers, called the Tyndarids in 4.145, are also known as the Dioscuri and are referred to as such in 2.43 and 2.50.

32 Cadmus is associated with the Phoenicians (5.58–9) and his sister is Europa, the woman who Cretans abducted from Tyre in Phoenicia according to the account Herodotus reports in 1.2.

33 'Mr Right' is Lateiner's translation for Themison (2012: 164) – the name pointing to a folk tale – for a man who earns his moniker by managing to act in a morally correct way while cleverly fulfilling the obligation by which he is morally bound, having sworn an oath to someone who at the time was his guest-friend (*xenia*).

34 As well as differences in the accounts of Cyrene's foundation, similarities can also be significant. In the Therean version, Delphi is consulted for the second time because a seven-year drought falls upon the city (4.151) while in the Cyrenean account Battus consults the oracle because of his stutter (4.155). For Dougherty (1993), the two versions can be seen as synonymous given the way Greek narrative personalizes public events and the way an individual's physical problem can be a substitute for civic problems of a broader kind. The two accounts are alike in progressing the narrative and, as Dougherty observes, Herodotus confirms their 'interchangeability' by noting how after Battus goes to Delphi but before the colony is established 'everything began to go wrong, both with Battus himself and the others on the island' (1993: 17). Dougherty goes on to provide a close reading of Pindar's *Pythian 5*, which celebrates a victory in a chariot race by a king of Cyrene, noting differences from Herodotus' account (1993: 103–19).

35 See also Osborne 2009: 8–13.

36 *Finnegans Wake* 275.N5 and 614.2; see n. 35, p. 263.

37 The name Garamantes here is possibly a corruption in the text, given the tribe of a different people (and with a historical record, see Sparavigna 2013) that is described in 4.183.

38 Most notably in the claim that Greeks learnt from the Egyptians the naming of their gods (2.50), though adding the qualification that the origins of Poseidon are Libyan (see p. 98). Intercultural contact that makes diffusion difficult is evident in the first recorded case of 'silent trade', between the Carthaginians and an unknown tribe 'beyond the Pillars of Heracles' (4.196).

Book Five

1 See Gray 2007 for a detailed look at the disproportionate nature of the detours in 5.55–69.

2   The earliest crossings between Europe and Asia, of course, being those that inaugurate the *Histories* (1.1–5)

3   Morgan 2016: 98–105.

4   For Herodotus' interest in kledonomancy and the idea that a person's name could be a clue to their essential character, see Lateiner 2004: 38–45; Irwin and Greenwood 2007: 46–7; and p. 283 below.

5   For an interesting gloss on the episode, reading it as a 'failed duel' in which, like the Thyreae story (1.82), the side that loses considers itself the victor in the duel, see Dillery 1996: 224–5.

6   The Indians as the most numerous of people in the world was stated earlier (3.94); an odd observation given that Herodotus knows so little about them.

7   The account of the polygamous Thracian tribe where women compete to be chosen as the best-loved wife who is then slain alongside their deceased husband (5.5) is seen by Munson to focalize the custom through the participants; an exemplary case of nonjudgementally describing a foreign culture whose *nomos* is clearly not shared by the ethnographer (2001a: 160–1).

8   'Herodotus has already accepted the theory that the Colchians, in modern-day Armenia, were colonists from Egypt (2.104); the connection made here, between inhabitants of modern Albania and Iran, seems no more unlikely' (Mensch 2014: 269, n.7).

9   The use by men of an eye-catching woman to impress others and ultimately satisfy their own needs has occurred earlier, first with Candaules showing his undressed wife to Gyges (1.8–10) and then with the stratagem of Peisistratus to gain power in Athens by using a woman – described just like the Paeonian woman as tall and beautiful (*eueidēsi*) – to appear in a chariot like the goddess Athena (1.60).

10 The account of Alexander at the Olympia competitions (5.22) as another instance of pro-Macedonian spin and the larger ambivalence that emerges from the *logos* of 5.17–22, also evident in the blurring of Greek, Macedonian and Persian *nomoi* and mythological dissonances, are all explored in Fearn 2007.

11 For the history of the Ionian revolt, see Murray 1988; Cawkwell 2005: 61–86; Scott 2005: 52–62; and Briant 2002: 146–56. Herodotus is the only source of information for the Ionian revolt and historians finding dissatisfaction with his account have proffered their own interpretation of events. Examining the Naxos affair and causes of the revolt, the nineteenth-century classical historian George Grote suggested that Herodotus' narrative points to a history that he fails to make explicit (2001: 151–2). A modern historian, George Cawkwell, does something similar but with different conclusions (2005: 71–6). Pierre Briant, the Achaemenid historian, finds Aristagoras' decision to revolt 'highly suspect': 'Herodotus does not ask the questions to which historians seek answers' (2002: 149,153)

12 For an article that seeks to render plausible the account Herodotus provides, see Keaveney 1988.

13 It has been dryly noted that 'if the slave was trusted enough to carry a message on his head then surely he was reliable enough to carry it in his head'.

(Cawkwell 2005: 69–70), but the tattoo makes it difficult for the slave to read the message he is carrying so he was not being trusted too much. Given the three-month journey from Susa to Miletus, plus time to allow for the slave's hair to regrow, Histiaeus must have planned for an Ionian revolt before the failure of the Naxos affair. Then again, maybe the tattooed message is a post-event fiction; Histiaeus and Aristagoras could have communicated in less time using sealed letters (Scott 2005: 64–5).

14 Cawkwell, with regard to the Aristagoras and Megabates in the Naxos affair, asserts that Herodotus misunderstands how the Persian Empire operates (2005: 62–8).

15 See Harrison 2011: 30–3 and pp. 20–6.

16 See pp. 71–2.

17 The motive of Dorieus echoes 4.147 when Thereas left Sparta (Baragwanath 2008: 165–6) and some details relate to future historical references, making a case for its organic connection to the main narrative (Hornblower 2007; 2013: 148).

18 The intellectual Anaximander, the first person said to have drawn a map of the world, came from Aristagoras' city of Miletus. For Cawkwell, the idea of Aristagoras having a map with him on his visit to Sparta is 'a fantastic invention' (2005: 77), echoing the judgement of Fehling (1998: 144) that such a map is 'clearly an object bordering on the miraculous'; Dover (1998: 227) demurs.

19 Irony arises in the light of the advice that Sandanis gave to Croesus, warning him that the Persians he was planning to attack were hardy people unaccustomed to luxury and wearing trousers made of hides (1.71); the concern of Sandanis for how they might acquire a taste for luxurious living is borne out by events and now Aristagoras uses Persian affluence as bait to try and entice the Spartans to attack them.

20 Two other treasuries (*thēsauroi*) have already made an appearance in the *Histories*: Croesus' at Sardis (1.30) and Deioces' at Ecbatana (1.98). When Solon was shown around the one at Sardis and asked to explain why he did not think what he saw impacted on Croesus' store of happiness it prompted him to introduce a consideration of time, the factor of temporality that is crucially being omitted from Aristagoras' account (Purves 2010: 138–9).

21 For a successful outcome in the ekphrastic tradition, the Shield of Achilles in the *Iliad*, see Purves 2010: 46–7.

22 4.47–58, see p. 137.

23 Compare Purves 2010: 135–7, Barker, Bouzarovski and Isaken 2016: 4–6 and Eide 2016: 316–18 with Rood 2012: 121–40 and Branscome 2010.

24 For a breakdown of the 'narratorial analepses' in 5.55–96, see de Jong 2002: 263–6.

25 For this and the way it is prepared for in the first digression about Athens in Book One, see Baragwanath 2008: 157–8.

26 The only time Herodotus refers directly to a family tradition, and then only to disagree with it, is in relation to the Gephyraean clan to which the murderers

of the tyrant Hipparchus belonged (5.57). Thomas (1989), using material in Thucydides and Aristophanes as well as Herodotus, investigates rival oral traditions – of the Alcmaeonids and those emanating from democratic *polis* sources – for Alcmaeonid family history; see pp. 186–9.

27 Cleomenes' claim has its basis in a Dorian lineage that goes back to the Achaean Perseus; see p. 181.

28 A remark of interest to historians who detect a tendentious Herodotus being disingenuous by not questioning the placing of blame on the messengers (Lateiner 2013: 207; Hornblower 2013: 218).

29 For a discussion of these two interpretations and likely sources for Herodotus' account of Athenian history in Book Five, see Forsdyke 2002: 533–45.

30 An example of the way in which a change in the political organization of a society can effect a transformational alteration in the behaviour and attitudes of its members; Jeremiah (2002: 110) cites 5.78 as exemplifying a profound advance in subjectivity: 'The development of the material conditions of society to a point where the individual may be posited as economically *for-itself* and therefore as constituting its own *telos*, puts in some groundwork for the abstraction of this orientation as the for-itself of consciousness prevalent in Hegel and Sartre.'

31 Herodotus is not inclined to believe in providentially shaped statues, neither kneeling ones here or the handless ones in the tale of Mycerinus (1.131).

32 See p. 119.

33 See p. 19.

34 Hence the length of 5.92, a result of the book's chapter divisions that were introduced in the early seventeenth century and which followed a self-imposed rule that every speech should be contained within its own chapter (Hornblower 2013: 2). The subdivisions also introduced for the speech in the seventeenth century are retained in some editions, the most recent being the translation by Mensch (2014).

35 Democracy as such is not mentioned by Socles; exclaiming 'you, Lacedaemonians, are destroying the rule of equals' (*isokratias*), the word he uses means 'equality of rights', the opposite of tyranny and semantically less ideological than the term democracy. See Barker (2009: 158–63) for the issues of freedom, inter-polis conflicts and the nature of Greek debate that emerge from Socles' speech.

36 Moles (2007) identifies nine readings of the speech and incorporates three of them in his own exhaustive analysis of 5.92 which also draws out parallels between Socles' view and Herodotus'.

37 The phrase *theiē tuchē* is also used when Heracles was in Scythia and when he was sleeping his horses, which were grazing nearby, disappeared by 'divine chance' (4.8). Griffths (2006: 140–1) finds a possibly suppressed folk motif – kind animals intervening to save the life of a hero figure – in Labda's hiding of her baby, a reshaping and rationalizing process that has a structural parallel in the alternative version of Gyges – he finds a magic ring which confers the power of invisibility on its wearer – recorded by Plato.

38 See pp. 122–4.

39 In 1.20 Periander does a favour for his friend (*xenia*) Thrasybulus, tyrant of Miletus, and this is returned in the wheat field story that Socles relates. It was from Periander's Corinth that Arion left on a journey and to where he returned after his fateful encounter with a dolphin (1.23–4). In Book Three there is the story of Periander and his son Lycophron (3.48–53) and the death of his wife Melissa is first mentioned, the peculiar consequence of which is related by Socles.

40 See Pelling (2006: 101–3) who also discerns a Homeric echo in the way Socles is present; for what was happening in 432, see the Corinthian speech in Thucydides (1.66–71) advocating intervention in Athens.

41 Murray 1988: 483–6.

42 Barker (2009: 155–8) compares Aristagoras' mission to Athens with his earlier one to Sparta and draws out useful observations. He sees Herodotus as drawing critical attention to the lack of discussion in Athens and 'the paradox of hearing a tyrant wax lyrical on freedom' seeming to pass unnoticed by 'all involved – bar, one cannot help thinking, our narrator' (157).

43 Pelling (2007: 183–4) discusses the meaning of *diaballein*, concluding that it means to 'throw words around' in a way that is not strictly honourable or honest, and translates its meaning here as 'to put one across'. For an interpretation of the 'easier to deceive many than one' sentence as the second part of a set (the first being 5.78), structurally similar but antithetical in meaning, that seriously reflects on Athens and the nature of government, see Munson 2001a: 206–11.

44 Wordplay arising from *arkhē* also having the meaning of 'empire' – an Athenian empire emerging after victory against the Persians – could perhaps be consciously intended for Herodotus' contemporary audience.

Book Six

1 For the division of the *Histories* into nine books, see Priestley 2014: 192. The original text will have been written in capital letters, lacking punctuation and spaces between the words and sentences and possibly without any division into books. It has been said that the length of a papyrus roll may have influenced the division into books.

2 See p. 169.

3 For *tisis*, see pp. 24–5.

4 For a detailed discussion, see Scott 2005: 63–73.

5 For the history of the final stages in the Ionian revolt, see Murray 1988: 487–90, and Cawkwell 2005: 63–5.

6 For the ambivalence in Ionian resistance at this stage of the revolt, see Baragwanath 2008: 186–9.

7 For the politics of Sicily at the time, see Scott 2005: 128–9.

8 The Samian exiles who take up the offer to found a colony in Sicily are the 'wealthy' ones (6.22) who were living under the rule of Aeaces and presumably

they knew that the Persians would restore him as the island's tyrant (6.25). It cannot be known if relations with the tyrant were a factor in their decision to leave their home. Incidentally, it being a small Greek world for the elite, Aeaces is the nephew of Polycrates of Samos and the son of the man who first received the tyranny of the island from Darius for his spontaneous gifting of his red cloak (3.139–40).

9 The telling of the collapse of the school roof is compared by Immerwahr (1954: 16–17) with Thucydides' tale of another loss of schoolchildren's lives (7.29) in order to bring out how Herodotus views and presents 'the significance of action in the historical process'.

10 If Herodotus is counting then he may be silently looking forward to a fourth occasion, the subjection by Athens after the Persian Wars.

11 For the presence of Perseus in Herodotus, see Gruen 2011: 256–60.

12 See Thomas (2013: 348–51) for speculation about what she calls a 'wild combination of mythical genealogizing and argument about ethnicity'; see also, Georges 1994: 152–5.

13 Heracles is discussed in 2.43, 44, 146; see p. 97.

14 The woman who apparently endows the infant with the gift of beauty appears at a Spartan temple to Helen and, like Helen of Troy, the infant becomes a married woman who attracts 'the love' (erōs) of another man (6.62).

15 For the nature and sanctity of oaths, see Sommerstein and Torrance 2014: 1–5.

16 Examples of the first kind, ethnic behaviour, are the elaborate Scythian oaths featuring blood, weapons and prayers and ones sworn by the Nasamonians over the tombs of noble countrymen (4.172). The drawing of blood from the bodies of oath-takers is also practised by Lydians (1.74). Lateiner includes in this category the oaths exchanged between Cambyses and an Arabian king, ratifying safe passage for the Persians through Arab land (3.7), although they could be regarded as an instance of his second type, oaths securing treaties between states like the ones between Zanclaeans and Samians (6.23). The third category are those sworn by individuals in very particular circumstances and the most remarkable example is that of the Carian women who see their families murdered by the Ionian conquerors of their country (Lateiner places it as an ethnic practice but its unique character forms a bridge with his third category). Their oath is to refrain from ever eating with the Ionian husbands forced on them or to call them by name (1.146), a joint exercise of female protest that is passed down to their daughters and in this way becoming a Carian tradition.

17 A variation of the craftily observed oath occurs when Themison ('Mr Right') does not break his oath to throw the daughter of Etearchus into the sea but saves her from being drowned by not leaving her in the water (4.154). In another case, Prexaspes knowingly swears a false oath to the Magi but is seen to be acting with honourable intent when he speaks the truth before committing suicide (3.74–5; see p. 122).

18 The circumstances of Demaratus' conception find a parallel in those of his distant ancestor Heracles whose mother, Alcmene, was visited by Zeus, disguised as her husband Amphitryon returning early from war. The real

Amphitryon happened to return later on the same day and Alcmene became pregnant.

19 This seems the most likely course of action he had in mind; for other oath-swearing options available to him, see Sommerstein and Torrance 2014: 318–19.

20 The idea of divine anger at perjury is found in Homer (*Iliad* 4.155–68) and expressions of misfortune as the consequence of oath-breaking are found in Assyrian epic and the Bible (West 1979: 125–6). Indications of a personified power that will pursue and punish perjurers are also traced by West in the work of Hesiod and she finds references to a primitive, demonic force of this type in Akkadian and Hittite sources.

21 For this interpretation, see Johnson 2001: 20–4.

22 'We have only to look forward a generation to the work of Thucydides, Herodotus' successor, to see how unthinkable by then was the very idea of telling a story to support a political argument' (Gould 1989: 41).

23 Curiosity is aroused, for instance, by the Pythia's reply to Glaucus' change of heart: 'to make trial of [*peirēthēnai*] the god and to do the deed were of like effect' (6.86). The precept has a biblical resonance ('But I say to you that everyone who looks at a woman with lustful intent has already committed adultery with her in his heart', Matthew 5.28), establishing an equivalence of guilt between thinking of something reprehensible and carrying it out. It has alarming existential consequences for Glaucus and a residual applicability to Athens. The city, having decided to refuse the Aeginetan request before listening to the didactic speech urging it to do otherwise, would still be guilty even if it had accepted there were a sacrosanct obligation to return the hostages.

24 For the history of the expedition of Datis and Artaphernes, see Hammond 1988a; Cawkwell 2005: 87–9; Briant 2002: 157–61; Osborne 2009: 311–13; and Holland 2005: 182–201.

25 For Delos as a boundary in the *Histories* between East and West, see Stadter 1992: 785–95.

26 For a discussion of Pan's possible role, see Hornblower 2001: 143–5.

27 The Battle of Marathon has famously exercised the minds and imaginations of many commentators, with the German historian Eduard Meyer seeing the end of Greek civilization if the Persians had won the battle, John Stuart Mill regarding it as a more important event in English history than the Battle of Hastings and Robert Graves beginning his 'The Persian Version' with 'Truth-loving Persians do not dwell upon / The trivial skirmish fought near Marathon' – a perspective that finds support in the work of Pierre Briant: 'from the Persian point of view, Marathon was nothing but a minor engagement that had no effect whatever on the Aegean strategy defined by Darius' (2002: 160–1). For some military-minded observations on the battle, see Tritle 2006: 214–15; Billows 2010; Krentz 2010. For a useful summary and review of the two books by Billows and Krentz, see Hyland 2011.

28 Baragwanath 2008: 27–34; for Iser, see p. 52 n23.

29 Another analogy would be that just as in quantum physics the observer would ideally be included in the observed objectivity of the situation so, in these chapters of the *Histories*, the virtual author of 6.121–3 is to be included as one of the narrative voices employed by the authoritative narrator in the orchestration of multi-sourced material. Herodotus is seen to be working with a set of oral traditions about the Alcmaeonids that jar against one another: the family's own traditions that protect its good name and noble achievements; patriotic traditions emanating from within the Athenian polis; and popular folk traditions that poke fun at the illustrious and the very wealthy.

30 For an investigative account of the Accursed, see Thomas 2008: 272–81, and for the stories about Alcmeon and Cleisthenes of Sicyon, see 262–81.

31 The idea that Herodotus is drawing on a popular folk tale as a source for the two stories of Alcmeon and Hippocleides finds support in Griffiths (2001a 167–8), who points to how both tales climax with 'a memorable image of aristocratic legs in motion': Alcmeon's in outsized boots overfilled with gold and Hippocleides' in his outré dance on the table.

32 The Pelasgians who are expelled to Lemnos are mentioned in 4.145.

33 For the Pelasgians' oddly persistent presence in the *Histories* (being also mentioned in 4.145, 5.26, 6.136–40, 7.94–5, 8.44), given their remoteness in time and pre-Greek identity, and how this may be related to the importance of origins in societies relying on oral tradition and memories for their knowledge of the past, see Sourvinou-Inwood 2003: 121–44; Munson 2014: 344–7. For Thomas (2000: 120–2), Herodotus is being mischievous in 6.137 by questioning the Athenians' claim to autochthony while for Gruen (2011: 240) there 'is more muddle than malice'; for Georges (1994: 131–4), there is also muddle and the perception that 'the closer we look at Herodotus' Athenians, the less absolutely Hellenic they appear' (131).

34 For the puzzling account of Miltaides' attempt to capture Paros with the assistance of Timo (6.134–5), see p. 42.

35 For a discussion of motivation in 6.137–9, see Baragwanath 2008: 136–42.

Book Seven

1 For a summary of the contributory causes of the war, see Harrison 2002: 555–8.

2 Grand assemblies are held in *Iliad* 1 and IX and divine ones in *Odyssey* 1 and V.

3 For the stories involving Atossa in the context of the attention Herodotus is seen to give to gender difference, see Dominick 2007. For Atossa's appearances in the *Histories* and the way Nazi historiography, looking to explain the collapse of the original Aryans (Persians), found helpful the image of powerful Oriental women influencing their manly husbands, see Sancisi-Weerdenburg 2013: 139–43.

4 The fears of Artabanus, Pelling argues (1991: 136), are only partly borne out by what does in fact take place. The Greeks do not destroy the bridge at the

Hellespont and, although a storm will (8.117), it does not affect the outcome of the Persian invasion. Artabanus, referring to what almost happened when Darius invaded Scythia, also mentions the threat of the Ionians deserting. The danger is real but at the Battle of Salamis they don't in the numbers required to make a difference (8.85). Artabanus is correct in his assessment of the prowess of the Greeks as a fighting force.

5   Baragwanath 2008: 247.

6   Artabanus' warning, that if Mardonius goes to Greece his body will become prey for dogs and birds, echoes the opening lines of the *Iliad* 1.4–5: Achilles' wrath 'hurling' the souls of Greeks to Hades and their bodies becoming 'delicate feasting of dogs, of all birds'.

7   Lloyd-Jones goes on to add that traces of such thinking are discernible in the 'Mediterranean superstition of the evil eye or in the Anglo-Saxon practice of touching wood' (1971: 69).

8   For this level of meaning in Herodotus, see Gould 1989: 81–2; for the role of contradictory gnomai in 7.8–10, see Shapiro 2000: 100–3.

9   For discussions of the apparition, see Baragwanath 2008: 249–53; Boedeker 2002: 103; Fisher 2002: 223; Gould 1989: 70–2; Harrison 2000: 132–7; Immerwahr 1954: 33–6; Saïd 2002: 144–5; Stahl 2012: 138–42.

10 As Evans also observes, *nomoi* can be changed and reformed (as Solon in Athens and Lycurgus in Sparta show) but, and this is what he calls the 'symbolic force' of Xerxes' dream, it is especially difficult in Persia because of what has been achieved with the *nomoi* instituted by Cyrus and maintained by Cambyses and Darius. Xerxes cannot ignore the dream as easily as Sabacos did his. The Ethiopian king successfully invaded Egypt and in a dream a man told him to slaughter the priests in the land he has conquered. Sabacos regarded it as a provocation from the gods and simply chose not to do so (2.138).

11 'Herodotus is not the first to compare past and present, but he is the first to connect the present with the past in an analytic manner, showing how causes – here, human desire, national character, and the forward logic of empire – intertwine in a complex way' (Marincola 2006: 17).

12 See n. 20, p. 274.

13 For Griffin, the tale of Xerxes is another example of the influence of Greek tragedy on Herodotus: 'The whole story of the expedition of Xerxes itself is, in one vital aspect, the story of divine temptation, superhuman presumption and aspiration, and eventual defeat and despair (7.17; 8.109.3). That is very Aeschylean' (2006: 49–50).

14 For a discussion of the differences between Artabanus' public speech and his private conversation with Xerxes, and the employment of the term *hybris*, see Fisher 2002: 220–3. For a suggested modification to Fisher's understanding of *hybris*, allowing the term to encompass 'thinking big' and include a god as a victim of insulting behaviour by a hubristic individual, see Cairns 1996. Cairns also considers the relationship between *phthonos*, seen as possessing moral and non-moral inflections, and *hybris* (17–22).

15 The only use of *hybris* with a possible connection to an act of impiety is when Leocedes is said to have committed an act of 'gross arrogance' (*hubrisantos*

megista) by expelling the stewards of the Olympic Games and taking over control of the games (6.127) and, as Mikalson observes (2003: 153), even in this case the insult may be to the stewards and not to Zeus. For the religious dimension that is evident, with Artabanus' warning about the god (using the term four times) feeling envy, and the way this co-mingles with a naturalistic discourse, see Pelling 1991: 136–40; for the near conflating of chance (*tuchē*) with Artabanus' warning and the role of the divine in Xerxes' decision making, see Scullion 2006: 194–7.

16 For accounts of the bridge-building, see Hammond 1988b: 527–32, and Hammond and Roseman 1996.

17 For maps of the Persian expedition by sea and land, see Hammond 1988b: 528–9; Waterfield 2008: Map J; Cartledge 2006: xxxiv. For the land journey from Doriscus to Therma, see n. 33 below. For Thermopylae, see n. 44 below.

18 For these two perspectives, see Baragwanath 2008: 254–65; for Genette, see p. 35.

19 The translations are those of, respectively, Godley, Blanco, Baragwanath (2008: 254), Immerwahr (1966: 177) and Holland (2013); de Sélincourt treads a middle line with 'mere ostentation'.

20 Immerwahr, one of the first to draw attention to the ambivalence, generalizes from the characterization of Xerxes: 'The ability to look at the same event, or the same person, from two different points of view without attempting to reconcile the resulting paradox is characteristically Herodotean' (1954: 26).

21 *Paradise Lost*, X, 300–11.

22 Aeschylus does not refer to fetters being thrown into the sea, or any whipping, harsh words or branding, but pictures the bridge as acting like a shackle in the way it enslaves the natural current of the sea; see also the following note. For the view that Herodotus was impressed enough by Aeschylus' metaphor to invent literal fetters, adding the whipping and branding to reinforce the moral, see Garvie 2009: 295.

23 On the differences between Aeschylus and Herodotus in their treatments of Xerxes crossing the Hellespont, see Romm 2006: 186–90. He notes, for instance, how the cables holding the two bridges together, said by Herodotus to possess 'beauty' (*kallonē*, 7.36), are 'the same cables, according to Aeschylus' tragic portrait of the same episode, that imprisoned the "holy" Hellespont and thus incurred the wrath of the gods' (190). For the absence of a religious dimension to Xerxes' behaviour at the Hellespont, see Scullion 2006: 193–4; for a different reading, see Lateiner 1989: 126–35.

24 For the view that a paradoxical play on words is at work in designating Xerxes as 'barbaric' because he violates his own 'barbarian' *nomos*, see Corcella 2013: 74, n. 102. For Xerxes, Darius and Cyrus as transgressors of natural boundaries and provokers of the gods, see Darbo-Peschanski 2013: 99–100; for Greek attitudes towards the Hellespont as a particularly dangerous boundary between Europe and Asia, see Boedeker 2013: 374.

25 For a discussion of 7.44–6 and a point of similarity with Solon and Croesus, see Flory 1978a: 145–9.

26 A Solonian echo is most pronounced with Artabanus' final remark to his king before he returns to Susa – about the conclusion to something being not always apparent at its start – recalling Solon's final remark to Croesus about the need to look to the end of matters because the divine, 'after giving many men a glimpse of happiness, overthrows them root and branch' (1.32, translated by Mensch).

27 For the way gnomai are used in their conversation as a form of historical explanation, see Shapiro 2000: 103–5.

28 For a discussion of Rollinger's account of Hittite texts and the possible Hellenizing of a Persian military purification rite, see Thomas 2012: 235–44.

29 For the probable size of the army (with estimates ranging from 30,000 to 300,000) and the fleet (thought to be 600 triremes at most), see Flower 2007.

30 For the 'hard' and 'soft' lifestyles that Demaratus' remarks touch on, see pp. 4–8.

31 For Demaratus as a rival inquirer to Herodotus, see Branscome 2013: 54–104; for an exegesis of the conversation between Demaratus and Xerxes, see Forsdyke 2002: 342–50.

32 For the ominous role laughter plays in the *Histories*, see Lateiner 1977.

33 Tuplin 2003: 400; Tuplin provides a remarkably empirical account and a detailed map of the possible routes taken by the army from Doriscus to Therma; see also Hammond 1988: 537–9.

34 As Bridges (2015: 51) points out, the story of the Persian heralds cannot easily be accommodated within a moralistic and canonical Greek–barbarian polarity that is sometimes seen to be at work in the *Histories*; the fact that Herodotus, unlike Thucydides (2.67), does not refer to a possible justification for the Athenians killing the sons of Sperthias and Bulis might suggest that another morally questionable action by Greeks is being brought to the reader's attention.

35 For a discussion of the mixed motives of different Greek cities responding to the Persian demand for 'earth and water' (7.132, 138), see Munson 2001a: 207–10.

36 Greenblatt 1992: 127 draws a noteworthy 'structural parallel' between the strategic value of the Scythians' nomadism against Darius (4.46) and the Athenian decision not to rely on their walled city and to take to ships instead.

37 For the historical background to Herodotus' apologetic tone – and the possibility that he is writing at a time when Athens could use her resistance to Persia as propaganda in justifying her own empire (as Thucydides indicates in *The Peloponnesian War*, 1.73–5) – and the question of dates, see Evans 1979.

38 Herodotus' counterfactual argument prompts comparison with a similar approach on his part to the proposition that Helen was never in Troy during the siege of the city (and where, see p. 106, he also refers to *alētheia*).

39 For a good discussion of 7.139 and what Herodotus admired about the Athenians, see Balot 2014: 92–107.

40 For a discussion of the different versions of the Argives' behaviour, see Munson 2001: 225–9, and Baragwanath 2008: 212–17.

41 The tendentious ways in which mythic discourse is used by Gelon and the emissaries, and earlier by Greeks seeking to discredit the Argives for their lack of support, are looked at by Bowie (2012: 279–82) and seen to be forms of 'diplomatic chicanery' and evidence of 'Greek difficulties with questions of leadership'.

42 For mixed motives in the responses of Gelon and a sympathetic understanding allowed for the possibly conflicted Corcyreans, see Baragwanath 2008: 217–22; for a sober gloss on the Homeric phrasing (*Iliad*, 7.125) of the Spartan envoy's shock at Gelon's suggestion that he be given overall command of the Greek forces, 'loud would lament Agamemnon son of Pelops', see Pelling 2006a: 89–90; for a more detailed commentary on intertextuality in the exchanges in Sicily, see Grethlein 2006.

   For the complex relationship between mainland Greeks and those in Sicily, part of Herodotus' intricately layered account which crystallizes around the Sicilians' claim that their defeat of the Carthaginians and the Battle of Salamis took place on the same day (7.166), see Feeney 2007: 45–6.

43 For the Thessalian response, see pp. 218–19.

44 Cawkwell (2005: 92–4), as part of a general criticism of the historical account of the Persian expedition in the *Histories*, finds fault with Herodotus' sense of geography over the naval movements of 7.183 and is unconvinced that the Greek fleet, by moving south to Chalcis on the west coast of Euboea, would have so recklessly exposed the land forces at Thermopylae to an enemy landing to their rear. For a map and historical account of Thermopylae, see Cartledge 2006: xxxv, 123–51; see also Foster 2012: 187–8, 195–203; Matthew and Trundle 2013; Tritle: 2006: 215–16; Grote 2001: 233–46.

45 For an account that questions the equating of Leonidas' last stand and his military objective with those of Japanese *kamikaze* pilots during the Second World War (Cartledge 2006: 130), see Matthew 2013; see also Evans 2011 and, for Thermopylae as fitting into a narrative pattern of the 'duel and sole survivor', see Boedeker 2003: 34–6.

46 Alluded to but not unpacked in the words of the oracle are the complexities, partly but not wholly genealogical, that manage to unite and oppose Spartan ancestry with both Perseus (6.53) and Heracles, intriguingly complicated by Persian claims to be descended from Perseus (7.61, 150) and by Heracles being a great-grandson of Perseus (7.220): either Sparta will be 'wasted by the sons of Perseus' (*Perseidēis*), the Persians that is, or mourn for the death of a king 'from Heracles' line descended'.

47 For the unmistakeable Homeric resonances in the struggle for Leonidas' corpse and, more generally, in the events leading up to Thermopylae, see Gainsford 2013: 120–30.

48 Cartledge (2006: 145) reminds readers that *ephialtis* is the modern Greek word for 'nightmare'. The functioning of the Panhellenic body that formally establishes Ephialtes' guilt (7.214) is similar to the Olympic body that declares Alexander of Macedon to be an ethnic Greek (5.22).

49 For the role of Demaratus, see Boedeker 1987.

Book Eight

1 For discussions of the way the wording in 8.3 can be translated to yield different readings of what Herodotus is saying or alluding to, see Baragwanath 2008: 199–201, and Munson 2001a: 214–17.

2 The provenance of the two oracles, the possibility that originally there was only one and that the last two lines of the 'wall of wood oracle' are a piece of 'Themistoclean spin used to alter a pre-existing prophecy about the destruction of Athens' are discussed by Matthew 2013: 85–7.

3 For Themistocles as possessing the qualities admired in Odysseus, see Detienne and Vernant 1991: 313–14. For Asheri, Themistocles is 'the Odysseus of the Persian wars' (2007: 48).

4 For an historical account of Artemisium unfolding alongside events at Thermopylae, see Hammond 1988b: 553–61.

5 See p. 182; Thrasybulus, the ruler of Miletus, provides another example (1.21–2).

6 For a succinct summary of political wrangling that bedevil Greek unity, see Osborne 2009: 321–4. At a very general level it is worth remembering that of the approximately 1,000 Greek communities living around the Mediterranean and the Black Sea only just over thirty of them constituted the anti-Persian alliance of Greek states. This cannot be explained simply by a reductionist assertion about inter-state rivalries but, as with the Thessalian–Phocian and Athenian–Aeginetan enmities, such contentions would have been a contributory factor.

7 See p. 25.

8 This is the way Herodotus presents the situation but historians debate the importance of an archaeological find in 1960, an inscription which points to an organized evacuation of the region around Athens planned *before* the Battle of Artemisium took place; see Hammond 1988b: 558–63, and, for a dismissal of the inscription's authenticity as 'bogus', Cawkwell 2005: 277–80.

9 The Greek debate is helpfully discussed by Barker (2009: 163–72), by way of comparison with the assembly scene in Book Two of the *Iliad*, and its perceived failure to accommodate dissent is traced to institutional difficulties due to the nature of inter-*poleis* debate.

10 For the contrast between the Persian and Greek debates, see Pelling 2006c: 111. Later, when the Greek commanders are arguing over Eurybiades' decision to stay and fight at Salamis (8.78), the words used to describe their quarrelling, *ōthismos logōn* (colloquially translated as 'a hot dispute'/ 'wrangling' / 'at loggerheads') connote a physical jostle, 'a thrusting and pushing of words' (as with the motion of shields in a mêlée). The relatively docile Persians display no such contentiousness in their debate.

11 For Cawkwell (2005: 92), her argument 'is absurd; they [Persians] had not fought their way in only to abandon it so lightly or to discuss abandoning it'.

12 See pp. 211–12.

13 For the language of *hybris* and *dikē*, see pp. 74 and 223.

14 For the first use of *hybris*, by Artanabus to Xerxes (7.16), see p. 201.

15 Macan (2013), in his commentary on 8.77, lists seven arguments against its authenticity; Enoch Powell, in his 1939 edition of Book VIII, labels 8.77 'spurious' (2003: 116–17); Bowie (2007: 166–7) gives three reasons which, taken together, he regards as 'a major case against the authenticity of the chapter'.

16 Dewald (1993) uses the case of the green shoot on the Acropolis as one of her examples for the way Herodotus foregrounds material objects, open to interpretation by different people and in different ways, without directing their meaning.

17 For details and maps of the battle, including Aeschylus' account, see Hammond 1988b: 569–9; Cawkwell (2005: 99) finds empirical problems for modern historians: exact locations cannot be established, other essential information is not supplied and, due to Herodotus' inadequate reporting, it is not certain in what directions the fleets faced each other; for Aeschylus and Herodotus, see Griffin 2006: 54–6; Souza 2003: 60–6; Saïd 2002: 137–45; for the nature of trireme warfare in Herodotus, see Hirschfeld 2007: 824–34; see also Tritle 2006: 216–18.

18 Munson 1988: 99–102.

19 By way of comparison, Pheretime's revenge (4.202–5) is deemed so excessive as to arouse the anger of the gods but no such authorial comment attaches itself to the tale of Hermotimus' demand for reciprocity and Hermotimus himself thinks the gods have delivered the wrongdoer to him for due punishment. The *tisis* that he feels is due to him has more similarity with the story of Pharnuches and his punishment of the horse that throws him (7.88) than with Pheretime. For the *tisis* of Hermotimus as a form of the symmetry that can be traced throughout the *Histories*, see Redfield 2013: 273–4.

20 After being ostracized from Athens around 470, Themistocles aided anti-Spartan groups in the Peloponnese and after Sparta accused him of being corrupted by Persia he fled to the East and eventually became a provincial governor for the Persian king. Thucydides gives an account of his life and his qualities but does not mention his alleged offences (1.38).

21 For an account of hostile sources for Themistocles' second message to the Persians, see Marr 1995. Marr finds it highly improbable that a second message could have been sent and this is also the view of Blösel (2012) who, regarding it as a duplicate of the first and historically more viable dispatch of a secret message, sees Herodotus presenting a complex portrayal of Themistocles. For a summary of Themistocles' role in the *Histories*, see Moles 2002: 43–8.

22 *The Persians*, 65–72, 130–2, 186–96, 721–6, 743–5; for a discussion that draws a distinction between Aeschylus' viewpoint and that of Herodotus, see Scullion 2006: 193–6.

23 For interpretations along these lines, see Immerwahr 1966: 182–3. Flory (1987: 58–60) also links it thematically with the story of Pythius (7.27–9), as does Gray (2002: 295). Strid (2006: 393–4) reads it as an instance of Herodotus' interest in 'the extraordinary and exceptional in respect of requital and revenge'.

24 Messages hidden inside a dead hare (1.123); tattooed on a slave's head (5.35); secretly concealed beneath a layer of wax (7.239).

25 For a discussion of 8.144 and in particular to what extent the reference to 'the shrines of gods and the sacrifices we have in common' can be taken as proof of Greek religious unity, see Polinskaya 2010.

26 For the implications of taking the context of the speech in 8.144 into account, see Thomas 2013: 341–2.

27 Assmann writes of 'hot memory' as a use of the past 'to create a self-image and to provide support for hopes and for intentions' (2011: 62) and the term could be applied to the two speeches of the Athenians. Assmann adds to his definition that 'This [hot memory] is called myth'.

28 Raaflaub 2002: 165.

29 For the organization of time in the *Histories*, see Cobet 2002.

Book Nine

1 Cawkwell (2005: 115) finds Plataea a 'needless' battle for a set of different practical reasons.

2 The literary, intertextual potential of fire beacon imagery is amply explored in Baragwanath's reading of 9.3 (2012: 303–8).

3 The tragic overtones of this scene allow Saïd (2002: 123) to view it as modelled on the conversation of Cassandra and the chorus in Aeschylus' *Agamemnon* (1296–8); and the sentiment of the sorrow that accompanies a knowledge that cannot be acted is seen to 'precisely' echo lines in Aeschylus *Suppliants* (453–4). For a wide-ranging look at the different uses of *anankē* in Herodotus, with comparisons in Thucydides, see Munson 2001b.

4 The Tegean boast about killing the son of Heracles may be diplomatically crass for in the past the Heraclidae were threatening the security of the Peloponnese and this is what the Persians are doing in the present.

5 For Solmsen (1944: 249), the speech of the Tegeans is merely a pretext for giving space for what the Athenians say about their own achievements, primarily at Marathon. The bravery of the Athenians has just been displayed in their encounter with Masistius' cavalry but in the battle to come they will not play a major role and the victory will be all Sparta's. For Solmsen, Herodotus is balancing the books and reminding his audience of what the Athenians have already achieved.

6 As Saïd (2002: 147) observes, this is a truth borne out by Croesus' transformation from foolishness to wisdom and the reverse movement in the case of Cyrus.

7 The seer Megistias is mentioned in relation to Thermopylae (7.221).

8 Melampus first appears in the *Histories* when he is credited by Herodotus with introducing the cult of Dionysus to Greece (2.49).

9 Munson (2001a: 59–62), for whom mythical history 'is never the focus of Herodotus' exposition', reads Tisamenus' achievement as a metaphor for the obtainment of kingly power. For Gray (2012: 170–4), the tales of Tisamenus and Melampus share characteristics that place them in a narrative constellation alongside the story of how the Spartans, anxious to gain the upper hand over the Tegeans, who at that time were regularly defeating them in battles, acquired the bones of Orestes (1.67–9). The Spartans, like the Argives, have to rely on the assistance of an outsider who is unaware of their power, though there are some differences as well (the bargaining motif is absent) and the Melampus story abbreviates the pattern to bare essentials. The art of Herodotus is seen to show itself in the way he tailors a traditional story pattern to suit the occasion, thus the bargaining is accentuated in the seer stories because they stress the urgency felt by one party and the power play exercised by the other, factors which arise because of the crises at hand (the imminent threat of the Persians and the madness afflicting the women of Thebes).

10 For the view that Alexander is hedging his bets in case the Greeks are victorious, see Irwin and Greenwood 2007: 121, 124–5.

11 For an account of the Battle of Plataea, see Barron 1988: 599–609; Cartledge 2013: 105–17; Cawkwell 2005: 113–16; Flower and Marincola 2002: 20–8; Lazenby 1993: 217–47; de Souza 2003: 68–71; Tritle 2006: 218–20.

12 For hoplite warfare in Herodotus, see Lee 2007.

13 'Time present and time past / Are both perhaps present in time future / And time future contained in time past.'

14 In narratology, the term for the temporal distance that extends from the moment representing the present within the narrative to either the past or the future is 'reach' (Genette 1983: 47–8). For a look at the Sophanes tale within a discussion of how characters in Herodotus use narratives where the temporal reach is the legendary past, see Baragwanath 2012b: 40–3.

15 Pausanias' later collusion with the Persians, in the expectation of becoming a satrap of Greece, has been alluded to (5.32) and the Athenians are able to capitalize on the decline in his reputation (8.3).

16 See pp. 208–9.

17 For the Pausanias of the future, see Thucydides 1.94–5, 1.128–35 (especially 1.130). For a reading that sees Herodotus shrewdly playing with the luxury motif, 'a series of inversions that entangled Persian and Greek', see Gruen 2011: 28; for 'ill-considered greed, and ambiguous laughter' in the depiction of the scene, see Munson 2001a: 70; for the view that Pausanias' ridicule of Persian opulence 'serves as an ironic symbol of the corruption of Greeks by eastern wealth and luxury', see Forsdyke 2006: 232.

18 For the taking of the messenger's name as a good omen, another instance of kledonomancy, see p. 269, n. 4 and 167 (when Cleomenes arrives at the Acropolis).

19 Griffiths (1999: 176) also reminds readers of a resemblance to the annual festival of the Scythians (4.7) where if the person appointed to guard the gold falls asleep (outdoors, during the day, not at night in a cave) his days are numbered (the punishment) but he is granted a large amount of land (the reward).

20 See pp. 118–19.

21 The omen that Cleomenes received at Argos was accepted by the Spartans as a credible explanation of his decision not to take Argos (6.82) and Herodotus interprets the earthquake on Delos as a sign from the heavens (6.98).

22 For accounts of the Battle of Mycale, see Barron 1988: 611–15; Cawkwell 2005: 199, for his customary scepticism about Herodotus' accounts of battles.

23 For the scholarly division over the ending of the *Histories*, see Boedeker 2013: 359–61, and Dewald 2013a: 393–4.

24 Herington (1991a) discerns a triple ring composition giving coherence and closure to the ending of the *Histories*; see also Lateiner (1989: 49–50) and Desmond (2004); Moles (2002: 49) reads the story of Cyrus' advice as a Herodotean warning about emerging Athenian imperialism.

25 Flory, peculiarly perhaps, calls Candaules' desire 'asexual' (1978a: 151), aligning it with Croesus' longing for others to view his wealth and Xerxes' wish to view his fleet.

26 See pp. 201–2.

27 Harrison's suggestion (2011: 61) is that the shawl may be a symbol of sovereignty and that the story may be an allegory, misunderstood by Herodotus, of rivalry between brothers for the throne.

28 For the view that there is an authorial warning here to the incipient imperialism of Athens, see Georges 1994: 130; Pelling 2013: 60ff.; Rood 2007: 116; Forsdyke 2006: 229–30. A similar kind of adumbration could also be at work in the siege of Andros (8.111).

29 See pp. 227, 243 and Forsdyke 2006: 231–2.

BIBLIOGRAPHY

Adkins, A. W. H. (1960), *Merit and Responsibility: A Study in Greek Values*, Oxford: Oxford University Press.

Althusser, L. (1971), *Lenin and Philosophy and Other Essays*, New York, London: Monthly Review Press.

Armayor, O. K. (1978a), 'Did Herodotus Ever Go to the Black Sea?', *Harvard Studies in Classical Philology* 82: 45–62.

Armayor, O. K. (1978b), 'Did Herodotus Ever Go to Egypt?', *Journal of the American Research Center in Egypt* 15: 59–63.

Aro, S. and Whiting R. M. (eds) (2000), *The Heirs of Assyria (Melammu Symposia 1)*, Helsinki: Neo-Assyrian Text Corpus Project.

Ash, R., Mossman, J. and Titchener, F. (eds) (2015), *Fame and Infamy: Essays for Christopher Pelling on Characterization in Greek and Roman Biography and Historiography*, Oxford: Oxford University Press.

Asheri, D. (2007a), 'General Introduction', in D. Asheri et al., *A Commentary on Herodotus Books I–IV*, 1–56, Oxford: Oxford University Press.

Asheri, D. (2007b), 'Book 1', in D. Asheri et al., *A Commentary on Herodotus Books I–IV*, 57–218, Oxford: Oxford University Press.

Asheri, D. (2007c), 'Book 1II', in D. Asheri et al., *A Commentary on Herodotus Books I–IV*, 379–527, Oxford: Oxford University Press.

Asheri, D., Lloyd, A., Corcella, A., Murray, O. and Morenco, A. (eds) (2007), *A Commentary on Herodotus Books I–IV*, with a contribution by M. Brosius. Tr. B. Graziosi, M. Rossetti, C. Dus and V. Cazzato. Oxford: Oxford University Press.

Assmann, J. (2011), *Cultural Memory and Early Civilization: Writing, Remembrance, and Political Imagination*, Cambridge: Cambridge University Press.

Austin, N. (1994), *Helen of Troy and her Shameless Phantom*, Ithaca, NY: Cornell University Press.

Bakker, E. J. (2002), 'The Making of History: *Historiēs Apodexis*', in E. J. Bakker, I. J. F. de Jong and H. van Wees (eds), *Brill's Companion to Herodotus*, 3–32, Leiden, Boston and Cologne: Brill.

Bakker, E. J., de Jong, I. J. F. and van Wees, H. (eds) (2002), *Brill's Companion to Herodotus*, Leiden and Boston: Brill.

Bakker, M. de. (2012), 'Herodotus' Proteus: Myth, History, Enquiry, and Storytelling', in E. Baragwanath and M. de Bakker (eds), *Myth, Truth, and Narrative in Herodotus*, 107–26, Oxford: Oxford University Press.

Bal, M. ([1985] 1997), *Narratology: Introduction to the Theory of Narrative*, Toronto, Buffalo and London: University of Toronto Press.

Balot, R. K. (2014), *Courage in the Democratic Polis: Ideology and Critique in Classical Athens*, Oxford: Oxford University Press.

Baragwanath, E. (2008), *Motivation and Narrative in Herodotus*, Oxford: Oxford University Press.

Baragwanath, E. (2012a), 'Returning to Troy: Herodotus and the Mythic Discourse of his own Time', in E. Baragwanath and M. de Bakker (eds), *Myth, Truth, and Narrative in Herodotus*, 287–312, Oxford: Oxford University Press.

Baragwanath, E. (2012b), 'The Mythic Plupast in Herodotus', in C. B. Krebs and J. Grethlein (eds), *Time and Narrative in Ancient Historiography: The 'Plupast' from Herodotus to Appian*, 35–56, Cambridge: Cambridge University Press.

Baragwanath, E. and Bakker, M. de. (eds) (2012), *Myth, Truth, and Narrative in Herodotus*, Oxford: Oxford University Press.

Bard, R. (ed.) (1999), *Encyclopedia of the Archaeology of Ancient Egypt*, London and New York: Routledge.

Barker, E., Bouzarovski, S., Pelling, C. and Isaken, L. (eds) (2016), *New Worlds from Old Texts: Revealing Ancient Space and Place*, Oxford: Oxford University Press.

Barker, E., Bouzarovski, S. and Isaken, L. (2016), 'Introduction: Creating New Worlds out of Old Texts', in E. Barker, S. Bouzarovski, C. Pelling and L. Isaken (eds), *New Worlds from Old Texts*, 1–21, Oxford: Oxford University Press.

Barker, E. T. E. (2009), *Entering the Agon: Dissent and Authority in Homer, Historiography and Tragedy*, Oxford: Oxford University Press.

Barnes, J. ([1979] 1982), *The Presocratic Philosophers*, London and New York: Routledge.

Barron, J. P. (1988), 'The Liberation of Greece', in J. Boardman, N. G, L. Hammond, D. M. F. Lewis and M. Ostwald, *Cambridge Ancient History Second edition, Volume IV, Persia, Greece and the Western Mediterranean c.525 to 479 B.C.*, 599–622, Cambridge: Cambridge University Press.

Barthes, R. ([1984]1989), *The Rustle of Language*, trans. R. Howard, Berkeley and Los Angeles: University of California Press.

Barton, J. (ed.) (2016), *The Hebrew Bible: A Critical Companion*, Princeton, NJ, and Oxford: Princeton University Press.

Beard, M. (2017), 'Women in Power', *London Review of Books* 39, no. 6: 9–14.

Beasley-Murray, T. (2013), 'On Some Motifs in Walter Benjamin: Seed, Sperm, Modernity and Gender', *Modernism/modernity* 19, no. 4: 775–91.

Bernadette, S. (1969), *Herodotean Inquiries*, The Hague: Martinus Nijhoff.

Billows, R. A. (2010), *Marathon: How One Battle Changed Western Civilization*, New York and London: Overlook Duckworth.

Blanco, W. (trans.) (2013), *The Histories Herodotus*, ed. W. Blanco and J. T. Roberts, New York and London: Norton.

Blösel W. (2001), 'The Herodotean Picture of Themistocles: A Mirror of Fifth-century Athens', in N. Luraghi (ed.), *The Historian's Craft in the Age of Herodotus*, 179–97, Oxford: Oxford University Press.

Blösel, W. (2012), 'Thucydides on Themistocles', in E. Foster and D. Lateiner (eds), *Thucydides and Herodotus*, 185–214, Oxford: Oxford University Press.

Boardman, J., Hammond, N., Lewis, D. and Ostwald, M. (1988), *Cambridge Ancient History Second edition, Volume IV, Persia, Greece and the Western Mediterranean c.525 to 479 B.C.*, Cambridge: Cambridge University Press.

Boedeker, D. (1987), 'The two faces of Demaratus', *Arethusa* 20: 185–201.

Boedeker, D. (1993), 'Hero Cult and Politics in Herodotus: The Bones of Orestes', in C. Dougherty and L. Kurke (eds), *Cultural Poetics in Archaic Greece: Cult, Performance, Politics*, 164–77, Oxford: Oxford University Press.

Boedeker, D. (2001), 'Heroic Historiography: Simonides and Herodotus on Plataea', in D. Boedeker and D. Sider (eds), *The New Simonides: Contexts of Praise and Desire*, 120–34, Oxford: Oxford University Press.

Boedeker, D. (2002), 'Epic Heritage and Mythical Pattern in Herodotus', in E. J. Bakker, I. J. F. de Jong, and H. van Wees (eds), *Brill's Companion to Herodotus*, 97–116, Leiden, Boston and Cologne: Brill.

Boedeker, D. (2003), 'Pedestrian Fatalities: the Prosaics of Death in Herodotus', in P. Derow and R. Parker (eds), *Herodotus and his World: Essays from a Conference in Memory of Georg Forrest*, 17–36, Oxford: Oxford University Press.

Boedeker, D. (2011), 'Early Greek Poetry as/and History', in A. Feldherr and G. Grant (eds), *The Oxford History of Historical Writing Vol. One: Beginnings to AD 600*, 122–47, Oxford: Oxford University Press.

Boedeker, D. ([1988] 2013), 'Protesilaos and the end of Herodotus' *Histories*', in R. V. Munson (ed.), *Herodotus: Volume 1 Herodotus and the Narrative of the Past*, 359–401, Oxford: Oxford University Press.

Boedeker, D. and Sider, D. (eds) (2001), *The New Simonides: Contexts of Praise and Desire*, Oxford: Oxford University Press.

Bouzarovski, S. and Barker, E. (2016), 'Between East and West: Movements and Transformations in Herodotean Topology', in E. Barker, S. Bouzarovski, C. Pelling and L. Isaken (eds), *New Worlds from Old Texts*, 155–79, Oxford: Oxford University Press.

Bowie, A. M. (2012), 'Mythology and the Expedition of Xerxes', in E. Baragwanath and M. de Bakker (eds), *Myth, Truth, and Narrative in Herodotus*, 269–86, Oxford: Oxford University Press.

Bowie, A. M. (ed.) (2007), *Herodotus: Histories Book VIII*, Cambridge: Cambridge University Press.

Branscome, D. (2010), 'Herodotus and the Map of Aristagoras', *Classical Antiquity* 29, no. 1: 1–44.

Branscome, D. (2013), *Textual Rivals: Self-Presentation in Herodotus' Histories*, Ann Arbor: University of Michigan Press.

Braund, D. (1998), 'Herodotus on the Problematics of Reciprocity', in C. Gill, N. Postlewaite and R. Seaford (eds), *Reciprocity in Ancient Greece*, 159–80, Oxford: Oxford University Press.

Brettler, M. Z. (2014), 'Historical Texts in the Hebrew Bible?', in R. A. Rauflaub (ed.), *Thinking, Recording, and Writing in the Ancient World*, 213–33, Chichester: Wiley Blackwell.

Briant, P. ([1996] 2002), *From Cyrus to Alexander: A History of the Persian Empire*, trans. P. T. Daniels, Warsaw, IN: Eisenbrauns.

Bridges, E. (2015), *Imagining Xerxes*, London and New York: Bloomsbury.

Budelmann, F. and Michelakis, F. P. (eds) (2001), *Homer, Tragedy and Beyond: Essays in Honour of P. E. Easterling*, London: Society for the Promotion of Hellenic Studies.

Burkert, W. ([1972] 1983), *Homo Necans: The Anthropology of Ancient Greek Sacrificial Ritual and Myth*, trans. P. Bing, Berkeley and Los Angeles: University of California Press.

Burrow, J. (2007), *A History of Histories: Epics, Chronicles, Romances and Inquiries from Herodotus and Thucydides to the Twentieth Century*, London: Penguin.

Bury, J. B. (1957), *History of Greece*, 3rd edn, revised by R. Meiggs, London: Macmillan.

Buxton, R. G. A. (1999), From *Myth to Reason? Studies in the Development of Greek Thought*, Oxford: Oxford University Press.

Cairns, D. L. (1996), 'Hybris, Dishonour, and Thinking Big', *Journal of Hellenic Studies* 116: 1–32.

Calasso, R. ([1988] 1994), *The Marriage of Cadmus and Harmony*, trans. T. Parks, London: Vintage.

Cartledge, P. (1993), *The Greeks: A Portrait of Self and Others*, Oxford: Oxford University Press.

Cartledge, P. (1998), *Cambridge Illustrated History: Ancient Greece*, Cambridge: Cambridge University Press.

Cartledge, P. (2006), *Thermopylae: The Battle that Changed the World*, London: Macmillan.

Cartledge, P. (2013), *After Thermopylae: The Oath of Plataea and the End of the Graeco-Persian Wars*, Oxford: Oxford University Press.

Cawkwell, G. (2005), *The Greek Wars; The Failure of Persia*, Oxford: Oxford University Press.

Chiasson, C. (1983), 'An Ominous Word in Herodotus', *Hermes* 111, no. 1: 115–18.

Chiasson, C. (2001), 'Scythian Androgyny and Environmental Determinism in Herodotus and the Hippocratic περὶ ἀέρων ὑδάτων τόπων', *Syllecta Classica* 12: 33–73.

Chiasson, C. (2003), 'Use of Attic Tragedy in the Lydian *Logos*', *Classical Antiquity*, 22. 1: 5–36.

Chiasson, C. (2012), 'Myth and Truth in Herodotus' Cyrus' *Logos*', in E. Baragwanath and M. de Bakker (eds), *Myth, Truth, and Narrative in Herodotus*, 212–32, Oxford: Oxford University Press.

Christ, M. R. ([1994] 2013), 'Herodotean kings and historical inquiry', in R. V. Munson (ed.), *Herodotus: Volume 1 Herodotus and the Narrative of the Past*, 212–50, Oxford: Oxford University Press.

Clark, M. J., Currie, B. G. F. and Lyne, R. O. A. M. (eds) (2006), *Epic Interactions: Perspectives on Homer, Virgil and the Epic Tradition*, Oxford: Oxford University Press.

Cobet, J. (2002), 'The Organization of Time in the *Histories*', in E. J. Bakker, I. J. F. de Jong and H. van Wees (eds), *Brill's Companion to Herodotus*, 387–412, Leiden, Boston and Cologne: Brill.

Collingwood, R. G. ([1946]1994), *The Idea of History: Revised Edition*, Oxford: Oxford University Press.

Corcella, A. (2007), 'Book IV', in D. Asheri et al., *A Commentary on Herodotus Books I–IV*, 543–721, Oxford: Oxford University Press.

Corcella, A. ([1984] 2013), 'Herodotus and analogy', trans. J. Kardan, in R. V. Munson (ed.), *Herodotus: Volume 2 Herodotus and the World*, 44–77, Oxford: Oxford University Press.

Cowling, M. and Martin, J. (eds) (2006), *Marx's 'Eighteenth Brumaire': (Post) modern Interpretations*, London and Sterling, VA: Pluto Press.

Curthoys, A. and Docker, J. (2006), *Is History Fiction?*, Sydney: University of New South Wales.

Dale, E. M. (2014), *Hegel, the end of History and the Future*, Cambridge: Cambridge University Press.

Darbo-Peschanski, C. ([2007] 2013), 'Herodotus and historia', in R. V. Munson (ed.), *Herodotus: Volume 2 Herodotus and the World*, 78–105, Oxford: Oxford University Press.

Derow, P. (1994), 'Historical Explanation: Polybius and his Predecessors', in S. Hornblower (ed.), *Greek Historiography*, 73–90, Oxford: Oxford University Press.

Derow, P. and Parker, R. (eds) (2003), *Herodotus and his World: Essays from a Conference in Memory of George Forrest*, Oxford: Oxford University Press.

Desmond, W. (2004), 'Punishments and the Conclusion of Herodotus' Histories', *Greek, Roman and Byzantine Studies* 44: 19–40.

Detienne, M. and Vernant, J.-P. ([1974] 1991), *Cunning Intelligence in Greek Culture and Society*, trans. J. Lloyd, Chicago and London: University of Chicago Press.

Dewald, C. (1987), 'Narrative Surface and Authorial Voice in Herodotus' *Histories*', *Arethusa* 20: 147–70.

Dewald, C. (1993), 'Reading the World: The Interpretation of Objects in Herodotus' *Histories*', in R. M. Rosen and J. Farrell (eds), *Nomodeikes: Greek Studies in Honor of Martin Ostwald*, 55–70, Ann Arbor: University of Michigan Press

Dewald, C. (2003), 'Form and content: the question of tyranny in Herodotus', in K. Morgan (ed.), *Popular Tyranny*, 25–58, Austin: University of Texas Press.

Dewald, C. (2006), 'Humour and danger in Herodotus', in C. Dewald and J. Marincola (eds), *The Cambridge Companion to Herodotus*, 145–64, Cambridge: Cambridge University Press.

Dewald, C. (2008), 'Introduction and Notes', in R. Waterfield, *Herodotus The Histories*, ix–xivi and 591–744, Oxford: Oxford University Press.

Dewald, C. (2012), 'Myth and Legend in Herodotus' First Book', in E. Baragwanath and M. de Bakker (eds), *Myth, Truth, and Narrative in Herodotus*, 59–86, Oxford: Oxford University Press.

Dewald, C. ([1997] 2013a), 'Wanton kings, pickled heroes, and gnomic founding fathers: Strategies of meaning at the end of Herodotus' *Histories*', in R. V. Munson (ed.), *Herodotus: Volume 1 Herodotus and the Narrative of the Past*, 379–401, Oxford: Oxford University Press.

Dewald, C. ([1981] 2013b), 'Women and culture in Herodotus' *Histories*', in R. V. Munson (ed.), *Herodotus: Volume 2 Herodotus and his World*, 151–79, Oxford: Oxford University Press.

Dewald, C. (2015), 'The Medium is the Message: Herodotus and his *Logoi*', in R. Ash, J. Mossman and F. Titchener (eds), *Fame and Infamy: Essays for Christopher Pelling on Characterization in Greek and Roman Biography and Historiography*, 67–82, Oxford: Oxford University Press.

Dewald, C. and Marincola J. (eds) (2006), *The Cambridge Companion to Herodotus*, Cambridge: Cambridge University Press.

Dillery, J. (1996), 'Reconfiguring the Past: Thyrea, Thermopylae and Narrative Pattern in Herodotus', *American Journal of Philology* 117, no. 2: 217–54.

Dodds, E. R. (1951), *The Greeks and the Irrational*, Berkeley and Los Angeles: University of California Press.

Dominick, V. H. (2007), 'Acting Other: Atossa and Instability in Herodotus', *Classical Quarterly* 57, no. 2: 432–44.

Dougherty, C. (1993), *The Poetics of Colonization: From City to Text in Archaic Greece*, New York and Oxford: Oxford University Press.

Dougherty, C. and Kurke, L. (eds) (1998), *Cultural Poetics in Archaic Greece: Cult, Performance, Politics*, Oxford: Oxford University Press.

Douglas, M. (2007), *Thinking in Circles: An Essay on Ring Composition*, New Haven, CT: Yale University Press.

Dover, K. (1998), 'Herodotean Plausabilities', *Bulletin of the Institute of Classical Studies* 42: 219–25.

Drews, R. (1973), *The Greek Accounts of Eastern History*, Cambridge, MA: Harvard University Press.

Eide, Ø. (2016), 'Verbal Expressions of Geographical Information', in E. Barker, S. Bouzarovski, C. Pelling and L. Isaken (eds), *New Worlds from Old Texts*, 301–18, Oxford: Oxford University Press.

Eidinow, E. (2011), *Luck, Fate & Fortune: Antiquity and its Legacy*, London and New York: I.B. Tauris.

Eiland, H. and Jennings, M. W. (eds) (2002), *Walter Benjamin Selected Writings: Volume 3, 1935–1938*, trans. J. Jephcott, H. Eiland and others, Cambridge, MA, and London: Harvard University Press.

Elsner, J. and Rutherford, I. (eds) (2005), *Pilgrimage in Graeco-Roman and Early Christian Antiquity: Seeing the Gods*, Oxford: Oxford University Press.

Emlyn-Jones, C. J. (1980), The *Ionians and Hellenism: A Study of the Cultural Achievements of the Early Greek Inhabitants of Asia Minor*, London and New York: Routledge.

Eschenbaum, N. E. and Correll, B. (eds) (2016), *Disgust in Early Modern English Literature*, London and New York: Routledge.

Evans, J. A. S. (1961), 'The Dream of Xerxes and the "nomoi" of the Persians', *Classical Journal* 57, no. 3: 109–11.

Evans, J. A. S. (1968), 'Father of History or Father of Lies', *Classical Journal* 64, no. 1: 11–17.

Evans, J. A. S. (1979), 'The Evidence of the Encomium', *L'Antiquité Classique* 48: 112–18.

Evans, J. A. S. (1991), *Herodotus, Explorer of the Past: Three Essays*, Princeton, NJ: Princeton University Press.

Evans, J. A. S. (2011), 'The "Final Problem" at Thermopylae', *Greek, Roman, and Byzantine Studies* 5, no. 4: 231–7.

Evans, R. (2001), *In Defense of History*, London: Granta.

Fantham, E., Foley, H., Kampen, N. B., Pomeroy S. B. and Shapiro, H. A. (1994), *Women in The Classical World: Image and Text*, Oxford, Oxford University Press.

Fearn, D. (2007), 'Narrating ambiguity: murder and Macedonian allegiance (5.17–22)', in E. Irwin and E. Greenwood (eds), *Reading Herodotus: A Study of the Logoi in Book 5 of Herodotus's Histories*, 98–127, Cambridge: Cambridge University Press.

Feeney, D. (2007), *Caesar's Calendar: Ancient Time and the Beginnings of History*, Berkeley and Los Angeles: University of California Press.

Fehling, D. ([1971] 1989), *Herodotus and his 'Sources': Citation, Invention and Narrative Art*, trans. J. H. Howie, Prenton, UK: Francis Cairns Publications.

Fehling, D. (1994), 'The Art of History and the Margins of the World', in Zweder von Martels (ed.), *Travel Fact and Travel Fiction: Studies on Fiction, Literary Tradition, Scholarly Discovery and Observation in Travel Writing*, 1–15, Leiden, Boston and Cologne: Brill.

Feldherr, A. and Grant, G. (2011) (eds) *The Oxford History of Historical Writing Vol. One: Beginnings to AD 600*, Oxford: Oxford University Press.

Fentress, J. and Wickham, C. (1992), *Social Memory*, Oxford: Blackwell.

Finkelbeg, M. (1995), 'Sophocles' "Tr." 634–69 and Herodotus', *Mnemsoyne* 48, no. 2: 146–52.

Fisher, N. R. E. (1979), '*Hybris* and Dishonour: II', *Greece and Rome* 26: 32–47.

Fisher, N. R. E. (1992). *Hybris: A Study in the Values of Honour and Shame in Ancient Greece*, Warminster: Aris & Phillips.

Fisher, N. R. E. (2002), 'Popular Morality in Herodotus', in E. J. Bakker, I. J. F. de Jong and H. van Wees (eds), *Brill's Companion to Herodotus*, 199–224, Leiden, Boston and Cologne: Brill.

Flory, S. (1978a), 'Laughter, Tears and Wisdom in Herodotus', *American Journal of Philology* 99, no. 2: 145–53.

Flory, S. (1978b), 'Arion's Leap: Brave Gestures in Herodotus', *American Journal of Philology* 99, no. 4: 411–21.

Flory, S. (1987), *The Archaic Smile of Herodotus*, Detroit: Wayne State University Press.

Flower, H. I. ([1991] 2013), 'Herodotus and Delphic traditions about Croesus', in R. V. Munson (ed.), *Herodotus: Volume 1 Herodotus and the Narrative of the Past*, 124–53, Oxford: Oxford University Press.

Flower, M. A. (2007), 'The Size of Xerxes' Expeditionary Force', in R. B. Strassler (ed.), *The Landmark Herodotus*, 819–23, New York: Anchor Books.

Flower, M. A. and Marincola J. (eds) (2002), *Herodotus: Histories Book IX*, Cambridge: Cambridge University Press.

Fludernik, P. ([2006] 2009), *An Introduction to Narratology*, trans. P. Häusler-Greenfield. and M. Fludernik, London and New York: Routledge.

Fornara, C. W. (1971), *Herodotus: An Interpretative Essay*. Oxford: Oxford University Press.

Fornara, C. W. ([1971] 2013), 'Herodotus' Perspective', in R. V. Munson (ed.), *Herodotus: Volume 1 Herodotus and the Narrative of the Past*, 321–33, Oxford: Oxford University Press.

Forsdyke, S. (2001), 'Athenian Democratic Ideology and Herodotus' *Histories*', *American Journal of Philology* 122, no. 3: 329–58.

Forsdyke, S. (2002), 'Greek History c.525–480 BC', in E. J. Bakker, I. J. F. de Jong and H. van Wees (eds), *Brill's Companion to Herodotus*, 521–50, Leiden, Boston and Cologne: Brill.

Forsdyke, S. (2006), 'Herodotus, political history and political thought', in C. Dewald and J. Marincola (eds), *The Cambridge Companion to Herodotus*, 224–41, Cambridge: Cambridge University Press.

Forster, E. M. ([1927] 2005), *Aspects of the Novel*, London: Penguin.

Foster, E. (2012), 'Thermopylae and Pylos', in E. Foster and D. Lateiner (eds), *Thucydides and Herodotus*, 185–214, Oxford: Oxford University Press.

Foster, E. and Lateiner, D. (2012), *Thucydides and Herodotus*, 154–84, Oxford: Oxford University Press.

Fowler, R. (1996), 'Herodotus and his Contempories', *Journal of Hellenic Studies* 116: 62–87.

Fowler, R. (2006), 'Herodotus and his prose predecessors', in C. Dewald and J. Marincola J. (eds), *The Cambridge Companion to Herodotus*, 29–45, Cambridge: Cambridge University Press.

Frankopan, P. (2015), *The Silk Roads: A New History of the World*, London: Bloomsbury.

Gainsford, P. (2013), 'Herodotus' Homer: Troy, Thermopylae, and the Dorians', in C. Matthew and M. Trundle (eds), *Beyond the Gates of Fire: New Perspectives on the Battle of Thermopylae*, 117–37, Barnsley: Pen & Sword.

Garland, R. (2017), *Athens Burning: The Persian Invasion of Greece and the Evacuation of Attica*, Baltimore, MD: Johns Hopkins University Press.

Garvie, A. F. (ed.) (2009), *Aeschylus Persae*, Oxford: Oxford University Press.

Genette, G ([1972] 1983), *Narrative Discourse: An Essay in Method*, trans. J. E. Lewin, Ithaca, NY: Cornell University Press.

Georges, P. (1994), *Barbarian Asia and the Greek Experience*, Baltimore, MD: Johns Hopkins University Press.

Gera, D. L. (2000), 'Two Thought Experiments in the Dissoi Logoi', *American Journal of Philology* 121, no. 1: 21–45.

Gera, D. L. (2003), *Ancient Greek Ideas on Speech, Language and Civilization*, Oxford: Oxford University Press.

Giangiulio, M. (2001), 'Constructing the Past: Colonial Traditions and the Writing of History. The Case of Cyrene', in N. Luraghi (ed.), *The Historian's Craft in the Age of Herodotus*, 116–37, Oxford: Oxford University Press.

Gill, C., Postlewaite, N. and Seaford, R. (eds) (1998), *Reciprocity in Ancient Greece*, Oxford: Oxford University Press.

Gill, C. and Wiseman T. P. (eds) (1993), *Lies and Fiction in the Ancient World*, Exeter: Exeter University Press.

Godley, A. D. (trans.) (1920–5), *Herodotus, The Persian Wars*, Vols 1–4, Cambridge, MA, and London: Harvard University Press.

Goldhill, S. (2002), *The Invention of Prose*, Oxford: Oxford University Press.

Goodridge, J. (2006), 'The Case of John Dyer's Fat-Tailed Sheep and their Tail-Trolleys: "A Thing to Some Scarce Credible"', *Agricultural History Review* 54, no. 2: 228–39.

Gorman, V. and Robinson, E. (eds) (2002), *Oikistes: Studies in Constitutions, Colonies, and Military Power in the Ancient World, Offered in Honor of A. J. Graham*, Leiden: Brill.

Gould, J. (1989), *Herodotus*, New York: St. Martin's Press.

Gould, J. (2001), *Myth, Ritual, Memory, and Exchange: Essays in Greek Literature and Culture*, Oxford: Oxford University Press.

Gould, J. ([1994] 2013), 'Herodotus and religion', in R. V. Munson (ed.), *Herodotus: Volume 2 Herodotus and his World*, 183–97, Oxford: Oxford University Press.

Grant, M. (1995), *Greek and Roman Historians: Information and Misinformation*, London and New York: Routledge.

Gray, V. (2002), 'Short Stories in Herodotus' *Histories*', in E. J. Bakker, I. J. F. de Jong and H. van Wees (eds), *Brill's Companion to Herodotus*, 291–317, Leiden, Boston and Cologne: Brill.

Gray, V. (2007), 'Structure and Significance (5.55–69)', in E. Irwin and E.
    Greenwood (eds), *Reading Herodotus: A Study of the Logoi in Book 5 of
    Herodotus's Histories*, 168–78, Cambridge: Cambridge University Press.
Gray, V. (2012), 'Herodotus on Melampus', in E. Baragwanath and M. de Bakker
    (eds), *Myth, Truth, and Narrative in Herodotus*, 167–91, Oxford: Oxford
    University Press.
Greenblatt, S. ([1991] 1992), *Material Possessions: The Wonder of the New World*,
    Chicago and London: University of Chicago Press.
Greene, D. and Lattimore R. (eds) (1991), *Sophocles 1*, Chicago and London:
    University of Chicago Press.
Grethlein, J. (2006), 'The Manifold Uses of the Epic past: The Embassy Scene in
    Herodotus 7.153–63', *American Journal of Philology* 127, no. 4: 485–509.
Grethlein, J. (2009a), 'How Not to Do History: Xerxes in Herodotus' Histories',
    American Journal of Philology 130, no. 2: 195–218.
Grethlein, J. (2009b), 'Philosophical and Structuralist Narratologies – Worlds
    Apart?', in J. Grethlein and A. Rengakos (eds), *Narratology and Interpretation:
    The Content of Narrative Form in Ancient History*, 153–76, Berlin: De Gruyter.
Grethlein, J. (2011), 'The Rise of Greek Historiography and the Invention of
    Prose', in A. Feldherr and G. Grant (eds), *The Oxford History of Historical
    Writing Vol One: Beginnings to AD 600*, 148–70, Oxford: Oxford University
    Press.
Grethlein, J. and Rengakos, A. (eds) (2009), *Narratology and Interpretation: The
    Content of Narrative Form in Ancient History*, Berlin: De Gruyter.
Griffin, J. (2006), 'Herodotus and Tragedy', in C. Dewald and J. Marincola (eds),
    The Cambridge Companion to Herodotus, 46–59, Cambridge: Cambridge
    University Press.
Griffiths, A. (1987), 'Democedes of Croton. A Greek doctor at Darius' Court', in
    H. Sancisi-Weerdenburg and A. Kuhrt (eds), *The Greek Sources: Proceedings of
    the Groningen 1984 Achaemenid History Workshop*, 37–51, Leiden:
    Nederlands Instituut voor het Nabije Ooste.
Griffiths, A. (1999), 'Euenius the Negligent Nightwatchman (Herodotus 9.92–6)',
    in R. G. A. Buxton, *From Myth to Reason? Studies in the Development of
    Greek Thought*, 167–82, Oxford: Oxford University Press.
Griffiths, A. (2001a), 'Kissing Cousins: Some Curious Cases of Adjacent Material in
    Herodotus', in N. Luraghi (ed.), *The Historian's Craft in the Age of Herodotus*,
    161–78, Oxford: Oxford University Press.
Griffiths, A. (2001b), 'Behind the Lines: The Genesis of Stories in Herodotus', in
    F. Budelmann and P. Michelakis (eds), *Homer, Tragedy and Beyond: Essays in
    Honour of P. E. Easterling*, 75–89, London: Society for the Promotion of
    Hellenic Studies.
Griffiths, A. (2006), 'Stories and storytelling in the *Histories*', in C. Dewald and
    J. Marincola (eds), *The Cambridge Companion to Herodotus*, 130–43,
    Cambridge: Cambridge University Press.
Grote, G. ([1846–56] 2001), *A History of Greece: From the Time of Solon to
    403 B.C.*, London and New York: Routledge.
Gruen, E. S. (2011), *Rethinking the Other in Antiquity*, Princeton, NJ, and Oxford:
    Princeton University Press.
Hall, A. M. (1997), *Ethnic Identity in Greek Antiquity*, Cambridge: Cambridge
    University Press.

Hall, E. (1989), *Inventing the Barbarian: Greek Self-Definition through Tragedy*,
    Oxford: Oxford University Press.
Hall, E. (2008), *The Return of Ulysses: A Cultural History of Homer's Odyssey*,
    London and New York: I.B. Tauris.
Hammond, N. G. L. (1988a), 'The Expedition of Datis and Artaphernes', in J.
    Boardman, N. G. L. Hammond, D. M. Lewis and M. Ostwald, *Cambridge
    Ancient History Second edition, Volume IV, Persia, Greece and the Western
    Mediterranean c.525 to 479 B.C.*, 491–517, Cambridge: Cambridge University
    Press.
Hammond, N. G. L. (1988b), 'The Expedition of Xerxes', in J. Boardman,
    N. G. L. Hammond, D. M. Lewis and M. Ostwald, *Cambridge Ancient History
    Second edition, Volume IV, Persia, Greece and the Western Mediterranean
    c.525 to 479 B.C.*, 518–91, Cambridge: Cambridge University Press.
Hammond, N. G. L and Roseman, L. J. (1996), 'The Construction of Xerxes'
    Bridge Over the Hellespont', *Journal of Hellenic Studies* 116: 88–107.
Hanson, W. (2002), *Ariadne's Thread: A Guide to International Tales Found in
    Classical Literature*, Ithaca, NY: Cornell University Press.
Hanson, W. (1996), 'The Protagonist on the Pyre: Herodotean Legend and Modern
    Folktale', *Fabula* 37: 272–85.
Harrison, T. (2000), *Divinity and Herodotus*, Oxford: Oxford University Press.
Harrison, T. (2002), 'The Persian Invasions', in E. J. Bakker, I. J. F. de Jong and
    H. van Wees (eds), *Brill's Companion to Herodotus*, 550–78, Leiden, Boston
    and Cologne: Brill.
Harrison, T. (2003a), 'Herodotus and the origins of history', in P. Derow and R.
    Parker (eds), *Herodotus and his World: Essays from a Conference in Memory of
    George Forrest*, 237–55, Oxford: Oxford University Press.
Harrison, T. (2003b), 'Upside Down and Back to Front: Herodotus and the Greek
    Encounter with Egypt', in R. Matthews and C. Roemer (eds), *Ancient
    Perspectives on Egypt*, 145–55, London: UCL Press.
Harrison, T. (2011), *Writing Ancient Persia*, London: Bloomsbury.
Hartog, F. (1988), *The Mirror of Herodotus: The Representation of the Other in
    the Writing of History*, trans. J. Lloyd, Berkeley, Los Angeles and London:
    University of California Press.
Hartog, F. ([1979] 2013), 'Imaginary Scythians: Space and Nomadism', in
    R. V. Munson (ed.), *Herodotus: Volume 2 Herodotus and his World*, 245–66,
    Oxford: Oxford University Press.
Hashhozheva, G. (2016), 'Indecorous customs, rhetorical decorum, and the
    reception of Herodotean ethnography from Henri Estienne to Edmund Spencer',
    in N. E. Eschenbaum and B. Correll (eds), *Disgust in Early Modern English
    Literature*, 85–105, London and New York: Routledge.
Hau, L. I. (2016), *Moral History from Herodotus to Diodorus Siculus*, Edinburgh:
    Edinburgh University Press.
Haubold, J. (2007), 'Athens and Aegina (5.82–9)', in E. Irwin and E. Greenwood
    (eds), *Reading Herodotus: A Study of the Logoi in Book 5 of Herodotus's
    Histories*, 226–44, Cambridge: Cambridge University Press.
Hegel, G. W. F. ([1899] 1956), *The Philosophy of History*, trans. J. Sibree, New
    York: Dover Publications.
Hegel, G. W. F. (1975), *Lectures on the Philosophy of World History: Introduction*,
    trans. H. B. Nisbet, Cambridge: Cambridge University Press.

Hegel, G. W. F. (1984), *The Letters*, trans. C. Butler and C. Seiler. Bloomington: Indiana University Press.

Heinz, M. and Feldman M. H. (eds) (2007), *Representations of Political Power: Case Histories from Times of Change and Dissolving Order in the Ancient Near East*, Warsaw, IN: Eisenbrauns.

Henderson, J. (2012), 'Old Comedy and Popular History', in J. Marincola, L. Llewlyn-Jones and C. Maciver (eds), *Greek Notions of the Past in the Archaic and Classical Eras: History Without Historians*, 144–59, Edinburgh: Edinburgh University Press.

Herington, J. (1991a), 'The Closure of Herodotus' *Histories*', *Illinois Classical Studies* 16: 149–91.

Herington, J. (1991b), 'The Poem of Herodotus', *Arion* 1, no. 3: 5–16.

Hirchfield, N. (2007), 'Trireme Warfare in Herodotus', in R. B. Strassler (ed.), *The Landmark Herodotus*, 824–34, New York: Anchor Books.

Holland, T. (2005), *Persian Fire: The First World Empire and the Battle for the West*, London: Little, Brown.

Holland, T. (trans.) (2013), *Herodotus The Histories*, London: Allen Lane.

Hornblower, S. (2001), 'Epic and Epiphanies: Herodotus and the "New Simonides"', in D. Boedeker and D. Sider (eds), *The New Simonides: Contexts of Praise and Desire*, 135–47, Oxford: Oxford University Press.

Hornblower, S. (2002), 'Herodotus and his Sources of Information', in E. J. Bakker, I. J. F. de Jong and H. van Wees (eds), *Brill's Companion to Herodotus*, 373–86, Leiden, Boston and Cologne: Brill.

Hornblower, S. (2003), 'Panionius of Chios and Hermotimos of Pedasa', in P. Derow and R. Parker (eds), *Herodotus and his World: Essays from a Conference in Memory of George Forrest*, 37–57, Oxford: Oxford University Press.

Hornblower, S. (2004), *Thucydides and Pindar: Historical Narrative and the World of Epinkian Poetry*, Oxford: Oxford University Press.

Hornblower, S. (2007), 'The Dorieus episode and the Ionian Revolt (5.42–8)', in E. Irwin and E. Greenwood (eds), *Reading Herodotus: A Study of the Logoi in Book 5 of Herodotus' Histories*, 168–78, Cambridge: Cambridge University Press.

Hornblower, S. (2011a), *Thucydidean Themes*, Oxford: Oxford University Press.

Hornblower, S. ([1983] 2011b), *The Greek World: 479–323 BC*, London and New York: Routledge.

Hornblower, S. (ed.) (1994), *Greek Historiography*, Oxford: Oxford University Press.

Hornblower, S. (ed.) (2013), *Herodotus Histories Book V*. Cambridge. Cambridge University Press.

Hyland, J. (2011), 'Contesting Marathon: Billows, Krentz, and the Persian Problem', *Classical Philology* 106, no. 3: 241–53.

Immerwahr, H. R. (1954), 'Historical Action in Herodotus', *Transactions and Proceedings of the American Philological Association* 85: 16–45.

Immerwahr, H. R. (1966), *Form and Thought in Herodotus*, Cleveland, OH: American Philological Association.

Immerwahr, H. R. ([1956] 2013), 'Aspects of historical causation in Herodotus', in R. V. Munson (ed.), *Herodotus: Volume 1 Herodotus and the Narrative of the Past*, 157–93, Oxford: Oxford University Press.

Irwin, E. (2009), 'Herodotus and Samos: Personal or Political', *Classical World* 102, no. 4: 395–416.

Irwin, E. and Greenwood, E. (eds) (2007), *Reading Herodotus: A Study of the Logoi in Book 5 of Herodotus's Histories*, Cambridge: Cambridge University Press.

Jennings, M. W., Eiland, H. and Smith, G. (eds) (1999), *Walter Benjamin Selected Writings: Volume 2, Part 2 1931–1934*, trans. R. Livingstone and others, Cambridge, MA, and London: Harvard University Press.

Jeremiah, E. T. (2002), *The Emergence of Reflexivity in Greek Language and Thought: From Homer to Plato and Beyond*, Leiden, Boston and Cologne: Brill.

Johnson, D. M. (2001), 'Herodotus' Storytelling Speeches: Socles (5.92) and Leotychides (6.86)', *Classical Journal* 97, no. 1: 1–26.

Johnson, M. and Ryan. T. (eds) (2005), *Sexuality in Greek and Roman Society and Literature: A Sourcebook*, London and New York: Routledge.

Jong, I. J. F. de. (2002), 'Narrative Unity and Units', in E. J. Bakker, I. J. F. de Jong and H. van Wees (eds), *Brill's Companion to Herodotus*, 245–66, Leiden, Boston and Cologne: Brill.

Jong, I. J. F. de. (2012a), 'The Helen *Logos* and Herodotus' Fingerprint', in E. Baragwanath and M. de Bakker (eds), *Myth, Truth, and Narrative in Herodotus*, 127–42, Oxford: Oxford University Press.

Jong, I. J. F. de. (ed.) (2012b), *Space in Ancient Greek Literature: Studies in Ancient Greek Narrative*, Leiden, Boston and Cologne: Brill.

Jong, I. J. F. de. (ed.) ([1999] 2013), 'Narratological aspects of the *Histories* of Herodotus', trans. J Kardan, in R. V. Munson (ed.), *Herodotus: Volume 1 Herodotus and the Narrative of the Past*, 253–91, Oxford: Oxford University Press.

Jong, I. J. F. de. and Nünlist, R. (eds) (2007), *Time in Ancient Greek Literature: Studies in Ancient Greek Narrative, Volume Two*, Leiden, Boston and Cologne: Brill.

Joyce, J. ([1939] 1964), *Finnegans Wake*, London: Faber and Faber.

Joyce, J. ([1922] 1986), *Ulysses*, ed. Hans Walter Gabler et al., London: Bodley Head.

Kapuściński, R. (2007), *Travels with Herodotus*, trans. K Glowczewska, London: Penguin.

Karttunen, K. (2002), 'The Ethnography of the Fringes', in E. J. Bakker, I. J. F. de Jong and H. van Wees (eds), *Brill's Companion to Herodotus*, 457–74, Leiden, Boston and Cologne: Brill.

Keaveney A. (1988), 'The Attack on Naxos: A "Forgotten Cause" of the Ionian Revolt', *Classical Quarterly* 38, no. 1: 76–81.

Kramer, L. and Maza, S. (eds) (2002), *A Companion to Western Historical Thought*, Oxford: Blackwell.

Krebs, C. B. and Grethkein, J. (eds) (2012), *Time and Narrative in Ancient Historiography: The 'Plupast' from Herodotus to Appian*, Cambridge: Cambridge University Press.

Krentz, P. (2010), *The Battle of Marathon*, New Haven, CT: Yale University Press.

Kuhn, T. ([1962] 2012), *The Structure of Scientific Revolutions*, Chicago: University of Chicago Press.

Kuhrt, A. (2002), 'Babylon', in E. J. Bakker, I. J. F. de Jong and H. van Wees (eds), *Brill's Companion to Herodotus*, 475–96, Leiden, Boston and Cologne: Brill.

Kuhrt, A. (2007), 'Cyrus the Great of Persia: Images and Realities', in M. Heinz and M. H. Feldman (eds), *Representations of Political Power: Case Histories from Times of Change and Dissolving Order in the Ancient Near East*, 169–91, Warsaw, IN: Eisenbrauns.

Lateiner, D. (1977), 'No laughing matter: a literary tactic in Herodotus', *American Philological Association* 107: 173–82.

Lateiner, D. (1989), *The Historical Method of Herodotus*, Toronto: University of Toronto Press.

Lateiner, D. (1990), 'Deception and Delusion in Herodotus', *Classical Antiquity 9*, no. 2: 230–46.

Lateiner D. (2005), 'Signifying Names and Other Ominous Accidental Utterances in Classical Historiography', *Greek Roman and Byzantine Studies* 45: 35–57.

Lateiner, D. (2012), 'Oaths: Theory and Practice in the *Histories* of Herodotus and Thucydides', in E. Foster and D. Lateiner (eds), *Thucydides and Herodotus*, 154–84, Oxford: Oxford University Press.

Lateiner, D ([1984] 2013), 'Herodotean historiographical patterning: "The Constitutional Debate"', in R. V. Munson (ed.), *Herodotus: Volume 1 Herodotus and the Narrative of the Past*, 194–211, Oxford: Oxford University Press.

Lattimore, R. (trans.) (2011), *The Iliad of Homer*, Chicago and London: University of Chicago Press.

Lazenby, J. F. (1993), *The Defence of Greece*, Warminster: Aris & Phillips.

Lee, J. W. I. (2007), 'Hoplite Warfare in Herodotus', in R. B. Strassler (ed.), *The Landmark Herodotus*, 798–804, New York: Anchor Books.

Lévi-Strauss, C. ([1989–2002] 2016), *We Are All Cannibals*, trans. J. M. Todd, New York: Columbia University Press.

Lewis, M. W. and Wigen, K. E. (1997), *The Myth of Continents: A Critique of Metageography*, Berkeley and Los Angeles: University of California Press.

Lianeri, A. (2016a), 'Ancient Historiography and "Future Past"', in A. Lianeri (ed.), *Knowing Future Time in and through Greek Historiography*, 59–77, Berlin and Boston: De Gruyter.

Lianeri, A. (ed.) (2016b), *Knowing Future Time in and through Greek Historiography*, Berlin and Boston: De Gruyter.

Liddell, H. G. and Scott, R. (2000), *Intermediate Greek Lexicon: Founded upon the Seventh Edition of Liddell and Scott's Greek–English Lexicon*, Oxford: Oxford University Press.

Lincoln, B. (2007), *Religion, Empire and Torture: The Case of Achaemenid Persia with a Postscript on Abu Ghraib*, Chicago and London: University of Chicago Press.

Llewellyn-Jones, L. (2013), *King and Court in Ancient Persia*, Edinburgh: Edinburgh University Press.

Lloyd, A. (1999). 'Herodotus', in K. Bard (ed.), *Encyclopedia of the Archaeology of Ancient Egypt*, 444–5, London and New York: Routledge.

Lloyd, A. (2002), 'Egypt', in E. J. Bakker, I. J. F. de Jong and H. van Wees (eds), *Brill's Companion to Herodotus*, 415–35, Leiden, Boston and Cologne: Brill.

Lloyd, A. (2007), 'Book II', in D. Asheri et al., *A Commentary on Herodotus Books I–IV*, 219–378, Oxford: Oxford University Press.

Lloyd, G. E. R. (1987), *The Revolutions of Wisdom: Studies in the Claims and Practice of Ancient Greek Science*, Berkeley and Los Angeles: University of California Press.

Lloyd-Jones, H. (1971), *The Justice of Zeus*, Berkeley and Los Angeles: University of California Press.

Luraghi, N. (2001a), 'Local Knowledge in Herodotus' *Histories*', in N. Luraghi (ed.), *The Historian's Craft in the Age of Herodotus*, Oxford: Oxford University Press.

Luraghi, N. (2006). 'Meta-*historiē*: Method and Genre in the *Histories*', in C. Dewald and J. Marincola (eds), *The Cambridge Companion to Herodotus*, 76–91, Cambridge: Cambridge University Press.

Luraghi, N. ([2005] 2013), 'The stories before the *Histories*: Folktale and traditional narrative in Herodotus', in R. V. Munson (ed.), *Herodotus: Volume 1 Herodotus and the Narrative of the Past*, 87–112, Oxford: Oxford University Press.

Luraghi, N. (ed.) (2001), *The Historian's Craft in the Age of Herodotus*, Oxford: Oxford University Press.

Macan, R. W. (ed.) ([1908] 2013), *Herodotus: The Seventh, Eighth and Ninth Books*, Cambridge: Cambridge University Press (available at http://www.perseus.tufts.edu/hopper/text?doc=Peresus:text:1999.04.0038; accessed 17 November 2017).

Marincola, J. (2001), *Greek Historians*, Cambridge: Cambridge University Press.

Marincola, J. (2006). 'Herodotus and the Poetry of the Past', in C. Dewald and J. Marincola (eds), *The Cambridge Companion to Herodotus*, 13–28, Cambridge: Cambridge University Press.

Marincola, J. (2012), 'Introduction: A Past Without Historians', in J. Marincola, L. Llewlyn-Jones and C. Maciver (eds), *Greek Notions of the Past in the Archaic and Classical Eras: History Without Historians*, 1–13, Edinburgh: Edinburgh University Press.

Marincola, J. (ed.) (2007), *A Companion to Greek and Roman Historiography: Volume One*, Oxford: Blackwell.

Marincola, J., Llewlyn-Jones, L. and Maciver, C. (eds) (2012), *Greek Notions of the Past in the Archaic and Classical Eras: History Without Historians*, Edinburgh: Edinburgh University Press.

Marks, H. (ed.) (2012), *The English Bible: King James Version. Volume One, The Old Testament*, New York and London: W. W. Norton.

Marr, J. (1995), 'Themistocles and the supposed second message to Xerxes: the anatomy of a legend', *Acta Classica* 38: 57–69.

Marwick, A. (1995), 'Two Approaches to Historical Study: The Metaphysical (Including "Postmodernism") and the Historical', *Journal of Contemporary History* 30, no. 1: 5–35.

Matthew, C. (2013), 'Was the Greek Defence of Thermopylae in 480 BC a Suicide Mission?', in C. Matthew and M. Trundle (eds), *Beyond the Gates of Fire: New Perspectives on the Battle of Thermoplyae*, 60–99, Barnsley: Pen & Sword.

Matthew, C. and Trundle, M. (eds) (2013), *Beyond the Gates of Fire: New Perspectives on the Battle of Thermopylae*, Barnsley: Pen & Sword.

Matthews, R. and Roemer C. (eds) (2003), *Ancient Perspectives on Egypt*, 145–55, London: UCL Press.

Mayor, A. (2014), *The Amazons: Lives and Legends of Warrior Women in the Ancient World*, Princeton, NJ, and Oxford: Princeton University Press.

McConnell, J. (2013), *Black Odysseys: The Homeric* Odyssey *in the African Diaspora since 1939*, Oxford: Oxford University Press.

McInerney, J. (ed.) (2014), *A Companion to Ethnicity in the Ancient World*, Chichester: Wiley Blackwell.

Mensch, P. (trans.) (2014), *Herodotus Histories*, Indianapolis, IN: Hackett Publishing Company.

Mikalson, J. D. (2003), *Herodotus and Religion in the Persian Wars*, Chapel Hill, NC, and London: University of North Carolina Press.

Millender, E. G. (2002), 'Spartan Obedience and Athenian Lawfulness in Fifth-Century Thought', in V. Gorman and E. Robinson (eds), *Oikistes: Studies in Constitutions, Colonies, and Military Power in the Ancient World, Offered in Honor of A. J. Graham*, 35–59, Leiden: Brill.

Moles, J. (1993), 'Truth and Untruth in Herodotus and Thucydides', in C. Gill, and T. P. Wiseman (eds), *Truth and Fiction in the Ancient World*, 88–120, Exeter: Exeter University Press.

Moles, J. (2002), 'Herodotus and Athens', in E. J. Bakker, I. J. F. de Jong and H. van Wees (eds), *Brill's Companion to Herodotus*, 33–52, Leiden, Boston and Cologne: Brill.

Moles, J. (2007), 'Saving Greece from the "ignominy" of tyranny? The "famous" and "wonderful" speech of Socles (5.92)', in E. Irwin and E. Greenwood (eds), *Reading Herodotus: A Study of the Logoi in Book 5 of Herodotus's Histories*, 245–68, Cambridge: Cambridge University Press.

Momigliano, A. ([1958] 1966a), 'The Place of Herodotus in the History of Historiography', in A. Momigliano, *Studies in Historiography*, 127–42, London: Weidenfeld and Nicolson.

Momigliano, A. (1966b), *Studies in Historiography*, London: Weidenfeld and Nicolson.

Morgan, J. (2016), *Greek Perspectives on the Achaemenid Empire: Persia through the Looking Glass*, Edinburgh: Edinburgh University Press.

Morgan, K. (ed.) (2003), *Popular Tyranny*, Austin: University of Texas Press.

Moyer, I. (2006), 'Golden Fetters and Economies of Cultural Exchange', *Journal of Ancient Near Eastern Religion* 6: 225–56.

Munson, R. V. (1988), 'Artemisia in Herodotus', *Classical Antiquity* 7, no. 1: 91–106.

Munson, R. V. (1993), 'Herodotus' use of Prospective Sentences and the Story of Rhampsinitus and the Thief in the *Histories*', *American Journal of Philology* 114, no. 1: 27–44.

Munson, R. V. (2001a), *Telling Wonders: Ethnographic and Political Discourse in the Work of Herodotus*, Ann Arbor: University of Michigan Press.

Munson, R. V. (2001b), '*Anankē* in Herodotus', *Journal of Hellenic Studies* 121: 30–50.

Munson, R. V. (2007), 'The trouble with the Ionians: Herodotus and the beginning of the Ionian Revolt (5.28–38.1)', in E. Irwin and E. Greenwood (eds), *Reading Herodotus: A Study of the Logoi in Book 5 of Herodotus's Histories*, 146–67, Cambridge: Cambridge University Press.

Munson, R. V. ([2009] 2013), 'Who are Herodotus' Persians?', in R. V. Munson (ed.), *Herodotus: Volume 2 Herodotus and the World*, 321–35, Oxford: Oxford University Press.

Munson, R. V. (2014), 'Herodotus and Ethnicity', in J. McInerney (ed.), *A Companion to Ethnicity in the Ancient World*, 341–55, Chichester: Wiley Blackwell.

Munson, R. V. (ed.) (2013a), *Herodotus: Volume 1 Herodotus and the Narrative of the Past*, Oxford: Oxford University Press.

Munson, R. V. (ed.) (2013b), *Herodotus: Volume 2 Herodotus and the World*, Oxford: Oxford University Press.

Murray, O. (1988), 'The Ionian Revolt', in J. Boardman, N. G. L. Hammond, D. M. Lewis and M. Ostwald, *Cambridge Ancient History Second edition, Volume IV, Persia, Greece and the Western Mediterranean c.525 to 479 B.C.*, 461–90, Cambridge: Cambridge University Press.

Murray, O. ([1987] 2001a), 'Herodotus and Oral History', in N. Luraghi (ed.), *The Historian's Craft in the Age of Herodotus*, 16–44, Oxford: Oxford University Press.

Murray, O. (2001b), 'Herodotus and Oral History Reconsidered', in N. Luraghi (ed.), *The Historian's Craft in the Age of Herodotus*, 314–25, Oxford: Oxford University Press.

O'Malley, S. (2015), *Making History New: Modernism and Historical Narrative*, New York and Oxford: Oxford University Press.

Osborne, R. (2007), 'The Paeonians', in E. Irwin and E. Greenwood (eds), *Reading Herodotus: A Study of the Logoi in Book 5 of Herodotus's Histories*, 88–97, Cambridge: Cambridge University Press.

Osborne, R. (2009), *Greece in the Making: 1200–479 BC*, London and New York: Routledge.

Osborne, R. (2011), 'Greek Inscriptions as Historical Writing', in A. Feldherr and G. Grant (eds), *The Oxford History of Historical Writing Vol. One: Beginnings to AD 600*, 97–121, Oxford: Oxford University Press.

Ostwald, M. (1969), *Nomos and the Beginning of the Athenian Democracy*, Oxford: Oxford University Press.

Ostwald, M. (1991), 'Herodotus and Athens', *Illinois Classical Studies* 16, no. 1/2: 137–48.

Pascal, B. (1995), *Pensées and Other Writings*, trans. H. Levi, Oxford: Oxford University Press.

Peissel, M. (1984), *The Ant's Gold: The discovery of the Greek El Dorado in the Himalayas*, New York: HarperCollins.

Pelling, C. (1991), 'Thucydides' Archidamus and Herodotus' Artabanus', in M. Flower and M. Toher (eds), *Georgica, Greek Studies in Honour of George Cawkwell*, 120–42, London: University of London, Institute of Classical Studies.

Pelling, C. (2000), *Literary Texts and the Greek Historian*, London and New York: Routledge.

Pelling, C. (2006a), 'Homer and Herodotus', in M. J. Clark, B. G. F. Currie and R. O. A. M. Lyne (eds), *Epic Interactions: Perspectives on Homer, Virgil and the Epic Tradition*, 75–104, Oxford: Oxford University Press.

Pelling, C. (2006b), 'Talking and Learning in Herodotus' Lydian *Logos*', *Classical Antiquity* 25, no. 1: 141–77.

Pelling, C. (2006c), 'Speech and Narrative in the *Histories*', in C. Dewald and J. Marincola (eds), *The Cambridge Companion to Herodotus*, 103–21, Cambridge: Cambridge University Press.

Pelling, C. (2007), 'Aristagoras (5.49–55, 97)', in E. Irwin and E. Greenwood (eds), *Reading Herodotus: A Study of the Logoi in Book 5 of Herodotus' Histories*, 179–201, Cambridge: Cambridge University Press.

Pelling, C. ([1997] 2013), 'East is East and West is West – Or are they?', in R. V. Munson (ed.), *Herodotus: Volume 2 Herodotus and the World*, 360–79, Oxford: Oxford University Press.

Pitcher, L. V. (2007), 'Characterization in Ancient Historiography', in J. Marincola (ed.), *A Companion to Greek and Roman Historiography*, 102–17, Oxford: Blackwell.

Plato (1997), *Complete Works*, ed. J. M. Cooper, Indianapolis, IN: Hackett Publishing Company.

Polinskaya, I. (2010), 'Shared Sanctuaries and the Gods of Others: On the Meaning of "Common" in Herodotus 8.144', in R. M. Rosenm and I. Sluiter (eds), *Valuing Others in Classical Antiquity*, 43–70, Leiden: Brill.

Powell, E. ([1939] 2003), *Herodotus Book VIII*, Bristol Classical Press, Cambridge: Cambridge University Press.

Press, P. G. A. (1982), *The Development of the Idea of History in Antiqutiy*, Montreal: McGill-Queen's University Press.

Priestley, J. (2014), *Herodotus and Hellenistic Culture: Literary Studies in the Reception of the* Histories', Oxford: Oxford University Press.

Pritchett, W. K. (1993), *The Liar School of Herodotus*, Amsterdam: J. C. Gieben.

Purves, A. C. (2010), *Space and Time in Ancient Greek Narrative*, Cambridge: Cambridge University Press.

Raaflaub, K. A. (1987), 'Herodotus, Political Thought and the Meaning of History', *Arethusa* 20: 221–48.

Raaflaub, K. A. (2002), 'Herodotus and the Intellectual Trends of his Time', in E. J. Bakker, I. J. F. de Jong and H. van Wees (eds), *Brill's Companion to Herodotus*, 149–86, Leiden, Boston and Cologne: Brill.

Raaflaub, K. A. (ed.) (2014), *Thinking, Recording, and Writing in the Ancient World*, Chichester: Wiley Blackwell.

Redfield, J. ([1985] 2013), 'Herodotus the tourist', in R. V. Munson (ed.), *Herodotus: Volume 2 Herodotus and the World*, 267–91, Oxford: Oxford University Press.

Renehan, R. (2001), 'Herodotos Philanthropos', *Hermes* 129: 173–87.

Ricoeur, P. ([1983] 1984), *Time and Narrative: Volume 1*, trans. K. McLaughlin and D. Pellauer, Chicago and London: University of Chicago Press.

Ricoeur, P. ([1985] 1988), *Time and Narrative: Volume 3*, trans. K. Blamey and D. Pellauer, Chicago and London: University of Chicago Press.

Roberts, J. T. (2011), *Herodotus: A Very Short Introduction*, Oxford: Oxford University Press.

Rollinger, R. (2000), 'Herodotus and the Intellectual Heritage of the Ancient Near East', in S. Aro and R. M. Whiting (eds), *The Heirs of Assyria (Melammu Symposia 1)*, 65–83, Helsinki: Helsinki University Press.

Romm, J. (1989), 'Herodotus and Mythic Geography', *Transactions and Proceedings of the American Philological Association* 119: 97–113.

Romm, J. (1998), *Herodotus*, New Haven, CT: Yale University Press.

Romm, J. (2006), 'Herodotus and the natural world', in C. Dewald and J. Marincola (eds), *The Cambridge Companion to Herodotus*, 178–91, Cambridge: Cambridge University Press.

Rood T. (2006), 'Herodotus and foreign lands', in C. Dewald and J. Marincola (eds), *The Cambridge Companion to Herodotus*, 290–305, Cambridge: Cambridge University Press.

Rood, T. (2007), 'Herodotus', in I. J. F. de Jong and R. Nünlist (eds), *Time in Ancient Greek Literature: Studies in Ancient Greek Narrative*, Vol. Two, 115–30, Leiden, Boston and Cologne: Brill.

Rood, T. (2010), 'Herodotus' Proem: Space, Time, and the Origins of International Relations', *Ariadne* 16: 43–74.

Rood, T. (2012), 'Herodotus', in I. J. F. de Jong (ed.), *Space in Ancient Greek Literature: Studies in Ancient Greek Narrative*, 121–40, Leiden, Boston and Cologne: Brill.

Rosen R. M. and Farrell J. (eds) (1993), *Nomodeikes: Greek Studies in Honor of Martin Ostwald*, Ann Arbor: University of Michigan Press.

Rosen, R. M. and Sluiter, I. (eds) (2010), *Valuing Others in Classical Antiquity*, 43–70, Leiden: Brill.

Rutherford, I. (2005), 'Down-Stream at to the Cat-Goddess: Herodotus on Egyptian Pilgrimage', in J. Elsner and I. Rutherford (eds), *Pilgrimage in Graeco-Roman and Early Christian Antiquity: Seeing the Gods*, 131–49, Oxford: Oxford University Press.

Rutherford, R. B. (2012), 'Structure in Epic and Historiography', in E. Foster and D. Lateiner (eds), *Thucydides and Herodotus*, 13–38, Oxford: Oxford University Press.

Saïd, S. (2002), 'Herodotus and Tragedy', in E. J. Bakker, I. J. F. de Jong and H. van Wees (eds), *Brill's Companion to Herodotus*, 117–45, Leiden, Boston and Cologne: Brill.

Saïd, S. (2012), 'Herodotus and the "Myth" of the Trojan War', in E. Baragwanath, E. and M. de Bakker (eds), *Myth, Truth, and Narrative in Herodotus*, 87–105, Oxford: Oxford University Press.

Samuels, T. (2015), 'Herodotus and the Black Body: A Critical Race Theory Analysis', *Journal of Black Studies* 46, no. 7: 723–41.

Sancisi-Weerdenburg, H. ([1989] 2002), 'The Personality of Xerxes, King of Kings', in E. J. Bakker, I. J. F. de Jong and H. van Wees (eds), *Brill's Companion to Herodotus*, 579–90, Leiden, Boston and Cologne: Brill.

Sancisi-Weerdenburg, H. ([1983] 2013), 'Exit Atossa: Images of women in Greek historiography on Persia', in R. V. Munson (ed.), *Herodotus: Volume 2 Herodotus and the World*, 135–50, Oxford: Oxford University Press.

Sancisi-Weerdenburg, H. and Kuhrt, A. (eds) (1987), *The Greek Sources: Proceedings of the Groningen 1984 Achaemenid History Workshop*, 37–51, Leiden: Nederlands Instituut voor het Nabije Ooste.

Scanlon, T. F. (2015), *Greek Historiography*, Chichester: Wiley-Blackwell.

Schepens, G. (2007), 'History and *Historia*: Inquiry in the Greek and Roman Historians', in J. Marincola (ed.), *A Companion to Greek and Roman Historiography*, 39–55, Oxford: Blackwell.

Scott, L. (2005), *Historical Commentary on Herodotus: Book 6*, Leiden, Boston and Cologne: Brill.

Scullion, S. (2006), 'Herodotus and Greek religion', in C. Dewald and J. Marincola (eds), *The Cambridge Companion to Herodotus*, 192–208, Cambridge: Cambridge University Press.

Sebeok, T. A. and Brady, E. (1978), 'The Two Sons of Croesus: A Myth about Communication in Herodotus', *Journal of the Folklore Institute* 15: 5–22.

Sélincourt, A. de. (trans.) ([1954] 2003), *Herodotus The Histories*, London: Penguin.

Shapiro, S. O. (1994), 'Learning Through Suffering: Human Wisdom in Herodotus', *Classical Journal* 89, no. 4: 349–55.

Shapiro, S. O. (1996), 'Herodotus and Solon', *Classical Antiquity* 15, no. 2: 348–64.

Shapiro, S. O. (2000), 'Proverbial wisdom in Herodotus', *Transactions of the American Philological Association* 130: 89–118.

Shaw, I. (2004), *Ancient Egypt: A Very Short Introduction*, Oxford: Oxford University Press.

Sinos, R. H. (1993), 'Epiphany and Politics in Archaic Greece', in C. Dougherty and L. Kurke (eds), *Cultural Poetics in Archaic Greece: Cult, Performance, Politics*, 73–91, Oxford: Oxford University Press.

Solmsen, L. (1944), 'Speeches in Herodotus' Account of the Battle of Plataea', *Classical Philology* 39: 241–53.

Sommerstein, A. H. and Torrance, I. C. (2014), *Oaths and Swearing in Ancient Greece*. Berlin and Boston: De Gruyter.

Sourvinou-Inwood, C. (2003), 'Herodotus (and others) on Pelasgians: Some Perceptions of Ethnicity', in P. Derow and R. Parker (eds), *Herodotus and his World: Essays from a Conference in Memory of George Forrest*, 103–44, Oxford: Oxford University Press.

Souza, P. de. (2003), *The Greek and Persian Wars 499–386 BC*, Oxford: Osprey Publishing.

Sparavigna, A. C. (2013), 'Outlining the Garamantian Kingdom, from Herodotus to the Google Maps', *Archaeogate*, https://papers.ssm.com/sol3/papers.cfm?abstract_id2753485 (accessed 18 November 2017).

Stadter, P. (1992), 'Herodotus and the Athenian Arche', *Annali della Scuola Normale Superiore di Pisa* 22: 781–809.

Stadter, P. A. (2002), 'Historical Thought in Ancient Greece', in L. Kramer and S. Maza (eds), *A Companion to Western Historical Thought*, 35–59, Oxford: Blackwell.

Stahl, H.-P. (1968), 'Herodotus Gyges-Tragödie', *Hermes* 96: 385–400.

Stahl, H.-P. (1975), 'Learning Through Suffering? Croesus' conversations in the history of Herodotus', *Yale Classical Studies* 24: 1–36.

Stahl, H.-P. (2012), 'Blind Decisions Preceding Military Action', in E. Foster and D. Lateiner (eds), *Thucydides and Herodotus*, 125–53, Oxford: Oxford University Press.

Stavrakopoulou, F. (2016), 'The Historical Framework: Biblical and Scholarly Portrayals of the Past', in J. Barton (ed.), *The Hebrew Bible: A Critical Companion*, 24–53, Princeton, NJ: Princeton University Press.

Stern, J. (1991), 'Narratives in Herodotus', *Hermes* 119, no. 3: 304–13.

Strassler, R. B. (ed.) (2007), *The Landmark Herodotus*, New York: Anchor Books.

Strid, O. (2006), 'Voiceless Victims, Memorable Deaths in Herodotus', *Classical Quarterly* 56, no. 2: 393–403.

Thomas, O. (2016), 'Greek Hymnic Spaces', in E. Barker, S. Bouzarovski, C. Pelling and L. Isaken (eds), *New Worlds from Old Texts*, 25–46, Oxford: Oxford University Press.

Thomas, R. (1989), *Oral Tradition and Written Records in Classical Athens*, Cambridge: Cambridge University Press.

Thomas, R. (1997), 'Ethnography, proof and argument in Herodotus' *Histories*', *Proceedings of the Cambridge Philological Society* 43: 128–48.

Thomas, R. (2000), *Herodotus in Context: Ethnography, Science and the Art of Persuasion*, Cambridge: Cambridge University Press.

Thomas, R. (2001), 'Herodotus' *Histories* and the Floating Gap', in N. Luraghi (ed.), *The Historian's Craft in the Age of Herodotus*, 198–210, Oxford: Oxford University Press.

Thomas, R. (2006), 'The intellectual milieu of Herodotus', in C. Dewald and J. Marincola (eds), *The Cambridge Companion to Herodotus*, 60–75, Cambridge: Cambridge University Press.

Thomas, R. (2012), 'Herodotus and Eastern Myths and *Logoi*: Deioces the Mede and Pythius the Lydian', in E. Baragwanath and M. de Bakker (eds), *Myth, Truth, and Narrative in Herodotus*, 233–53, Oxford: Oxford University Press.

Thomas, R. ([2001] 2013), 'Ethnicity, genealogy, and Hellenism', in R. V. Munson (ed), *Herodotus: Volume 2 Herodotus and his World*, 339–59, Oxford: Oxford University Press.

Thucydides. (2009), *The Peloponnesian War*, trans. M. Hammond, Oxford: Oxford University Press.

Török, L. (2014), *Herodotus in Nubia (Mnemosyne Supplements)*, Leiden, Boston and Cologne: Brill.

Tritle, L. (2006), 'Warfare in Herodotus', in C. Dewald and J. Marincola (eds), *The Cambridge Companion to Herodotus*, 209–23, Cambridge: Cambridge University Press.

Tuan, Y.-F. (1977), *Space and Place: The Perspective of Experience*, Minneapolis: University of Minnesota Press.

Tucker, A. (ed.) (2009), *A Companion to the Philosophy of History and Historiography*, Chichester: Wiley Blackwell.

Tuplin, C. J. (2003), 'Xerxes' March from Doriscus to Therme', *Historia* 52: 385–409.

Turnbull, D. (2007), 'Maps, narratives and trails: performativity, hodology and distributed knowledges in complex adaptive systems – an approach to emergent mapping', *Geographical Research* 45: 140–9.

Van der Dussen, J. (2016), *Studies on Collingwood, History and Civilization*, Dordrecht: Springer.

Vandiver, E. (2012), '"Strangers are from Zeus": Homeric *Xenia* at the Courts of Proteus and Croesus', in E. Baragwanath and M. de Bakker (eds), *Myth, Truth, and Narrative in Herodotus*, 142–66, Oxford: Oxford University Press.

Vannicelli, P. (2001), 'Herodotus' Egypt and the foundations of universal history', in N. Luraghi (ed.), *The Historian's Craft in the Age of Herodotus*, 211–40, Oxford: Oxford University Press.

Van Seters, J. (2011), 'Historiography in Ancient Israel', in A. Feldherr and G. Grant (eds), *The Oxford History of Historical Writing Vol. One: Beginnings to AD 600*, 76–96, Oxford: Oxford University Press.

Vašíček, Z. (2009), 'Philosophy of History', in A. Tucker (ed.), *A Companion to the Philosophy of History and Historiography*, 26–43, Chichester: Wiley Blackwell.

Veen, J. E. van der (1995), 'A Minute's Mirth . . .: Syloson and his Cloak in Herodotus', *Mnemosyne* 48: 129–45.

Versnel, H. S. (2011), *Coping With the Gods: Wayward Readings in Greek Theology*, Leiden and Boston: Brill.

Vidal, G. (1981), *Creation*, New York: Random House.

Volney, C.-F (1788), *Travels through Syria and Egypt, in the years 1783, 1784 and 1785*, 2nd edn, Vol. 1, https://archive.org/details/b2877050x_0001 (accessed 18 November 2017).

von Martels, Zweder (ed.) (1994), *Travel Fact and Travel Fiction: Studies on Fiction, Literary Tradition, Scholarly Discovery and Observation in Travel Writing*, Leiden and Boston: Brill.

Waterfield, R. (2009), 'On "Fussy Authorial Nudges" in Herodotus', *Classical World* 102, no. 4: 485–94.

Waterfield, R. (trans.) (2008), *Herodotus The Histories*, intro. and notes C. Dewald, Oxford: Oxford University Press.

Waters, K. H. (1970), 'Herodotus and the Ionian Revolt', *Historia* 19: 504–8.

Wayters, K. H. (1985), *Herodotos the Historian: His Problems, Methods and Originality*, London: Croom Helm.

Węcowski, M. (2004), 'The hedgehog and the fox: form and meaning in the prologue of Herodotus', *Journal of Hellenic Studies* 124: 143–64.

Wesselmann, K. (2016), 'No Future? Possibilities and Permanence in Herodotus' *Histories*, in A. Lianeri (ed.), *Knowing Future Time in and through Greek Historiography*, 195–214, Berlin and Boston: De Gruyter.

West, M. L. (1997), *The East Face of Helicon: West Asiatic Elements in Greek Poetry and Myth*, Oxford: Oxford University Press.

West, S. (1985), 'Herodotus' Epigraphical Interests', *Classical Quarterly* 35, no. 2: 278–305.

West, S. (1991), 'Herodotus' Portrait of Hecataeus', *Journal of Hellenic Studies* 111: 144–60.

West, S. (2002), 'Scythians', in E. J. Bakker, I. J. F. de Jong and H. van Wees (eds), *Brill's Companion to Herodotus*, 437–56, Leiden, Boston and Cologne: Brill.

West, S. (2007), 'Rhampsinitos and the Clever Thief (Herodotus 2.121)', in J. Marincola (ed.), *A Companion to Greek and Roman Historiography*, 322–7, Oxford: Blackwell.

White, H. (1973), 'Interpretation in History', *New Literary History* 4, no. 2: 281–314.

White, H. ([1973] 2014), *Metahistory: The Historical Imagination in Nineteenth-Century Europe*, Baltimore, MD: Johns Hopkins University Press.

Williams, B. (2004), *Truth and Truthfulness: An Essay in Genealogy*, Princeton, NJ: Princeton University Press.

Wilson, N. G. (2015), *Herodotea*, Oxford: Oxford University Press.

Winkler, J. (1990), *The Constraints of Desire: The Anthropology of Sex and Gender in Ancient Greece*, London and New York: Routledge.

Wolf, E. R. ([1982] 2010), *Europe and the People without History*, Berkeley and Los Angeles: University of California Press.

Yerushalmi, Y. H. (1982), *Zakhor: Jewish History and Jewish Memory*, Seattle: University of Washington Press.

Žižek, S. (1989), *The Sublime Object of Desire*, London: Verso.

INDEX